D0875714

R.V.W.

A BIOGRAPHY
OF
RALPH VAUGHAN WILLIAMS

by

Ursula Vaughan Williams

London
OXFORD UNIVERSITY PRESS
NEW YORK TORONTO
1964

Oxford University Press, Amen House, London E.C.4.
GLASGOW NEW YORK TORONTO MELBOURNE WELLINGTON
BOMBAY CALCUTTA MADRAS KARACHI LAHORE DACCA
CAPE TOWN SALISBURY NAIROBI IBADAN ACCRA
KUALA LUMPUR HONG KONG

Printed in Great Britain
by Richard Clay and Company, Ltd.,
Bungay, Suffolk

Contents

List of Illustrations		vii
Acknowledgements		ix
Chronology		xi
Short Bibliography		xiii
Note on names		xv
I.	Family background	1
II.	1872–92	8
III.	1892–97	35
IV.	1897–1905	52
V.	1906–11	77
VI.	1912–14	100
VII.	1914–19	115
VIII.	1919–22	133
IX.	1923–30	147
X.	1930–34	183
XI.	1934–39	201
XII.	1939–45	229
XIII.	1945–51	264
XIV.	1951–53	310
XV.	1953–55	339
XVI.	1956–58	369
Appendix I.	Hugh the Drover	400
Appendix II.	Vaughan Williams and Bach	423
Index of Works		431
Index		434

List of Illustrations

R. V. W., December 1897 — *Frontispiece*
Leith Hill Place — *facing page* 32
Arthur Vaughan Williams — 33
Margaret Vaughan Williams — 33
Ralph, aged about three, six, and thirteen — 33
(*a*) Ralph Wedgwood and R. V. W. — 48
(*b*) Nicholas Gatty — 48
(*a*) Rough music at Hooton Roberts — 49
(*b*) Adeline Fisher, about 1896 — 49
(*a*) George Butterworth — 96
(*b*) Meggie Vaughan Williams, 1904 — 96
Adeline, 1908 — 97
A Walking Tour. Gustav and Ralph — 112
(*a*) R.A.M.C., 1915 — 113
(*b*) R.A., 1917 — 113
(*a*) Margaret Vaughan Williams at Leith Hill Place, 1917 — 160
(*b*) Ralph and Adeline at Cheyne Walk, 1917 — 160
Ralph, 1925 — 161
Ralph, 1938 (*Howard Coster*) — 176
Ursula Wood, 1938 (*J. Somerset Murray*) — 177
(*a*) Ralph about 1942 with Foxy (*Dudley Styles*) — 336
(*b*) Down Ampney, 1948 — 336
(*c*) Sirmione, 1953 — 336
Rehearsing at Buffalo, 1954 (*Alex Wilson*) — 337
Rehearsing 'The Lark Ascending' with Frederick Grinke in Gloucester Cathedral, 1956 (*Gloucestershire Newspapers Ltd.*) — 352
At Hanover Terrace, 1957 (*Douglas Glass*) — 353

Acknowledgements

So many people have helped me by giving or lending letters and other documents, by writing their memories of my husband or by reminding me of sources of information that a comprehensive list of their names would almost make another chapter. Though I have not been able to use directly all the material placed at my disposal, every letter, every incident and every memory has shed some light on the story and is therefore part of this book, and I thank all those who have so generously shared their friendship for Ralph with his biographer. They include members of the Vaughan Williams, Darwin, Wedgwood, and Fisher families, people who knew Ralph at Charterhouse, Cambridge and The Royal College of Music, his companions of army days, his colleagues and pupils as well as a very wide circle of other friends. It is sad that some of the older ones among them died before the book was finished and so cannot know how much it owes to their contributions.

I must also thank those who deciphered and typed my manuscript, my friends who have read and criticized the work in all its stages and who have undertaken proof reading, particularly Sir Gilmour Jenkins and Mr. Roy Douglas. The Publisher and his staff at the Oxford University Press have given me invaluable help, and Mr. Michael Kennedy, the writer of the companion volume, *The Works of Ralph Vaughan Williams*, has shared his discoveries and material with me and has advised and encouraged me in all difficulties.

I hope that Ralph's own writings, the letters of others and the happenings recorded here will show that all his qualities and defects, generosities and withdrawals were no contradictions but aspects of a whole man of whom it is difficult to write in the past tense.

U. V. W.
January 1964

Chronology

1872 Born 12 October at Down Ampney, Gloucestershire
1890 Entered Royal College of Music as a student: September
1892 Entered Trinity College Cambridge. Continued weekly lessons at the R.C.M.
1894 Mus.B. Cantab.
1895 B.A. (Cantab.). Re-entered Royal College of Music. Became organist of St. Barnabas, South Lambeth
1897 Married Adeline Fisher, 9 October. Went to Berlin and studied with Max Bruch
1898 Obtained F.R.C.O. diploma by examination
1899 Passed Mus.D. Cantab. examination; took the degree May 1901
1902 Gave University Extension Lectures (and wrote articles for *The Vocalist*) for several years
1903 Started to collect folksongs. Wrote the articles on *Conducting* and *Fugue* for Grove's Dictionary (1904)
1904 Started work on editing the English Hymnal
1905 First Leith Hill Festival
1908 Studied with Ravel in Paris
1909 *On Wenlock Edge; The Wasps*
1910 *A Sea Symphony*, first performed at Leeds Festival. *Tallis Fantasia*, first performance at Three Choirs Festival, Gloucester
1912 Conducted and arranged music for Benson's seasons of plays at Stratford-upon-Avon
1914 *A London Symphony* first performed
Enlisted as a private in the R.A.M.C.
1916 Posted to France and later Salonika
1917 Commissioned as a Lieut. R.G.A. Posted to France
1918 Served in France. Appointed Director of Music, First Army B.E.F.
1919 Demobilized. Appointed Professor of Composition, R.C.M. Hon. D.Mus., Oxford
1921 Appointed Conductor of the Bach Choir
1922 *A Pastoral Symphony*. First visit to America
1922 *Mass in G minor*
1924 *Hugh the Drover*
1925 *Flos Campi: Concerto Accademico*

1926 *Sancta Civitas*
1928 Resigned from Bach Choir.
1929 Moved to Dorking. *Sir John in Love*. R.C.M.
1930 *Job*. First performance at Norwich Festival
1931 *Job* staged in London
1932 Gave the Mary Flexner Lectures at Bryn Mawr College (Penn.)
1933 *Piano Concerto*
1934 Death of Gustav Holst
1935 *Symphony No. 4 in F minor*. Created O.M.
1936 *The Poisoned Kiss. Dona Nobis Pacem. Five Tudor Portraits*
1937 *Riders to the Sea*
1938 *Serenade to Music*
1939–1943 Film music, war work, lecturing, writing
1943 *Symphony in D major (No. 5)*
1944 *Oboe Concerto*
1945 *Thanksgiving for Victory*
1948 *Symphony in E minor (No. 6)*
1950 *Folk Songs of the Four Seasons. Concerto Grosso*
1951 *Pilgrim's Progress*
Adeline Vaughan Williams died, 10 May
1952 *Romance for Harmonica. An Oxford Elegy*
1953 *Sinfonia Antartica (No. 7)*
Married Ursula Wood (daughter of Major General Sir Robert Lock, K.B.E., C.B., and Lady Lock) widow of Lieut. Colonel Michael Forrester Wood
Moved to London
1954 *Tuba Concerto. Hodie. Violin Sonata*
Lectured at Cornell University, N.Y. Lecture tour across U.S.A.
1956 *Symphony in D minor (No. 8)*
1958 *Symphony in E minor (No. 9)*
Died on August 26 of coronary thrombosis

Short Bibliography

A Century of Family Letters, Emma Darwin, edited by Henrietta Litchfield. London: John Murray, 1915.

A Romantic Man and Other Tales, Hervey Fisher. London: Martin Secker, 1920.

Unfinished Autobiography, H. A. L. Fisher. London: Oxford University Press, 1940.

An Autobiography of an Historian and other Essays, G. M. Trevelyan. London: Longmans, Green and Co. Ltd., 1949.

Musicians' Gallery, M. D. Calvocoressi. London: Faber and Faber, 1933.

Tales of a Field Ambulance 1914–1918, told by the Personnel. Printed for private circulation, 1935.

George Butterworth, a memorial volume printed for private circulation, 1918.

Gustav Holst, Imogen Holst. London: Oxford University Press, 1938.

The Three Choirs Festival, H. Watkins Shaw. Worcester and London: Ebenezer Baylis and Son Ltd., 1954.

Offspring of the Vic. A history of Morley College, Denis Richards. London: Routledge and Kegan Paul, 1958.

Period Piece, Gwen Raverat. London: Faber and Faber, 1952.

Grove's Dictionary of Music and Musicians, 1894 onwards. London: Macmillan and Co. Ltd.

Leith Hill Musical Festival 1905–1955. Epsom: Pullingers Ltd.

Principal Writings by Vaughan Williams

National Music (based on his Mary Flexner Lectures on the Humanities, given in 1932 at Bryn Mawr, Pennsylvania). London: Oxford University Press, 1934.

Some Thoughts on Beethoven's Choral Symphony, with writings on other musical subjects (extending from 1920 to 1952). London: Oxford University Press, 1953.

The Making of Music (lectures given in 1954 at Cornell University, N.Y.). London: Oxford University Press, 1955.

National Music and other essays (containing the three books listed above with a preface by Ursula Vaughan Williams), Oxford Paperbacks, No. 76. London: Oxford University Press, 1963.

'Who Wants the English Composer?', *R.C.M. Magazine*, Christmas Term, 1912. Vol. IX. No. 1.

English Folk Songs (Pamphlet based on lecture given on 10 January 1912), London: Joseph Williams, 1912. (Also reprinted in *Vaughan Williams*, by Percy M. Young. Dennis Dobson, 1953.)

Correspondence

Heirs and Rebels. Letters written to each other and occasional writings on music by Ralph Vaughan Williams and Gustav Holst, edited by Ursula Vaughan Williams and Imogen Holst. London: Oxford University Press, 1959.

Principal Books edited or part-edited by Vaughan Williams

Welcome Songs of Purcell, Part I (Purcell Society, *Works of Henry Purcell*, Vol. XV. London: Novello & Co., 1905). Part II (Purcell Society, *Works of Henry Purcell*, Vol. XVIII. London: Novello & Co., 1910).

The English Hymnal (music editor. London: Oxford University Press, 1906, revised 1933).

Songs of Praise (music editor with Martin Shaw). London: Oxford University Press, 1925, revised 1931.

The Oxford Book of Carols (music editor with Martin Shaw). London: Oxford University Press, 1928.

The Penguin Book of English Folk Songs (with A. L. Lloyd). London: Penguin Books, 1959.

Principal Writings about Vaughan Williams

Ralph Vaughan Williams: A Study, by Hubert Foss (containing 'A Musical Autobiography' and reprint of 'Who Wants the English Composer?', both by R. Vaughan Williams). London: Harrap & Co., 1950.

Vaughan Williams, by Percy M. Young (containing reprint of 'English Folk Songs' by R. Vaughan Williams). London: Dennis Dobson, 1953.

The Music of Ralph Vaughan Williams, by Frank Howes. London: Oxford University Press, 1954.

Ralph Vaughan Williams: A Discovery of his Music, by Simona Pakenham. London: Macmillan & Co., 1957.

Vaughan Williams, by James Day (The Master Musician Series). London: J. M. Dent & Co., 1961.

Vaughan Williams, by A. E. F. Dickinson. London: Faber & Faber, 1963.

The Works of Ralph Vaughan Williams, by Michael Kennedy. London: Oxford University Press, 1964

For comprehensive bibliography of articles by and about Vaughan Williams see *The Works of Ralph Vaughan Williams*, by Michael Kennedy.

Note on Names

Ralph's grandfather, Sir Edward Vaughan Williams, seems to have been the first member of the family to use the double-barrelled but unhyphenated name. All his sons were so named and though occasionally—at school or in the army—Ralph was called Williams it is not correct. Ralph's name was pronounced Rafe, any other pronunciation used to infuriate him.

Ralph's elder brother and one of Adeline's brothers both had the name of Hervey. Ralph's mother and sister were both called Margaret but his sister is always called Meggie as that was the usage among her family and friends. As far as possible people are called by the names Ralph used for them. Gustav Holst was *von* Holst when Ralph first met him, and all the early letters are addressed to VH or sometimes V. By the time Holst dropped the *von* Ralph was writing to him as Gustav. R. O. Morris was always called either R.O. or Morris, his wife, Emmeline Fisher, was always known as Emmie.

CHAPTER I

Family Background

Ralph Vaughan Williams was, on his father's side, of mixed English and Welsh descent. On his mother's he came from the families of Wedgwood and Darwin, so often intermarried. He drew his inheritance partly from Celtic sources, from a family chiefly of lawyers and parsons, and partly from the strong and inventive stock of craftsmen, manufacturers, and scientists. These provided a family background and tradition of integrity, directness, alert interest, and lively intelligence.

Ralph's great grandfather, John Williams, was born at Job's Well, Carmarthen, in 1757. He married Mary Clarke of Foribridge, Staffordshire, in 1789, and moved to London. He became sergeant at law, and his obituary in the Annual Register for 1810 says that he was 'gifted by nature with extraordinary powers of memory and excellent understanding . . . patient and persevering application to the study of law . . . luminous expositions, sound deductions and clear reasoning.' A portrait, painted perhaps at the time of his marriage, shows a sensitive face with a broad forehead, huge dark eyes, a roman nose and dark, slanting eyebrows. John and Mary Williams had seven children; the eldest son went into the Church, the third became a Colonel in the Royal Engineers, the fourth son seems not to have had any profession and the three daughters all married. The second son, Edward Vaughan Williams, followed his father in the legal profession and became a Judge—the first to be given the title of Judge of Common Pleas. His wife, Jane Bagot, was black-eyed and proud, a descendant of that Bagot known to Shakespeare as 'a creature of Richard II', but this discreditable view of her forbear did not affect her esteem for her ancestry. Ralph remembered her as an unapproachable figure in a black dress, for he only knew her as a widow living in a house in Queen Anne's Gate, which he said was dark and stuffy and alarming, but her few surviving letters show her to have been a loving and entirely friendly mother-in-law and affectionately concerned with her grandchildren.

She and her husband had six sons and one daughter. The boys were educated at Westminster School and their parents rented Tanhurst on the slopes of Leith Hill, a house with a view of the South Downs which had all the facilities for riding, shooting, walking, and country pleasures that an energetic family needed in the holidays. A charming water colour sketch still hangs there showing flowers in the square white panelled hall, and a youth with curly hair running up the stairs.

The eldest son, Hervey, born in 1829, died when he was twenty-three. The second and third sons, Edward and Arthur, born in 1833 and 1834, both went into the Church, the fourth, Lewis, born in 1836, joined the Rifle Brigade and died young, while the two youngest, Roland and Walter, were the third generation to make the law their profession—Roland becoming a Lord Justice of Appeal. The one girl, Henrietta Maria, died when she was nine. Lewis kept a diary for some part of 1854, the year his sister died, and when he was eighteen. He was still at Westminster, apparently idling through his last year at school, for he records playing pool, going to see the boat race, smoking, shooting, rolling the cricket ground, walking, fishing, and taking part in amateur theatricals. He had financial difficulties too, for one entry is, 'Got up early went up town and popped ring and pin'. As far as work is concerned there were a few days when he did 'Latin with Papa' probably the result of 'got 27 for my epigram'—he put down his failures—'tried to mend a gate' and 'tried to stuff a bird'. Lewis's brother, Edwardie—they all used diminutives—became rector of North Tedworth in Wiltshire, devoted to the quiet pursuits of country life. Arthur went to Christchurch in 1854. There he became friends with Herbert Fisher and brought him to stay at Tanhurst. This was the beginning of a friendship which was a foreshadowing of the future and of a linking of lives still to come.

Arthur took his B.A. in 1857 and his M.A. in 1860, the same year in which he won a silver tankard in a foot steeple-chase. Also in 1860 he was ordained Deacon by the Bishop of Oxford. His first appointment as curate was to George Herbert's parish of Bemerton, near Salisbury. He was happy there and his talents were appreciated, for the vicar wrote to his father:

April 7. 1863

My dear Sir Edward,

I cannot allow your son to leave this weekend without writing to you to express my deep regret at the separation which will so soon take place between us. It is now more than two years since he came here, and I can assure you he has endeared himself to everyone in the Parish, and especially to the school children in whose welfare he has taken the deepest interest and over whom he has watched with the tenderest care. It was quite affecting to see them all on Sunday in tears at his leaving and I can assure you they were not the only ones. We have worked together during the time he has been here in perfect harmony. He has been to me everything I would have wished or hoped for; and I trust that his ministry may prove a lasting blessing to the Parish. I am sure that wherever he goes he will be loved and respected and the more he is known the more he will be valued. I hope you will not think I have written this to flatter him, but that it is the outpouring of my heart. I am also truly happy to know that his health has not suffered but improved during his residence here; so that I can return him to you in the enjoyment of bodily strength. My prayers for him will be that he may long continue to enjoy health and be a blessing to you, Lady Williams, and those over whom he may be called to minister.

I will not trouble you with a longer letter, but only add my kind remembrances to Lady Williams, and trust you will believe me.

Ever truly yours,
Wellesley Pole Pigott

Arthur's next appointment was at Halsall near Ormskirk in Lancashire, from 1863 until 1865, when he was sent to the parish of Alverstoke in Hampshire. From Alverstoke it was easier for him to get to London or to Tanhurst.

The nearest house to Tanhurst is Leith Hill Place. It had been bought by Josiah Wedgwood (the third of that name, grandson of the potter), in 1847. It is one of those houses added to and adapted by successive owners to suit their needs or to conform to the taste of their time. Built about 1600 on earlier foundations, modernized in the mid-eighteenth century, it had been, as well as the home of several different families in succession, a school for a few years. When Josiah bought it he was fifty-two and had been married for ten years to his cousin Caroline Darwin. It was a marriage warmly approved by both families though by the time it came about they had almost given up hope that the idea would occur to the couple themselves.

After their marriage Josiah and his wife left Staffordshire and settled at Downton near Salisbury. There their four daughters were born, the eldest dying in infancy. When they came to Leith Hill Place their three little girls were old enough to enjoy all the pleasures the house and surrounding countryside could afford. A high brick wall enclosed four acres of land as a kitchen garden with glass houses and potting sheds next to the home farm. Here, and in orchards and coach houses there was endless scope for games and adventure.

To the south of the house the ground slopes steeply, a slope that has given pleasure to generations of tobogganers; the wide view stretches as far as Chanctonbury to the south and to the hills by Haslemere to the west. In the woodland between Leith Hill Place and Tanhurst the Wedgwoods planted rhododendrons and azaleas among the native trees, achieving a fairy-tale forest that is both exotic and romantic, unexpected and entirely natural. Another charm for the children, Sophy, Margaret, and Lucy, in living at Leith Hill Place was the daily hope that their walks or drives might be enlivened by the sight of kangaroos, for the Evelyns, Lords of the Manor, and enthusiastic naturalists, had established these shy creatures on the common where they were sometimes to be seen leaping through the bracken.

The nurseries were in the attics of the house, a kingdom from which the little girls descended sedately to say good morning to their parents and to receive a teaspoonful of cream from the grown-ups' breakfast table. One day they all solemnly refused this treat and persisted in their refusal. At the end of a week they demanded, and were given, a whole jugful. They grew up in an easy world, with the discipline, good manners, and sense of responsibility towards those less fortunate than themselves usual in such households. They were free of the grown-up world, welcomed in the kitchen and on the farm, and lived the secret lives of childhood in their nursery. As they grew older they went with their parents to visit their many cousins, and for holidays abroad, and they joined in dancing classes and children's parties in the neighbourhood. Conscious of inadequacies in her own education Caroline Wedgwood was determined that her daughters should have the best masters available and that any talent they had should be fostered. They all learned music, and Lucy's flair for composition was encouraged, as was Margaret's interest in sketching. They were not beautiful girls and fashion was a conception as remote as untidiness in dress would have been; but their clear cut features, large eyes and fine skins gave them an air of distinction and they had the poise that comes from unquestioned security.

Their uncle, Charles Darwin, recruited them to help him with earthworm experiments, and all sorts of botanical problems.

My Dear Lieutenant Lucy,

If the book with many volumes with coloured plates be the Botanical Mag., please look at Pl. 356 and see whether it mentions the flowers of the plant, viz. Erica Massoni, are glutinous, or the leaves—and whether the glutinous matter is secreted by glandular hairs.

How about the Paeony seeds—do the pods open, are they brilliantly coloured? Do birds eat them? Have the seeds a thin fleshy coat?

Yours affectionate Uncle and Commander,

C. L. Darwin

A long letter to 'My Dear Sophy' asks her to observe whether bird's-nest orchis break through the ground with flower stems straight or arched.

Lucy worked hard at earthworms, following elaborate instructions; the result of her probing with knitting needles, and Sophy's observation of casts, brought glowing thanks: 'you are worth your weight in gold', and later:

My Dear Angels!

I can call you nothing else. I never dreamed of your taking so much trouble. The enumeration will be invaluable . . . but I write now to ask whether you will be more angelic than angels and send me in tin, not tightly packed, with *little* damp (*not wet*) moss (perhaps tied round stems?) 2 or 3 flowers of both forms of Hollonia; I much wish to measure pollen and compare its grains.

My dear angels,

C. Darwin

There is a family tradition that when Sir Edward Vaughan Williams was asked why he had chosen the Leith Hill district for his country home he answered 'Because it is full of charming young heiresses'. They must have been very young indeed when he said this, but from Lewis's diary it is clear that there was a lot of sociability among the young people in the neighbourhood who had grown up together, and there was a close friendship between the households at Leith Hill Place and Tanhurst. So it was no surprise to their families when Arthur Vaughan Williams and Margaret Wedgwood became engaged in September 1867. Nothing could have been more suitable, or have given more pleasure to their respective parents.

Lady Vaughan Williams wrote to her son:

> No piece of news could have made me so happy and I am sure I may use the same words as regards your Papa. We had been for a long time hoping we might some day see Margaret Wedgwood your wife—and now the wished-for tidings have come, we are made still happier by hearing both Mr. & Mrs. Wedgwood so cordially approve the engagement, and that they and their girls have expressed themselves so kindly about it. It must be very pleasant for you to know that every one of your own brothers will be delighted to have Margaret for their sister-in-law, and that Laura [Roland's wife] has always been so fond of her——

Both Margaret's parents wrote equally glowing letters, Josiah to explain that he did not believe in long engagements, and

> if you can make up your minds to a small income at first I see no objection to the marriage taking place as soon as you can be released from Mr. Walpole, but all these matters you can talk over and settle when next you see her. . . . I propose allowing Margt. £500 a year, and ultimately she will have 1/3 of my property which latterly has yielded about £4,000 a year. The amount is uncertain as it depends almost entirely on railroads. . . .

Margaret wrote to Arthur giving an account of her doings each day, worried over his colds, and tried spasmodically to learn to cook, starting a large exercise book with soup and milk pudding recipes. It took some months for Arthur to end his work at Alverstoke, but at last he was free, and after Christmas he accepted the living at Down Ampney, near Cricklade, on the borders of Gloucestershire and Wiltshire.

Margaret and he were married at Coldharbour Church on 22 February 1868, and after their honeymoon they moved into Down Ampney vicarage. Their eldest child, Hervey, was born at

Leith Hill Place, the two younger ones, Margaret (Meggie) and Ralph at Down Ampney, Ralph on Saturday, 12 October 1872. The old rhyme says 'Saturday's child has far to go' but Ralph's journey very nearly ended on the day of his christening for the officiating clergyman dropped him at the font and he was only saved by his mother catching the long skirts of his christening robe.

CHAPTER II

1872–1892

Ralph remembered only two things from the two and a half years he lived at Down Ampney. Coming home from an outing in his perambulator he pointed to the darkly shadowed pathway that ran between shrubs and the garden wall: 'Take me there,' he said to his nurse. He remembered the moment in photographic detail when he saw the garden in 1947 on his way back from Worcester, though he had forgotten whether his command was obeyed. The other memory was of coming home, bandaged and triumphant, after having had his finger caught in a slamming door and having been taken to the doctor, and saying: 'I've got a new finger.' The accident had been a matter for concern, for Lady Vaughan Williams wrote:

24 Queen Anne's Gate,
November 18th (1874)

My dearest Margaret,

We take every comfort from your last letter that the joint of poor little Ralph's finger is safe, even if a scar should be permanent, but we are very sanguine that such prompt bandaging and careful watching will avert that slight evil—we have very moving *visions* of him in his sling. It tells most pleasantly for his disposition that he wears it so patiently. That he has not suffered more pain after the first ten minutes, which must have been terrible, is a great comfort.

We are glad to hear of Lucy's and her husband's and Sophy's expected visit this week to Down Ampney, but we hope *this* was not the one day fixed upon—drizzling rain and mist, and a good deal of wind in our drive in Hyde Park this morning, made us decide not to encounter it again this afternoon, which gives me a little time for writing to you. I please myself with thinking that Hervey and Meggie have like their Grandmama many happy recollections of their visit to the 'Church House'. If we live to another summer the Judge has a great wish to take a house at Seaford, which is within half a mile of the Fishers—and in that case it would be delightful to have you and Arthur and the children our guests at the sea-side. . . .

Give my love to my three dear grandchildren as well as to Arthur and yourself, dearest Margaret,

Ever yr. aff*te* Mother
Jane Vaughan Williams.

Arthur took as much interest in the schoolchildren at Down Ampney as he had taken in those at Bemerton. He was a School Manager, and from the schoolmaster's log book he is recorded as having given lessons in arithmetic, writing on 'Sclates',[1] as well as a vicar's normal work in those days, teaching scripture and catechism, while Margaret visited the school and sometimes inspected the children's sewing.

The schoolmaster's log book gives the only account that has survived of Arthur's death.

February 9th, 1875.

Today, at 3.35 p.m. our Manager (the Rev. A. V. Williams) died, after an illness which only began on the morning of the 7th. He had been ailing some time but for the few days before he was taken ill he was in unusually good health and spirits. There will be no more night school in consequence of his death. He will be greatly missed and lamented in our village.

He had been working on a sermon. Margaret kept it, with another letter from her mother-in-law:

24 Queen Anne's Gate,
April 2nd (1875)

My dearest Margaret,

You are so continually in my thoughts that I do not feel it is so long as it really is since I wrote to you—and now I have a second dear letter of yours to answer and to dwell upon with such a full heart of love and sympathy and respect. It is soothing to me to think that these first spring days giving such beautiful evidence in the opening of leaves and flowers of the resurrection of nature have the same comforting charm for you that they have for myself—and in so many ways are, as to me, mingled with sweet and happy thoughts of Arthur . . . I find much to like in the photograph you have sent me—there is a good deal of a speaking look in the expression. . . . I am grateful to you for your gift of the photographs of the house and church. They are beautiful I think, but dearly as I love to possess and to look at them I find them most intensely affecting. The little flowers on the mound so distinct, my tears could not be kept back—I so often think of dear

[1] Writing slates: the schoolmaster spelt it as in Middle-English usage.

little Hervey's words, so simple and touching 'and now I can't——' I am glad to hear so nice and good an account of the children—I trust, dear Margaret, you will try to make the effort to go out of doors with them. . . .

Margaret had returned to her parents' home, and her mother-in-law's letter continues:

I can so well imagine all the pains that are lovingly taken that you mention for the arrangements of your rooms within doors and your comfort in everything. . . .

Emma Darwin, writing to her daughter, Henrietta Litchfield ('Aunt Etty'), told her:

I am just returned from a call . . . at L.H.P. I went after luncheon and the drive was lovely. I sat out with them most of the time and Margaret soon joined us. She looks very thin and speaks in a low voice as if she was weak, but was quite calm and joined in everything; she looks very pretty in her widow's cap. Hervey was playing about all the time and the other two came after. Little Ralph has regular features and might be like Lucy or Susan.[1]

Lucy had married James Harrison, a naval lieutenant, in April 1874, and, though she was sometimes at his parents' home at Ewhurst, she lived the usual nomadic life of a sailor's wife. Sophy had not married and she and her parents were glad to have Margaret and the children in the house. The year after, Caroline Wedgwood was dangerously ill, and it was thought that she would not recover. But five months later she was well enough for her sister-in-law, Emma Darwin, to stay. After this visit to Leith Hill Place, she wrote to her son George:

It was so pleasant and so wonderful to see Aunt C. quite her old self. . . . We saw the girls by themselves after she was gone to bed and I never had so much talk with Margaret in my life and I thought her very nice and feeling and prettier than ever she was. She seems a capital mother, very intelligent and yet firm enough to carry off little Ralph remorselessly when he screams, which he does on slight provocation. She says that he's so heavy that she will not be able to do so much longer, but I daresay it will not be needed.

By the following spring Ralph had learned to read. His grand-

[1] His aunt, Lucy Harrison, and his great-aunt, Susan Darwin, who died in 1866.

mother, now completely recovered, taught him from the New Edition, 1837, of *Cobwebs to Catch Flies*: it had been recommended as a reading book by Erasmus Darwin in his *Plan for the Conduct of Female Education in Boarding Schools* published in 1797, and this copy was the one she had used when she taught her young brother Charles Darwin to read. At some point in its history a careful child had painted the little wood engravings in bright colours. By April 1877, Ralph had reached longer words and the farmyard they described cannot have been very different from the one across the road from which the buttercup-coloured Jersey butter came for nursery tea, as well as the cream which was so ordinary that the children found custard far more interesting.

Photographs taken at this time show him with the shoulder-length hair and the short skirts still worn by little boys: his face has already the wide brow and firm mouth of later life, though his expression is more sceptical than serious. His great-aunt wrote:

> The children have pleasant, open expressions but their grandfather[1] and grandmother had exactly the same defect of little dark eyes very near together, the two eldest have the same.

The children had settled into the old nursery in the attic, and their nurse, Sarah Wager, was Ralph's friend in particular. She trained the children very strictly, table manners had to be perfect, and obedience was enforced, but she never expected them to dress themselves, fold their clothes, or tidy up. She was a passionate radical and planted her political opinions in the nursery. They were not unlike those of her employers, but both would have been surprised had they made this discovery.

Ralph was by nature left-handed. His earliest letters, written between ruled lines half an inch wide, are in careful copybook script and look as if he had been struggling to write with his right hand.

> My dear
> mother
> I am going
> again to

[1] Presumably Vaughan Williams, as this is written by the Darwin–Wedgwood side of the family.

Vivian[1]
today. Aunt
Sophy and
I went to church
in the shandri-
dan. i am going
a drive with
Aunt S.
your affec
ralph.

By the time his writing became formed and characteristic, it was already the leaping, sprawling handwriting all his friends knew well, and no letters of his middle childhood have survived to show the transition.

Margaret's letters suggest that he had already a sociable disposition.

My dear Ralphy,

You will have a great deal of news to tell me when I come back. I shall want to hear all about your parties, the Wickhams, the Bosanquets and the others. I wish I could pack up this little baby[2] and bring her to Leith Hill Place but I am afraid Aunt Lucy would not spare her. She went out of doors yesterday for the first time and is out in the garden now.

Goodbye dear Ralphy till tomorrow.

Your affec. Mother.

In all surviving letters her affection and common sense are apparent, and Ralph remembered an episode that happened when he was six or seven. The publication of Charles Darwin's *The Origin of Species* had shaken the family and the country to their foundations: echoes of the controversies it had aroused still surrounded Great Uncle Charles, who seemed an august but unpredictable person. Ralph was alone with him in the dining-room before breakfast when his grandson, three year old Bernard Darwin,[3] rushed into the room: pink and defiant he announced 'I've just hit my Nana.'

'Why did you do that?' asked Charles.

[1] Vivian Bosanquet whose family now lived at Tanhurst. The Vaughan Williams family had moved to High Ashes, another house in the neighbourhood.

[2] Lucy Harrison's daughter Anne, born in 1877.

[3] Who later became the writer on golf and a leader-writer for *The Times*.

'Because I wanted to,' said Bernard.

Ralph waited for the skies to fall: instead Charles said mildly:

'A very good reason too.'

After this Ralph asked his mother about *The Origin of Species*, and what it meant. She answered:

'The Bible says that God made the world in six days, Great Uncle Charles thinks it took longer: but we need not worry about it, for it is equally wonderful either way.'

This answer completely satisfied Ralph at the time: nor did he ever forget it, for it seemed typical of her good sense, bringing difficult problems within the scope of the children's understanding. A little later, when he was ten or eleven and had made some progress with violin playing, she asked him to play for some visitors. He, with a mixture of shyness and offended pride, refused and rushed out of the room. Margaret followed him. In the voice of an equal she said, 'Ralph, I told them you would play and you are making me look *such* a fool.' He was completely won over and, as he said, 'played rather well'.

Music had always been important in the family. When Ralph's grandmother Caroline went to stay with the Charles Darwins at Down, there was always music for her: her sister-in-law played the piano very well and was a keen and critical concertgoer, and Caroline had liked singing in her youth. Though Lucy was the officially musical one of her daughters, it was Sophy who gave Ralph his early music lessons. He had been fascinated by the sound of a piano even in his earliest days and tried to reach the keyboard, and he wrote his first pianoforte piece when he was six. It was four bars long and he called it *The Robin's Nest*. Aunt Sophy took him through a textbook published in 1819 called *A Child's Introduction to Thorough Bass*. Like Mrs. Markham's history of France, and other lesson books of the period, the questions and answers give a pleasant picture of intelligent children being sensibly treated, and the information compares well with that in far more modern textbooks.

Ralph corresponded also with Sarah Wager's brother who was an organist and taught at Gorse Hill Board Schools. In answer to Ralph's inquiry about writing for the viola he wrote:

The music for the viola or Tenor Violin is written in the C (alto) clef, and the compass of the instrument in the *1st position* ranges from

C to E . By playing in the higher positions the 2nd, 3rd, 4th, or 5th and so on the same compass can be reached relatively as on the violin, but it is not often that the viola is used in this way. Sometimes passages for the 1st string and above the first position are introduced and are written in the Treble clef to avoid the use of the many ledger lines. Scale of the instrument.

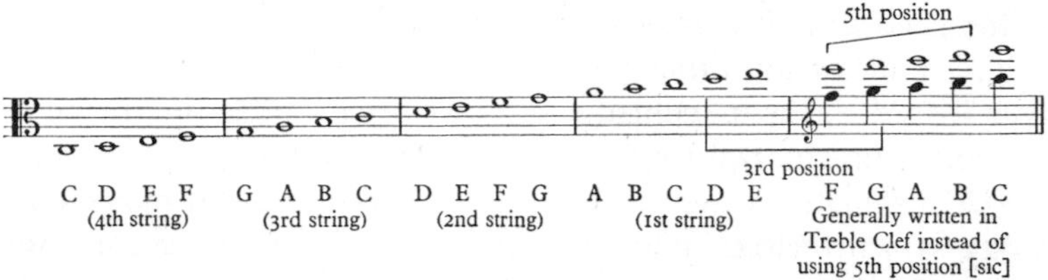

I send by this same post the viola part of one of Schubert's beautiful quintets which can be returned any time.

Drum music is written for Bass and Side Drums, generally a note for each beat of the Drum corresponding to its length, that is, duration of time. As the sound produced is the same in pitch, the notes vary only in length, not in position. The roll on the Side Drum is generally indicated:

The above has been scribbled at my sister's request.

Your obedient servant,

Henry Wager.

Stainer's *Harmony*, and a correspondence course organized by Edinburgh University, undertaken by Ralph when he was about eight, and in which he passed both preliminary and advanced examinations, kept him busy, and also occupied Aunt Sophy, to whom he was allowed to dictate his examination answers because his writing was so bad. He had been given a toy theatre for which he wrote operas, a manuscript book labelled 'Overtures by Mr. R. V. Williams' gives the subjects 'The Major', 'The Ram Opera', 'The Galoshes of Happienes', and there are several piano works 'respectfully dedicated to Miss Sophy Wedgewood' [*sic*].

The actors in the operas were china dogs known collectively as The Obligers, the largest one being called 'The Judge' after Ralph's Uncle Roland. These animals also ran a newspaper called *The Obligerton Journal*, which Ralph wrote when he had nothing else to do. Not many numbers appeared.

Ralph and Meggie were companions in the nursery. Hervey's four years' seniority was felt very much by both brothers, and he assumed a slightly severe and critical attitude to Ralph which persisted all through their school days. It was Ralph and Meggie who shared the ownership of Coffee, a puppy who belonged to their nursery life. Ralph very much disliked the other pets which children were supposed to keep. Silkworms, guinea pigs and a savage little fledgling owl called Fluffy had no charms for him, and the owl's early death was a matter for relief. He had not yet discovered cats, for they lived on the farm and in the kitchen and had not pet status.

Margaret wrote:

My dear Ralphy,

Will you tell Meggie with my love that I was quite surprised to receive her letter this morning and very much pleased with it. I wish the puppy would come. Aunt Lucy is very glad you like the name 'Coffee'.

I have been into two shops to try to get a chain for him but could not find one, so I must try again.

I hope Rushbrook brought a little box last night for you three children. It is a little box of figs—and I advise you to have one each for luncheon—and one for supper every day and to ask Sarah if she would like one too. Perhaps the first day one will not be enough at a time, if so I advise you to take two apiece.

It is snowing again a little today, and I am afraid you will not be able to go out. . . .

There is a windmill just at the top of the hill behind this house and I can watch it from my bedroom window going round and round.

Goodbye dear Ralphy,

Your affec.
Mother.

Another letter was addressed to the nursery from Ralph's grandfather, and formally sealed with red wax, and it still has the indentation of the half crown it held.

Oct 12

Dear Ralph,

Thank you very much for your invitation to tea. I think I ought to pay for my share of the feast—so I fold up a piece of silver in this note.

Your affectionate grandpapa,
J. Wedgwood.

He had also invited his mother:

dear mother w—
ill you come to
tea with
me on my
birth
day
Your
affec. ralp.

This was his sixth birthday, and the hard labour of writing with his right hand is painfully apparent.

The family were much given to visiting. Harrison, Langton, Darwin, and Massingberd cousins abounded, and another letter from his grandfather followed him on one of these visits:

Nov 29.

Dear Ralph,

I have to thank you for your letter that I got yesterday, and I am glad to hear you are enjoying yourselves with your cousins. Poor Coffee is very well but goes about with his tail very low, being unhappy I suppose for want of somebody to take him out walking. I have been riding Black Tommy this morning, and invited Coffee to come with us, and he was very glad to come. A letter came today directed Ralph Williams. I guess it is from Mademoiselle.

Your affectionate Grandfather,
J. W.

Mademoiselle, also away for a holiday, was another addition to the children's lives. She and Sarah did not get on well together, and said dark things about each other. But Ralph liked them both and he very much enjoyed playing Bezique with Mademoiselle, who made it a desperate and emotional game. 'Quel désespoir—que ferai-je?' echoed through the nursery, though she had to curb her cries of 'Mon dieu! mon dieu!' which horrified Margaret who thought it blasphemous. However, she was a good teacher and, instead of grammar and irregular verbs, she taught the children to write stories in French or to listen to the exciting ones she made up for them.

For Christmas Ralph had been given a diary which he kept all through the holidays. He said it was rather dull, for the entry was the same each day. 'Wet. In morning painted, in afternoon pasted.' He never tried again.

One holiday, perhaps in 1879, they had stayed at Down,[1] and Charles Darwin wrote:

My dear Margaret,

Thank you for your letter but much more for your most welcome visit of very real advantage as well as pleasure to my children—at their age as an educational benefit better I believe than any other.

I was going to write to you to tell you of a trait of Ralph more than amusing—when I gave his tip I said 'don't mention it till after you are in the carriage'. He presently afterwards said to me, 'I suppose I ought to give it back to you for I have told Aunt Sophy.' A proof of pleasure which he could not forbear to show, and of honesty which he could not resist.

With kindest regards and wishes for you all,

Your ever affectionate Uncle,

C. D.

They also visited their Vaughan Williams cousins, and when the children were staying at Tedworth with their uncle Edwardie,[2] he took Ralph to the bell ringers' practice, and even allowed him to hold the card and call the numbers guiding the team through the changes.

Every Christmas holidays brought parties and, in those early days, party clothes for the little boys were black velvet suits. Ralph said that, when the children and their cousins were being dressed one afternoon, he discovered that his was velveteen, and that his cousin, Stephen, had real velvet. He was much perplexed, and asked his mother why his was not velvet too. She said that she was not as rich as Stephen's mother, and that he

[1] The Darwins' house in Kent: now spelt Downe.

[2] Edward Fraser Vaughan Williams, 1833–1914. Rector of Tedworth, 1869–1911.

looked very nice as he was. This was the first time he had ever thought about money, for until then he had supposed all grown-ups were rich and all children poor. Another revelation came after a winter party. It was rather late in the evening and the children were bundled into the carriage, wrapped in rugs for the drive home. The others slept, but Ralph, fascinated by the moonlit frosty night and the sound of the hoofs on the road, stayed awake. He heard the sound of a bell as they drove by a village church: the regular tolling at this strange hour filled him with wonder, and he asked why it should ring at night and so slowly. Sarah explained it was the passing bell and told him it was ringing for someone who had just died: so his first realization of death came through a country custom and by means of music.

The first death in the family of which he was conscious was that of his grandfather, Josiah Wedgwood (his other grandfather had died only a few months after his father).

The Evelyns' bailiff came the same night to claim Heriot, a custom still obtaining, by which the Lord of the Manor could claim the best beast in the possession of anyone who died holding Manor land. The family paid an agreed price and kept the horse. It was very exciting, and Ralph remembered that, and complications about the funeral cortège and a right of way, far more clearly than the death which had set these ancient customs in motion.

In the following December Charles and Emma Darwin stayed at Leith Hill Place. In a letter to their son, Emma wrote:

> Our visit has been well worth while. It seems to have roused poor Aunt C. and done her real good . . . she came down about 11 and sat all day having a great deal of talk with F [Father] and me for the whole day till 9. F. exerted himself enormously, and with the daughters also and liked Margaret very much. Poor Sophy strikes one anew every time one sees her as utterly dead and quite as much dead to mother and sisters as to the outsiders. I felt the house with that long dark passage and no carpet so depressing and wondered how they would ever get thro' the winter. The children keep them alive.

'The dark passage' was a place of terror to Ralph. Going to bed by candlelight makes shadows move with the progress of the light. The sinister threats lurking outside that little curve of brightness are forgotten now in a world of electric light, but they were very real terrors, every night of every winter, to almost all children in those days.

Ralph hated illness—he remembered the hushed discomfort of a house interrupted in the usual pattern of daily life and how he used to pray that his grandmother would either die or get quite well, so that things could be ordinary again. She did get well, and in 1881 Margaret took the children to Down. Emma Darwin wrote to her son telling him that Margaret was taking her two boys up to see a surgeon: 'They are both troubled with the sinking of the instep.'

Besides having his music lessons with his Aunt Sophy, Ralph played duets with his brother and sister from 'funny old volumes containing choruses from *Messiah* and *Israel*, and arias from *Don Giovanni* and the overture to *Figaro*, which we used to play *Andante Sostenuto*! We also played *Non più mosta* by Rossini which I found had remained in my head, like Longfellow's song, when, years after, I heard *Cenerentola* at Covent Garden.'[1] When Ralph and Meggie first heard works from their repertoire played by orchestras the pace seemed slightly shocking.

During these years Ralph had music lessons from Mr. Goodchild at Ockley, riding over on his pony with a neighbour of the same age, Vivian Bosanquet, or with Meggie. Mrs. Goodchild, who also gave Ralph lessons, remembered him as 'this naughty boy' when she told a story of his arriving in a huge, brightly coloured knitted tam o' shanter with a pom-pom on it, which she had admired. Ralph pulled it off indignantly. 'I think it's awful,' he said, 'you know what I'll do with this?' and he threw it on the muddy ground and jumped on it.

Music was one of the daily pastimes at Leith Hill Place; there was an atmosphere of leisure, with time for such pleasures as sketching, reading and playing. When Ralph was seven he began violin lessons with an old German music-teacher called Cramer, who lived at Eastbourne where Margaret had taken the children to stay for some weeks. He soon discovered that he felt much happier with a stringed instrument than he had ever done with the pianoforte, and sometimes, when they had hymn singing after tea on Sundays, he would play a voice part, although he had a clear treble voice and enjoyed singing. He had made a list in his copy of

[1] *Musical Autobiography*. R.V.W. Reprinted in *National Music and Other Essays*. Oxford University Press, 1963.

Hymns Ancient and Modern, called 'Hymns I like'—it included *Miles Lane*, the *Old Hundredth*, and the *Old Hundred and Fourth*.

Hervey went away to boarding school at Rottingdean, and he came home for holidays with new ideas: he realized that the family life at Leith Hill Place was unlike the home life of his school friends and throughout his school and university career he tried to guide his mother, aunt, and brother into more usual habits. Their unorthodox half past seven breakfast, and the proper way to dress, preoccupied him, but breakfast continued to be at that time, and his efforts about correct clothing were only partly successful, as Margaret provided for her sons according to the Dorking tailor's advice, and sometimes his ideas and Hervey's were very far apart. It took Hervey many years to emancipate Ralph as well as himself from this guidance.

A curious family custom, an economy practised by Aunt Sophy, was to provide newspaper in the lavatories. It was cut into neat squares and threaded on string. Newspapers were forbidden in the nursery, but Ralph read these cuttings with avidity: his knowledge of crime and politics from which the children were supposed to be sheltered was inevitably patchy, and he always found it difficult to remember not to talk about the things he had learned from fragments of *The Times* or the local paper which 'were not there to read'.

Among the favourite nursery books were Thackeray's *The Rose and the Ring*, *The King of the Golden River* by Ruskin, *Sintram and his Companions* by de la Motte Fouquet, *The Adventures of Ulysses* by Charles Lamb, Grimm's *Fairy Tales*, *Prince Prigio* by Andrew Lang, and various adventure stories. After tea in the winter Margaret read aloud, Scott or Shakespeare or story books by Henty and Ballantyne. When it was Shakespeare she left out or altered unsuitable words or passages as she went. Ralph discovered this and contrived to lean on her chair so that he could read over her shoulder. He, at any rate, preferred the text unexpurgated.

The June after Hervey had gone to boarding school, Margaret drove Meggie and Ralph to stay at the seaside for a holiday. It took two days in the pony cart, going through lanes not yet white with the dust of high summer. They spent a night at an inn, which was in itself an adventure, and the leisurely journey was one of the episodes Ralph remembered all his life. There were other holiday journeys, sometimes to the Three Choirs Festivals where Ralph heard choral music for the first time. Later, he was taken to concerts at the Crystal Palace. In the summer of 1882 Margaret took the three children to Normandy. It was their first visit abroad and they spent most of it sightseeing. At Rouen the boys climbed the Cathedral tower, and Ralph said it was an excitingly frightening experience. But the best part of the whole expedition was their visit to Mont St. Michel. He remembered his first sight of the grey and golden buildings rising beyond the salt marshes, the steep streets, the mazes of halls and chapels with a ghost of incense seeming to linger in their darkness, and the great wheel where the prisoners used to walk to wind the pulley ropes lifting loads of supplies up the battlements. He did not go back there for seventy years but that first impression of romance never faded.

He had become passionately interested in architecture, and he explored books about Norman and Gothic buildings, lecturing Meggie and Sarah on any castles or cathedrals they visited. His mother gave him a well-illustrated and informative 'Pictorial Architecture of the British Isles' for Christmas in 1883 and from it he learned to know enough for Emma Darwin to tell her son George in a letter written in March 1884: 'Ralph is great on architecture.' This interest bore fruit in later years when he studied the work of Tudor composers, for he found then that he was familiar with another aspect of their world, and he could apprehend the attitude of mind of musicians whose contemporaries had built the chapels of King's College at Cambridge, St. George's at Windsor, and of Henry VII at Westminster.

Ralph was enjoying his last months of freedom. When Bernard Darwin came to stay at Leith Hill Place in 1883, Emma Darwin wrote: 'Bernard was perfectly happy with Ralph and they had a pistol each and were rushing down the bank as two young lieutenants. . . .' Margaret took the children to stay with her at The Grove, Cambridge, the following March, probably for the Easter holidays, and Emma Darwin wrote to her son: 'It is pleasant to see how much Bernard enjoys having Ralph Williams here. I hear constant giggling in the dining room below. The tricycle is a great resource too. . . .' In her next letter she says: 'Bernard is in a state of rapture all day with Ralph who is apparently quite well amused with him 'tho so much younger than himself.' Ralph had not forgotten the 'because I wanted to' episode, and had great respect for his cousin.

Ralph followed Hervey to Rottingdean in September 1883. Their school, Field House, is now called 'St. Aubyn's'. It is a white house in the High Street with a gravel half-moon drive and steep slate steps up to the front door. In Ralph's time it was run by two Mr. Hewitts and their sister, and the boys had a fairly hard life. They got up at half past six for half an hour of preparation followed by practice of a musical instrument, which excused the player from prayers, before eight o'clock breakfast which consisted of tea, bread and butter with a small piece of cold beef. There were lessons all the morning, then luncheon—large and coarse joints and lots of stodge-pudding. The boys went to a shop near by for kippers and chocolate with pink cream inside to supplement Miss Hewitt's housekeeping economies. Games and walks filled the afternoon, followed by tea and bread and butter at five, and after that preparation, punctuated by baths once a week. There were four tin hip-baths filled by the school menservants, 'David and Solomon', so that four boys could scrub simultaneously and briskly before returning to their prep. until bedtime at eight. The uniform was black suits, white shirts and stiff collars, which they did not change for games.

Ralph slept in the cottage over the way, above the masters' Common Room, and had his violin lessons in the same building. Describing his school days, he said:

We learned Latin and Greek. The mathematical teaching was far the best. Hewitt was a magnificent teacher. I doubt if he knew any Latin or Greek himself, though of course we never knew that. His brother, Billy Hewitt, the second master, was really a very fine musician, and I am sorry I did not take more advantage of it. The music teaching, by two visiting masters from Brighton, was very good. I learned pianoforte from Mr A. C. West who, after giving me one or two ordinary pieces, realised I was more musical than most of his boys, and introduced me to a delightful little volume called *The Bach Album*, edited by Berthold Tours, which contained some of the easier preludes and movements from the Suites, among others, the 'Cross-hands Gigue'. My violin master was a Manxman, called Quirke, a fine player and a good teacher, but not a very cultivated musician. He made me learn Raff's *Cavatina*, which was the fashionable piece at that moment, and I played it at a school concert. The year after I again appeared at a school concert and played the rather too popular Bach–Gounod *Prelude*. I remember on that occasion Billy Hewitt showed me the original which, by the way, is the first of the forty-eight, and, with curious, but characteristic, lack of curiosity, I did not examine the whole book, which I did not get to know until years later.

It was during my time at Rottingdean that Billy took me to a Richter concert in Brighton. The programme consisted, I remember, of the Weber–Berlioz *Invitation à la Valse* which I was at that moment learning as a pianoforte piece; also the *Eroica* Symphony, which passed me by completely, the Prelude to *Lohengrin* which thrilled me and, even more, *The Ride of the Valkyries*, on which theme I used to improvise to my friends at Rottingdean on the pianoforte, and called it *The Charge of the Light Brigade*.[1]

Music was absorbing a great deal of his time, and Emma Darwin,[2] writing from Brighton in the autumn of 1884 told her daughter-in-law:

Aunt Caroline (ask George who she is) and all the Leith Hill Prty. are within a few doors. They are come for masters etc. for Meggie and Ralph who is at school near Brighton comes every half holiday for some hours. He got into a scrape the other day for playing his violin after he had gone to bed which set the boys dancing in their shirts and the masters came in. However nothing very severe was awarded to him.

This Ralph himself seems to have forgotten. He said:

The community music at Rottingdean was not much to boast of—for our annual concert we used to sing such popular successes as Crow's vocal waltz *The Fairies*. The masters also used to perform, and I remember one of them reciting *The Revenge*. We also did a children's play in which I took part, called *Our Toys*; the title was a parody on a popular farce called *Our Boys*. I took the part of a wooden soldier, but my voice cracked at the critical moment and I had to act but not sing

'For I'm a wooden soldier bold
and used to war's alarms,
I've got a pair of wooden legs
and little wooden arms. . . .'

The words were mostly adapted to tunes out of popular French operas, such as *La Fille de Madame Angot*, so our musical education

[1] Dictated to U.V.W. 1957, see p. 379.
[2] Widow of Charles Darwin.

was not very advanced. I learned a lot from a remarkable undermaster, Suttlery, who tried to add a little general culture to our rather meagre book learning. He used to read translations of the great speeches out of Greek plays, and I remember once his explaining the philosophy of the thirteenth chapter of I. Corinthians. I wish we had had more of him, for this was, of course, all off the record.

Jimmy Hewitt once took me to a performance by a well-known reciter called Brandrum who recited a bit of *Twelfth Night*, which I loved, and later to another by Mr. Ellaby who, among other things, recited Coleridge's *Ode to Mont Blanc*, which has been among my favourite poems ever since. It may be worth while noting that, on one of these occasions, probably a concert, we came home cold and tired, and Jimmy insisted on my drinking some whisky and hot water. This did not lead to my downfall, so all is well.

I think on the whole the general education was good. I certainly got further in Latin (Public-School Primer) and Greek (Farrar's *Greek Card*) and Mathematics than I did for years later on, at Charterhouse. Towards the end of my time a visiting German master came in from Brighton once a week and any boy who wished could—I need hardly say for an extra fee—attend his classes. The little German I know now I learned from him.

Another good lesson Jimmy Hewitt used to give us was the spelling class. He used to read out dozens of difficult words and we had to write them down and were marked according to the number of mistakes we made. As a result of this my spelling is on the whole better than my other general education. Hewitt used to read out almost impossible words like *eschscholtzia* and *diarrhoea*. I remember when one of the under-masters took the spelling class and read something out of the newspaper we were all at sea.

Most of the boys thought the country round was dull. I thought it lovely and enjoyed our walks. The great bare hills impressed me by their grandeur. I have loved the Downs ever since.[1]

Ralph learned a number of things from other boys. Sarah had interested him in politics and from his earlier years he had shared her radical views. Now he met rabid conservatism, as well as class consciousness and snobbery which shocked him. One boy was fascinatingly an atheist who said: 'If I go to war and they pray for the soldiers they must leave me out of their prayers, *I will not* be prayed for.' Ralph found this both impressive and reasonable. Sex was also discussed; the boys' information was, he said, in-

[1] A life-long inconsistency. Ralph said he hated a treeless landscape, but loved both the Downs and Salisbury Plain: but he never wanted to live near either.

accurate and depressing. 'If it's so dangerous,' he said, 'why do they do it?' 'Because it's awfully nice,' one of his friends answered. This was quite as new an idea as atheism.

During these years he played games at school with fair success but without pleasure. He hated the holiday cricket matches—and he soon contrived to avoid the cricket and yet to go to the dances which always followed. There were other dances in the holidays for which friends and cousins came to stay, and sometimes there were mornings devoted to chamber music for which Ralph would arrange works for what ever instruments were available in the house.

In January 1887 Ralph followed Hervey to Charterhouse. The cross-country journey from Ockley to Godalming was always prefaced by a ritual meal of coffee and little cakes 'because the boys would miss their tea'. This melancholy feast, following rather closely on luncheon, was eaten while the boxes were piled on to the pony carriage.

He joined the Headmaster's house, Saunderites, and his form was IV.B. His first term was as unhappy as most first terms at a new school. The change from being a senior boy, an influential person in a familiar world, to becoming an unnoticed junior in a much larger and more complex organization was hard, and the spring term, though it is the shortest in the school year, is the coldest and most depressing of the three. He still did not like games, and to those who are not naturally adept they can be a futile waste of time, cold, boring, and pointless. But he did not achieve the splendid individualism of Max Beerbohm, who never played any game and was never expected to do so. He and Ralph were contemporaries, though Max had arrived a term or two earlier. Ralph saw him on his first day at school, coming out of the Library, reciting:

I was some ice,
So white and so nice,
Which nobody tasted
And so it was wasted.

He did not know Edward Lear's alphabetical rhymes then, but he was amused and interested.

After his first term he settled in to the school life and accepted its conditions. He had learned enough Latin and Greek to do moderately in class, he read a great deal, and, if the teaching of mathematics had been better, he would have done well for it was a subject he liked when it was made interesting. He enjoyed the freedom of half-holiday expeditions, long walks and conversation, as well as the opportunities for music making. He wrote of his memories:

It is a mistake to suppose that the Public Schools of that period were entirely philistine and ignored the arts; probably this false idea arose from the equally false legend that in the sixties an Etonian who was caught practising a musical instrument was subjected to the extreme penalty. However, by the eighties, at all events at Charterhouse, the arts, even the art of music, were mildly encouraged.

There were in my time two presiding authorities over Carthusian music, Mr H. G. Robinson, the organist, and Mr Becker who taught the pianoforte and also played the horn. Robinson was a sensitive musician and a kind-hearted man, and gave me, and others, leave to practise on the chapel organ. There was in my time at least one competent organist among the boys, H. C. Erskine, who was able to give a very good performance of Bach's *St Anne Fugue*. Mr Becker was a very remarkable man and a fine teacher. I am sorry I never came directly under his influence. He was brother to the well-known Miss Lydia Becker, one of the forerunners of the suffragist movement. Among the piano pupils were several remarkable performers, H. V. Hamilton, N. G. Smith (later Swainson), who both became well-known in the professional world, and Ramsbotham who later made his name as a musicologist. And I also ought to mention a boy whose name became vicariously famous—Gordon Woodhouse.[1]

One cannot write of Carthusian music without mentioning 'Duck' Girdlestone. He was a keen amateur musician and conducted weekly practices of the school orchestra. I was one of the two violas, the other being the famous Mr Stewart ('Stewfug') whose chief business in life was to preside with complete inefficiency at 'extra school': however, he was a good viola player and a great help in the orchestra. One of my first practical lessons in orchestration came from playing the viola part in the slow movement of Beethoven's first symphony, when I was excited to find that my repeated notes on the viola were enriched by a long holding note from Mr Becker's horn.

Then there was, of course, the school choir which practised once a week in the time otherwise devoted to extra French, and was therefore very popular. Choir and orchestra used to meet once a year for a grand concert at the end of the summer, and occasionally for an oratorio. I

[1] His wife, Violet, was a noted harpsichord player, She died in 1947.

remember taking part in *Judas Maccabaeus*. Girdlestone also lives in my affectionate remembrance because in the winter months he used to invite some of us to his house on Sunday afternoons and there we played through many of the Italian Concerti Grossi from old band parts. The performances were pretty rough ('Duck' himself was an execrable violoncellist) but I learned much from the experience.

One of the most astounding events of my school musical life took place when Hamilton and I decided to give a concert. . . . It was my task to approach Dr Haig Brown, the Headmaster, for leave to use the school hall. Dr Haig Brown was a formidable man, and in later life I should never have dared to make the request, but leave was obtained, and we gave the concert, and it was attended by several of the masters and their wives and even some of the boys. I was complimented after the concert by Mr Noon, the mathematical master, who said in his well-known sepulchral voice, 'You must go on.' That is one of the few words of encouragement I have ever received.

Partly as a result of this concert, Girdlestone, who organized the Sunday evening 'Entertas', decided to devote four of them to national programmes and I was ordered to provide a Welsh concert. This was my first introduction to the beautiful melodies of the Principality. Another vivid reminiscence is the annual concert given by the Misses Haig Brown. Two of them played the pianoforte, and they invited six of us boys to join them in music for sixteen hands on four pianofortes. As I was one of the performers I never appreciated the full horror of the result.[1]

A letter to his sister postmarked 15 October 1889, is written on a sheet from an exercise book—it probably refers to one of these concerts:

Dear Meggie,

Please excuse this paper but I suddenly find that I have run out of all my notepaper. I hope to find you at no very distant period singing at a concert that I shall give at Charterhouse (a hypothetical one of course). Hamilton (O. C.) has been staying with Robinson and slept in my room, the consequence was that we talked from 10.30 PM till 3 AM. and as I got up at 6 15 AM I only had (about) three hours sleep. As I suppose you know he is going to be a pro. he has been to Bayreuth and now is a Wagnerite. We now have to believe that Mendellsohn [*sic*] is NOT a great composer, that though Beethoven is great he is old-fashioned. As to Handel, etc. they are quite out of date. I know Behinke and Pearce's book. I think brown, are they not? The concert

[1] *The Carthusian*, 1952.

was not so bad as I expected, but I and another fellow had to play one of (*illegible*) duets with $\frac{1}{2}$ hours practice.

Yours truily, [*sic*]
Ralph Vaughan Williams

For mother
I have got no tin boxes
I do not want gloves yet
I was bilious and am all right
Will ask Nicholson
Small cakes not big ones thanks very much.

Then, written round the corners:

For mother: will do all sorts of things which you tell me,

and,

Since H has been here, I started a practising mania yesterday. I practised 2 1/2 hours of piano besides counterpt.

After two years in Dr. Haig Brown's house he moved to the house of G. H. Robinson, the school organist, and spent his last four terms as head of the house.

During these years he was working at music in the holidays. An organ had been put in the hall at Leith Hill Place for him, and he would practise before breakfast. He always found it easy to get up early, though here it meant being very early, for breakfast was still at half past seven. The trouble about the early morning was finding a blower for the organ, and Ellis Cook (whose family came to Leith Hill Place with the Wedgwoods in 1847) recalled the consternation this caused:

It was very disturbing to the servants. . . . Phillips, the old butler, would try to steer clear, having the dining room breakfast to lay. At times he [Ralph] would get the service of maids, this made them late with their work, at times he would have to call in the help of groom or gardener. On Sundays he would be practising long after all the rest of the household had started to walk to church, two miles distant, and he usually arrived just as the service was starting. The service over, the three children would walk home with their young friends, whose parents, Mr and Mrs Bosanquet, were tenants at Tanhurst. They would call at Tanhurst and then walk home through the rhododendron woods and the park, generally arriving late for lunch, for which there was a severe scolding.[1]

[1] *R.C.M. Magazine*. Easter 1959.

There were other diversions, visits to London for theatres and concerts, tennis and croquet, the only game Ralph played left handed. At one of the winter dances he was delighted to overhear someone say, 'Why don't you ask that pretty Mrs. Vaughan Williams to dance?', though, until then, he had never thought about his mother's looks. At another party he was standing at the door of the ballroom, feeling horribly shy because he was rather younger than anyone else, a little uncertain of his evening clothes and not confident of his dancing, when the three beautiful Miss Maxses caught sight of him and called out: 'Oh, *look* where you're standing, Ralph.' He looked up and found he was under a branch of mistletoe and fled blushing as the girls laughed at his discomfiture. In the summer holidays of 1890, when he left Charterhouse, Aunt Sophy, Margaret, Hervey, Meggie, and Ralph all went to Oberammergau for the Passion Play. Ralph did not enjoy the experience. He found the play tedious, and disliked all the beards and the fervent and rapturous atmosphere. Nor did he much care for the place with its hotels full of enthusiasts; though he was amused to discover that it was always possible to see which rooms were occupied by English visitors as they all hung their sponge bags out of the windows. This visit made him realize how little religion meant to him. He had been confirmed at Charterhouse, taking it as a matter of course in his school career, and he continued to go to church fairly regularly 'so as not to upset the family'. This attitude did not affect his love of the Authorized version of the Bible. The beauty of the idiom of the Jacobean English was established in his mind long before he went away to school and, like the music of Bach, remained as one of his essential companions through life. He was far too deeply absorbed by music to feel any need of religious observance. He was an atheist during his later years at Charterhouse and at Cambridge, though he later drifted into a cheerful agnosticism: he was never a professing Christian.

Another much more successful event of that holiday was a visit to Munich where he heard his first Wagner opera.

We found that *Die Walküre* was down for that evening. The opera, we were told, would start at seven, so at six o'clock we sat down to have a preliminary meal. Hardly had we started when the waiter rushed in—he had made a mistake—on a Wagner *abend* the opera started at six. The rest decided for dinner, but I, like the hero of a novel, 'left my food untasted', and rushed off to the Opera House. I arrived just in time to hear that wonderful passage for strings when Sieglinde offers Siegmund the cup. This was my first introduction to later Wagner, but I experienced no surprise, but rather that strange certainty that I had heard it all before. There was a feeling of recognition, as of meeting an old friend, which comes to us all in the face of great artistic experiences. I had the same experience when I first heard an English folksong, when I first saw Michelangelo's *Day and Night*, when I suddenly came upon Stonehenge or had my first sight of New York City—the intuition that I had been there already.[1]

At this time Ralph felt he had the makings of a good string player; he had given up the violin for the viola, an instrument he loved, and he would have dearly liked to become an orchestral player. But the whole weight of family opinion was against him. If he had to be a musician he must be an organist, which was a safe and respectable career. So with dogged determination he worked at the organ at home, and at the one in the church at Coldharbour, which he had permission to use. He would walk down through the woods after tea and work until almost dinner time. In spring and summer this was agreeable enough, but in the winter he was frightened by the rustling blackness of the woods, until one night there was a great storm and he watched balls of fire tossing along the hillside and found to his surprise that he did not mind the dark road ever again.

Ralph left Charterhouse in July 1890 and in September, after the summer holidays, entered the Royal College of Music as a student. The College had been founded in 1883 and the first Director, Sir George Grove,[2] was still in office. Before devoting all his time to music, Grove had been a civil engineer with a distinguished and sometimes exciting career. His interests were wide, scholarly, and ranged through the arts. Under his direction the College gave a sound musical education, with active encouragement to its students to explore beyond the limits of their immediate studies, and to be aware of literature and painting, history and science as well as of the music of the past and the present. Ralph remembered:

[1] *Musical Autobiography*.

[2] Perhaps better known as the founder and first editor of Grove's *Dictionary of Music and Musicians*.

I was determined if possible to study composition under Parry. I had first heard of Parry some years before, when I was still a schoolboy. I remember my cousin, Stephen Massingberd, coming into the room full of that new book *Studies of Great Composers*. 'This man Parry,' he said, 'declares that a composer must write music as his musical conscience demands.' This was quite a new idea to me, the loyalty of an artist to his art. Soon after that I got to know some of his music, especially parts of *Judith*, and I remember, even as a boy, saying to my mother that there was something, to my mind, peculiarly English in his music. So I was quite prepared to join with the other young students of the R.C.M. in worshipping at that shrine, and I think I can truly say I have never been disloyal to it. . . .

By a wise ruling of the College, which I fear no longer obtains, no one was allowed to study composition until he had passed Grade V in harmony. So for two terms I did my theoretical work with Dr. F. E. Gladstone. Under his guidance I worked through every exercise in Macfarren's *Harmony*, a discipline for which I have ever since been grateful.

After two terms I passed my Grade V harmony and was allowed to become a pupil of Parry. I will not try to describe what this experience meant to a boy. I was very elementary at the time. I blush with shame now when I think of the horrible little songs and anthems which I presented for his criticism. Parry's great watchword was 'characteristic'. He was always trying to discover the character revealed in even the weakest of his students' compositions.

Before telling the following story, I ought to explain that Parry, not content with the official lesson, used to keep his pupil's compositions to look at during the week. One day, through pure carelessness, I had written out a scale passage with one note repeated and then a gap. Parry said, 'I have been looking at this passage for a long time to discover whether it is just a mistake or whether you meant anything characteristic.'

I was painfully illiterate in those days. Parry could hardly believe that I knew so little music. One day he was talking to me about the wonderful climax in the development of the *Appassionata* Sonata. Suddenly he realised that I did not know it, so he sat down at the pianoforte and played it through to me. There were showers of wrong notes, but in spite of that it was the finest performance that I have ever heard. So I was told to study more Beethoven, especially the posthumous Quartets, 'as a religious exercise'. At that time I hated Beethoven. I was suffering from an overdose of Gounod, and I could not understand why the tune in the finale of the *Eroica* Symphony was good music while the 'Judex' from *Mors et Vita* was bad music. . . .

Parry was very generous in lending scores to his pupils. (This was long before the day of miniature scores and gramophone records.) I borrowed *Siegfried* and *Tristan* and Brahms's *Requiem*, and for some time after my compositions consisted entirely of variations of a passage near the beginning of that work.[1]

There were about fourteen students in the Harmony and Counterpoint classes. A fellow pupil[2] of Ralph's remembers him as very hard working, frequently agitated and in no way outstanding as a musician. She also had lessons with Parry and sometimes she came in at the end of Ralph's, and listened to the last few minutes. One day Parry said, after Ralph had left him: 'That's a very strange young man. He says he can't sleep at all for two nights after he's heard one of Wagner's operas.' Ralph's account continued:

I remember one day when I came in for my lesson I found a fellow student, Richard Walthew, borrowing the score of the Prelude to *Parsifal*. Parry condemned it as the weakest of the Wagner Preludes—'mere scene painting' was, I think, his description of it. He was always very insistent on the importance of form as opposed to colour. He had an almost moral abhorrence of mere luscious sound. It has been said that Parry's own orchestration was bad; the truth is, I think, that he occasionally went too far in deliberate eschewal of orchestral effect. . . .

Parry's criticism was constructive. He was not merely content to point out faults, but would prescribe a remedy. The last two bars of my early song *The Willow Song* were almost certainly composed by Parry.

Parry once said to me: 'Write choral music as befits an Englishman and a democrat.' We pupils of Parry have, if we have been wise, inherited from him the great English choral tradition, which Tallis passed on to Byrd, Byrd to Gibbons, Gibbons to Purcell, Purcell to Battishill and Greene, and they in their turn, through the Wesleys, to Parry. He has passed on the torch to us and it is our duty to keep it alight.

I have already mentioned Richard Walthew. We became great friends . . . this however is not a record of friendships, but of musical influences, and I pick out Walthew's name among friends of that period because I learnt much from him. I used occasionally to go to his house at Highbury and play duets with him—or rather, he played and I stumbled behind him as best I could. In this way I learnt to know a lot of music, including, I remember, Stanford's *Irish Symphony*. In those days, before the gramophone and the wireless and the miniature score, the pianoforte duet was the only way, unless you were an or-

[1] *Musical Autobiography*. [2] The Dowager Lady Farrer.

Leith Hill Place

Arthur Vaughan Williams

Margaret Vaughan Williams

Ralph, aged about three

Ralph, aged about six

Ralph, aged about thirteen

chestral player, of getting to know orchestral music, and one really got to know it from the inside; not in the superficial way of lazily listening to a gramophone record. One day, Walthew, who had a holy terror of anything high-falutin' in art, insisted on taking me to hear *Carmen*. By that time I had quite recovered from my Gounod fever and had become the complete prig. Bach, Beethoven (*ex officio*), Brahms and Wagner were the only composers worth considering, so I went to *Carmen* prepared to scoff; but Walthew won the day, and I remained to pray. It must have been about the same time that I had another salutary disturbance of my musical prejudices; I heard Verdi's *Requiem* for the first time. At first I was properly shocked by the frank sentimentalism and sensationalism of the music. I remember being particularly horrified at the drop of a semitone on the word *Dona*. Was not this the purest 'village organist'? But in a very few minutes the music possessed me. I realized that here was a composer who could do all the things that I, with my youthful pedantry, thought wrong—indeed, would be unbearable in a lesser man; music which was sentimental, theatrical, occasionally even cheap, and yet was an overpowering masterpiece. That day I learnt that there is nothing in itself that is 'common or unclean'; indeed, that there are no canons of art except that contained in the well-worn tag, 'To thine own self be true'.[1]

During this time Ralph lived at Leith Hill Place though he would have prefered to stay in London during term-time. It had been difficult to persuade his family to allow him to go to the R.C.M. instead of staying on at Charterhouse, and he did not like to ask for further concessions—though living at home meant that he was not able to go to all the concerts or theatres he would have liked. He sometimes managed to slip into a Music Hall and catch a later train home, or to spend a night with friends, such as Walthew, whose families lived in London.

Caroline Wedgwood died in 1888, and the ownership of Leith Hill Place passed to Sophy, who had begun to show the eccentricities that made her more and more difficult to live with as time went on. She had a curious, squirrel-like way of hiding biscuits in cupboards, or announcing that she had told the servants, 'we will just have oranges and biscuits instead of tea'. Emerging from a long afternoon, battling with Kyrie or quartet, Ralph would find a sour orange a dreary alternative to the cakes and home-made bread and butter, the jam and cream that were his favourite kinds of food. She was devoted to her nephews, but she

[1] *Musical Autobiography.*

all too easily forgot that their appetites were larger than her own bird-like needs. But it was a minor hardship, and on his College days he used to go out with his friends and have enormous teas of muffins and cake.

On 15 June 1892, Mahler gave the first performance of *Tristan* in London since Wagner had conducted it in 1875. It was an exciting occasion, with Max Alvary and Rosa Sucher singing. After the opera Ralph, standing on the murky platform of the underground railway at Charing Cross with his score under his arm, met a fellow student from the R.C.M. and, with him, a Cambridge undergraduate, George McCleary. They talked for a few moments, and George thought he had not cared for the opera, but many years later Ralph told him that he had been deeply shaken by it. This chance meeting was the beginning of a long and pleasant friendship—one of the many gifts Cambridge gave him—for after the summer holidays he entered Trinity College as an undergraduate, a few days before his twentieth birthday. There his independence and emancipation started, and his real life began.

CHAPTER III

1892–1897

Cambridge gave Ralph the right life precisely when he was ready to appreciate it. He was fortunate in his contemporaries, particularly in his cousin Ralph Wedgwood who came from Clifton to Trinity fully fledged with worldly knowledge and with friendships already established. The two Ralphs shared Darwin relations at Cambridge to whose houses they were both welcome. One of the youngest of the cousins, Frances (later Cornford), was about six when 'a towering presence' was brought up to her Cambridge nursery. 'I was told this was my new undergraduate cousin, Ralph. I remember it was a misty day in late autumn, of exciting, premature snow. He lifted me up to the window-seat to look out. I remember too quite well how clumsily yet gently he did it, and also my sense that he really appreciated the snow in the field and liked the blue-grey afternoon just before tea time in the same way that I did.'[1]

Another house at which he was always welcome was the Lodge at Downing. The Vaughan Williams and Fisher families had been friends since Ralph's father and uncles had known Herbert Fisher at Christchurch and the Fishers had taken houses in Surrey, not far from Dorking, in summer holidays, so the younger generations were acquainted. The eldest of Herbert Fisher's daughters, Florence, had married Frederic Maitland, who held the Chair of the Laws of England, and there was a great deal of music-making in their home at Downing College. Ralph admired both Maitland, a vivid and attractive man whose lectures and writings illuminated the dusty archives of legal history with humanity and wit, and his wife, who was a beautiful and original young woman and a fine amateur violinist. Among the most constant visitors to their house were Ralph's friends Nicholas and Ivor Gatty; Nicholas was a violinist, Ivor played the horn, Ralph the viola, and other undergraduate musicians joined the group for 'scratch' chamber music. Sometimes Florence's younger sister, Adeline, stayed at the

[1] *R.C.M. Magazine*, Easter 1959.

Lodge and, as she was able to play the cello if no one else was available to do so, though her real talent was for the piano, she was a welcome addition to the party. She was staying when Tchaikovsky visited Cambridge in June 1893 to receive an honorary degree. He too stayed at Downing and Florence and Adeline played for him, and pinned roses in his buttonhole before he joined Boito, Saint-Saëns, and Max Bruch for the ceremonies at which they all received their honorary degrees. During the week they all performed at concerts to which Ralph went.

Ralph's official study was history, a subject chosen because the lectures at Cambridge did not conflict with Parry's teaching days at the R.C.M.: he spent as much time on music as he could, travelling to London for his lessons. There was some difficulty in arranging this, for Parry wrote to him at the very beginning of his first term:

October 9th 1892

My dear good soul,

It won't do for you to be missing such a lot of time. It's just throwing away your property! Can you come up on *Tuesday* instead. I'll keep 11 o'clock in the morning or 12.20 for you if you can. Send me a telegram or something to say which, if you can. It's my only chance as I have to go to Oxford on Tuesday night.

Very sincerely yours,
C. Hubert H. Parry

Besides these excursions to London he had lessons from Charles Wood in preparation for the degree of Bachelor of Music.

Charles Wood was the finest technical instructor I have ever known, I do not say necessarily the greatest teacher. I do not think he had the gift of inspiring enthusiasm or of leading to the higher planes of musical thought. Indeed, he was rather prone to laugh at artistic ideals, and would lead one to suppose that composing music was a trick anyone might learn if he took the trouble. But for the craft of composition he was unrivalled, and he managed to teach me enough to pull me through my B.Mus. I also had organ lessons from Alan Gray. Our friendship survived his despair at my playing, and I became quite expert at managing the stops at his voluntaries and recitals.[1]

In those days attendance at Chapel was compulsory, and one morning when Ralph's absence had been noted he was sent for by authority:

[1] *Musical Autobiography*.

'I did not see you in Chapel this morning, Mr. Vaughan Williams.'

'No, Sir.'

'Perhaps, however, you were in the organ loft?'

'Yes, Sir, I was.'

'Well, you can pray as well in the organ loft as in any other part of the Chapel.'

'Yes, Sir—but I didn't.'

The first year he had rooms at 17 Magdalene Street, then he moved to 2 Whewells Court, where he remained for the rest of his time at Cambridge, and for these rooms he chose prints and china with excited pleasure. He and Randolph (his name for Ralph Wedgwood) used to lunch together almost every day, and their usual meal was biscuits and jam. They planned to go right through an alphabet of biscuits, but the grocer supplied a seven-pound tin of Abernethys to start with and on that rock the plan foundered.

A great pleasure of these years was bicycling. Ralph and his friends all bought bicycles, which made longer excursions possible, and on them they explored much of the country around and sometimes, at the end of term, Ralph bicycled to London. One winter, the frosts were so hard that it was possible to skate from Cambridge to Ely. The stronger skaters did the journey both ways, but Ralph was one of the many who preferred to return by train. It was a journey he knew well, for he often went to hear the Cathedral morning service on summer Sundays, and the exciting moment when the towered hill appeared from the surrounding fens was one that never ceased to delight him. The train arrived in time for him to slip in just after the service had started and the sound of the choir's singing set new musical ideas flowing. He always carried little manuscript notebooks in his pocket and filled them with pencilled jottings to be worked out later.

Besides the Gatty brothers, G. E. Moore, Maurice Amos, and George Trevelyan became close friends, and when H. P. Allen[1] came as an organ scholar to Christ's, another life-long friendship began. Ralph and Hugh Allen belonged to the University

[1] G. E. Moore, O.M., the philosopher; Maurice Sheldon Amos, K.B.E., K.C.; George Trevelyan, O.M., the historian, Master of Trinity; Sir Hugh Allen, later Director of the R.C.M.

Musical Club, the main purpose of which was to study chamber music, and concerts were given by the members every Saturday evening. Ralph went to them regularly, and it was at one of them he heard the first public performance of one of his own works, a quartet for men's voices. Hugh Allen organized an encore, but even after a second hearing nobody liked it except Haydn Inwards, a professional violinist and a member of the teaching staff of the R.C.M.

At this time Ralph was rather a dandy, with a liking for the fashionable, large, floppy ties. He was tall, broad-shouldered, and good looking, with dark hair that curled a little unless he kept it cut very short, and eyes, between grey and blue, that looked bluer in summer when he was sun-burned. He enjoyed himself among his friends, and the independence of living away from home was intoxicating. Besides music and history, conversation and cousins, there were girls. All through his life Ralph was romantically susceptible to beauty, and at Cambridge he was as liable to fall in love as any one of his age. His first flame there was a girl who, he said, was not conventionally pretty, but most deliciously attractive. He met her at dances, at Sunday tea-parties and at tennis parties. Once Ralph Wedgwood accused him of faking the toss, so that he could partner her, and Ralph brazenly agreed that he had. This springtime fancy never grew beyond the quivering expectation of meeting and the melancholy rapture of parting at the end of dances. Nothing was said, and she remained a delightful memory. They never met again, though he knew when and whom she married, and even sixty years later the steps of her house recalled moments of tremulous expectation.

Shyness, and the conventions of romance, the inaccessibility of distant beauty, almost in the medieval troubadour manner, were his natural element: this was a curious paradox in a man of passionate disposition and warm, human affection, who all his life enjoyed both the decorative gaieties and the lively companionship of women, all of whom gave him unchanging affection that a word from him could have warmed into far more. Brought up in the rigid moral code of his age, he admired the freer ways of others and of later generations but any physical indulgence was impossible or inhibited for him by his own inner discipline, which allowed flirtation, friendships, and emotional turmoils, but forbade anything that he thought might hurt or injure another person. In later years he said that he had never been brave enough to plunge into what he called 'affaires', and it seemed, to an onlooker, that there was a subconscious saving of all emotion for the deeper needs of creation. He also maintained for many years that he had never been in love. Be this as it may, his nature was deeply romantic in all its responses to life.

Among the pleasures of the Cambridge years were reading parties. One summer, he, Ralph Wedgwood, George Moore, and George Trevelyan were in Skye and it was there he heard a Gaelic preacher at an open-air service. Not understanding the language, he listened to his voice and noted how emotional excitement, and having to speak so that the words would carry, changed speech rhythm into song. He remembered the melodic formula into which the sermon grew

and recognized it when he started his work on folk song, and found it common to the opening of many English and Scottish songs.

Ralph left before the end of the party and George Trevelyan wrote to him:

Dear V.W.,

Have you left a sweater, Jersey, Guernsey, Alderney, or Sark (not shirt) behind you here? There is great distress here because there is a nameless jersey left, whether yours or Wedgwood's is unknown. . . . I went up Ben Tillett another way, just the other side of John Burns to where we climbed up together on the first memorable occasion. I have been to Miss Scott's and had strawberries and cream. They had been very much impressed by you and your music. I hope you are enjoying yourself as much as you expected.

We are all in an anti-jam and anti-more-than-one-helping-of-pudding league, so help us God!

Yrs sincerely,
G. M. Trevy.

Another summer the same party went to Penzance, and at Easter 1895 to Seatoller in Cumberland. This time they kept a log book, which Maurice Amos, a fifth friend who had joined the party, illustrated. They were all great walkers, and hardy enough

The Seatoller Reading Party; from left to right: Ralph L. Wedgwood, M. S. Amos, G. E. Moore, G. M. Trevelyan, R.V.W.

to bathe, as the log book records. There is a note each day on who was down last; who was the day's president; and what was the day's subject for discussion—these ranged from theology to battles sham and real, *Punch*, Thackeray, the unjust steward, and tips.

Each of them contributed stories and rhymes: among Ralph's offerings were a limerick, a Meredithian fragment of dialogue and a Swinburnian poem on climbing Glaramara. George Trevelyan wrote an Arthurian fragment, a brief topical *roman à clef*, in which they all figured as talkative, giant-slaying knights; taking coffee in Sir Behemoth's (Ralph's) rooms in Cambridge. It ends with Marshish (Eddie Marsh), a visitor, sweeping them all off to the Incantation Club. Ralph was the first to leave this holiday and George Moore gave him a sonorous epitaph—

In memory of
Ralph Vaughan Williams
who passed away with the utmost complaisance
March 29th 1895

Interiit, miti multis qui praefuit unus
Ingenio: in conclos moriger ille fuit
Idem, ubi maturum deposeunt fata recessum.
Annuit ipse libens obsequitur que Deo.[1]

A summer of hard work followed, with examinations, in which, to his great pleasure, he took a good degree—a second in history. He had taken his B.Mus in 1894 so he left Cambridge with a solid achievement and returned to the Royal College of Music.

Alan Gray foresaw many difficulties for him and he wrote from Cambridge to the Professor teaching organ-playing at the R.C.M.

My dear Parratt,

I wish you would let me have a line as to your opinion of Vaughan Williams. He is leaving here next term and is uncertain as to his future. I cannot tell him that I think he is justified in going in for an organist's career which is his pet idea. He seems to me so hopelessly 'unhandy'. He has got to a certain point and sticks there. I can never trust him to

[1] Here lies a man, who in his gentle wit
Surpassed the crowd, obsequious to all;
When God and Fate demand his ripe retreat
With pious joy he straight obeys the call.
Tr. William LeFanu.

play a simple service for me without some dread as to what he may do. And this he combines with considerable knowledge and taste on organ and music matters generally.

He said once that you had been 'rushing him through' pieces before he knew them, from which I gathered that you had noticed the same defects in him. I have tried the same but I cannot say with success.

In fact he seems to me somewhat hopeless, but I should be very glad if you could give me your opinion, as of course you have had far wider experience than I have in such matters.

Yours very truly,
Alan Gray.

Besides belonging to the amateur University Musical Club, whose rehearsals under Hugh Allen Ralph had attended until he knew Schumann and Brahms pianoforte quintets by heart, he conducted a small choral society which met on Sundays to sing Schubert's Masses. Ralph knew that this experience of practical music making was vital knowledge for a composer. If his teachers were puzzled about his future he was in no doubt himself that he would write music, even if he had to start his musical career as an organist. When he re-entered the R.C.M. in 1895 he did not wait for the beginning of the academic year, but joined for the second half of the midsummer term. This was the year of Oscar Wilde's trial; Shaw had finished his two years as music critic for *The World*; Ellen Terry, in her later forties, was acting in his plays; Duse and Bernhardt were at the height of their fame; Sir George Henschel had left Glasgow for London, and many young musicians, including Ralph, learned to know the classics from his authoritative performances.

Manet and Tennyson had been dead for two years; Verlaine was fifty-one; Monet, Zola, Daudet, and Hardy were all fifty-five; Dvorak and Cézanne a year older; Maupassant ten years younger, and George Meredith sixty-two. Young talents were rising. Debussy and Delius were thirty-three, Elgar thirty-eight. Henry Wood, twenty-six that year, had already started conducting Promenade Concerts and was enthusiastically ready to include new and little-known music in his programmes. It was a time of promise, and the Royal College of Music had a brilliant generation of musicians among its pupils.

What one really learns from an Academy or College is not so much from one's official teachers as from one's fellow students. I was lucky in my companions in those days; other students at the College were Dunhill, Ireland, Howard-Jones, Fritz Hart and Gustav Holst. We used to meet at a little teashop in Kensington and discuss every subject under the sun from the lowest note of the double bassoon to the philosophy of *Jude the Obscure*. I learnt more from these conversations than from any amount of formal teaching, but I felt at a certain disadvantage with these companions; they were all so competent and I felt such an amateur. . . .[1]

This feeling persisted, but it was more probably due to the fact that he was searching for his own individual language than to any lack of diligence or application. No one can guide explorations of a place as yet unknown, and the steps on an unmapped journey are naturally more faltering than those on a well made road. In the discipline of his working hours, in his eager study of his craft, and in his anxiety to learn about all kinds of music, Ralph was professional, but when he compared what he had achieved with what his friends had achieved, he often felt he was not 'good enough'. Then, as later, he suffered from despair, jealousy, and frustration, as all composers probably do, but he kept these darknesses to himself and they never became obsessions or spoiled friendships he made at college.

Chief among these friendships was that with Gustav von Holst. He was two years younger than Ralph and he came from a family of professional musicians. From the first they seemed to be complementary in character, and Ralph spoke of him as 'the greatest influence on my music'. While Ralph was impressed by von Holst's professional attitude and his experiences in the holidays as an orchestral player, Ralph's wider reading and more sophisticated Cambridge background provided contact with a world outside music for von Holst. From their College days they started playing their works over to each other for criticism and help, 'field days' which became more important to both as time went on.

One of the great moments of the Autumn term of 1895 was the first performance in modern times of Purcell's *Dido and Aeneas*. It was given by R.C.M. students at the Royal Lyceum Theatre, with scenery lent by Sir Henry Irving, Mr. Johnston Forbes Robertson, Mr. Frederick Harrison, and Mr. I. Cohen; the properties and some dresses were lent by Sir Augustus Harris.

[1] *Musical Autobiography.*

Agnes Nicholls was Dido, and Stanford conducted. Ralph was a member of the chorus, and because of his height he was dressed impressively as a high priest. The make-up man refused to believe that he belonged to the ranks and spent most of the allotted time in making him up, neglecting the real principals in spite of all Ralph could say. He enjoyed himself thoroughly, and from then on he and von Holst were firm devotees of Purcell's music.

Among the pleasant activities of this second period at the R.C.M. was the debating society which met on Saturday afternoons. Ralph's contributions included papers on Purcell, The Rise and Fall of the Romantic School, Bayreuth, and Didactic Art. There was a debate on his motion 'that the moderate man is contemptible'. Other contributions were equally diverse and provocative and the society sometimes devoted their meeting to reading Shakespeare or to discussing recently published books such as Max Nordau's *Degeneration*. After the meetings ended the whole society removed to Wilkins' tea shop in Kensington High Street where the talk continued over tea and buns.

Parry was now Director of the R.C.M., so Ralph went to Stanford for lessons.

Stanford was a great teacher, but I believe I was unteachable. I made the great mistake of trying to fight my teacher. The way to get the best out of instruction is to put oneself entirely in the hands of one's instructor, and try to find out all about his method regardless of one's own personality, keeping, of course, a secret *eppur si muove* up one's sleeve. Young students are much too obsessed with the idea of expressing their personalities. In the merest harmony exercise they insist on keeping all their clumsy progressions because that is what they 'felt', forgetting that the art cannot mature unless the craft matures alongside with it.

The details of my work annoyed Stanford so much that we seldom got beyond these to the broader issues, and the lesson usually started with a conversation on these lines:

'Damnably ugly, my boy. Why do you write such things?'

'Because I like them.'

'But you can't like them, they're not music.'

'I shouldn't write them if I didn't like them.'

So the argument went on and there was no time for constructive criticism. Stanford tried—I fear in vain—to lighten my texture. He actually made me write a waltz. I was much bitten by the modes at that time, and I produced a modal waltz! I really must have been unteachable and fearfully obstinate.

Stanford never displayed great enthusiasm for my work. I once showed him a movement of a quartet which had caused me hours of agony, and I really thought it was going to move mountains this time. 'All rot, my boy,' was his only comment. But his deeds were better than his words—later on he introduced my work to the Leeds Festival, thus giving me my first opportunity of a performance under those imposing conditions. When all is said and done, what one really gets out of lessons with a great man cannot be computed in terms of what he said to you or what you did for him, but in terms of the intangible contact with his mind and character. With Stanford I always felt I was in the presence of a lovable, powerful and enthralling mind. This helped me more than any amount of technical instruction.[1]

Ralph was still under the influence of his Cambridge friends as far as clothes were concerned, dressing with a worldly dash remarkable among young musicians. There was a story current at the R.C.M. that he appeared there after a wedding dressed in a morning coat and top hat: leaving later with some friends, they met a man playing a barrel-organ, who told them he had had a very bad day. Ralph pushed the organ into Kensington High Street and turned the handle and collected nearly a pound before he gave it back to its owner. He was fortunate because an allowance from his family saved him from the necessity of having to earn his living, but in spite of this he took an organist's post in 1895 at the church of St. Barnabas, South Lambeth. The advantage of this was that he had to live in London. He had rooms first in Smith Square, later near his church in St. Barnabas Villas.

As I have already said, I never could play the organ, but this post gave me an insight into good and bad church music which stood me in good stead later on. I also had to train the choir, and give organ recitals, and accompany the services, which gave me some knowledge of music from the performer's point of view. I also founded a choral society and an orchestral society, both of them pretty bad, but we managed once to do a Bach Cantata, and I obtained some of the practical knowledge of music which is so essential to a composer's make-up. Composers who think that they will achieve their aim by ranging apart and living the life beautiful make the great mistake of their lives.[2]

[1] *Musical Autobiography*. [2] Ibid.

In these small concerts Ralph was helped by a very young fellow organ pupil of Dr. Parratt's, William Harris,[1] who had come to take over his church duties during the summer holidays. He was then a lad of sixteen or so, and already a very promising organist whose support was invaluable when Ralph conducted.

After two years' work with Stanford and organ lessons with Parratt, Ralph felt he needed a change and he decided to go to Germany. This was against Stanford's advice, who urged him to visit Italy, to hear opera at the Scala rather than to take definite lessons. He thought Ralph was too Teuton already so did not approve of his choice of Berlin where the great attraction was *The Ring* given without cuts, for at that time Ralph had an insatiable appetite for Wagner.

He had another reason for wanting to go abroad: he had long wanted to marry Adeline Fisher, and she had at last accepted him. He knew how closely knit a family she belonged to and how difficult it would be for her to break away from that devoted circle into which he had no wish to be absorbed, so he thought it would be easier for them both if they could start their married life away from everyone and in a place neither of them knew.

Adeline's father, Herbert Fisher, was the son of a Canon of Salisbury, and one of his great uncles had been Constable's friend and patron; his mother was a cousin of Wordsworth. He was a brilliant young man, practising at the Bar, when the Dean of Christ Church, Henry Liddell, recommended him to the Prince Consort as 'guide and mentor' for the Prince of Wales to supervise his studies at Oxford and Cambridge. This was a brief appointment and before long Herbert Fisher returned to his legal work. But he was soon offered the post of private secretary to the Prince of Wales, which he accepted as he had a great personal affection for the Prince though less liking for Court life.

He married the beautiful, young Mary Jackson. Her ancestry was as romantic as her looks. Her grandfather, Antoine de L'Etang, a dashing page of Marie Antoinette's household, whose name rumour connected with hers, was hurried away from Versailles to Pondicherry. Many reasons for this were imagined, none known for certain. The fine-boned and aristocratic features of the Chevalier persisted through many generations of his descendants, and Mary Jackson, who as a girl was the model for Una in Watts's

[1] Later Sir William Harris, organist of St. George's Chapel, Windsor.

picture of Una and the Red Cross Knight, inherited this beauty. The family had remained French in many of its habits. Above all they had an immense clannishness, a cult of family so passionate and intense that even the husbands and wives they married remained outsiders, although officially accepted and loved.

The Herbert Fishers had a family of eleven, all good looking and talented, with a mutual devotion, almost like the emotional closeness usual in twins, which was fostered and encouraged by their mother's selfless devotion to them all. There was very little money to go round among the needs of so many young people, but Mrs. Fisher was a great contriver and had charmingly inventive talents. She painted furniture with landscapes of birds and flowers, so that any old odds and ends for the nursery or for children's bedrooms became enchanted points of departure for stories and daydreams. Dresses would be invented out of a length of book muslin, and, because the wearer was lovely and enjoying herself, the insufficiencies of the sewing did not mar the pleasure of a grand ball.

Perhaps the happiest time for all the family was during the years they lived at Brockenhurst, where their father inherited a house from three old aunts, maiden ladies, who left a miscellany of ancient furniture, trunks full of old dresses and, in the house itself, a world of romance and surprise which all the young Fishers enjoyed and remembered as a place of happiness for the rest of their lives.

Hervey Fisher, the invalid brother, who was a writer of short stories, described Adeline as a girl in this New Forest setting—she is Marjorie, he Kenneth:

> Marjorie was a flaxen haired girl of sixteen—four years older than Kenneth—with heavy-lidded grey eyes and the light of June in her cheeks . . . to the brothers the girls were on the whole Olympian and mysterious. . . .
>
> Their beauty, virginal and dewy, gave a shape in his mind to those lovely Greek legends that already stirred in his heart a vague yet passionate desire. He saw in them the embodiment of myths, the rosy realisation of immortal shadows. Marjorie was a more human goddess. She played hide-and-seek sometimes, read aloud fairy tales, caught newts and butterflies, paddled in the river, sailing boats with the boys. Though sixteen, her hair still hung over her shoulders in a yellow cascade . . . she was still a child's playmate with the warmth of the

nursery yet upon her. Only her flashes of superior wisdom revealed to her brothers that she had descended from the heights.[1]

Another brother, William,[2] going to sea as a midshipman at fifteen, wrote of his return, three years later:

> Half way up the hill I see figures in white in the dusk and the next moment I am out of the carriage and surrounded by sisters. Sisters let themselves go in a way that brothers don't and I shall never forget those soft yet excited voices and the sudden realisation of what I had been banished from so long and so completely. . . . I am home again, surrounded, protected and understood, no longer alone.

Florence and Adeline had worked together at music, but, after Florence's marriage to Fred Maitland, the partnership of violin and piano could be renewed only when Adeline stayed in Cambridge or Florence visited her parents. But Adeline continued to practise, and her most devoted audience were her youngest sister and brother, Cordelia and Edwin. She also used to read aloud to them and they went through all of Scott's novels, Adeline's vivid characterization making the stories memorable. She was a good photographer, having learned from her aunt, Julia Cameron.[3] It was a cumbrous business and called for patience in both sitter and photographer, and a lot of messy work in the developing and printing of the plates. So with helping her mother with housekeeping, looking after family invalids, reading, and with the correspondence that kept brothers far away in almost daily touch with home events, her life passed agreeably and almost eventlessly. Her cousin, Stella Duckworth, stepdaughter of Leslie Stephen, was like another sister, and perhaps her only confidante. The Fishers were not anxious for their daughters to marry, home life seemed to fulfil every demand. 'Adeline could have married anyone,' was often said, but quite obviously she didn't want to, and no one succeeded in touching what many must have believed to be a heart of ice. Besides her beauty she had a quick wit, a lively intelligence, and an ability to be cruelly critical. She and Ralph had met frequently during his years at Cambridge. Ralph had

[1] 'An Afternoon', from *A Romantic Man and other Tales*, by Hervey Fisher (Martin Secker, 1920).

[2] Later Admiral Sir William Fisher.

[3] Mrs. Cameron was well known as a photographer, and particularly for her portraits of eminent Victorians.

Ralph Wedgwood and Ralph V. W.

Nicholas Gatty

Rough music at Hooton Roberts (Ralph on right)

Adeline Fisher, about 1896

been a constant visitor to Hove, where the Fishers now lived, during the spring and summer and Adeline had stayed at Leith Hill Place in January. But she was staying in London with the Leslie Stephens when he proposed to her and was accepted. She telegraphed to her parents, and a letter followed next morning. Cordelia remembers her father reading it at breakfast and saying gloomily: 'So it's a *fait accompli.*'

Adeline had gone to London to be with Stella, who had recently married, had returned ill after a short honeymoon in Paris, and had been unwell ever since. However, at this moment she was reassuringly better and Mrs. Fisher's visit to London to spend the day with the newly engaged couple was unmarred by anxiety.

There was everything in the way of background and interest to draw them together. Ralph, deep in pre-Raphaelite poetry, saw all romance alive in her beauty, and devoted himself to writing piano music to give her pleasure. Both families were pleased by the engagement, though one of Adeline's brothers said in his letter of congratulation:

> I only know of one fault that he has or rather defect, and that is that he cannot discriminate between good and bad food. I don't know whether you intend to trade on this or cure it. . . .

Money was not thought of as a necessary qualification on either side. Mrs. Fisher's diary for that summer gives a picture of the comings and goings of a large family, and of many visits exchanged between Hove and Leith Hill Place. Ralph bicycled down from London to arrive at breakfast time with his present for Adeline on her birthday morning: he had hoped to spend a few days with her, but Stella was ill again, so she and her mother rushed to London. Three days later, on 19 July, Stella died. Adeline's grief and despair excluded everything else, and nearly brought the engagement to an end. But after the funeral she went to stay with Ralph's grandmother, Lady Vaughan Williams, at Queen Anne's Gate, and while there she managed to come to terms with life, though the happiness of the first bright days of their engagement was never wholly recaptured.

Ralph had left the R.C.M. in the summer of 1896, but he continued to study, to see his friends, and to manage the musical affairs of St. Barnabas, though the work there was becoming more and more uncongenial. He thought that von Holst might be able to take it over for the months he had arranged to spend studying and honeymooning in Berlin. It would mean a small but regular income and Gustav had helped him out before, playing for services. But for a regular post, more was required. He wrote:

Dear V.H.

It's awfully hard to know what you had better do. I don't think the communication business would matter—as a matter of fact I always did it when there was choral communion because I thought it looked picturesque as I had a hood and went up first and was generally part of the show—all the same he will probably ask you 'what your position is and whether you will do your best to promote reverent conduct of the service' to which I answered that I was broad (not physically) and that everyone ought to do the sort of praying that suited them best—and that I would do my best etc. This is a very useful evasion. I suppose you consider me very wicked to have done all this but I consider it more important to take every chance of improving one's talents (?!?) than to save one's soul. Again the Vicar will not be back till Sunday, when he comes I will tell him that if he wants you he must close with you at once—put off signing your agreement as long as you can.

My dear V.H. I wish to goodness I could offer you anything more definite than this—I *cannot* do anything like promise you will get it as the Vicar is quite mad. Only I will do my best—only I am not sure that Crouch-end in the hand is not worth St. Barnabas in the Bush.

I want you for Wed 4th at 7.0 THURSDAY 5th at 8.15 you must do Thursday or you're no good and Sunday 8th. Will 30/– be enough for the whole show. By the way I promised the Vicar that you would provide a testimonial from Stanford! also a word from Hoyte[1] would be good also Parry and above all if possible Parratt—the Vicar is very great on testimonials—also your last Vicar would be good also a good-character one from Somebody—I gave him two! Besides musical ones.

Yours in esparation [*sic*]
R. Vaughan Williams.

V.H. does not appear to have got the job.

René Gatty, brother of his Cambridge friends Ivor and Nicholas, was already living in Berlin, and promised to find rooms for the honeymooners, so, while Mrs. Fisher shopped for the trousseau, Ralph and Adeline played duet arrangements of

[1] W. S. Hoyte, von Holst's organ teacher.

Wagner's operas, preparing themselves for the delights of *The Ring*. They also went to stay with the Maitlands, who spent holidays at a house Fred had inherited near Gloucester. There they were the object of passionate admiration to the two little daughters, Fredegond and Ermengard, who remembered them as 'a first step from Fairyland into Romance—a very short step, for he and Adeline were much like our princes and princesses in grace and beauty, and we were wide-eyed in excitement over their engagement. . . .'

Ralph wrote to these children from Leith Hill Place—using their family nicknames:

Dear Gaga and Vuff,

I wrote you a letter last week but I tore it up; so then I thought I would write to you from here; so that you might see where to write me a telegram whenever you want to. Adeline and I think you might like to see some designs for my trousseau.

The first pattern represents my wedding suit, the general colour is puce the spats being of a sandy colour the boots to be light blue with red heels.

Pattern 2. represents a good working suit for every day wear being made of good strong material with plaid stockings.

Two other pictures are supposed to be guesses of what I shall look like when I come back from Germany—I don't know which is the most likely to be true.

And last of all two pictures of a giraffe one by Adeline and one by me; the head of my one is wrong, but the tail is better than in Adeline's.

I want to see the new monkey of which also I will give you a picture and end up. This is not much like a monkey.

Ralph Vaughan Williams.

On 9 October Ralph and Adeline were married at the Parish Church, All Saints, Hove, by W. J. (later Canon) Spooner,[1] an old friend of Herbert Fisher's. The two Maitland children were Adeline's bridesmaids and Ralph Wedgwood was the best man. Adeline was twenty-seven, and Ralph would be twenty-five three days later.

[1] Of 'Spoonerism' fame.

CHAPTER IV

1897–1905

Ralph had an introduction to Heinrich von Herzogenberg, head of the Department of Theory and Composition at the *Hochschule für Musik* in Berlin, who looked at his work and suggested lessons from Max Bruch, the school's chief professor of composition. Bruch had been Director of the Liverpool Philharmonic Society from 1881–83, and Ralph had heard some of his music at College concerts and elsewhere. He proved an encouraging and friendly teacher with whom Ralph worked hard, and after Stanford's brusque discouragements Bruch's helpfulness was good for him and gave him confidence.

Besides the long working hours when he battled with music, there were amusing lessons in German which he and Adeline shared. She, having more time to devote to reading, got on faster, but they were both soon able to enjoy plays. René Gatty took them sightseeing, to cafés as well as to theatres, and all three were ardent opera-goers. Gatty's presence was a help in all practical matters and a great pleasure to them both. He was a journalist and also wrote verse which he showed to Adeline who was a sympathetic critic.

Adeline's parents and some of the family had gone to San Remo early in December. Adeline and Ralph joined them there for Christmas. On the way, changing trains at Bolzano, they had time for a long walk, and Adeline took a romantic photograph of Ralph lying on the sunny hillside, with a background of mountains. They stopped for a night at Genoa and joined the family the next day. It was pleasant weather and they were able to hire bicycles. Ralph made many expeditions and went for long walks, sometimes with Adeline but often alone, for she was happy to be with her mother and sister again and spent most of her time with them.

After the holidays they went back to Berlin until April, when they visited Dresden, and reported to René Gatty in Berlin:

Webers Hotel,
Dresden.
April 1st.

Dear Herr Gatty,

I am just writing to say Dresden's not a Reizendes Dörfchen but that there has been a good lot of Donnerwetter about today. You may be surprised to hear that we said to our waiter 'Wir werden ein Flasche Champagner haben,' to which he replied, 'Ha! Champagner,' but brought Rotwein at 2 pf. the bottle which I after described as a 'guter reiner Wein'. We can't make out this hotel has anything to do with 'Der Freischütz' but Paderewski stays here, so that it has some musical reputation. They are doing 'Die Neunte Symphonie' at the opera concert on Saturday, and Othello on Sunday evening.

Saturday morning—another mind now prevails—it is still raining but we are going off to the pictures to admire the San Sisto—or not as the case may be.

Yours always and affectionately,
R. Vaughan Williams.

Ralph was still the official organist of St. Barnabas, so when Adeline wrote next day to thank René for forwarding a letter to Dresden she told him it was from the Vicar. 'Alas—no reprieve.' She said they had survived eight courses at the *table d'hôte*, and, though it was still wintery and wet, they were able to dry their clothes on hot pipes in their room; and that they would see him tomorrow if he could get tickets for the Nikisch concert in Berlin. It was their last jaunt before returning to England.

By the end of the following week they were back at Leith Hill Place, and Ralph wrote in German to say that he hoped René had received the two pounds they owed, 'which proved better than ten thousand telegrams', that they had arrived safely and that they thought of him going to the *Matthew Passion*.

A visit to Hove followed, and Adeline wrote to say they had found somewhere to live in London:

Three very small rooms in a curious old panelled house (16 North Street, Westminster) close to Westminster Abbey, and closer still to Queen Anne's Footstool Church in Smith Square. . . . Ralph I hope will not find it too far from S. Lambeth. We went to church at St. Barnabas last Sunday morning—the choir stared and Mr. Ireland,[1] the deputy, was very much upset at sight of R. Mr. Stanley preached a long ineffectual sermon and afterwards Ralph went into the vestry and was kindly greeted by the choir who hoped he had enjoyed his holiday in Switzerland! Ralph did not like this. . . .

I am staying at home for a few days. Ralph is in my brother's lodgings at Westminster practising 5 hours a day at organ and piano and singing '*The Revenge*' in S. Lambeth.

Letters to René followed each other fast and give an idea of their lives. In London they had been to a rather poor performance of Schumann's Second Symphony and *Casse-Noisette*—Ralph had read *The Portrait of a Lady* by Henry James, and was sending 'an account of the battle of Albara which is rather good'. A few weeks later Adeline wrote to give their new address—5 Cowley Street—for they had been turned out of their first lodgings as

the landlady objected very strongly to my having influenza. We have been looking at flats in Battersea Park, but find it very difficult to determine what we want. . . . My husband heard a bit of your brother's Quartet played at the Royal College; he thought it beautiful and your brother played a good deal of it to us on the piano. . . . My husband has not done any composition since he set foot in England—nor has he wished to—he works tremendously hard at his choir and organ and piano and is having lessons from Mr. [Howard] Jones. . . . We have been to no operas or concerts but on Friday we go to *Tristan*. We watched the procession last Saturday—it was most interesting to see the House of Commons and Lords. . . .

Ralph and Adeline sometimes wrote to their 'Herr Gatty' in German, and both wrote long letters after hearing a performance of Nicholas's Quartet—Ralph said:

I want to tell you how much we enjoyed Nicholas's Quartet; it was performed last Friday at the Royal College of Music by students. The first movement was very good, but the Andante quite excellent—a completely new tune, really filled with the deepest feeling—the Scherzo also was extraordinarily good and very well composed for the instruments, as was everything else in this work. The Variations were not so good, but maybe they weren't so well played, and the *Fuga Finale* was beautiful. . . . I enclose a programme. . . . We hear with

[1] The composer John Ireland 1879–1963.

pleasure that you will soon be coming to England, and we have received with pleasure an invitation to Hooton Roberts—perhaps you could spend a few days with us on your way to Yorkshire?[1, 2]

This visit to the Gattys' home in Yorkshire was an entirely happy one. It was the vicarage of a remote village in a quiet and beautiful part of the county. The house was filled with old, locally made, oak furniture, collected from farmers who were anxious to raise money to help to survive hard times. The vicar himself was a man who appreciated the character of his people and understood their ways. He delighted Ralph by telling him that when anyone came to communion looking a bit under the weather, he always gave 'a good swig'. All the family were full of interests—Mrs. Ewing, who was their aunt, might well have modelled the Yorkshire household in *Six to Sixteen* on them. There was one daughter, Margot, who was much younger than the boys, and very shy. Adeline won her heart for life by drawing her in to share the grown-up holiday pleasures and by treating her with the same easy friendship as her brothers. They walked, picnicked and, when either Nicholas or Ralph or both had written music for the odd combination of instruments available, they played—sometimes in the garden, for a faded photograph shows a group outside the front door, with Adeline as cellist. Mrs. Gatty found Ralph's preoccupation and sudden absorbed silences at meals a little worrying, for he would forget to help himself to salt or sugar or bread and butter, so she arranged for Margot to sit opposite him and look after all his needs.

Visits to Hooton Roberts became a regular pleasure each year, but London and Leith Hill Place claimed them too, and Adeline's family often needed her help and support. London was dull, Ralph wrote to René:

What operas and concerts have there been in Berlin lately? You are lucky to be in the midst of music which we, with all our concerts and operas and Queen's Halls and things, will never be.

They were both missing René's company and worrying about his health and his finances. A short trip to Holland to hear the organ at Haarlem and see the Amsterdam pictures was reported to him, and how Adeline's fur coat was lost and returned, 'so that

[1] Hooton Roberts, a village in Yorkshire where the Gattys' father was the vicar.
[2] Translated.

I can go on looking like a weasel', with an invitation to come 'at any day and at any moment'. Adeline was copying his poems and sending them round to magazines for him, a task that employed her while a series of bad colds kept her indoors. She wrote on 31 December:

Did I mention our new Quartet *Abends*, or rather *Nachmittags*? Ralph plays viola, Herr Nicholas 1st violin or cello as wanted and Mr. von Holst 2nd. We have met only once, but I hope it may become an institution. . . . Ralph has just signed the lease and we are furnishing our house as soon as possible. He is writing a new serenade for orchestra, which is turning out rather Dvorak-y. . . .

At this time von Holst was often out of London, touring with the Carl Rosa Opera or with the Scottish Orchestra, so the quartet evenings were irregular. Ralph missed him:

Dear V.H.

How when and where are you? When I don't hear from you for some time I'm afraid always that you've resolved into your constituent elements or disappeared into the air like the Cheshire cat. I did write to Gatty about W.W.[1]—did I tell you, and he said he would write to Wallace again—I don't know if he did—I will worrit him up again now he's back in London. When do you come back? Do come soon and lift the cloud that has settled on the metropolis since your departure.

I have written a new coda and a new movement for my serenade and most of my degree exercise.[2] Have you been writing anything—also you haven't said how your hand is for about a year. Do tell us how it is and how you are generally.

We heard Tchaikovsky's 1812 at Queen's Hall the other day. I've never heard such a row. Band, organ, bells, and someone apparently hitting a tub.

Yours,

R. V. W.

My wife says she hopes you are coming back soon.

About the same time he wrote to René:

I wish there was a good choral society in London. We have only three—the Albert Hall and the Queen's Hall—which can sing but do *not* and the Bach Choir, which does good things but can't sing. . . .

[1] William Wallace.

[2] For his Mus.D. Cambridge, 1899 (a setting of the Mass still exists at Cambridge).

How is Bruch and do you see anything of him now? Ivor was in London a little while ago and told us about *the* choral society.[1] . . . I hear you are going to make them do the Song of Miriam—do you like it—it seems to me to be rather dull what I know of it.

I suppose you know of Nick's organ appointment. I'm afraid he doesn't care for it very much but I think a little routine work is good for everyone—even a composer!

My choral society had a most successful show . . . we did Mendelssohn's 95th Psalm as our chief thing and Brahms's 'How lovely' and Sullivan's 'O Gladsome Light' as side dishes.

In April they settled at 10 Barton Street, Westminster, a pretty little house which they furnished very simply with rush mats and white curtains, oak furniture they had picked up at sales, and two ancient chests from Hooton Roberts. There was no bathroom, so hot water had to be carried from the kitchen to fill a brown tin bath, and the lavatory was in the back yard, but it was quiet and there was a spare room for visitors. The drawing-room on the ground floor was also used as a study for Ralph.

Adeline wrote to René in April. She was still copying poems for him and reported that Ivor was painting her portrait, but the sittings were interrupted as she was wanted at Hove to nurse one of her brothers. She continued:

Herr Nicholas says he is doing nothing but I believe he has a great work pursuing its quiet way in the background, but his sympathies are all military just now like most people's, I expect any day to meet him in khaki.

Ralph gives himself very important airs as a householder, turning off the gas and locking every window and door every night. But he has set Matthew Arnold's 'Dover Beach' to music and has got an article accepted by 'The Londoner',[2] a new rag (weekly) which has just started up—his literary aspirations are growing at this unexpected success. . . .

Surviving letters give the impression of a happy and intimate group, René urging Adeline to read Verlaine, Adeline reporting that they had been reading Ibsen's new plays and Anatole France, and all of them making music. It was a new pleasure for Ralph to

[1] At Hooton Roberts. Where *Linden Lea* and *Blackmwore by the Stour* were first sung by J. Milner: in September 1902.

[2] This article must have been unsigned as nothing signed by R.V.W. can be traced.

be able to have friends to his own house, and, although there were breaks in the easy flow of day to day doings when Adeline had to go back to her family, he was working steadily and uninterruptedly and the first years in Barton Street were some of the happiest they were to know.

In spite of his choral society and the use of the discipline of a regular job, Ralph disliked his work at St. Barnabas. He had given up taking communion, even as 'part of the show', so when a new vicar was appointed who made this a condition of his continuing as organist, he resigned his post with great thankfulness. Always untidy about his possessions, he neglected to clear up before he left, and a large cardboard box of French novels, chiefly Maupassant, Zola, and Balzac, was sent on to Barton Street, with a chilly note saying that, as they were found in the organ loft, they were presumably his.

At this time he was working for his Mus.D. and thinking critically of other people's music as well. He was able to write to René:

> We were so glad to get your letter. I am going to confine myself to a few remarks about Nick's Serenade. It *came off* most tremendously, the scoring was effective without straining after effect and the parts must have been very well written for the instruments as it went so well the first try over. Awfully jolly tunes in it too—and those not isolated but welded together into a whole—altogether a complete success and a distinct advance even on the Quartet. He has gone the right way to work and the quality of his ideas and the mastery over the means of expression advance side by side without one outstripping the other.
>
> I envy you the *Singakademie*—what a way to get to know Bach.

And at the end of another letter commenting on a performance of *The Devil and Kate*:

> The Dvorak was very good and characteristic all the time he was with the village scenes, but when he got down to Hell he lost himself and became a bad imitation of *Nibelheim* in the *Rheingold.* I don't think they are the coming *Volk*. Smetana and Dvorak were the result of a national movement but I think they will now become cosmopolitan.

René's health and finances were a continual anxiety, and letters to him put Ralph's feelings about his own independent means—

not at that time very large—into words, which gave his life-long attitude to money:

> You *must get well* by hook or by crook. Now I consider that between friends and especially between musicians there is a kind of freemasonry which binds us all together like a happy family and makes it the duty of each one of the band not to stand aloof from the rest when he may give them the opportunity of showing him the value of their friendship. Remember that it's not only for yourself that you've got to get well and not even only for your family, but it's for all your friends. You *owe it them* as a proof of any affection you have for them to neglect no opportunity of putting them out of anxiety. You owe it them not to disappoint the expectation we have all formed of your doing something big some day.
>
> Therefore, please do not despise the little we can do but just receive it and so prove the strength of our friendship. You know that we'd all make you well ourselves if we could, but we can't, so we must do it by proxy.
>
> For heaven's sake do go away from the *cheap*, *incompetent*, *dishonest* quack who has been doing his best to *keep you in his clutches*; and go to the *best* doctor in Berlin and *stick to him*—please use what the postman will bring for that purpose.
>
> Yours always,
> R. V. W.

After this passionate but practical advice, René did change his doctor, and with the return of his health he secured a good position as a foreign correspondent on *The Morning Post.*

About the turn of the century, Ralph and Adeline had a summer holiday in Yorkshire with Ralph Wedgwood. They hired a boat which the men took it in turns to row, they picnicked at midday and stayed at inns for the night. It was lovely weather and they took their time idling between the flowery banks of blue cranesbill and meadow-sweet. One evening they reached an inn where they were looked at very doubtfully, they were all three sunburned and probably none too tidy, and they had very little luggage. But Ralph saw a piano and, telling Randolph to find the prettiest girl in the room as a partner, he started to play dance tunes. It was irresistible, and soon everyone left the bar to dance. When they were all exhausted, the landlord drew pints of beer for them, offered Ralph a job for as long as he liked, turned his son out of his room for Ralph and Adeline to sleep there, and made up a bed for Randolph in the bar. He was sadly disappointed when they left the next morning.

In the autumn of 1900 Ralph took a teaching job at a small school for girls in Ladbroke Grove, where he taught class singing and pianoforte to about twenty young ladies. His shyness, his brown suit, and his choice of music made them give him the nick-name of 'the nut-brown maid', and his lessons were much enjoyed. One of his pupils, Maud Brackenbury, kept her school reports, during the four terms he was there:

'Has much improved in power and attack.'
'Plays Beethoven with great intelligence and has worked hard.'
'Has great appreciation of good music.'
'An extremely intelligent pupil. Understands Bach and Beethoven in a way which is uncommon at her age.'

Ralph's training as a historian had made him see both music and painting with a certain historical sense, and to be aware of the roots and growth of art related to the life of times and places. Besides teaching enthusiastic and merry girls, he had undertaken a course of university extension lectures and, in preparation for this, he took lessons in voice production. He had already had some singing lessons from Madame Careño, a large and formidable lady from whom he learned much that was useful to him both as a conductor of choirs and as a writer of songs.

Adeline spent the early months of 1901 at Hove. The Boer War was filling everyone's minds, and her brother, Jack, one of the brilliant and more unstable of the family, was fighting in South Africa. Anxiety for him as well as the need to nurse Hervey, who was by now a confirmed invalid, made her presence at her parents' home a great comfort and, it seemed to her, an urgent need. Ralph spent his time in London, making flying visits to Hove, staying some nights at Leith Hill Place, working and teaching. He had an attack of sciatica early in March, but recovered in time to go to Bournemouth a few days later where Dan Godfrey gave a performance of his *Serenade*.

At midsummer Gustav von Holst married Isobel Harrison. He had met her in 1897, and he had told Ralph and Adeline about his plans perhaps in 1900 or early in 1901. The only clue is an undated letter from Ralph:

My dear V.

I can't tell you what pleasure it gives me that you should consider us old friends enough to confide in—also it enables me to behave like an old friend and tell you how absolutely right I feel you are—after all what's the good of waiting—I *was* glad when I came upon your news—characteristically sandwiched in between two operas; you've got something that's better than all the concerts in the world put together—I'm afraid I'm very disjointed but I want to express more than I can in words. You say that you are going to 'drop your laziness'—you never were lazy—but you had not a sufficient idea of the value of your time—you must really learn to be rather more churlish and not be ready to work yourself to the bone for any man who meets you in the street—not only without any pecuniary reward but with the certain knowledge that (i) the result cannot possibly be anything like commensurate with the pains expended and (ii) that the results however good will not be appreciated.

Do remember that it's your duty to keep all your energies *in reserve* for the moment when they can be used to advantage (For instance don't make a new copy of 'Sita' but show me the old one when you come back)—There: I've been preaching you a sermon. . . .

Their other great event that summer was a performance of Ralph's Quintet. By this time Adeline was free for a while, as Hervey was in hospital and the Fishers staying in Oxford. In September she and Ralph both went to Somerset with his mother, staying near Kilve. Here Ralph was able to go for the long afternoon walks he enjoyed after a morning of writing and before he plunged into an after-tea period of more work, refreshed by the heathery air of Exmoor, by the views of the Welsh hills beyond the Bristol Channel, as well as by cream and honey and cake in which The Castle of Comfort, a temperance hotel, specialized.

When they returned to London he started work on a series of articles which were published in *The Vocalist* in 1902. The titles cover a wide range of subjects—*A School of English Music*, *The Soporific Finale*, *Palestrina and Beethoven*, *Good Taste*, *Bach and Schumann*, *The Words of Wagner's Music Dramas*, *Brahms and Tschaikowsky*, *A Sermon to Vocalists*, and *Ein Heldenleben.*[1] He found he had much to say and the discipline of writing clarified his own thought.

In March 1902 another Bournemouth concert gave Ralph a chance to hear his *Bucolic Suite* at the Winter Gardens, where von

[1] First performed in England December 1902.

Holst's *Cotswold Symphony* also had a performance. For that he went to both rehearsal and concert, and his admiration was a much needed support to the composer, who was nervous and worried. The Magpie Madrigal Society included Ralph's *Rest* (Christina Rossetti) in their May concert at St. James's Hall, and repeated it again in June. His settings of William Barnes's *Linden Lea*, *Blackmwore by the Stour*, and *The Winter's Willow* were being noticed favourably in musical papers, and by music critics in dailies and weeklies, and were having a fair number of performances at recitals.

The year 1902 brought the Boer War to an end, and Adeline's brother, Jack, returned home, suffering from what was later known as shell shock: he had been full of life and gaiety but he came back wrecked and destroyed; the household at Hove revolved round him—even when he had to leave it for hospital. The months before his death were so agonizing to the family that, even years later, none of them could bear to speak of it. As usual, much of the burden fell on Adeline. Her passionate devotion helped them all through the first break in the enchanted family circle, though it told on her, and indirectly on Ralph, who could help her only by leaving her entirely free to be where she felt she belonged.

Among the families living near Leith Hill who were long-standing friends of the Vaughan Williamses and Wedgwoods were the Broadwoods of Lyne. In 1843 John Broadwood had published a volume of songs collected from the country people in Surrey and Sussex. His niece, Lucy, another musician, descended from a line of Tschudis as well as Broadwoods, followed in his footsteps and collected more songs from people in the same district. These were added to John Broadwood's collection and published in 1889 with harmonies by H. F. Birch Reynardson, as *Sussex Songs*. With these Ralph was familiar, as with her later volume published in 1893 in collaboration with J. A. Fuller Maitland, *English County Songs*. This volume was a landmark in the history of English music, for it made the musical world aware of the treasures preserved in the memories of unlettered country people. Stainer and Bramley's book of Carols had introduced Ralph to *The Cherry Tree Carol* during his childhood, and these tunes, following that early impression, made him realize that here was a musical tradition that was both rich and simple, classical yet romantically national, so, when he was asked to give university extension lectures on music, a subject lay ready to his hand.

His first series was given at the Technical School at Pokesdown, Bournemouth, during the winter of 1902. It was fully reported by a bewildered local journalist, but she, like the audience, found it much easier going than she had expected because the lectures 'were appropriately illustrated by vocal and instrumental music. This is an entirely new idea and one which enhances the value of the lectures and make them more intelligible to those who possess only a rudimentary knowledge of music.' Lucy Broadwood, herself a charming singer, illustrated one of the lectures, and as the subject that day was *The Characteristics of National Songs in the British Isles*, her collection was the mainstay of his talk. Her reward from the audience was a bouquet of chrysanthemums and maidenhair fern with orange streamers. Ralph always believed that music must be heard, and it was a principle of his lectures from those early days to let his audience hear for themselves the points he made, even if it meant playing or singing to them himself. Among the other subjects on which he spoke during this course were *Are we a musical nation?*, in which he said firmly, 'When England has its municipal-aided music, so that every town of decent size possesses its own permanent orchestra as is the case in Germany, we shall have conductors of our own, and with increased musical activity our composers will grow. Until the good time comes, the protest against foreign music and foreign conductors is futile.' This subject was filling his mind and von Holst's at this time. Dan Godfrey in Bournemouth and Henry Wood in London were both doing much for English composers, giving works by the young and unknown as often as possible but, in spite of their efforts, it was very hard for the English musician to get a hearing and harder still for people in the provinces to hear any English music beyond that which they could make among themselves.

His penultimate lecture was on church music: 'A remarkably able and hard one, and though we may differ from the lecturer on some points we cannot but admire his sincerity, for he certainly has the courage of his opinions. . . . After a very able summary of what folk song had done for religious music the lecturer touched on modern church music and made a well-deserved attack on the false sentimentalism of many of our modern hymns as compared with the true feeling and dignity of earlier examples.' This was undoubtedly the fruit of his years at St. Barnabas. A historical survey of the music of the Church, with some deeply felt criticisms of congregational singing, bad choirs, and inept organists, sent everyone away argumentative and happy. The course ended with a summing up: 'The Importance of Folk Song', and at the end of the series there was an examination, which two of the candidates passed—one with distinction. It is amusing to picture the one hundred and twelve students and the reporter looking forward to the next season, for which the proposed alternatives were either 'Science' *or* 'The Napoleonic Era Illustrated by Lantern Slides'.

Ralph gave his lectures again at Gloucester, starting the course early in January. Adeline was staying at Hove again and she was there when her father died. For the next few months she went to and fro helping her mother to look for a house and prepare to move to London, contriving to be in London to go to the concerts at which Ralph's new songs were performed. Two young singers, Francis Harford and Campbell McInnes, who were giving recitals in London at the St. James's Hall and the Bechstein Hall, included many new songs in their programmes, among them some of Ralph's. In February Ralph took part in two performances of his Quintet for Pianoforte, Clarinet, Horn, Violin and Violoncello at the Oxford University Musical Club, playing the piano.

In March, one of Gustav von Holst's songs, *Invocation to the Dawn*, was sung by Campbell McInnes in the same programme as *Whither Must I Wander?*—a happy occasion for both composers. At a third recital by Francis Harford *Silent Noon* was one of six songs by British composers which received a first performance, others were *A Countryman's Song* by Nicholas Gatty and *Idyll* by Cecil Forsyth.

Even more important, on 12 March Campbell McInnes, accompanied by Howard-Jones, gave the first performance of *Willow-Wood* at one of the Broadwood concerts at St. James's Hall. The work was a series of four Rossetti sonnets, Nos: XLIX, L, LI, and LII, turbulent, shadowy, and melancholy. It was noticed by many papers and, although the critics varied from bewilderment to excited interest, it was clear that they felt a promise for the future lay in these songs. Ralph also made a setting for women's voices of Christina Rossetti's poem, *Sound Sleep*, at Margaret

Massingberd's request, and in April he stayed at Gunby to hear it sung at the East Lincolnshire Music Festival.

Barnes, Tennyson, both Rossettis, and Stevenson were the poets Ralph had found most apt for tunes; a second D. G. Rossetti cycle, *The House of Life*, in which *Silent Noon* was included, and the Stevenson *Songs of Travel* belong to this time: but another, and very different, kind of writer was beginning to fill his mind. Walt Whitman's *Leaves of Grass*, in several editions, from a large volume to a selection small enough for a pocket, was his constant companion. It was full of fresh thoughts, and the idea of a big choral work about the sea—the sea itself and the sea of time, infinity, and mankind, was beginning to take shape in many small notebooks. It was an ambitious and terrifying project, for the scope was to be unlike that of any choral work he had yet attempted. Perhaps von Holst knew of it in early days; perhaps Nicholas Gatty; but he kept it very much to himself, sketching and re-sketching the text, using, discarding, and re-arranging poems.

Gustav and Isobel von Holst were having their first holiday abroad and Gustav wrote long and excited letters to Ralph, carrying on the conversations on which they both depended.[1] Ralph's *Solent*[2] was played through in June, and Adeline and her mother brought the invalid Hervey to hear it. In July they took Mrs. Fisher to Salisbury for a holiday and, having settled her in lodgings, they joined Randolph for a boating trip down the Avon from Salisbury to Christchurch. Their only adventures were when one or other of them forgot the lock keys and they tossed for who should walk upstream to retrieve them. They probably spoke of G. E. Moore whose *Principia Ethica* was published that year: he had sent a copy which Ralph found 'difficult but wonderful'. Back at Salisbury for a few more days, they visited Edwardie Vaughan Williams, at Tedworth, and made an expedition to Stonehenge. Ralph had seen it first when he was bicycling in the west country, after a visit to Holst's family at Cheltenham, and he had found it a terrifying place, but there was hardly a hint of its dark power on that summer afternoon when it was the setting for a family picnic.

[1] Quoted in *Heirs and Rebels*.

[2] Later withdrawn: but a theme from this work reappears in *A Sea Symphony* and the *Ninth Symphony* and in music for the film *The England of Elizabeth*.

They had no holiday by themselves during the summer, for when they had taken Mrs. Fisher back to London they went to Swanage with Ralph's mother and Meggie. In fact they were not often alone, for nearly all the Fisher family stayed at Barton Street from time to time or were there for meals or to meet each other, so Adeline's time was fully occupied when she was at home. The family round is fully chronicled in Mrs. Fisher's diary, with Adeline always at the centre of the picture. When the Broadwood concerts started again it was pleasant to see that Ralph's works were promised as well as those of Walford Davies, Balfour Gardiner, Josef Holbrooke, and Cyril Scott.

Yet another of his courses of lectures on folk song took Ralph to Brentwood in Essex during the autumn. After one talk two middle-aged ladies told him that their father, the vicar of Ingrave, was giving a tea-party for the old people of the village and some of them possibly might know country songs; he would be very welcome, they said, if he would care to come. Though Ralph was rather shy of a Parish Tea, and though he felt it was most unlikely that anyone there would know any folk songs, he accepted the invitation. The vicar's daughters introduced him to an elderly labourer, Mr. Pottipher, who said of course he could not sing at this sort of party, but if Ralph would visit him next day he would be delighted to sing to him then. The next day, 4 December, Mr. Pottipher sang *Bushes and Briars*: when Ralph heard it he felt it was something he had known all his life.

After this discovery at Ingrave, Ralph explored the country round Leith Hill Place where he and Adeline stayed for a few days after Christmas. To his surprise and delight these bicycling trips, on which he went equipped with notebook and pencil, proved extremely fruitful and he gathered songs almost at his own doorstep. He visited Mr. Pottipher again at the beginning of the New Year on his way back from a visit to Cambridge and took down more songs.

At this time Bartók and Kodály were beginning to collect songs from Hungarian peasants. In England, Cecil Sharp, staying at Hambridge in Somerset during the summer of 1903, heard his host's gardener sing *The Seeds of Love*, a tune which started him on his life's work of collecting the songs of England.[1] He and Ralph had known each other for several years but it was some

[1] He had started collecting dances earlier—in 1899.

time before they spoke about this music that had become so vital to each of them. Ralph declared that his new enthusiasm bored most of his friends to death, and it was ironic that Cecil Sharp was among those who, he thought, would be most likely to find it dull.

He had recently arranged some traditional French songs, which he had come across when preparing his lectures, *L'Amour de Moy*, *Réveillez-vous*, *Piccars*, and the sombre ballad, *Jean Renaud*; these were sung by Francis Harford at a Broadwood Concert on 4 February in a programme which included songs by Hurlstone, Ernest Walker, and Donald Tovey.

He managed to spend a few days in Essex in February, pursuing songs, while Adeline and her mother were much at Leslie Stephen's house during his last illness. After his death Adeline and her sister Emmie went to Paris for a week but they returned in time to go to Bournemouth where, on 7 March, Dan Godfrey and the Bournemouth Symphony Orchestra gave a performance of Ralph's *Symphonic Rhapsody*. The programme note quotes in full Christina Rossetti's poem, *Come to me in the Silence of the Night*. *The Bournemouth Guardian*, with little space at its disposal for reporting the concert, said: 'it showed the hand of a thorough musician throughout', but *The Bournemouth Observer* thought otherwise.

The Bournemouth concert was followed by a performance of his *Heroic Elegy and Triumphal Epilogue* on 11 March, recorded in Mrs. Fisher's diary without any details of where or by whom the concert was given, and on 22 March by his arrangements of *Adieu*, *Think of me*, and *Cousin Michael*, which were sung at the Steinway Hall. The accompanist at this concert was Donald Tovey, and songs by Roger Quilter were also in the programme.

One day at the end of March Ralph was delighted to hear ballad singers in Barton Street. He bought copies of all the broadsheets they had, and took down another song, *William and Phillis*, which they sang for him. A month later he went to Brentwood for ten days, and bicycled round the neighbourhood collecting songs at Willingale, Ingrave, Little Burstead, East Horndon, and Billericay. It was a successful trip for he brought home, among other songs, *The Farmer's Boy*, *The Poacher's Song*, *Green Bushes*, *John Barleycorn*, and four versions of *The Lost Lady Found*. But perhaps the greatest prize was the carol he collected a little later from Mrs. Verrall of Monk's Gate near Horsham; he bicycled over from Leith Hill Place on 24 May and she sang *On Christmas Night* to him.

Ralph took another teaching appointment, this time at James Allen's Girls' School at Dulwich, where he was succeeded by von Holst a year later. His life was even busier now, for he had been asked to edit a volume of *Welcome Songs* for the Purcell Society[1]—'This necessitates days at the British Museum copying rare manuscripts. He likes this work very much, unpaid though it is,' Adeline wrote to René Gatty. It also meant a visit to the library at Buckingham Palace. Thinking of the work to be done and not of the social implications, he had gone in his everyday suit; it had not occurred to him that he should wear a top hat; this much upset Barclay Squire who conducted him to the Palace and, because he was wrongly dressed, took him in and out through the kitchen premises.

He had also been commissioned to write the articles on Fugue and on Conducting for the new edition of *Grove's Dictionary of Music and Musicians*. Conducting was a subject he had discussed with von Holst, whose experience in the Scottish Orchestra and with the Carl Rosa Company was illuminating, but the friend who gave him most help in writing his article was Henry Wood. It was a long and difficult task, but one he enjoyed, and his work for *The Vocalist* had given him some confidence in his ability to write prose.

Ralph's present to Adeline for her thirty-fourth birthday in July was a short piano piece. He was away in Yorkshire working on his choral symphony, which at that time he called *The Ocean*: he found this solitary and concentrated attack was immensely valuable: he would take rooms, hire a piano and drive himself hard, particularly in the mornings and evenings. The afternoons he usually spent in walking or bathing, and this time he collected a few songs in Westerdale and at Robin Hood's Bay. He was nearly drowned one afternoon bathing on a deserted and rocky beach: the sea was rougher than he thought and, after swimming, he found he could not scramble back on to the rocks. He had almost decided to give up and let himself drown, when a wave washed him on to the shore—he crawled out of reach of the sea

[1] *The Works of Henry Purcell*, Volume XV—*Welcome Songs*, part I—Novello & Company Ltd., 1905.

and lay exhausted until he felt able to climb to the place where he had left his clothes. After that he took care to bathe in safe places, it was an adventure he kept to himself and did not tell Adeline when he joined her and the Fishers in Salisbury at the end of August. But he made them laugh by describing how his landlady brought his supper one evening when he had been playing through the music he had just been writing. 'It's nice,' she said, 'our postman plays it, but he plays it much faster.'

While they were at Salisbury Ralph visited the workhouse, or Union as it was called, and found old people who were delighted to sing to him and to find a visitor interested in the music which they loved and which belonged to their happier times. He bicycled in the district and added more songs to his notebook, collected at Coombe Bissett, Ramsbury, and Stratford Tony.

During the autumn *The Morning Post* published some correspondence on folk songs. Mr. Stewart Gowe wrote a letter complaining of the poverty of songs in Essex. Ralph took up this challenge with excitement:

Sir,

My attention has been called to the paragraph in your issue of 1st October referring to my letter to *The Morning Post* in which I described how I noted down a large number of folk songs in Essex. It may interest your readers to know that the village where I made my collection was Ingrave, near Brentwood. My thanks are due to the Misses Heatley of Ingrave Rectory for discovering singers in the parish who still sing 'the old ballads' and introducing me to them, so that I could note down the songs as they sang them. It is interesting to note that though these ladies have lived at Ingrave for several years and are intimate with the village people, they had no idea that the folk song still survived there until I suggested the possibility to them some time ago.

Now I believe that Ingrave is not an exceptional village from this point of view. I imagine if every village, not only in Essex, but all over England, were investigated, an equally rich store of traditional song will be found; but it will not be found without some trouble. The younger singers, it must be confessed, very seldom sing the old country ballads, it is the elder people to whom we must go and they are often shy, or have forgotten the old songs, and they will require a little persuasion and to be assured that they are not being laughed at.

But if anyone cares to undertake the search he will find the results amply repay him. I am sure that your readers would be astonished at the beauty and evident antiquity of many of the tunes which I noted down, many of them being founded on the old 'Church modes'. The collections of 'Songs of England' and the like give no idea of the real nature of English folk music; indeed I believe that we are only now beginning to realize what a store of beautiful melody has existed in our country; and this is not a mere individual opinion, but is supported by a perusal of the collections of folk music made in Sussex and Somerset by such well-known authorities as Miss Lucy Broadwood and Mr. Cecil Sharp.

But whatever is done in the way of preserving traditional music must be done quickly; it must be remembered that the tunes, at all events, of true folk songs exist only by oral tradition, so that if they are not soon noted down and preserved they will be lost forever.

This is the work which the 'Folk Song Society' is attempting to do. The Society has already published six numbers of its 'Journal', each containing about forty traditional ballads collected from all parts of England, besides which the Society has an immense quantity of material still in manuscript which it is only prevented from publishing from lack of funds. May I add that the Hon. Secretary of the Society is Miss Lucy Broadwood, 84 Carlisle Mansions, Victoria Street, S.W., and if any of your readers know any traditional ballads, or any information concerning them, they would be doing a good work by sending them to the Hon. Sec. when they will be considered by the Editing Committee: or if anyone knows of traditional songs but does not feel able to note them down correctly, I myself should be happy, wherever possible, to come and note down the songs from the mouths of the singers.

Yours, etc.
R. Vaughan Williams
4th October 1904

Another task was started during the year. Ralph described its beginning:

It must have been in 1904 that I was sitting in my study in Barton Street, Westminster, when a cab drove up to the door and 'Mr. Dearmer' was announced. I just knew his name vaguely as a parson who invited tramps to sleep in his drawing room; but he had not come to me about tramps. He went straight to the point and asked me to edit the music of a hymn book. I protested that I knew very little about hymns but he explained to me that Cecil Sharp had suggested my name, and I found out afterwards that Canon Scott Holland had also suggested me as a possible editor, and the final clench was given when I understood that if I did not do the job it would be offered to a well-known Church musician with whose musical ideas I was much out of sympathy. At this opening interview Dearmer told me that the new book was being sponsored by a committee of eight clerics who were dissatisfied with the new *Hymns Ancient and Modern* which they considered unsatisfactory. He told me that these eight founders had put down five pounds each for expenses, and that my part of the work would probably take about two months.

I thought it over for twenty-four hours and then decided to accept, but I found the work occupied me two years and that my bill for clerical expenses alone came to about two hundred and fifty pounds. The truth is that I determined to do the work thoroughly, and that, besides being a compendium of all the tunes of worth that were already in use, the book should, in addition, be a thesaurus of all the finest hymn tunes in the world—at all events all such as were compatible with the metres of the words for which I had to find tunes. Sometimes I went further, and when I found a tune for which no English words were available I took it to Dearmer, as literary editor, and told him he must write or get somebody else to write suitable words. This was the origin of Athelstan Riley's fine hymn *Ye Watchers and Ye Holy Ones* . . . another fine hymn of Dearmer's is *Holy God we offer here* which was written to carry the *choral* tune from Wagner's *Die Meistersinger*.[1]

As musical editor Ralph asked composers to write tunes for some of the hymns with difficult metres for which he could find no suitable music; among them were W. H. Bell, Thomas Dunhill, Nicholas Gatty, and Gustav Holst: some tunes he wrote himself but these he did not sign and they appeared anonymously in the first edition. He searched for the best versions of the older tunes, and he adapted folk songs, continuing the ancient practice of the Church of taking secular music and using it for her own purposes.

The Committee had long and frequent meetings which were enlivened for Ralph by Athelstan Riley's demands for him to play 'something to act as a musical olive to clear our artistic palates', or by his arrival on horseback at Barton Street, where fortunately Adeline's young brother Edwin was available to hold the white steed during the discussion.

Ralph was fascinated by the odd language appertaining to hymnology and, when he came across 'dear Lord Jesus bring us thistles' in a proof he thought it could easily be correct, and did

[1] *The First Fifty Years, A brief account of the English Hymnal, 1906–1956*, Oxford University Press.

not realize that 'thistles' was anything so humdrum as a misprint for 'thither'.

When the first announcements of the 'forthcoming New Hymn Book' were made in the press, *The Standard*, in a half column of speculative criticism, remarked:

> Dr. Vaughan Williams is the musical editor, a selection which ensures purity of musical taste, perhaps even a leaning to the side of severity. . . .

Ralph was in fact trying to put right some of the things that he had found wrong with Church music in his short career as an organist. The eventual value of that uncomfortable job was his discovery that for many people the music the Church gave them each week was the only music in their lives and that it was all too often unworthy both of their faith and of music itself.

Towards the end of the year he gave a concert at the Bechstein Hall of his own and Gustav's songs. The most substantial works in the programme were Ralph's two song cycles, sung respectively by Edith Clegg and Walter Creighton, *The House of Life* and *Songs of Travel*.

When he and Adeline went to Leith Hill Place for Christmas, he had a year of achievement to look back on. In fact he probably did not look back at all but spent his evenings studying maps, for as usual he was out all day collecting songs, mostly in Sussex, though on New Year's Eve he went as far as Gravesend. Early in January he stayed at King's Lynn in a small commercial hotel, where to his surprise the landlady greeted him as an old friend and asked tenderly after his dogs. He found out, after a bewildering conversation, that she was certain he had stayed there before with a troupe of performing dogs when a circus had been visiting the town, and nothing he could say would convince her otherwise. He came to the conclusion that she suspected him of having failed with his performers and disposed of them, probably in some horrible and brutal way which he was unwilling to confess. In the week he was there he collected about thirty songs. Many of them were sea songs, *The Bold Princess Royal*, *Loss of the Ramillies*, *Spanish Ladies*, *On Board a Ninety-Eight*, and among the others there were versions of *Barbara Allen*, *Erin's Lovely Home*, *Lord Bateman*, and *The Golden Glove*. They came from retired sailors in the Union, from fishermen, from sailors still going to sea, from labourers, from a sexton, and from a sailmaker. Most of the singers were over seventy and, though their memories were good the thin voices of old age sometimes made it difficult to note the tune. But with each foray after songs he was getting more experienced and more able to capture both tune and words without asking for too many repetitions.

In January, too, he conducted his *Heroic Elegy* in Leeds, travelling up with Adeline to stay there for two days to rehearse with the Leeds Municipal Orchestra. Another project for the spring took up a great deal of his time. This was the beginning of the Leith Hill Musical Festival. In 1904, Lady Farrer, who had been Ralph's fellow student at the R.C.M. before he went to Cambridge, and his sister, Meggie, met to discuss the musical festivals which, under the leadership of Miss Mary Wakefield, had come into being in the North of England. Petersfield had been among the earliest followers of this venture, and these two friends had been to the 1904 festival there. It was so exciting, so gay, and the choirs were so enthusiastic that they had decided it was an example to follow. After several meetings at Lady Farrer's house, Abinger Hall, the framework of the Leith Hill festival was decided, and a circular was drafted to set out the plans:

Object To raise the standard of music generally in towns and villages in the district, by stimulating existing societies and by encouraging new societies.

Method By arranging annually, after Easter

i) Public competition of Local Societies at some convenient centre.

ii) A concert or concerts which shall include a combined performance by the Local Societies.

In January the Minutes record:

The Committee decided to ask Mr. R. Vaughan Williams if he would conduct the evening concert and would coach the various choirs in the combined music beforehand.

The Committee also noted that they must secure a guarantee of seventy-five pounds. Three committees shared the work—General, Music Selection, and Reference. An accompanist and judge were needed, and obligatory sight-reading classes were included in the programme.

Teaching small choirs the chosen work—for the first Festival it was *Judas Maccabaeus*—and preparing them for the competitions, male voice, female voice, madrigal and quartet, meant a lot of work. Meggie, the Festival Secretary, was indefatigable, and she and Ralph bicycled to all the villages, took rehearsals during the winter months, and helped the village conductors in their work. Of the seven choirs who entered for the Festival, four were conducted by women. One of the conductors was Elizabeth Trevelyan, wife of the poet Robert, an elder brother of Ralph's Cambridge friend, G. M. Trevelyan, the historian. Elizabeth, who was always called Bessie, was herself a violinist, and she and her husband were close friends of Donald Tovey, of Casals, and later of Jelly d'Aranyi and Adila Fachiri, as well as of many other musicians. They had built a house between Tanhurst and Leith Hill Place, where Bob (Robert) Trevelyan haunted the woods, writing out of doors under the beeches or in the glades where rhododendrons and azaleas flourished, a landscape that recurs in very many of his poems. They called their house The Shiffolds and shared with Leith Hill Place, and several other houses where members of the committee lived, the pleasure of having soloists, judge or accompanist to stay for the Festival. Lady Farrer became President, Lord Farrer and Colonel Lewin, at whose home Ralph had played chamber music as a schoolboy, were both on the Reference Committee: Lucy Broadwood and Sir Walter Parratt served on the Music Committee with Henry Bird, who was the Festival Accompanist, Miss Craig Sellar, Mrs. Julian Marshall and Ralph. The Festival was on 10 May, the morning was devoted to competitions, the afternoon to rehearsal and the evening concert followed at seven forty-five: these all took place in the hall that has since become the Dorking fire station. It was a great success and, as has been the case ever since, it ended with everyone making plans for next year.

Ralph had had a busy spring, for before the Leith Hill Festival he had prepared and conducted music for the Stratford Revels, at which Ben Jonson's *Pan's Anniversary* was performed for the first time since 1625. Ralph was asked to provide incidental music for this Masque. Holst helped him with the work and they explored early seventeenth century dance tunes, while Cecil Sharp found Morris dancers and Maypole dancers for the spectacle, which took place in the Bancroft Gardens. The music was performed by the Choral Union Orchestra, amateur choirs, one Stratford soloist, and two professional singers from Benson's Shakespeare Company. The whole entertainment was a success and useful to both Holst and Ralph in discovering how to arrange old music for modern instruments and how to use unaccompanied songs as incidental music.

The lease of the house in Barton Street was coming to an end and the landlord wanted a much higher rent if it was renewed. The lack of a bathroom, the outdoor lavatory, and the distance from Chelsea where Mrs. Fisher was now living—and where Adeline spent part of every day with her—were all reasons for moving. During May they saw and liked No. 13 Cheyne Walk, and decided that it would suit them. Though it is not so beautiful as some of the neighbouring houses it has some distinction. Its red brick walls, well spaced windows, and little garden seemed light and airy after Barton Street, but the greatest attraction was the view over the river. Since decorations had to be done and the tenancy agreement settled, Ralph and Adeline spent most of the summer in London.

In July *The Times Literary Supplement* devoted most of a page to the review of the new edition of *Grove*, particularly noticing Ralph's article on conducting. He had done a fair amount of conducting himself during the year, and during the autumn he had the chance of playing in an orchestra again for Holst was preparing a performance of *Sleepers Wake!* with the choir and orchestra of the Passmore Edwards Settlement.[1] It was their first performance of a Bach Cantata, which Ralph enjoyed in spite of the long bus ride to rehearsals, his nervousness of his fellow players in the viola section, and a tremendous fog on the night of the concert.

The move to Cheyne Walk on 1 November was managed easily, and after a week spent in arranging the house and taking books upstairs to his new study, Ralph went to Leith Hill Place to spend a few days in song collecting. He had finished his new quintet and in mid-December he played it to Adeline and her family the day before the first concert performance.

It is very hard to unravel the many strands of work that made the substance of each year. Dates of first performances are little guide to dates of composition because Ralph always put his work

[1] Now Mary Ward Settlement.

aside until he could see it in some sort of perspective. Other new works filled this interval, to be 'put into cold storage' in their turn. It is clear that the first years of the century were fruitful and that he was starting to find his way as a composer. It is also clear that he was becoming known to his fellow musicians and to a discerning though small public. He was learning a great deal from hearing performances of his works. He was fortunate in having his songs sung by excellent singers and his orchestral works interpreted by those sturdy professional conductors, Henry Wood and Dan Godfrey.

He had learned a great deal from his work in editing the Purcell manuscripts and the varied material for *The English Hymnal*, and from training choirs in Surrey and from writing down tunes as they were sung to him by country people. But he still felt that his technical equipment was not equal to the demands he would need to make of it.

CHAPTER V

1906–1911

The move to Cheyne Walk was the beginning of Ralph's maturity. His study on the top floor of the house with its view across to Battersea Park, of sunsets over the river, and of the river itself (for the plane trees had not yet obscured it from the windows), was the room where some of his most important work was done. The *Sea Symphony* was growing slowly, and his experience in conducting the Leith Hill Festival choirs was useful, for it helped him to discover what choirs could do and could not do, what, as he said, would 'come off', and what blurred the words or lay beyond the capacity of choral singers.

It was in some ways a time of restlessness and dissatisfaction. Others of his contemporaries seemed to be doing so much more, so much better. It was not entirely a question of success, though that came into it too, for success is a great encouragement, a stretching of wings suggesting of how great a flight they may be capable.

There were also family anxieties. Adeline's brother Hervey was a perpetual invalid for whom she felt a share of responsibility as well as great affection. Her brother-in-law, Fred Maitland, was a flame burning towards extinction. For some years he and his family had spent winters in Madeira, hoping the gentle climate might help him, and Adeline was always concerned with their departures and returns.

In spite of these worries the house was frequently full of friends; there was talk, music-making and concert-going, and expeditions to collect folk songs. The Journal of the Folk Song Society issued in May presented a collection of tunes Ralph had gathered from seven counties. He wrote a short preface to the volume:

> ... Although the field covered by the tunes in this journal is in one sense very large, in another it is very small—since it is only a small part of each county which I have searched for songs, and the time spent has been of necessity very short.

What results might be obtained from a systematic and sympathetic search through all the villages and towns of England!—And yet this precious heritage of beautiful melody is being allowed to slip through our hands through mere ignorance and apathy.

I could imagine a much less profitable way of spending a long winter evening than in the parlour of a country inn taking one's turn at the mug of 'four-ale'—(surely the most innocuous of all beverages) —in the rare company of minds imbued with that fine sense which comes from advancing years and a life-long communion with nature—and with the ever-present chance of picking up some rare old ballad or an exquisitely beautiful melody, worthy, within its smaller compass, of a place beside the finest compositions of the greatest composers. . . .

Ralph and Adeline took The Warren at Meldreth, near Cambridge, for a month during July and August, where he collected songs in the district. They were there when Holst sent his *Two Songs Without Words*, and Ralph wrote to thank him for the dedication, adding, 'I've just finished scoring the second movement of *The Ocean*'. With all these works in hand he was still writing songs, among them a setting of Mrs. Dearmer's translation of *Le ciel est pardessus le toit*. She wanted to use it in a play and had sent her MS to Ralph asking for a tune. He said he did not feel much like doing it, Verlaine was not a poet he particularly liked; but going up to his study one afternoon he saw how hideously untidy it was and realized that he must either tidy up or write the song, so he wrote the song.

Early in December came the news of Fred Maitland's death. Florence and her daughters had gone ahead to Canary to prepare the villa they had taken for the winter. Fred followed a few days later, became ill, and died at Las Palmas. Ralph went out immediately to bring his sister-in-law and nieces home. It was his first and only visit to the island, where he spent two or three weeks while the packing up of the recently unpacked possessions was completed.

When he returned he worked on a setting of Whitman's poem, *Toward the Unknown Region*, which he had made in 1904 or early 1905. 'Gustav and I were both stuck—so I suggested we shd. both set the same words in competition—suggesting "Darest thou". The prize was awarded by us to me.'[1] He used the music as a

[1] Letter from R. V. W. to Imogen Holst from The White Gates—undated.

memorial, and he dedicated it to Florence Maitland. The first performance was at the Leeds Festival of 1907: this made it clear that a new voice was speaking with authority and originality; but Ralph was still restless: not forced by lack of money to have a regular job like most of his friends, he felt guilty about having all his time for himself and feared he was not using it fully. The acute conscience he inherited from both the Darwin and the Wedgwood families nagged: he consulted his friends and came to the conclusion that he should go to France. His first idea was to work with d'Indy but, on the advice of M. D. Calvocoressi, who gave him an introduction, he asked Ravel to accept him for lessons. He wrote to acknowledge Ravel's invitation to come to see him and sent the draft to Calvocoressi.

Cher Monsieur,

Selon votre très aimable invitation j'écris de vous prévenir que j'espère me trouver à Paris le soir de jeudi, le douze Décembre; et je me ferai l'honneur de vous faire une visite le jour prochain si cela ne vous gênera pas.

Mon addresse sera l'Hôtel de l'Univers et du Portugal, Rue Croix des Petits-Champs.

Agréez mes salutations sincères
Ralph Vaughan Williams.[1]

P.S. This is my best attempt to write a letter in French. I hope it is fairly correct.

Ralph wrote of his meetings and lessons with Ravel:

He was much puzzled at our first interview. When I had shown him some of my work he said that for my first lessons I had better '*écrire un petit menuet dans le style de Mozart*'. I saw at once that it was time to act promptly, so I said in my best French, 'Look here, I have given up my time, my work, my friends and my career to come here and learn from you, and I am *not* going to write a *petit menuet dans le style de Mozart*'. After that we became great friends and I learned much from him. For example, that the heavy contrapuntal Teutonic manner was not necessary. '*Complexe mais pas compliqué*' was his motto. He showed me how to orchestrate in points of colour rather than in lines. It was an invigorating experience to find all artistic problems looked at from what was to me an entirely new angle.

[1] Following your very kind invitation I write to tell you that I hope to be in Paris on the evening of Thursday the twelfth of December, and I shall do myself the honour of calling on you the following day if that will not inconvenience you. My address will be . . .

Brahms and Tchaikovsky he lumped together as '*tout les deux un peu lourds*'. Elgar was '*tout à fait Mendelssohn*', his own music was '*tout à fait simple, rien que Mozart*'. He was against development for its own sake—one should only develop for the sake of arriving at something better. He used to say there was an implied melodic outline in all vital music, and instanced the opening of the C minor symphony as an example of a tune which was not stated but was implicit. He was horrified that I had no pianoforte in the little hotel where I worked. '*Sans le piano on ne peut pas inventer des nouvelles harmonies.*' I practised chiefly orchestration with him. I used to score some of his own pianoforte music and bits of Rimsky and Borodin to which he introduced me for the first time.[1]

Ralph wrote to Calvocoressi:

I must write you one line to thank you for introducing me to the man who is *exactly* what I was looking for. As far as I know my own faults he hit on them all exactly and is telling me to do exactly what I half felt in my mind I ought to do—but it just wanted *saying*.

I have got *Antar*[2] and have set to work on him. It is awfully kind of you to have been present at the lesson, it was such a help.

In other, undated, letters from Paris to Calvocoressi he said:

I go to Ravel today at 6.0. I'm afraid you won't be there. If you happen to know of any nice and cheap hotel or any other place where I c^{d} get an appartment somewhere nearer to Ravel than I am at present I should be very grateful if you could let me have the name on a postcard.

Have you a *partition* of the *Symphonie Montagnarde* of d'Indy—I see it is being performed shortly.

I am getting a lot out of Ravel—I hope it doesn't worry him too much—only I feel that 10 years w^{d} not teach me all I want.

W^{d} you mind telling me ought I to pay him for the lessons I have had or wait till the end—I have had more than 10 already.

A letter to Gustav written from Paris ends: 'This was to have been about Ravel, but I am too sleepy and I can tell you all about it later—only it is doing me just the good I hoped it would—I go to him 4 or 5 times a week. . . .'

Ralph spent three months in Paris. Adeline came over once or twice for a week or two, but even then he did not do much sight-

[1] *Musical Autobiography.* [2] *Symphony No. 2*, Rimsky Korsakov.

seeing or theatre-going but worked for the greater part of each day. He was unable to find suitable rooms nearer to Ravel's home, so he continued to stay at l'Hôtel de l'Univers et du Portugal although it was not particularly comfortable and the management was rather haphazard, for there were two or three fires during the time he was there. He enjoyed lunches and dinners in crêmeries and cafés, but when Ravel asked him and a publisher friend to dinner at a restaurant he felt himself unequal to choosing the food. He excused himself as a barbarous foreigner, and was glad he had done so when he saw what a serious matter it was, for the preliminary discussion lasted nearly twenty minutes. It was a splendid meal, and the publisher ate silently throughout. After the coffee he suddenly turned to dig Ralph in the ribs saying: 'Now we go see some jolly tarts, ha?' Ralph was surprised and interested, but the girls were disappointing. It was seven years since the death of Toulouse Lautrec,[1] but the types he had painted still persisted, a style not embraced in Ralph's canon of beauty, and guaranteed, he said, not to tempt any young man to lose his virtue.

There was a plan to have one of his works performed, possibly *In the Fen Country*,[2] and two letters from Ravel show how he busied himself on Ralph's behalf after Ralph had returned to London.

[Translation] 3.3.08.

Before everything, forgive me for not having written to you sooner. I have had an appalling amount of work lately. Colonne must have my *Rapsodie Espagnole* by March 15th and only the 4th part was orchestrated.

Now about your work—when you get this letter send your score and parts to Mr Marcel Labey c/o Maison Pleyel, Rue Rochechouart. If the Société National can give two concerts they will perform your *Fantasia*. If not, a performance will be more difficult as the French composers must naturally come first with a Society that calls itself *national*. . . .

In any case I need not tell you that I will do my uttermost to arrange a performance of the work of a pupil of whom I am proud.

[1] 1864–1901.

[2] The MS. score of the pianoforte reduction has written on it, '*Dans les Landes d'Angleterre*'. It was probably this work to which Ravel refers as a 'Fantasia'.

G

25.3.08

I have now got through all sorts of boring work and I can tell you what happened to your composition. You sent it to me too late, the first Committee meeting had already taken place. I could not manage to be present at the second meeting as Colonne's rehearsal was at the same time and at the other end of Paris. It would have been risky to have had your *Fantasia* considered in my absence and, as *I did not want it to be refused* I decided not to send it in.

Anyhow you have nothing to regret. The programme was excessively long and your work would not have been sufficiently rehearsed and the performance would have been bad. This will have to be put right next season. Let me know what you are working at. You know how interested I am.

Ralph wrote:

I came home with a bad attack of French fever and wrote a string quartet which caused a friend to say that I must have been having tea with Debussy, and a song cycle with several atmospheric effects, but I did not succumb to the temptation of writing a piece about a cemetery, and Ravel paid me the compliment of telling me that I was the only pupil who '*n'écrit pas de ma musique*'.[1]

The song cycle was *On Wenlock Edge. A Shropshire Lad*, published in 1896, had proved a gift for composers, and for the next quarter of a century Housman's clear-cut poems with their nostalgic and vivid emotion were often set to music. The poet was known to dislike this, especially when the musician omitted verses, though Ralph always asserted that any poet who had written such lines as

The goal stands up, the keeper
Stands up to keep the goal,

should be grateful to have them left out.

The Leith Hill Musical Festival was well established after three successful seasons and the choirs had grown from seven to nine. In spite of having spent so much of the winter in Paris, Ralph was home in time to rehearse *Sleepers Wake!*, the first of a long series of Bach cantatas that he conducted at Dorking. In the programme the name of Isidore Schwiller appears as a member of

[1] *Musical Autobiography*.

the orchestra, beginning an association with the Festival that was to last for many years. He had known Gustav von Holst as a trombone player in the Carl Rosa Company where Isidore was leader of the orchestra and deputy conductor. Isidore led the Schwiller quartet and Ralph may have consulted him about his setting of the Housman poems that made up the *On Wenlock Edge* cycle; he used pianoforte and string quartet to accompany the tenor voice, and the Schwiller Quartet took part in the first performance eighteen months later, when they also played Ralph's quartet in G minor, another first performance.

In late May Ralph spent four days adjudicating at the Bucks., Beds., and Oxon Festival with Walford Davies, Maurice Sons, and Henry Bird as his fellow judges. In June he conducted *Toward the Unknown Region* at Cambridge, and it is probable that he was then asked to write the music for the 1909 Greek play, *The Wasps* of Aristophanes. He spent some of the summer at Leith Hill Place, collecting songs in Surrey and Sussex, and he went to Hereford, probably to the Three Choirs Festival, though the main reason of his visit was an invitation from Mrs. Leather, the wife of a solicitor living in Weobley. Mrs. Leather, who had spent all her life in Hereford, had written an article on local customs, *Memorials of Old Herefordshire*, and when her friends pointed out that no systematic record had been made of county beliefs and traditions, rapidly dying out, she undertook the work. She was well equipped to do so by her life-long knowledge of the county, and the people, and by her affection for both. She learned hop-picking from the casual labourers in the fields, for working beside them she learned their stories and their songs. Not being a musician she wrote to Ralph to ask his help. She discovered the singers, and he recorded the songs. It was a fruitful venture, and he collected many carols including several versions of *The Bitter Withy*, *The Carnal and the Crane*, *Christ Made a Trance*, *The Moon Shines Bright*, *The Truth Sent from Above*, and, best of all, *The Seven Virgins*, as well as *A Brisk Young Soldier* and a beautiful version of *The Unquiet Grave*.

One evening in Ledbury he heard a girl singing a ballad to two men. The pubs were just closing and these three, standing in the road outside in the light of the still open door, looked like a group in a story. He asked if they knew other songs, and one of the men said his old father did, would Ralph care to visit him?

As it was so late Ralph suggested that some other time might be more convenient, but the man insisted on taking him then and there. They went down wet lanes and stopped in a very muddy track where two tramps were sheltering in a barn. The guide left Ralph, saying his parents lived in a tent near by and he would go and see if they were still awake. The tramps took no notice of Ralph's arrival, but went on talking—'Did you ever hear the harmonium?' one asked. 'No.' 'It's sweet music.' Ralph waited and waited until the man returned and said his parents had been asleep and did not feel like singing now—perhaps in the morning? So they retraced their way, Ralph keeping a careful lookout for landmarks. He went back in the morning: the old couple were friendly, but had no songs worth collecting, though he found some among their neighbours.

In 1907 Holst had been appointed Musical Director at Morley College. He set to work to improve the repertoire of choir and orchestra, and before long the enthusiasm for music he generated had made the musical life of the College exciting and stimulating. The earliest performances he gave with his students were of Rossini's *Stabat Mater* on Good Friday at the Old Vic, and, the following year, of Purcell's *King Arthur*. Ralph was, naturally, involved in both. During the winter of 1908–9 he gave a course of extension lectures 'From Haydn to Wagner'—music having been the subject chosen by the students themselves by a large majority for the extension course. Ralph was an old friend of the College, and was always ready to help in any way he could. When promising students could not afford the £1 a term fee, he often came to the rescue, and Holst gave them free tuition: between them they saw that no talent or real musical enthusiasm was lost to the College for want of money.

A song belonging to this year can be dated by a letter of 29 November 1908 from Max Gate:

Dear Sir,

I quite approve of your calling the soldiers' song Buonaparty that you have set to music from *The Dynasts*. Please state where it comes from.

Yours very truly,
Thomas Hardy.

P.S. My impression is that one of my lyrics of more general application would be more popular.

Ralph read all Hardy's novels, and one summer followed Tess's footsteps in her walk from Flintcomb Ash to Emminster. He thought *Tess* the greatest of the novels and his other favourite was *Far from the Madding Crowd*. He felt there were too many overheard conversations in *The Mayor of Casterbridge*, though the first chapter of that and the majestic beginning of *The Return of the Native*—Holst's as well as Hardy's *Egdon Heath*—were often re-read. But he found the many rustic conversations were almost always unbearably tedious, and he went so far as to say that they sounded as if Hardy had kept a little book of country talk to use when needed: (an idea probably suggested by the story that executors had found a notebook labelled 'Good second subjects' among Brahms's papers). When the cinema became capable of great themes Ralph longed for a film to be made of *The Dynasts*, so naturally suitable for the screen, and he would have liked to write the music for it.

Through the winter of 1908 and the early part of 1909 he was working on the music for *The Wasps*. He enjoyed this, and his Greek was still in good enough repair for him to manage the songs and choruses without trouble. The fair copy looks as if the words were written with no more difficulty than that needed for writing English words under the notes.

Adeline, who was always prone to prolonged colds and influenza, was very ill early in March. While she still had a high temperature she went, against all advice, to look after her mother who was recovering from a fall and had a relapse that gave anxiety. Adeline insisted on visiting her, though both her sisters, Emmie and Cordelia, were at home and doing all that was necessary. This unwise action was thought to have been the first cause of her own long suffering from arthritis: Ralph certainly believed it to be so. He took her to Weymouth for a few days at the end of March, and on 2 April she seemed quite well again and saw the Boat Race from the Holsts' house at Barnes.

Later in April Ravel answered their invitation to stay.

[Translation]
4 Avenue Carnot 13.4.09
Cher Monsieur,

Your invitation is so kind that I cannot do anything but accept. I am even more grateful because I must admit I felt frightened of being in a country of which I don't know the language. I arrive in

London on the 25th. I don't yet know at what time. I will write from there.

Please give my respectful greetings to Mrs. Williams. . . .

He was a pleasant visitor. Ralph enjoyed taking him sight-seeing, and was fascinated to find that he liked English food—the one thing the Cheyne Walk household had foreseen as a problem. But it was no problem at all: it appeared that steak and kidney pudding with stout at Waterloo station was Ravel's idea of pleasurably lunching out. He also wished to be taken to something he described as 'Vallasse', which Ralph rightly interpreted as the Wallace collection. His thank-you letter shows that he had enjoyed himself.

[Translation] 5.5.09

Chère Madame,

Here I am, once again a Parisian: but a Parisian home-sick for London. I have never before really missed another country. And yet I had left here with a certain fear of the unknown. In spite of the presence of Delarge, in spite of the charming reception of my colleagues I should still have felt a real stranger. I needed the warm and sensitive welcome waiting for me at Cheyne Walk to make me feel at home in new surroundings, and to give me a taste of the charm and magnificence of London, almost as if I were a Londoner.

One can never say all these things in the emotion and hurry of a departure and I should like to express my gratitude here, to you and to Mr. Williams just as I feel it—Please will you give your mother my most respectful greetings as well as to your brother, and I apologize again for not having been able to accept their kind invitation.

The second week after Easter was, as usual for Ralph, occupied by the Leith Hill Festival, then there were people to stay, a day or two in Oxford, then back to Leith Hill, and, in early June, to Paris. At midsummer there were the Darwin centenary celebrations at Cambridge, and it was strange to realize that the well-remembered Great-Uncle Charles of his childhood could have become this centre of veneration.

The rest of the summer passed in visits, concerts, going to the Follies, a few days at Woodhall Spa hoping the treatment there might help Adeline more than the massage she had been having regularly, and on 28 September they both went to the Music

League's Festival at Liverpool to hear the new version of *Willow-Wood* which Ralph had re-written and rescored, adding a chorus part. In his own copy of the vocal score he wrote 'first (and last) performance' beside the date and added: 'complete flop!'

On 15 November the Schwiller Quartet with Frederick Kiddle and Gervase Elwes gave the first performance of *On Wenlock Edge* at the Aeolian Hall, a first performance that satisfied Ralph and realized all his intentions as few first performances do. The next day he went to Cambridge. He had been there several times for rehearsals of *The Wasps*, when he had had opportunities of getting to know the distinguished young cast. Among those who later became well known in the arts were Miles Malleson, Denis Browne, James Friskin—then playing timpani—and Steuart Wilson whose friendship and whose singing were to be important in Ralph's life. The orchestra was led by Haydn Inwards who had liked Ralph's undergraduate compositions. It must have been pleasant for him to hear how *The Wasps* music was hummed and whistled and discussed by those taking part in the play. Ralph enjoyed himself enormously as he always did when he was involved in anything to do with the stage.

Another, less elaborate, theatrical venture, was a performance of scenes from *Pilgrim's Progress*, being acted and produced by friends at Reigate Priory, for which he was asked to write incidental music. This was limited by the instruments available and by the smallness of the stage, and his work had to be within the scope of the singers and players. But he found the acting version of the story, not re-read since nursery days, full of dramatic possibility for an opera:[1] an idea shelved for many years but never wholly forgotten, even to some details of production which were germane to music to be written forty years later.

The year finished in the usual pattern of much family visiting and Christmas at Leith Hill Place. Ralph was tremendously busy. *The Ocean*, now re-named *A Sea Symphony*, was to have its first performance at the 1910 Leeds Festival; the finishing touches to the score had to be made in time for the choir to learn it and the

[1] The music contained several features which had associations with Bunyan for Ralph. Principally the Roundhead tune 'York' and the folk song 'Our Captain Calls', which appears in *The English Hymnal* ('He who would valiant be'). One theme for contralto is fully developed in *The Shepherds of the Delectable Mountains*.

orchestra parts to be copied. There was the usual round of country rehearsals with each choir taking part in the Leith Hill Festival, then the Festival itself. This was a programme typical of the following years, work being written, other work being revised, proofs and band parts being corrected, and, at the same time, for Leith Hill, the checking and correction of hired parts and scores, the writing of programme notes, the engaging of orchestra and soloists, and the planning of rehearsals so that the best use should be made of every available minute. He had to teach inexperienced singers and their enthusiastic conductors to become a united choir, able to tackle music unfamiliar to many of them: this was something which he loved doing and to which he gave energy and devotion, patience and infectious enthusiasm and from which he learned a great deal about music.

Besides all this he was commissioned to write a work for the Three Choirs Festival at Gloucester. This was admission to a very special world of music: the Three Choirs Festivals had been founded in the early eighteenth century and had a long tradition of oratorio singing. In 1910 Elgar was the established light of their being. Ralph had been asked for an orchestral work, the first step over that sacred threshold. While he had been immersed in hymns he had used one of the nine tunes Thomas Tallis had written for Archbishop Parker's metrical Psalter of 1567 to accompany Addison's words, 'When rising from the bed of death'. He took this tune as a theme for a fantasia, using the strings of the orchestra grouped as a solo quartet, a small string band, and a larger body of players: with the Norman grandeurs of Gloucester Cathedral in mind and the strange quality of the resonance of stone, the echo idea of three different groups of instruments was well judged. It seemed that his early love for architecture and his historical knowledge were so deeply assimilated that they were translated and absorbed into the texture and line of the music. The audience in the cathedral that September evening had come to hear Elgar conduct *Gerontius*, but before that work Ralph stood in front of them, looking taller than ever on the high platform, dark haired, serious, inwardly extremely nervous, and the grave splendour of the *Fantasia on a Theme by Thomas Tallis* was heard for the first time.

Less than a month later rehearsals for *A Sea Symphony* were in full swing. Orchestral rehearsals took place at the Royal College of Music and Mrs. Fisher records the presence of her family on 3, 5 and 6 October. The performance was at Leeds on the 12th where Ralph and Adeline were joined by many friends who had come up to hear the new work: among them Henry Ley and another young man first known to Ralph at Oxford, who had become an ally in the world of folk music. This was George Butterworth, who had worked on *The Times*, been a master at Radley, and had then decided to go to the R.C.M. in 1910. Hugh Allen was there, of course, and the Stanfords, but Ralph was scarcely aware of their presence, being completely absorbed in the terrors of his first really big work. He had lived with the symphony on paper for so long, and now its moment of sound had come. He said that when the orchestra played the opening chords and the chorus came in, fortissimo, 'Behold the sea itself', he was nearly blown off the rostrum by the noise. He had hardly been able to sleep or eat for the last few days, and the timpanist, Henderson, fully appreciating his nervous state, gave him this comforting assurance: 'Give us a square four in the bar and we will do the rest.' Whether he did or not, he could not remember. Campbell McInnes, the baritone soloist, equally nervous, had not helped matters in the few minutes they stood together waiting to go on the platform: 'If I stop you'll go on, won't you?' he said. Somehow the symphony began, continued, and ended, and Ralph became aware that he was very hungry and very tired. Lady Stanford touched Adeline's shoulder and murmured: 'You must be very proud of him,' but she was unable to answer. It had been a major ordeal for them both and perhaps the most memorable birthday of Ralph's life. One letter survives that first performance—it came from Lucy Broadwood.

Oct. 13. 10.

Dear Ralph,

Thank you so very much for the keen pleasure which your noble setting of those splendid words gave me last night. I hope that your anxiety (owing to hurried rehearsals etc.) didn't prevent you yourself from enjoying it. The glorious sounds that you draw from your orchestra are a delight indeed.

You are every bit as wicked as most composers of your time in expecting human larynxes to adapt themselves to impossible feats and to stretch or contract their vocal chords to notes not in their registers, but the Leeds chorus and your two soloists (tho' they may send their throat doctors' bills to you later!) did wonders and wove themselves with glorious energy into the lovely texture of the whole.

It was delightful dining with your mother and Margaret. I wish I could have seen you both; I thought of you in your lodgings clasping your boiled ham as I took my flight to Bradford. . . .

Ralph thought that it had not been a very good performance, but the musicians in the audience realized the quality of the work and Hugh Allen at once planned an Oxford performance to consolidate the impression it had made. As Ralph discovered later, many of the younger generation first became aware of the music of their contemporary world through *A Sea Symphony*, and awoke to the fact that they lived in an age when music did not belong only to the past.

Adeline had not been well for a long time; she suffered from rheumatic or arthritic pain, and she was no longer able to go for bicycle rides or long walks. She saw many doctors, going to each new one in a spirit of hope which soon changed to despair, for none was able to curb the pain or arrest the increasing stiffness of her joints. But she did not allow illness to interfere with her life, perhaps unwisely, for her mother's diary notes her almost daily visits and the many hours various members of the family spent at '13'. During these years Margot Gatty became a student at the Royal College of Music and she too spent much time at Cheyne Walk, going to concerts with Adeline and Ralph, and eventually coming to stay in the house during term time. Fredegond Maitland was often there too, writing poems which she showed to Adeline and sometimes to Ralph. The household was looked after by a devoted couple, Mr. and Mrs. Mott, who lived in the basement, and to whose little girl Ralph attempted to teach music.

Margot Gatty remembered the house very vividly—the long white curtains bordered with blue linen in the drawing-room, chairs and sofa covered in dark blue, a table at one end where the afternoon light fell on them as they sat at tea, and the huge early Erard piano which Julia Cameron had owned and which had survived many journeys in the Isle of Wight from her house to Faringford so that Edward Lear could use it when he stayed there with Tennyson. This room in Chelsea, seen through the loving eyes of a girl happy to be with people who were to her the enchanted beings of her childhood, was still real to Margot fifty years later. She described a party at which Martin Shaw was to play some of his piano music for friends and to try over some new songs. Adeline arranged the room, having the piano placed so that the marred side of Martin's handsome face would be turned away from the audience. Then, as some of the refreshments had disastrously not arrived, she took a taxi to make some hasty last minute additions, but was so delayed that Martin Shaw, Gordon Craig,[1] and several other guests arrived before her. She heard them talking upstairs, but when she went into the room silence fell. Saying good night to Margot, she spoke of this: 'I shall give a party some day and not be there,' she said. She was always aloof, even frightening to those who did not know her well: partly from shyness, reserve, and a capacity for silence which could be alarming. Added to this was the effect of her particular kind of stately beauty: she made no concession to fashion, or the choice of anything which would enhance it. She showed pleasure at the presence of close friends particularly her own family: or if anyone was in any distress or was ill she was all consideration, warmth and solicitude, as if it needed this to bring tenderness out of the carapace of her reserve. But when Martin Shaw wrote to thank them for his party his P.S. to Adeline was: 'Dare I say it? I must, I love you.' It was to her he turned in a moment of distress when his sister had decided to become an artists' model. 'Would anyone know us?' he asked. 'Would you?' Both Ralph and Adeline, touched and amused, reassured him, with their easy attitude of 'Why not, if she wants to?'

Gustav of course was another regular visitor; he used to come in dead tired after a day of teaching and have a sleep on the sofa: Mrs. Mott knew that when Mr. Holst came it was to be boiled eggs for everyone for Adeline firmly believed in the reviving power of boiled eggs for tea. When Margot was ill Adeline nursed her, and spent hours telling stories of her youth in the New Forest as she sat by the bedroom fire, or brought drinks of hot milk in the night. She always found time to be with Hervey, the companion of those Forest days, and though he seemed to others a perpetual burden, he was never so to her, and she gladly gave him her service, devotion, and love.

The great excitement of the summer was Gustav's performance of Purcell's *Fairy Queen* on 10 June. It was the first performance since the seventeenth century, for the manuscript had been lost

[1] The stage-designer: son of Ellen Terry.

and had come to light only in 1910. The preparations had involved copying, sometimes transposing, fifteen hundred pages of manuscript for vocal and instrumental parts. The performance took place at the Victoria Hall and Ralph introduced the numbers. Although the hall was not full, the achievement was acclaimed by the critics, who had come in force, and the reputation of Morley College in the world of music was assured. Finances were difficult, for every new performance raised problems which had to be overcome somehow, whether it was paying for professional players to strengthen the orchestra or finding money for copying parts. Ralph, deeply interested in the work Gustav was doing, backed him to the uttermost, lecturing, bringing an orchestra to illustrate a talk, or helping in any other way he could devise—getting from the work there as much as he gave in terms of interest, musical experience, and friendship.

In a long letter from abroad in 1903[1] Gustav had written:

> I wonder if it would be possible to lock oneself up for so many hours every day. If so, it would be far easier for me than for you as you have so many friends. . . .

This was so indeed: among them were Cecil Sharp, S. P. Waddington, Hugh Allen, Percy Grainger, the Gattys, George Butterworth, Henry Ley, Theodore and Crompton Llewelyn Davies, George and Robert Trevelyan, G. E. Moore, Maurice Amos, Martin Shaw, and of course Gustav, of whom he probably saw more than of anyone else. Beyond these was a wider circle of acquaintances among musicians, younger men who were beginning to see in Ralph and Gustav the new leaders of English music, and to follow them.

As always in the profession both time and place dictate to a certain extent who are to be thrown together, sharing work for some project, meeting at rehearsals, or staying at the same place for festivals: a shifting pattern with music as the centre from which they drew their light and to which they gave their ardour.

This was an important year in music. Elgar's second symphony, Sibelius's fourth, and the first performance of *Petrouchka* were among the events of 1911. Mahler died, his tenth symphony unfinished. It was, too, the first year of King George V's reign. When Edward VII died, the flourish of the Edwardian age was

[1] See *Heirs and Rebels*, p. 17.

already fading into an era of social reform which had been growing imperceptibly. Crowns were about to fall, revolutions and armies to dominate a scene which the industrial revolution had been changing slowly for the last century. The interwoven pattern of life must affect the artist, sometimes directly, sometimes by indirect influence: though some periods seem static to those living through them, half a century later the perspective of years shows their movement and quality. That Holst should have brought to life a performance of a work unheard since the seventeenth century with the help of a college devoted to the education of working people was a symptom of the change of outlook and of promise for the future. The arts were for all, as folk songs, once the heritage of village life, were now to be given back to the people who had so nearly lost them when the effects of the Education Act had begun to be felt; when, instead of cherishing traditional lore, long richly stored memories and an inheritance of songs and dances of their forefathers, people were able to read and no longer had to rely on memory. The system of compulsory elementary education, evolving slowly, through trial and error, was bound to leave unintended victims of experiment strewing its way. It was left for evening classes, the Workers' Educational Association, Morley College and other pioneer bodies to fill the gaps and satisfy the adults in their urge to learn what schools had left untaught. Here was a new world of potential amateur performers, a new audience hungry for music.

As well as sharing some of Gustav's work at Morley, at Leith Hill Ralph was teaching people to take part in great music and to make it their own. Parry had written to Meggie after the 1911 Spring Festival:

> Thank you very much for your delightful letter. It is kind of you to write as you do. I enjoyed my day at Dorking immensely. It was enjoyable to see your brother devoting his abilities to such good purpose. You have reason to be proud of him and I hope Dorking and its neighbourhood is proud of him too. Please give him my love when you see him.

It must have been about this time that a very exotic luncheon party took place. Ralph had met Gordon Craig and there was some discussion of their writing a ballet together so a meeting was arranged with Diaghilev and Nijinsky at the Savoy. Nijinsky remained entirely silent throughout the meal, while Diaghilev proposed that he should dance both Cupid and Psyche, which was the story Gordon Craig wanted to use. Ralph objected very strongly to this idea. When the party broke up he and Craig walked home together. 'Let me have the music,' said Craig, 'and I'll fit in the story.' 'Impossible,' said Ralph, 'you must let me have the scenario and I will write music for it.' 'Impossible,' said Craig, 'just send the music'—and so they parted. Neither sent anything to the other and the projected ballet became another might-have-been.

Isadora Duncan and her brother were others he knew at this time. He found both to be charmers, and he was delighted by Isadora's dancing; he never cared for classical dancing, and the use of the body poised on the toe seemed to him a travesty of nature and made him feel uncomfortable. Isadora invited him to her studio to see her dance, as she wanted him to write music for her. She said sadly that had they been in Paris, she would have danced for him 'without costume'—but her English accompanist would not like her to do so. He found the melting beauty of her phrasing exactly the sort of movement for which he could write, and he started work on a choral ballet using Gilbert Murray's translation of *The Bacchae*. Sometimes she would collect him in her car and drive him about London at night. Generous and spectacular, she would make her chauffeur stop, and they would walk along the Embankment where she delighted to give half-crowns to the homeless who slept out on the benches there, often, like some eccentric fairy in her pale evening dress, waking them from their newspaper-wrapped sleep to press a coin into their hands.

Her brother, Raymond Duncan, who had lived for some time on a Greek island, was an equally decorative figure, for he always wore classical Greek dress and would arrive for tea at Cheyne Walk in short white tunic, cloak, and sandals, whatever the weather. He used to give public recitations of Whitman's poems and Ralph remembered on one occasion when he lost the thread in *A Song of Joys* and, flinging his cloak across his arm, strode across to the prompter and returned unabashed with slow magnificence to continue his oration with the words:

'Another time,—mackerel taking . . .'

Ralph himself did some dancing in these years. He used to go to

Cecil Sharp's holiday schools, sometimes conducting the singing and taking part, not very stylishly but with cheerful zest, in country dancing. He enjoyed these schools and festivals not only for the music but for the company: Maud and Helen Karpeles, George Butterworth, Douglas Kennedy, and others, all concerned in the organization and demonstration.

About this time he was beginning to think of a new symphony, which was, he said, Butterworth's idea:

> One of my most grateful memories of George is connected with my *London Symphony*: indeed I owe its whole idea to him. I remember very well how the idea originated. He had been sitting with us one evening, smoking and playing (I like to think it was one of those rare occasions when we persuaded him to play his beautiful little pianoforte piece, Firle Beacon) and at the end of the evening, as he was getting up to go, he said in his characteristically abrupt way: 'You know, you ought to write a symphony.' From that moment the idea of a symphony—a thing which I had always declared I would never attempt—dominated my mind. I showed the sketches to George bit by bit as they were finished, and it was then that I realized that he possessed, in common with very few composers, a wonderful power of criticism of other men's work, and insight into their ideas and motives.[1]

Perhaps Butterworth felt it was time Ralph thought more in terms of orchestral sound and less of choral possibilities. Like *A Sea Symphony*, the *London Symphony* took a long time to grow: Ralph described it as a symphony by a Londoner, and the river, the bustle, the street singers, the cabs, the crowds, the days and nights measured by Westminster chimes were all material that grew together in the sketches he was beginning to make.

Besides Hugh Allen, who was prepared to back his own judgement and to give the *Sea Symphony* a second chance at Oxford, and at Cambridge where a June performance was being prepared—but without the scherzo which seemed too difficult for the choir—Ralph had another champion at Bristol. This was Arnold Barter whose amateur choir had sung *Toward the Unknown Region* in 1909. His performance of the *Sea Symphony* followed the Oxford one, so it was the third performance of the work, which at that time showed no sign of being popular.

[1] *George Butterworth:* privately printed memoir and appreciation.

13 Cheyne Walk
S.W.
April 29. 1911

Dear Mr Barter,

When I received your letter this morning I thought that I could read between the lines and guessed that the performance of my *Sea Symphony* had been quite first rate. This guess of mine is now confirmed by the testimony of a niece of mine[1] of whose musical judgement I have a very high opinion, and who has heard the work both at Leeds and Oxford—she was present at your performance on Wednesday and says it was the nicest performance she has heard—'The chorus so fresh and lovely in its tone—the band small but so good and the whole thing so spontaneous and vigorous.'

Now first I want to thank *you* for all the immense labours and thought you have expended over the work, and for using all that musical capacity and insight, which I know you must possess to secure such a fine rendering.

Secondly I want you kindly to convey my very best thanks to the choir for their splendid determination to give a new work the very best possible chance. I know from bitter experience how hard the work is, and I know what self denial all those extra rehearsals must have entailed—I only hope that the success of their efforts has been some reward to them—and thirdly I must thank your orchestra who behaved like true artists in giving an extra rehearsal and thus contributing so much to the total success.

It is a great pleasure and encouragement to feel that my work has given pleasure to you and your performers—I hope I may one day have the pleasure of hearing your choir sing.

I thought that the two soloists[2] you chose were quite excellent. Thank you once again.

I remain yours very truly
R. Vaughan Williams.

In August Ralph and Adeline spent three weeks at Freshwater in the Isle of Wight, where he was busy with an opera, *Hugh the Drover*, being diverted from the new Symphony by the excitements of the stage.[3] The libretto was by Harold Child, a member of the staff of *The Times* to whom Ralph had been intro-

[1] Probably Ermengard Maitland who remembers going to several early performances.

[2] Laura Evans Williams and Jamieson Dodds.

[3] See Appendix I.

George Butterworth

Meggie Vaughan Williams

Adeline

duced by Bruce Richmond, the paper's literary editor.[1] The opera was set in the early nineteenth century but life in the English countryside still had some likeness to that past: and characters in the opera were not unlike singers Ralph had known in his folk song collecting days or the parents and grandparents of whom they had told him. He worked on the opera from 1910 to 1914: sometimes it took precedence of everything else, sometimes it lapsed into the background of his life but never for very long at a time.

The *Tallis Fantasia* had led to a new commission for the Worcester Festival, and Ralph chose poems by George Herbert for his *Five Mystical Songs*. He set them for baritone solo, choir, and orchestra, having Campbell McInnes's voice in mind.

Campbell McInnes had married one of Burne-Jones's granddaughters, Angela (later Thirkell), and her sister Clare Mackail remembered the performance as one of unearthly beauty. She also remembered seeing Ralph and Adeline at one of the concerts sitting in the nave of the cathedral 'with the sun shining through the windows on her hair which looked like pure gold. It was an unforgettable sight, the two of them. He had a thick thatch of dark hair, a tall, rather heavy figure, even then slightly bowed; and his face was profoundly moving, deep humanity and yet with the quality of a medieval sculpture——' Ralph's own memory of that Festival was different. He was probably aware that his work was awaited with curiosity: he was even more conscious of the lack of adequate rehearsal time, a nightmare almost every composer endures before almost every first performance. He had to conduct a new work, and the orchestra knew very little about it, and the choirs even less. 'I was thoroughly nervous. When I looked at the fiddles I thought I was going mad, for I saw what appeared to be Kreisler at a back desk. I got through somehow, and at the end I whispered to Reed,[2] "*Am* I mad, or *did* I see

[1] Bruce Richmond was a friend Hervey Vaughan Williams brought to stay at Leith Hill Place, the first Literary Editor of *The Times*, later founder and editor of *The Times Literary Supplement*. Though his work was with words, music was his recreation. He and Ralph soon became friends, and Ralph turned to him for advice on any literary problems.

[2] W. H. Reed, 1876–1941. Violinist, conductor, teacher, author and composer. He joined the London Symphony Orchestra when it was formed in 1904 and became its leader in 1912. He was a close friend of Elgar's and of many musicians including R. V. W.

Kreisler in the band?" "Oh yes," he said, "he broke a string and wanted to play it in before the Elgar Concerto and couldn't without being heard in the Cathedral." ' This became one of Ralph's favourite stories, and started: 'I have done something none of the grand conductors have. . . .' Years later he was telling it to some players and one of them completed it. 'I was sitting next to Kreisler, one of our people had been taken ill, so he slipped in beside me: just before we started, he said, "Nudge me if there's anything difficult and I'll leave it out." ' Kreisler did another memorable thing at that Festival; in the *St. Matthew Passion* it was he who played the solo accompanying the aria 'Have Mercy Lord' and no one who heard it ever forgot the matchless sound.

Most of November was spent at Leith Hill Place. Aunt Sophy, who had inherited the house that had been her home since childhood, died there on the 16th. She had become so crippled that her head was perpetually bowed: Bob Trevelyan once saw the maid who had wheeled her into the azalea woods lift it so that she could look up at the flowering trees. Her eccentricities had increased, she was tiresome and narrow-minded and she had had no part in Ralph's life for years. Though her death could not bring any grief to him it brought memories of her kindness when he was a child and she had given him his first music lessons. The ownership of the house passed to his mother and she and Meggie continued there with the same quiet dignity, the same mixture of hospitality and austerity that had hardly varied since the days of Caroline Wedgwood's widowhood.

In December Ralph and Adeline visited Cambridge again, and then Ralph went with George Butterworth on a short trip to collect songs in Norfolk. One night, in a pub where they had found several singers, one of them suggested it would be much quicker if he rowed them across the water than that they should bicycle round the Broad by road. It was a brilliantly starry night, frosty and still. They piled their bicycles into the boat and started. Their ferryman rowed with uncertain strokes, raising his oar now and then to point at distant lights, saying 'Lowestoft' or 'Southwold'. Before long they realized they were always the same lights and that he was taking them round and round in circles. The night air after the frowsty bar parlour and the beer had been fatal, and he was thoroughly drunk. Eventually they persuaded him to let them row. Luck guided them to a jetty among the reeds. By this time their singer was sound asleep and did not wake even when they extricated their bicycles from under him. So they tied the boat up and left him there while they bicycled down an unknown track and found their way back to Southwold. The singer survived and was found in the same pub the next evening. But this time they did not accept his offer of a short cut by water.

CHAPTER VI

1912–1914

During the past ten years Ralph had composed, lectured, taught, collected folk songs, examined, judged festivals—a job he hated, but one which brought in a useful addition to his small private income—edited, written articles and programme notes, and helped to found the Leith Hill Musical Festival, of which he became coach and musical adviser as well as conductor. In composition he had done a prodigious amount of work, some of which was already discarded. Though the mainstream of growth can be seen now, the tributaries are not clearly defined nor can one tell where they entered the course of the river or to what extent they enlarged the flow—but it is clear that the influence of folk song and Tudor music was important and enriching.

The effect of folk song in particular was immensely liberating. Ralph's thoughts on this absorbing subject were set forth very clearly in a lecture which he gave at a vacation conference on musical education on 10 January 1912, and which later was enlarged for publication. This he called *English Folk Songs*;[1] he began his talk by telling the audience:

> I have this excuse for standing up before you to-day—I am like a psychical researcher who has actually seen a ghost, for I have been among the more primitive people of England and have noted down their songs, and judging from these, and from songs collected by others, I have drawn some conclusions which I will try to put before you. . . .

The two main threads of his argument, after the nature of folk song has been very fully discussed, are its place as an art-form in its own right, and its place as the basis of a national music.

[1] Joseph Williams, 1912. See p. xiv.
In passing, it is interesting to compare this with articles on the same subject by Bartók (published in English in *Tempo*, Autumn and Winter 1949–50), whose collecting experience ran a parallel course in time and extent and whose conclusions were like Ralph's own.

The evolution of the English folk song by itself has ceased but its spirit can continue to grow and flourish at the hands of our native composers.

I do not wish to advocate a narrow parochialism in music. A composer's style must be ultimately personal, but an individual is a member of a nation, and the greatest and most widely known artists have been the most strongly national. Bach, Shakespeare, Verdi, Reynolds, Whitman—their appeal may be cosmopolitan, but the origin of their inspiration is national . . . we have made the mistake in England of trying to take over 'ready made' a foreign culture, a culture which is the result of generations of patient development, and of attempting to fit on to it our own incompatible conditions. This is merely to reap where we have not sown and the result must be failure.

He believed the remedy lay in acknowledging our own music as the natural language for our own composers:

Any direct and unforced expression of our common life may be the nucleus from which a great art will spring . . . and thus there will gradually be built up a musical structure which shall have that permanence and universal recognition which is only possible to an art which has grown out of the very lives of those who make it.

He enlarged on this theme, looking at it from another angle, in an article 'Who wants the English Composer?',[1] published in *The R.C.M. Magazine* in the Christmas term of 1912. It is headed with lines from Whitman's *Song of the Exposition*:

Come Muse, migrate from Greece and Ionia,
Cross out, please, those immensely over-paid accounts,
That matter of Troy and Achilles' wrath, and Aeneas, Odysseus' wanderings,
Placard 'removed' and 'to let' on the rocks of your snowy Parnassus,
Repeat at Jerusalem, place the notice high on Jaffa's gate, and on Mount Moriah,
The same on the walls of your German, French and Spanish castles, and Italian collections,
For know a better, fresher, busier sphere,
A wide, untried domain awaits, demands you.

He wrote:

. . . art for art's sake has never flourished in England. We are often called inartistic because our art is unconscious. Our drama and poetry,

[1] Reprinted in *Ralph Vaughan Williams: A Study* by Hubert Foss. London, Harrap, 1950.

like our laws and our constitution, have evolved by accident while we thought we were doing something else, and so it will be with music. The composer must not shut himself up and think about art, he must live with his fellows and make his art an expression of the whole life of the community—if we seek for art we shall not find it. . . .

Before either of these complementary articles was in print, Ravel's correspondence with Ralph was resumed.

[Translation] 4.1.12

My wishes would be too late for Christmas, so let me send them to you *à la française*, for the New Year, and ask Mrs. Vaughan Williams to accept them too.

We could not give a performance of your quartet last season. But the Committee of the *Société Indépendante* has decided to organise a concert of English music and to include in it either your 4tte or your song cycle with quintet accompaniment[1] which I find altogether remarkable. I must now apologize for not having told you this when you so kindly sent it to me. We might possibly perform both works. But if there is not time for that have you any preference? I would prefer the song cycle. The date of the concert is not yet settled. But you will be told in plenty of time. I do not think I shall come to London this year. But I hope I shall have the pleasure of seeing you in Paris for the performance of your works. . . .

2.2.12

I am delighted to tell you that the Committee of the S.M.I. has unanimously decided to include your song cycle with string quartet and piano in the programme of the concert on February 29. This concert will be exceptionally brilliant: Fauré will accompany on the pianoforte Jean Raunay. I am trying to persuade Cyril Scott to come and himself play his suite which is on the programme. And we will certainly have the British Embassy in the audience as well as the chief members of the British colony.

We have thought you should have Plamondon as soloist in your work, he is a well known tenor and an excellent musician and he sings in English. The Wuillaume Quartet will accompany. If you would play the piano part it would be perfect, otherwise I offer my services.

I hope, in any case, that I shall have the pleasure of seeing you. Your presence will really be necessary to give us the tempi. Please answer by return of post. It is important for the publicity we should have for this important occasion.

[1] *On Wenlock Edge.*

Obviously Ralph was at this concert, for Ravel's next letter, written from St. Jean de Luz, is glowing:

[Translation] 5.8.12

Here is a letter that has weighed on my conscience since the day you left Paris. My friend Godebski had sent it to me asking me to send it on to you. Every time I see him I promise to post it tomorrow as I have to write to you myself. You must wonder why I kept putting off from day to day the pleasure of congratulating you and telling you of my delight at your great success. In everyone's opinion your lyrical settings were a revelation. I mean to write about it soon in an article of which the greater part will be devoted to you.[1]

My different works performed during the last season and in particular *Daphnis and Chloë* have left me in a pitiable state. I had to be sent to the country for a rest to cure the beginnings of neurasthenia. I managed to return to the countryside where I was born.

I should have come to London last month but it seems to have been so hot that the concerts in which I should have taken part have been postponed until October. I hope I shall have the pleasure of seeing you again then.

I should like to have news of you and of your work.

Bruce Richmond introduced Ralph to Sir Frank Benson, who had asked for advice when he wished to find a musician capable of arranging the music for his Stratford season and also of conducting the orchestra. For Ralph this was an exciting idea, the dramatic experience for which he had wished. He was delighted to have a chance of working with a repertory company for a whole season, short though it was and given in two parts; a birthday season in April and a summer season later.

He decided that the music for the Histories must be contemporary with the action. He went down to Stratford armed with masses and plainsong as well as with many suggestions for the other plays. He found the Bensonians were, on the whole, as passionately wedded to their conventional incidental music as to their hockey and cricket, with no feeling at all for its suitability. He was allowed an absolutely free hand with only two plays,

[1] Rollo Myers, quoting this letter in his life of Ravel, says: 'I have been unable to trace this article but Ravel was constantly forming projects which were never carried out.'

Henry V and *Richard II*, in the birthday festival. Both were among his favourites.

It was his first introduction to the world of the theatre and he was delighted with it. He and Adeline had rooms in Stratford, and the friendliness of the company, the glamour of being part of two worlds, Shakespeare's and the players', was as constant a pleasure as Benson's utter disregard for music—except as something that had to be there—was an irritation. He became deeply interested in production, in lighting, in the whole process of illusion, and the magic worked for him at each performance in spite of all shortcomings. He made friends with the actor who was also stage manager, George Hannam Clark, who was a great ally, and was prepared to gather suitable recruits and compel them into extra rehearsal when, for example, Ralph wanted singers off-stage: on one occasion at least this went wrong, and Ralph was forced to sing an off-stage plainsong psalm by himself.

When it came to the summer season *The Merry Wives of Windsor* was one of the new plays. Taking Falstaff's words 'Let the sky rain potatoes, let it thunder to the tune of Greensleeves, hail kissing comfits and eringoes' as his cue, he invented entr'acte music based on this tune[1]—well known in Elizabethan days, and used for a dance tune, for a hymn, and for political ballads in later years—in its original form belonging traditionally to the great army of gold-diggers. In the middle section of this entr'acte he used *Lovely Joan* (which he had collected in Norfolk in 1908), both tunes that summed up the allurements used by the merry wives to entangle Falstaff. It was a play he had not known before and it captivated him: so much so that he began thinking of it in terms of opera, although *Hugh* was lying in draft at home, and the *London Symphony* was being written with infinite struggle.

He and Adeline were invited to a party at Marie Corelli's house which conferred great glory on them in the eyes of all the actors. When asked what it was like, for, of course, curiosity drove them to go, he said, 'Perfectly *awful*.' 'And she?' 'Perfectly awful too—but impressive in her belief in herself and all her surroundings, gondola, white dresses—everything.'

A summer custom of these years was outdoor performances at Leith Hill Place of plays based on folk songs, written by their

[1] He had also used *Greensleeves* in Richard II, 'the entrance of the Queen and her suite'.

neighbours, Bobby[1] and Margaret Longman who, with their father, had belonged to the Coldharbour choir since 1908. This was the choir which Meggie conducted, and for which Margaret Longman played the piano. Among the other performers dressed as villagers of a period that can only be described from the surviving photographs as 'Arcadian—Acting box', were Steuart Wilson and Clive Carey, as well as neighbours and other visitors to the Longmans. Ralph's part, for once, was spectator. He much enjoyed hearing the use to which some of the songs he had collected were put. Later he often asked Margaret Longman to sing illustrations for his folk song lectures. Another friend, Dorothy Fletcher, who was an accomplished violinist, was introduced to these players to help with their performances and Ralph always thought that it was owing to his perspicacity and encouragement that she and Bobby Longman eventually married.

In London, Rebecca Clarke, a young viola player from the R.C.M., James Friskin, one of *The Wasps* orchestra, Butterworth and other musicians—mostly people who had just left the R.C.M. and were starting their professional life—formed a group to sing early music. They called themselves the Palestrina Society and asked Ralph to be their conductor. This gave him great pleasure, for, with the intelligent musicianship of these young people, he was able to explore a great deal of music which he had not known before. They also sang through new works for him, from manuscript parts, including the ill-fated choral ballet, *The Bacchae*, of which only one choral number, '*Where is the home for me?*', survived into publication. Long before the work was completed Isadora Duncan had vanished from his life, though publishers who had undertaken other work for her kept writing to Ralph to ask for her address which he was unable to give them.

The Three Choirs Festival was at Hereford and Ralph's contribution was a *Fantasia on Christmas Carols*, for baritone solo, chorus, and orchestra. It included two Herefordshire carols, *The truth sent from above* and *There is a fountain* (tune only) with acknowledgements to Mrs. Leather as well as to Cecil Sharp (to whom the work is dedicated) for permission to include *Come all you worthy gentlemen*. As well as these tunes, he used the Sussex *On Christmas night*, and there are fragments of other carols

[1] R. G. Longman.

weaving in and out in the accompaniment. It is in the published score of this work that the first of his notes giving alternative instrumental possibilities is printed. This was the outcome of many years of making do, cueing in, and of not being able to afford or accommodate special extra players, so that such choirs and orchestra as those of Morley College and Leith Hill could attempt works otherwise out of reach. This note shows the possible alternatives:

> The work is scored for ordinary full orchestra with organ and set of bells (*ad lib*).
>
> It may, however, be accompanied in the following ways,
> a) String orchestra and organ (or pianoforte).
> b) Organ.
> c) Pianoforte and solo violoncello

This is followed by 'Important Note':

> The Chorus are required to sing in four different ways:
> 1. Singing the words
> 2. Singing with closed lips
> 3. Singing 'Ah'
> 4. Singing with humming tone—i.e. with open lips but with a short 'u' sound as in the word 'but'.

He had begun to realize the great help stage directions could give, not only to the chorus but also to inexperienced choir masters and amateur conductors. It was always his practice to read the words to the singers before they started rehearsing, so that they should understand what they were to sing before they struggled with notes.

After the Three Choirs Festival was over he went to Weobley again, collecting songs there and at Sutton St. Nicholas, and having a short holiday. This was welcome after the prolonged sitting on hard pews and after the many parties that make up the pains and pleasures, music apart, of these festivals.

He had been a member of the London Bach Choir since 1903 and the Monday evening practices were another regular pleasure, usually ending with a small supper party at Odone's near Victoria station, a habit that continued through many years. Once when they arrived, a band was playing in the restaurant and Ralph, who hated music used as a background noise for meals, sent for the manager. 'If you have music here,' he said, 'I shall leave and never have another meal in your restaurant.' The manager promised that the band would never play while Ralph was there.

On 4 February 1913 the *Sea Symphony* had its first London performance—Hugh Allen, who had succeeded Walford Davies as Musical Director of the Bach Choir in 1907, conducted, and the soloists were Agnes Nicholls and Campbell McInnes, with Harold Darke as organist. There is a very short programme note by the composer mentioning that the symphony, in a slightly revised form, had been performed at Oxford, Cambridge, and Bristol since its first performance at Leeds, and giving a laconic outline of the movements. From this evening there survives a menu of the celebration party given by Bobby Longman at Princes Restaurant, Piccadilly. The guests were Dr. Allen, Adeline V. W., R. Longman, Dorothy Fletcher, R. V. W., Margaret Longman, Steuart Wilson, Meggie V. W., for a sketched seating plan in pencil on the card shows them sitting in this order at a round table. Their supper was soup, sole, lamb cutlets, quails, and pineapple, which must have restored all of them after an exciting evening. The next day letters started arriving, some, like Bruce Richmond's, written directly after the concert:

Dear Ralph,

No one can say our generation hasn't accomplished anything first rate.

Yrs. B. L. R.

Three concerts during that spring were important both to Ralph and to Gustav. They were given by Balfour Gardiner who did much for English music, introducing new works by composers not yet widely known. On 11 February Ralph conducted the first London performance of his *Fantasia on a Theme by Thomas Tallis*. It was two and a half years since the Gloucester performance and after this first hearing in a concert hall he knew what revisions he wanted to make. On 28 February Gustav's *The Mystic Trumpeter* was revived, and on 4 March his *Cloud Messenger* was in the same programme as Ralph's *Fantasia on Christmas Carols*.

Being a Londoner, Ralph managed to do a fair amount of

opera-going and, when Thomas Armstrong,[1] then a very young man, told him that he had seen *Rosenkavalier* about a dozen times, Ralph, who never greatly cared for Strauss's work, said to him sadly, 'Tom, Tom, I hope you are not being taken in by that overheated music.' That opinion time did not change, nor did Ralph grow more sympathetic towards Strauss's other operas or the tone poems, though he admired some of the composer's technical brilliance. He had always seen as many operas as he could and was a passionate advocate of their being given in the language of the country in which they were being heard. Although he realized that poor translations were a stumbling block, he felt that the total ignorance of more than bare outline of plot, read hastily in a programme note before the curtain rose, was not enough for any audience. He was convinced that 'the original-language mystique' was a tiresome snobbery, and should not be tolerated in music any more than it was in drama. No one thought of performing Ibsen or Tchekov in England in the original language, and Shakespeare is played intelligibly all over the world, though the loss of the splendour of the language is incomparably more serious in drama than in opera. Ralph felt, too, that opera should be produced with some attention to the dramatic as well as to the musical necessities: Covent Garden 'celebrity performances' were apt to be undramatic and the star-crossed lovers of most plots were, in those ample days, better heard than seen. He realized that a romantic English opera would have very little chance of success, but he was none the less determined to write one.

He wrote incidental music for Maeterlinck's play, *Death of Tintagiles*: it was commissioned for a private performance in the early summer of 1913. Eddie Marsh described the evening in a letter to Rupert Brooke:

Poor Philip Sassoon gave a well-meant entertainment which was not so successful as it deserved. I arrived late and after being kept a few minutes on the landing was admitted into a place like the Black Hole of Calcutta. The door was shut behind me, the light which it admitted having shown for a second the flash of stars and tiaras, revealing the fact that all the ambassadors and Duchesses in London were present, but all that could be seen afterwards was a beautiful

[1] Later Sir Thomas Armstrong, Principal of the Royal Academy of Music.

little Norman Wilkinson[1] representing a heavy iron nail-studded door which flapped in the draught—and Lillah McCarthy beating against it and moaning inaudibly. Poor Mr. Balfour said, 'I'm deaf myself but I'm sure that even people who *can* hear can't hear this.' . . . If you know it you will realise that it is not the sort of thing to hold the attention of a fashionable London audience after a superb dinner. There was the most fearful fidgeting and bumping together of guardsmen at the back of the room struggling for a little air to breathe.

Granville Barker was the producer and besides Lillah McCarthy, Maire O'Neill and Arthur Wontner were in the cast. But in spite of this galaxy of talent the evening was as horrible as Eddie Marsh had said. The musicians were so placed that nothing could be heard—even if the audience hadn't talked all the time, and that particular audience was the worst mannered, Ralph said, that it had ever been his misfortune to meet. There was near disaster, too, for when they came back for the performance the cello, unwisely left unguarded after the rehearsal, was missing. Ralph sped down to the ballroom, for there was to be dancing later, and borrowed one from the dance band just in time. Afterwards, as he was invited to share the delicious supper prepared for the guests, he swept all the players along with him, not allowing them to be banished to a lowlier part of the house and to the inferior refreshment which it was the custom to provide for any entertainers whose names were not well known: he was determined that his band should have their compensating share of strawberries and champagne. He vowed never to get involved with another such entertainment and he would most thoroughly have agreed with Eddie Marsh's conclusion, 'it was very ill judged'.[2]

Ravel wrote from St. Jean de Luz: 'Where are you? Are you working hard? As for me—I am hard at work. I don't know what will come of it.' The letter arrived when Ralph was under pressure himself for the *London Symphony* was growing towards completion. But he was surely at Leeds for George Butterworth's *Shropshire Lad* Rhapsody on 2 October. At the beginning of November he was staying at King's Weston with Napier Miles,

[1] Norman Wilkinson 1883–1934. Stage designer. Known as N. W. of Four Oaks to distinguish him from his name-sake the artist.

[2] *Edward Marsh, A Biography*. By Christopher Hassall. Longmans Green and Co. Ltd. 1959.

an amateur composer and a wise patron of music, for whose Shirehampton and Avonmouth Choral Society he conducted arrangements of his Essex folk songs and *Three Elizabethan Songs*. At the year's end, he and Adeline, with some of the Fishers, went to Ospedaletti for Christmas, probably for the sake of Hervey's health.

This was the end of the last year of peace, the last winter when going to the Riviera would be an easy escape from the cold London climate, and, for many of Ralph's friends among the young musicians, the last winter of their lives.

Ralph returned alone from Italy while Adeline stayed on with her mother, Emmie and Hervey into the late spring. He was busy preparing for two important concerts, the first performance of his *Phantasy Quintet* on 23 March and of the *London Symphony* on 27 March. The Quintet has a short note in the programme:

> This 'Phantasy' was written at the request of Mr. W. W. Cobbett, as one of his series for various combinations of instruments. (The name 'Phantasy' was used by the Elizabethan composers, and it was suggested by Mr. Cobbett that the same title might serve to designate a modern work of much smaller scope than the ordinary full-grown quartet or quintet.) It is in four very short movements, which succeed each other without a break.

The players were the London String Quartet, led by Albert Sammons, with James Lockyer as second viola. The rest of the programme was interesting; *Gaspard de la Nuit* by Ravel,[1] *Variations, Interlude and Finale on a theme of Rameau* (for piano) by Paul Dukas, the *Italian Serenade* by Hugo Wolf, *Molly on the Shore* (for string quartet) by Percy Grainger and *Islamey* (for piano) by Balakirev. This was one of F. B. Ellis's chamber concerts at the Aeolian Hall, and in it is the advertisement and programme for the third concert of 'Modern Orchestral Music' at Queen's Hall on Friday evening, 27 March at 8.15, when the Queen's Hall Orchestra was to be conducted by Geoffrey Toye and F. B. Ellis. It was a programme which contained, besides the first performance of *A London Symphony*, the first performance of *Three Songs* with Orchestra by Arnold Bax, and of the revised edition of *In a Summer Garden* by Delius and the second London performance of Ravel's *Valses Nobles et Senti-*

[1] The pianist in this concert was M. Ricardo Viñes-Roda.

mentales. The *London Symphony* came second in the concert and was among the three works conducted by Geoffrey Toye. George Butterworth had been closely involved with its progress. Ralph wrote:

When Ellis suggested that my Symphony should be produced at one of his concerts, I was away from home and unable to revise the score myself, and George, together with Ellis and Francis Toye, undertook to revise it and make a 'short score' from the original—George himself undertook the last movement. There was a passage which troubled him very much, but I could never get him to say exactly what was wrong with it; all he would say was 'It won't do at all'. After the performance he at once wrote to tell me he had changed his mind:

> A work cannot be a fine one until it is finely played, and it is still possible that —— may turn out equally well. I really advise you not to alter a note of the symphony until after its second performance. The passages I kicked at didn't bother me at all, because the music as a whole is so definite that a little occasional meandering is pleasant rather than otherwise. As to the scoring, I frankly don't understand how it comes off so well, but it does all sound right, so there's nothing more to be said.[1]

Gustav, who had made notes at the rehearsal—a tremendous help to both composer and conductor—wrote of the performance:

You really have done it this time. Not only have you reached the heights, but you have taken your audience with you. . . . I wish I could tell you how I and everyone else was carried away on Friday. However it is probably unnecessary as I expect you know it already. . . .

Gustav's letter included an invitation to spend the next Sunday walking—a companion activity to their indoor field days, which gave both of them great pleasure. Sometimes they were day walks; sometimes, in holidays, when Holst was free, they would go away and walk for three or four days exploring new country or revisiting favourite places, doing a little mild sightseeing, not making rigid plans but feeling free to follow their fancies. This was entirely to Ralph's taste; roads were still almost empty of motor traffic, and they took maps, using lanes and trackways

[1] *George Butterworth*—memorial volume, privately printed. When the score was printed after the 1914–18 war Ralph dedicated *A London Symphony* to the memory of Butterworth.

whenever possible. This particular Sunday expedition was planned to end at the Edward Masons's to hear Rutland Boughton play through his new music drama. Boughton was another Old Collegian, whose part Ralph had taken when a work of his, given at a College concert, was condemned by Stanford as the ugliest thing he had heard apart from the work of Richard Strauss, which Ralph countered with 'Some of Strauss's uglinesses were better than Stanford's beauties'. Folk song variations by Boughton were given at the same Leeds festival as *Toward the Unknown Region*, and Boughton remembered Ralph's approval with pleasure. He was already writing the music dramas which were to be the main part of his life work, and to which both Ralph and Gustav gave some measure of support and interest.

On 1 May Guy's Hospital Musical Society gave an enterprising concert at which two nurses played the Bach Double Concerto, and Clive Carey sang the *Five Mystical Songs*. They also gave the first London performance of three of Ralph's *Five English Folk Songs*, freely arranged for unaccompanied chorus: *The Dark-eyed Sailor*, *Just as the Tide was Flowing*, and *Wassail Song*. Steuart Wilson joined Clive Carey for duets, and the concert ended with Parry's *Blest Pair of Sirens*. The conductor was Denis Browne[2], whose own beautiful *To Gratiana Dancing and Singing* was sung by Steuart Wilson. It was an immensely enterprising programme, and, remembering the conditions in which nurses then lived, with very long hours, very little comfort and few amenities, they must have had a passionate devotion to music to use so much of their free time for rehearsal. It was the sort of group that Ralph enjoyed working with and writing for, and that made him feel that the composer should be close to performers and aware of their needs and capabilities.

In June Ravel wrote to say he was not coming to London after all:

[Translation] 7.6.14

Alas, no, I shall not be coming to London, and the following letter[1] which I am sending to all the English papers will give you the reason.

Sir,

My most important work, *Daphnis et Chloë*, is to be produced at the Drury Lane Theatre on Tuesday, June 9. I was overjoyed; and

[1] The letter is in English in the original. [2] Organist at Guy's Hospital.

A walking tour, Gustav and Ralph

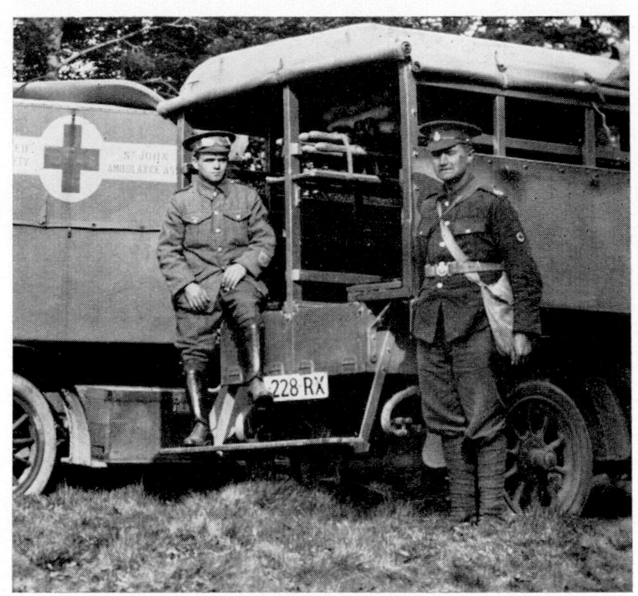

R.A.M.C., 1915

R.A., 1917

fully appreciating the great honour done to me, considered the event as one of the weightiest in my artistic career.

Now I learn that what will be produced before the London public is not my work in its original form, but a makeshift arrange- which I had accepted to write at M. Diaghilev's special request, in order to facilitate production in certain minor centres. M. Diaghilev probably considers London as one of the aforesaid 'minor centres' since he is about to produce at Drury Lane, in spite of his positive word, the new version, without chorus.

I am deeply surprised and grieved and I consider the proceedings as disrespectful towards the London public as well as towards the composer. I shall therefore be extremely thankful to offering my thanks in anticipation, [*sic*] I remain, dear Sir, faithfully yours.

Maurice Ravel.

This letter which mustn't mislead you as to my progress in English because it is only a translation, will appear in the Times, etc. If you have a chance to get it published anywhere else I shall be infinitely grateful to you. I owe this protest to the English public who acclaimed me in an unforgettable manner.

I advise you to hear the Nightingale by Stravinsky, it is a real masterpiece musically. The scenery and costumes are admirable. I want to thank you for your generous offer of hospitality which I should have taken advantage of without hesitation had it not been for these unfortunate circumstances. . . .

It is tantalizing not to know whether Ralph went to the cut version of *Daphnis and Chloë* so that he could report on the performance, or whether he angrily stayed away. Stravinsky's *Nightingale* he did see, and liked very much.

Having failed to find an English publisher willing to accept the *London Symphony*, Ralph posted his score to Breitkopf and Härtel of Leipzig who had published the first edition of the *Sea Symphony*, *Willow-Wood* and *Toward the Unknown Region*. It was his only copy and, being occupied with *Hugh the Drover*, he did not want to spend weeks in making a duplicate score and could not afford to send it to be copied—nor did there seem any reason to do so as posts were reliable.

A few months later when war was imminent George Butterworth realized that the score of the *London Symphony*, being now in Germany, might never be seen again, and organized its copying from the band parts which were still in London. He and

Edward Dent with Ralph's help made it their business to produce a working score, ready for the next performance when time permitted such things to be again.[1]

[1] This is the story as told by R. V. W. to U. V. W.

Inquiries at Breitkopf's were made in 1959, but they had lost so many of their records, as well as music, in two wars that they could give no help in tracing the original score.

It is possible, however, that it was sent to a conductor rather than a publisher—for R. V. W. told Michael Kennedy that the score was sent abroad, at Donald Tovey's suggestion, to Fritz Busch. Probably Busch was asked to take it to Breitkopf, or Breitkopf to send it to Busch. The recopied one is in the British Museum Library, given by Sir Adrian Boult.

CHAPTER VII

1914–1919

On 5 August, the day after war was declared, Ralph and Adeline left London to stay at Margate with Ralph's mother. They were old enough to remember the many young men that the South African war had claimed, the casualty lists and the losses and, though war was still the business of the professional soldier and sailor, it was also a lure to other young men, a siren voice that called to adventure and honour. It is imaginable how heavy with foreboding they felt and how anxiously they read the papers. Almost at once their younger friends rushed to enlist; public and personal anxiety filled everyone's minds and hearts: a war so close at hand was strange and horrifying.

Ralph, walking on the cliffs looking over the Channel, where the B.E.F. were already crossing towards the battlefields, sat down to write a tune he had thought of and grew absorbed in his music notebook. He was recalled to time and place by a small Boy Scout who gazed at him fiercely and told him that he was under arrest. 'Why?' asked Ralph, puzzled. 'Maps,' said the scout. 'Information for the enemy.' Feeling rather like Hugh the Drover accused of spying for Boney, Ralph allowed himself to be escorted to the police station, showed his suspicious MS paper and was let off with a caution.[1]

By the time they returned to London the regulars and reservists had mobilized, and Kitchener's appeal for recruits had gone to the nation. Many of Ralph's younger friends who found they had not the required qualifications to become officers immediately decided to enlist as privates—Butterworth among them, with R. O. Morris, F. B. Ellis, and Geoffrey Toye. Ralph joined the Special Constabulary and by 29 August, when Butterworth went to see him at Cheyne Walk, he had already become a sergeant. This was

[1] This was Ralph's own version of the story. Butterworth, in a letter written after a visit to Cheyne Walk, says that he was writing a lecture on Purcell.

a temporary measure, for a few weeks later he enlisted in the R.A.M.C. whose headquarters were at the Duke of York's School, Chelsea. Although he was otherwise fit, the medical examiners discovered that he had flat feet, a serious handicap; but the C.O., who had seen him and been impressed by his appearance, found a way round the difficulty—he was made a wagon orderly, where this disability would be of no consequence. Unfortunately for Ralph this was a purely theoretical appointment as there were no wagons available then. The recruits were drilled and given some medical instruction: as part of this Ralph was sent to Guy's Hospital, a strangely different visit from the one in May. Besides attending lectures he was sent to watch operations: on his first day in the theatre the surgeon who was operating and giving a running commentary, asked him if he'd ever seen the inside of a man's stomach: surprised to be addressed like this, he said 'No, Sir' in a tone of polite curiosity. 'There,' said the surgeon, slicing the visible bit of human flesh another six inches and displaying the contents to his interested eyes—'There you are.' Ralph felt that his 'Thank you, Sir' was inadequate, but he could not think of anything else to say.

They drilled, trained, and gradually acquired equipment through the autumn. Ralph was able to go to Morley College, and he was still living at home. On 1 January 1915 the unit was moved to Dorking and billeted there to continue their training. There were no wagons and no horses, so the wagon orderlies had to take part in route marches, sometimes to Guildford and back. Ralph's habit of long walks made it possible for him to manage, though army boots did nothing to help, and those days of marching called on all his powers of endurance and fortitude. Another part of the training was stretcher drill up and down the slopes of Box Hill and Ranmore Common. His group—now the 2/4th London Field Ambulance—had moved to Dorking with the 2/14th Battalion of the London Scottish, and Ralph was fascinated by the command of language possessed by some of their soldiers. He had never heard such rich incongruities of adjectives as they used in swearing, and he was much amused by this hitherto unexplored use of words. It was a bitterly cold winter, during which they attended a parade at Epsom, leaving Dorking at 4 a.m., to be inspected by Kitchener; they stood in thickly falling snow for over two hours, but Kitchener barely glanced at their unit: however they had seen this man who was an almost legendary figure to the armies.

Parry wrote from the R.C.M. on 19 January an answer to a letter consulting him on someone else's behalf: it starts affectionately, 'My dear old V. W.', and after offering to see what he could do about the problem troubling them both, he went on to say:

As to your enlisting, I can't express myself in any way that is likely to be serviceable. There are certain individuals who are capable of serving their country in certain exceptional and very valuable ways, and they are not on the same footing as ordinary folks, who if they are exterminated are just one individual gone and no more. You have already served your country in very notable and exceptional ways and are likely to do so again: and such folks should be shielded from risk rather than exposed to it. We may admit the generosity of the impulse, and feel—I will not say what.

Yours affect'ly,
C. Hubert Parry.

While Ralph was stationed at Dorking it was easy for him to go home for short periods of leave or for Adeline to visit him, which she did constantly. In February her elder sister, Emmie, married R. O. Morris, so another musician was added to the family.

Belgian refugees were pouring into London, and Adeline gave a home and work to Clemence Anique, the young wife of a Belgian miner who had come with a party escaping from occupied territory. Clemence was happy to find herself in a home where she could be understood; many of her compatriots found life none too easy once the first enthusiasm of their hosts had worn off. They had not only left their homes and familiar surroundings, but were unable to speak or understand the language of the country in which they found themselves, and friction was apt to develop between host and guest. This particular case was happier than most, and Clemence, and later her husband, became warmly attached. This experience of the refugees' difficulties stood Ralph in good stead when he met it again years later.

At this time he was himself fitting into a new group. Much older than most of his fellows, unused to the order expected at kit inspections, finding difficulty in wearing uniform correctly, in putting his puttees on straight and wearing his cap at the correct angle and in many other details of daily life, he found these minor afflictions called for elementary skills he had never needed before and had not got.

His cheerful acceptance of difficulties and his willingness to do everything that much younger men could do more easily impressed his comrades. Among them Harry Steggles, a lad who was his senior in the Ambulance by some weeks but his junior by more than twenty years, became his particular support. Their friendship had started with Ralph's interest in the fact that Harry played a mouth organ with real musicianship, and on the other side with Harry's protective help in looking after equipment. It became an affectionate partnership shared throughout Ralph's career in the Ambulance; Harry called him Bob, and treated him as both elder and younger brother. Coming from entirely different worlds, they were endlessly entertaining to each other; there was an undertone of the comradeship of the soldiers in *Henry V*, with discussions ranging over all subjects to which each brought totally different experiences, as well as a comedy partnership as entertainers, when Harry would sing 'When father papered the parlour', accompanied by Ralph on any available piano. When Ralph played for church parades, Harry would blow the organ for him, while both took musicianly pleasure in a voluntary which might be variations improvised on one of the very secular songs to which they marched.

In April 1915 the unit moved to Watford, where Ravel wrote to him at 76 Cassio Road:

[Translation]
My dear friend,

What has become of you? After such a long time I should be glad to have your news. As for me I am very busy doing nothing. It took me 8 months to manage to get into the 13th Artillery Regiment. Now I am awaiting my nomination as a *bombardier* in the Air Force for which I have asked and it can't be much longer in coming through.

I hope soon to have a few words from you. Give my homage and respectful affection to Mrs. Vaughan Williams and believe me my dear friend your affectionate

Maurice Ravel.

While stationed at Watford they took part in 'night operations' in Cassiobury Park, where mock casualties and stretcher parties disturbed young couples engaged in more romantic assignations.

The background to this period of training was the grim episode of the sinking of the S.S. *Lusitania* and the news of Italy's joining the Allies. In May they went on to Saffron Walden, and here Ralph spent much of his free time playing the organ in the church, Bach being the most certain refuge from the soul-destroying routine of an army in training. At Bishops Stortford a family called Machray had told the billeting officer that they would prefer to have someone interested in music, so, when the unit arrived, Ralph and Harry and Pte. Edwards, who had sung at the Palladium, were sent to them. This was a very happy arrangement, for the father played the viola, two sons the clarinet, another son the trumpet, one daughter the violin and the other the piano. The pianist's husband, Charles Mackrill, as well as one of the two clarinettists, were also in the Field Ambulance. All of them were stationed near enough to be at home on most Sundays, when there would be music. For Ralph this was the happiest time of all his army days and he enjoyed the sort of music-making he had had with the Gattys; though with Harry's repertoire of comic songs added, the evenings usually ended very light-heartedly. Ralph sometimes borrowed Mr. Machray's viola, and found that he could still conjure tolerable sounds from the strings.

Harry, besides singing, had 'arranged an early jazz drummer's outfit of flower pots, fire irons and a borrowed drum from the band'[1]—to add to the variety—and Ralph taught them all Morris and country dance tunes. He was so happy with the Machrays that he asked if he might stay with them for Christmas, exchanging leave so that Harry could go home. Ralph took his own leave at New Year when he spent a day or two at Cheyne Walk.

A marriage, one he was sure he had helped to make, had taken place in November when Ralph played the organ for Bobby Longman's wedding to Dorothy Fletcher. Bruce Richmond remembered a strange shuffling and scraping sound from the organ loft before the music started, which was afterwards explained as Ralph removing his army boots which were far too large and heavy to manage the necessary footwork; he had arrived at the same moment as the bride and her father, and had rushed to his place to start playing as they walked up the aisle.

Early in 1916 the unit left Hertford for Wiltshire, and Ralph

[1] R. C. M. Magazine Easter 1959.

and Harry had to give up their pleasant billet for the rigour of huts at Sutton Veny near Warminster on Salisbury Plain. Everyone started by calling his cold bare wooden shack interesting anatomical names: Ralph and Harry chose '1 Pancreas Place', but this levity was not permitted. The training programme continued, and the unit was fed on rumours throughout the spring. By June preparations for a move were apparent and Ralph wrote to Gustav:

We are on the eve—all packed and ready—I can't say more. . . . I feel that perhaps after the war England will be a better place for music than before. . . .[1]

Ravel, already on active service, sent a postcard dated 18 June:

[Translation]

If this reaches you I should be glad to have news of you. Are you still in England? I have been at the front for several months, the front where there is most action. It seems years since I left Paris: I have had moving, sometimes painful, and dangerous enough times to find it astonishing to have come out of here alive. However, I have hastened to throw off this adventurous life. For nearly a month I have been forced to rest, my vehicle is being repaired and I am very tired. And the life one leads in these parts is very boring. . . .

The unit left England on 22 June, and crossed to Le Havre by night. The boat was packed with troops and of course showed no lights: they disembarked in drizzling rain and entrained in cattle trucks—'40 men or 8 horses' was an inscription soon to become familiar. Their destination was Maizières, where they heard the ceaseless sound of gunfire on the Somme.

They took over from the Ambulance of the 51st Highland Division at Ecoives, and lived in outhouses round a big house which was the main dressing station. Although so near the trenches, it was sheltered by rising ground on which stood the village and ruined towers of Mont St. Eloi. Ralph was thankful to have something active to do at last and wrote to Gustav:

I should v. much like to have news of you—I wish I cd. write you an interesting letter—but one is hardly allowed to say anything. However I am very well and enjoy my work—all parades and such things cease. I am 'waggon orderly' and go up the line every night to bring back wounded and sick in a motor ambulance—all this takes place at night except an occasional day journey for urgent cases.

[1] See *Heirs and Rebels*.

Write and let me know all the news—I hear from my wife how all Thaxted is still singing Bach . . . I suppose I shall make you very angry with what I am going to say and I can't put it just as I mean—but I feel strongly that what you are doing at Thaxted is the real thing. . . .

Harry remembered:

He was more at peace with himself in the fighting areas for we were getting on with the war, not forming fours in squad drill, and what was more important, it didn't matter quite so much about dress, for he was on the motor ambulances between the trenches and our dressing station. 'Barns infested, rats for the use of' was his favourite description of our billets; in fact he loved the army method of cataloguing and in particular a medical pannier which contained, among others, the item 'tapes, pieces of, two', which he always quoted. . . . The trenches held no terrors for him—on the contrary, he was thrilled one day when he was allowed a peep at the German front line trenches.[1]

It was here at Ecoives that the *Pastoral Symphony* began to take shape in Ralph's mind; he wrote, long after:

It's really war-time music—a great deal of it incubated when I used to go up night after night with the ambulance waggon at Ecoives and we went up a steep hill and there was a wonderful Corot-like landscape in the sunset—it's not really lambkins frisking at all as most people take for granted.[2]

A bugler used to practise, and this sound became part of that evening landscape and is the genesis of the long trumpet cadenza in the second movement of the symphony:

les airs lointains d'un cor mélancolique et tendre.

Here, too, he continued training a choir, which he had formed among his fellow soldiers, that had survived, spasmodically, from Saffron Walden days, and he gathered whoever was available for practices whenever any opportunity offered. It was a welcome change from the fatigues that filled up every moment of a day not devoted to more vital duties. Besides the base dressing station, the unit was responsible for an advanced dressing station for urgent cases; the wounded could be brought down to Ecoives only under cover of darkness. There they were under direct

[1] H. Steggles, *R. C. M. Magazine*. Easter Term 1959.
[2] Letter to U.V.W.—4 October, 1938.

enemy observation but, even so, operations were performed and every kind of emergency treatment given to casualties awaiting transport.

Before the summer was over, there were personal sorrows enough. Charles Fisher, brilliant and most dashing of Adeline's brothers, died in the battle of Jutland: a blow from which she never recovered. F. B. Ellis, Denis Browne, and George Butterworth were killed in action, as were also many friends among those who had danced under Cecil Sharp's guidance or shared the work and pleasure of music in what seemed like another world. For Ralph, the loss of Butterworth's friendship and the unfulfilled promise of his music were a profound sorrow. It was a time when the casualty lists recorded almost every day the loss of some friend or acquaintance, and the wholesale slaughter of a generation of the youth of the nation left few homes untouched. Working in the ambulance gave Ralph vivid awareness of how men died.

He wrote to Gustav:

> I sometimes dread coming back to normal life with so many gaps—especially of course George Butterworth—he has left most of his MS to me—and now I hear that Ellis is killed—out of those 7 who joined up together in August, 1914 only 3 are left. I sometimes think now that it is wrong to have made friends with people much younger than oneself—because there will only be the middle aged left and I have got out of touch with most of my contemporary friends—but then there is always you and thank Heaven we have never got out of touch and I don't see why we ever should.

In the early autumn there were many rumours about the unit's next move: they supposed they would join the battle of the Somme. They marched through the autumnal landscapes, which seemed uncannily quiet, to Eaucourt sur Somme, a pleasant village within reach of the amenities of Abbeville which still existed almost untouched, though it was not far from the devastation to which they had become accustomed. While they were resting from their more active duties, they practised gas-drill, and from the issue of winter kit it looked as if they would stay in northern France. But they were ordered to entrain at Longpré for the south and, packed in cattle trucks, they started a long, slow journey to Marseilles where they embarked for Salonika.

Ralph described the voyage with pleasure. The ship was crowded and the food bad but, after a rough first night at sea, there was calm weather and sunshine. He said he had not the sort of imagination that made him fear torpedo attacks and he enjoyed the leisurely Mediterranean voyage and the warm weather. Their first camp was at Dudular and there, for the first time, they were introduced to mules which would provide their transport: an adventurous and uneasy partnership, in which the mules were usually the ruling partners. The weather was either dry and dusty beyond anything men accustomed to the English climate had imagined, or intolerably wet and muddy. They soon moved from Dudular, this time by paddle steamer, to Vromeri beach where there was no jetty of any kind. The men made a human chain and the stores were passed from ship to shore by hand. They lived on a breezy hillside overlooking the valley of the Pelikas, with Mount Olympus towering over the landscape. It was by now mid-December and, though the days were sunny, the nights grew colder and colder. The air was amazingly clear, and the nights brilliantly starry. Ralph and Harry shared a 'bivvy':

in the confined space of a 'bivvy' a little less than the area of a double bed . . . we had a ground sheet, a blanket apiece and all our worldly goods including razor, comb, lather brush, also Isaiah and Jeremiah. I must explain these for it was the name given by R.V.W. to two empty pineapple tins in which we lit charcoal and after whirling them round and round like the old-fashioned winter warmer we rushed them into the 'bivvy' and sealed up any air intakes we could find. I think we slept more from our rum ration plus carbon monoxide from Isaiah and Jeremiah than fatigue.[1]

One night when Ralph was on orderly duty in the main dressing station, a municipal building in Katerini where civilian cases were treated as well as army casualties, he was much surprised by the thirst that seemed to have attacked all the patients. Usually on such nights he curled up on blankets by the fire and slept, but this time, it was: 'Orderly, I want a drink', 'Can I have some water, orderly', all night long; eventually he had a drink himself and discovered the reason—the night's supply of drinking water had been sent up in rum casks and had a cheering,

[1] H. Steggles, *R.C.M. Magazine*, Easter Term, 1959.

faintly alcoholic taste. When they were free to leave the camp, Ralph and Harry explored the local wine shops in Katerini and in one they watched Greek soldiers dancing and Ralph took down the tune. They explored the wines too, failed with *ouzo* and *resinata*, and stuck to *Samos sec*, though sometimes romantic sounding names like *Mavrodaphne* lured them into further, and usually unrewarding, drinking.

Harry was much impressed by the wailing processions that accompanied funerals, so when one of the unit sprained his ankle badly and had to be carried down to the main dressing station by mule, he organized the cortège on the local model and appointed himself as chief wailer, the doleful sound echoing and growing fainter as they wound downhill and ceasing only when they neared the centre of authority.

Another experience, which no one who was there forgot, was carol singing on Christmas Eve: snow-capped Olympus, the clear night, the stars, and Ralph's choir singing carols of Hereford and Sussex with passionate nostalgia. The choir made that Christmas so far from home one that had a special quality, a special beauty, long remembered. To Ralph's friends who heard of it, it seemed as natural for him to be conducting carols on the slopes of Olympus as for Gustav to be conducting Bach in the cool aisles of Thaxted, part of the same universal bounty of music in the darkness of war.

After some months Ralph began to get restive. He had communicated his whereabouts to Adeline by sending a scale in the Dorian mode in one of his letters, and told her of his utter discontent:

> Salonika was too dilatory for him. He went on mosquito squad work, which consisted of filling in puddles to prevent mosquitos breeding: he thought this useful in an abstract way. But what caused him the most anguish was to sit down and wash red bricks, which were laid on the ground to form a red cross as protection from German 'planes. He swore one day, saying 'I will do anything to contribute to the war, but this I will not do.'[1]

Somewhere, someone in authority arranged for him to be sent back to England to train for a commission. He said good-bye:

[1] H. Steggles, *R.C.M. Magazine*.

'My only regret at leaving is that I shall cease to be a man and become an officer.'[1]

All letters were heavily censored, so Ralph had not been able to let Adeline know of his return and she was away when he arrived. He went to the Richmonds' house, and Bruce's wife, Elena, opening the door, was enchanted and amazed to find that the tired, rather grubby soldier who stood there was Ralph, demanding breakfast. He was welcomed and cherished by them, and he told them how, on arrival in England, he had been sent to London to report at the War Office, rather than having to go to an R.A.M.C. camp and continue stretcher drill on the sands at Blackpool as others less fortunate had done. This mysterious priority was due to the fact that his name had been put before an elderly officer with a repeated exhortation, 'You must do something about Vaughan Williams'—this unlucky man had fallen from his horse, become concussed and, lying semi-conscious, had gone on repeating, 'We must do something about Vaughan Williams'—so the word had gone forth to find Vaughan Williams, and on arrival Ralph had been rushed into a train, and hurried to London as if he were a visiting General. He was given a commission in the Royal Garrison Artillery,[2] and a new period of training began.

Musical life was still going on in London—Parry had written to him in February:

I have been wanting to write to you for ever so long, but the apparent difficulty of finding out where you were quite sufficed, on the top of being always rather busy, to stop my taking any opportunity to get under way. Now your dear old Uncle, Major Darwin, suggests what I ought to have thought of long ago, that I might get a letter through by asking your wife to forward it—and so, late as it is, I won't forego telling you how splendidly I thought the *Sea Symphony* came off at the Bach Choir Naval concert at Queen's Hall. Allen took any amount of trouble with it and it's worth it—and they all got into the spirit of it splendidly. I daresay you remember how enthusiastic

[1] He had not found the R.A.M.C. officers congenial. They were, in general, separated from their men by professional qualifications as well as by rank, and he had been aware of a great gulf fixed. He got on much better with the Gunner officers and found there was a far closer link there between officers and other ranks than he had known in the Ambulance.

[2] The part of the Royal Regiment responsible for the heavy guns and howitzers —60 pounder guns and 6 inch howitzers and upwards.

everyone was when they did it before and how they had you up and shouted with pleasure. It was quite the same this time and it does the public credit that they have found out what a splendid work it is—quite one of the finest and most genuine and characteristic things that has been achieved of late years—(illegible) and big! I wonder if . . . (illegible) . . . you to write something more in the strange conditions you must be in now. What experiences they must be! Perhaps you will extract something out of them!

I should like to have news of you.

Your ancient friend,
C. Hubert Parry

On 12 May the London String Quartet gave a performance of *On Wenlock Edge*, with Gervase Elwes singing. W. J. Turner wrote a very long, detailed and laudatory notice in *The New Statesman*, at the end of which he added:

The Carnegie United Kingdom Trust has sent me a list of the works accepted for publication under their scheme this year—it is as follows:

E. L. Bainton	Symphony for Contralto Solo, Chorus and Orchestra.	*Before Sunrise*
Granville Bantock	Symphony.	*Hebridean*
Rutland Boughton	Opera.	*The Immortal Hour*
F. Bridge	Symphonic Suite.	*The Sea*
H. Howells	Pianoforte Quartet in A Minor.	
Sir C. V. Stanford	Opera.	*The Travelling Companion*
R. Vaughan Williams	Symphony.	*London*

I don't think one can seriously quarrel with the selection, especially as the rule has now been made that no composer published under the scheme in any year shall be eligible the year following. . . . Now that Vaughan Williams's *London Symphony* is published, perhaps London will hear it again.

In August Ralph was posted to No. 32 Siege course at No. 2 R.G.A. Officer Cadet School at Maresfield, Sussex. The other cadets were mostly young men, some in their twenties, some direct from school, and very few of them had seen any service overseas. He wrote to Gustav:

Aug 4.

I wish we could have met again—but I was bunged off here all in a hurry—I'm *in* it now, though we don't really start work till Friday—

no leave till the middle of the course—about 2 months—it seems a fairly free and easy place at present, but a good deal of stupid ceremonial—*white gloves!!* (on ceremonial parades) (N.B. I believe there is a war on). I should have loved another long talk with you. Our house orderly is a funny little chap called Smith who has played with the 'worm'[1] sort of orchestra (violin) all over the place, he was at the R.C.M. 12 years ago and knows Schwiller.

My address is

Cadet R. Vaughan Williams,
3 Section 'H' Company,
No. 2 R.G.A. Cadet School,
Maresfield Park,
Uckfield, Sussex.

Yrs. R. V. W.

It was a noisy place, and Ralph found he needed every atom of concentration he had to grapple with unfamiliar subjects, for he was determined to do well in the passing-out examination. He therefore took a room in a cottage outside the grounds where he could work in privacy and silence, two qualities unknown in the cadet school. This arrangement was secret, for cadets were supposed to remain inside the grounds. He and a young cadet, John Tindall Robertson, and one or two others who were admitted to this working room, made a hole in a hedge, disguised with removable branches, through which they could come and go without passing a sentry. By this means, and by remembering to be in when they would be expected to be in, they achieved a measure of freedom, and Ralph was able to pass out not discreditably. Tindall Robertson took on Harry's rôle—

R. V. W. kept an avuncular eye on us, the rawest of raw schoolboys, and I, for my part, did my best to help him both with his work and in seeing that he got his equipment and so on right for parades. He was not one to whom the proper arrangement of straps and buckles and all those things on which the sergeant major is so keen, came easily. Neither was it easy for him, then in middle age, to learn and retain all the miscellaneous information which was pumped into us. But he achieved it by dogged perseverance and toil.[2]

[1] Stanislas Wurm was the conductor of the White Viennese Band in which Holst had played for some years. 'Worm' and 'worming' were words both composers used to describe that sort of conductor, band, or music, though it was now many years since Gustav had given it up.

[2] Letter to U. V. W., 1958.

Another cadet at the same course, Joseph Major, recalls the 7 a.m. parades consisting of 'a brisk march with some doubling along the country roads near Maresfield Park,'[1] and Ralph himself remembered that at one point they had to ride motor bicycles —and that one cadet who, at his test, which was once up and down the school drive, failed to turn round, had disappeared into the wilds of Sussex, on and on, till the petrol gave out.

After passing out in November 1917, and long weekend leave, his section was sent to Lydd for a firing course. It was desperately cold, and the cadets had to do physical jerks in shirtsleeves in a blizzard. This misery ended on 23 December, and there was the respite of Christmas leave for about three weeks before he was posted to Bordon. There he found Tindall Robertson was his room-mate while they waited for their overseas postings. Finally there was embarkation leave, and they left Southampton on 1 March 1918. They spent a few days at the base camp at Havre and then went up the line to Rouen. Ralph remembered how he had climbed the cathedral tower as a boy and found he had no desire to test his nerve by doing it again. He had joined 141 Heavy Battery[2] just before the big German attack on 21 March. He wrote to Gustav:

. . . The war has brought me strange jobs—can you imagine me in charge of 200 horses!! That's my job at present, I was dumped down into it straight away, and before I had time to find out which were horses and which were waggons I found myself in the middle of a retreat—as a matter of fact we had a very easy time over this—only one horse killed—so we were lucky.

He always felt that this was typical of the Army's wasteful methods: 'Having been trained as a 6″ Howitzer man I've been bunged into a 60 pdr!' The same had happened to Tindall Robertson who was stationed near; much of their work mastering the intricacies of the Howitzer and the use of motor transport was wasted for 60 pounders with horse transport were a different proposition. Both were put on the waggon lines but Ralph managed to acquire a bicycle, which he preferred to a horse for comings and goings. Part of his duty was to go up the line with the ammunition waggons, sometimes a very dangerous job. Some

[1] Letter to U.V.W., 1958.

[2] Equipped with 60 pounders—the only weapons of the R.G.A. drawn by horses.

reminders were scribbled into the cover of a little copy of *Leaves of Grass*:

1. 6 gun teams
   800 rounds of amm.
   Teams for (illegible)
   officers kit, waggon
   water cart to be up here at 6 p.m.
2. Lewis guns with am.

On one of these expeditions his driver, usually a very silent man, asked him in a worried tone: 'Do 'orses 'ave dreams, Mr. Williams, do they?' Ralph found the morning stables a bothersome inspection, as he was never sure what he ought to be looking for and the appearance of one horse seemed much like another to him, and two hundred horses all together had a nightmare quality. Another subaltern, W. A. Marshall, remembered this time:

> I first set eyes on Vaughan Williams in 1918, in April, I think at the battery horse-lines whither I had been sent down from the guns for a spell of duty. . . . It was during the retreat which began on March 21st, when the gun position was near Fontaine-les-Croiselles, some miles south of Arras and north of Bullecourt. We had retired twice and, when I first met Vaughan Williams, the guns were in position behind a wood, Athens Wood. I remember the Guards passing us in open order with fixed bayonets. Vaughan Williams had not been with us for long and was in charge at the horse lines—not a 'cushy' job by any means, especially at that time. He spent a lot of such spare time as he had in getting up concerts, vocal, by and for the troops, mostly drivers. I can't think he enjoyed them much, in view of the talent available. I saw him once or twice, drooping despondently over the keyboard of a ghastly wreck of a piano while drivers sang sentimental songs—execrably as a rule, to his accompaniment.[1]

Ralph had for batman a theological student, A. J. Moore (now Canon), who had enlisted as gunner, and been trained for observation work, but as he said: 'one does any job for which one is available'. He remembered one day when they were following up retreating Germans and were in action in the open—Ralph was suffering from a temporary indisposition and feeling so ill

[1] Letter to U. V. W., 1958.

that he could not stand, and so he was directing his section while lying on the ground:

The O.C. Battery came along past where I was standing, about fifty yards behind the guns, took in the situation at a glance, turned to me and said 'Moore! Tell Mr. Williams he is to go to bed.' 'Yes Sir. Mr. Williams, Sir, the O.C. says you are to go to bed.' 'Damn him!'

Later I suffered a temporary indisposition myself and still remember his kindness to me on this occasion. I think Lieut. Vaughan Williams had the respect of the whole battery as a kind, firm and considerate officer. In wartime, with heavy guns, powerful horses and all the work of dealing with the equipment necessary to the Battery, tempers can easily get frayed; with him this rarely happened.[1]

Gustav had tried to get some active war work, but he had been turned down at every attempt on grounds of health; at last he was offered a job as musical organizer in the Educational Department of the Y.M.C.A. in the Near East: he sailed for Salonika in October 1918. All through the war he had been teaching, lecturing, making music at Thaxted with his choirs, and Ralph had felt most deeply that Gustav and others so engaged were keeping the really important things alive. Ralph was aware of the danger of the springs of civilization becoming choked, even lost, in the war which was ostensibly to protect them; this became more and more his feeling as he lived through the years of battle and took part in it, though he could not have endured not to be sharing the common experience of the soldiers. He realized how much Gustav hated being left, however valuable his work, and was glad that he was at last getting a chance of foreign service.

Ralph wrote to him just after the Armistice:

Nov. 16th (1918)

I've been trying to write to you for many days—it's funny with the news so wonderful that I ought to be able to write pages—but somehow it's produced a complete slump in my mind, and I've never felt so fed up with my job.

I wonder how you are getting on and whether you are arrived at your job yet—I hope for your sake it's not that god-forsaken place Summer Hill Camp. Meanwhile we are probably going on a long journey—I don't look forward to it much—trekking all that way this

[1] Letter to U. V. W., 1958.

cold weather—nor our job when we get there but still one has to take things as they are.

Let me have a letter—and a less dull one than this—this is only to let you know I am alive and well—I feel incapable of anything else.

Yours always,

R. V. W.

His next letter is more biographical:

12.12.18

Dear Gustav,

I was so glad of your letter—what troubles you are having—I only hope you'll get refunded some time—luckily you don't depend on the army for it. I wonder what island you are at—I was at Milo for one day and bathed in the bay—I don't know Gallipoli—it was Taranto where I landed. I am still out here—slowly trekking towards Germany, not a job I relish, either the journey or its object. I've seen Namur and Charleroi and was disappointed in both—every village we pass is hung with flags and triumphal arches 'Gloire à nos vainqueurs' etc.

We usually march about 10 kilos or more a day and rest every 4th day—it's a tiresome job watering and feeding horses in the dark before we start (though I must confess that there being 8 subalterns in this Bty. my turn of turning out early for this only comes once a week). Then usually 2 or 3 waggons stick fast in the mud on the 1st start off and worry and delay ensues, and finally when one gets to one's destination one has to set up one's horse lines and find water and fill up nose bags etc. and if *this* has to be done in the dark it beggars description—so you see there's not much music-writing going on at present. But I've started a singing class and we are practising Xmas carols and 'Sweet and Low'.

Yrs. R. V. W.

Before long Ralph was separated from his horses and guns and made Director of Music, First Army, B.E.F. France. The authorities realized that it would be some time before demobilization could take place, and that recreation and educational opportunities must be given to men impatient to return to their ordinary lives. At this time the First Army H.Q. was at Valenciennes, and he settled into a billet and became a member of the H.Q. Mess. His successor (then Lieut.) E. R. Winship described his work

visiting the Divisions over a wide area, finding officers and other ranks from various units who were interested in music and getting them to act as conductors to a choral society, orchestra or to take a class in music. At the time of his demobilisation, in February 1919, there were already nine choral societies, three classes, an orchestra and a band. Included in these was the H.Q. Choral Society of which he was the conductor. He engaged recruits for this society himself, and once, after a church service in the town, came forward (rather an incongruous figure in uniform) and spoke of its activities. A friend of his at that time was Lieut. Col. G. A. Sullivan, a member of the H.Q. Choral Society (a talented pianist) and they sometimes played duets together. Once he played a piano piece by Grieg in the Mess and seemed very much amused afterwards at having been able to do so!

A rather unusual occupation for him at this time (evidently at the request of someone) was attempting to put together an organ which was lying in pieces on the floor of an out-building in the town. He spent some of his spare time here amidst the ruins of the instrument trying to sort things out.

This was evidently a restful and happy period for him back as he was at music and awaiting demobilization. Later on in life he sometimes referred to those happy old days spent at Valenciennes.[1]

At last he was demobilized, his war was over and he was free to go home.

Ralph had hated the war but he had taken part in what he believed had to be done. He knew that he could have stayed in England: he knew also that had he done so he would not have been able to write: he would have been burdened with a sense of evading his responsibility as a man, his duty as a citizen. Return was not a simple and joyful release. He was going back to a world that lacked many of his friends, and in familiar surroundings their loss would be more vivid than in the separation of war. He was also going back to discover how his own invention had survived the years of suppression, wondering whether it could come to life again or whether it was lost for ever, and, if so, what he could do with his life.

[1] Letter to U. V. W., 1958.

CHAPTER VIII

1919–1922

When Ralph was demobilized in February 1919, Gustav was still abroad as Musical Organizer for the Y.M.C.A. in their educational work for the Forces in the Near East. He was writing rapturous descriptions of the Parthenon and accounts of his time at Constantinople. He had been glad to have this opportunity of taking music to the Forces, but he was looking forward to returning to England, his friends, and, most of all, his work. He had missed the first public performance of *The Planets* which Adrian Boult had given in February and it was summer before he arrived home.

Ravel was demobilized—he wrote from St. Cloud:

[Translation]
Dear friend,

I have taken a long time to answer. I haven't even the excuse of work—I haven't managed to get down to it again—and yet my winter stay in the mountains has done me a lot of good, now it is my morale that must be restored and I don't know how to do it.

Aren't you coming to Paris soon? I should be very glad to see you after so many terrible years. I was meant to go to England during the next season but I think it would be better to work if I am still capable of it.

Will you give Mme Vaughan Williams my homage and respectful friendship and believe me, Your warmly devoted

Maurice Ravel.

Before Ralph returned to England, Adeline had moved into furnished rooms at Sheringham in Norfolk, hoping that the climate of the east coast might be good for her invalid brother, Hervey. She had looked after him since her mother had died after a street accident during the war. She may have felt thankful for the chance of devoting herself to the only one of her family the war had not swept into new activities. She was never quite free from pain, and, as her arthritis had not been helped by any of the treatments she had been persuaded to try, she gave up all hope of a cure and decided to ignore it as far as possible. In spite of having this charming, wayward, difficult, and demanding invalid on her hands, in spite of the shortage of domestic help and the inadequacies of furnished rooms, she was, more than ever, the centre of her family, the letter writer, the one to whom they all turned for advice, comfort, and reassurance.

So it was in rooms at the seaside that Ralph settled down to revising the *London Symphony* and *Hugh the Drover* and there that he started to shape the quiet contours of the *Pastoral Symphony*, recreating his memories of twilight woods at Ecoives and the bugle calls: finding sounds to hold that essence of summer where a girl passes singing. It has something of Rossetti's *Silent Noon*, something of a Monet landscape and the music unites transience and permanence as memory does.

Ralph, now forty-seven, was one of the older generation, a link with the English tradition through his masters Stanford and Parry. He was invited to teach at the Royal College of Music where Hugh Allen had become Director in 1918, after Sir Hubert Parry's death, and where his vitality and enthusiasm were devoted to making the College ready to take a lively part in training musicians for opportunities in a world of peace. But for Ralph, before the new academic year began, a spring and summer lay ahead at Sheringham. He wrote from there to William Rothenstein:

> Very many thanks for your kind letter. My plans are so vague that I don't like to make any promise to be at any particular place at any particular time. All I can suggest is that when you happen to be in London you should let me know of any times that are convenient to you—but I quite see that that would be a most awkward arrangement for you and that you would prefer to drop it altogether.

'It' was a proposed drawing of Ralph for *Music and Letters* for the first number of which Rothenstein had made a drawing of Elgar to accompany an article by G. B. Shaw on his music. Ralph did sit for him eventually, for when the autumn term started he was in London for at least one day of teaching every week. The result was not successful, the drawing being rather soft and sentimentalized, and not a good likeness. It is a pity, for though there are many photographs there are no portraits of Ralph in his youth or middle age and it would be illuminating to have an artist's record of him then which his contemporaries accepted as valid. The second issue of *Music and Letters* published this drawing with an article by the Editor, A. H. Fox Strangways, on Ralph's music, as well as Ralph's own contribution 'The Letter and the Spirit'.[1]

One tiny glimpse of the life at Sheringham remains, for Veronica,[2] daughter of Iris and Ralph Wedgwood (the 'Randolph' of Ralph's Cambridge days), was sent to convalesce there after some childish illness. She went to tea with Ralph and Adeline several times, and she remembers how, the night before she was to go home to her parents, Ralph, realizing that he had not said good-bye, came round to see her. He persuaded her nurse to let her get up, for it was long past an eight-year-old's bed-time in those stricter days, and paid a formal and affectionate farewell call which she much enjoyed.

The Honorary Degree of Doctor of Music was conferred on Ralph at Oxford. The *Monthly Musical Record* for July reported the ceremony:

> In convocation on June 19th the degree of D.Mus *honoris causa* was conferred on Ralph Vaughan Williams, M.A., Mus. Doc. Trinity College, Cambridge. In presenting Dr Williams the Public Orator, Dr A. S. Godley, spoke of his great services to English music. He had developed a style of his own which placed him in the front rank of English composers. His *Sea Symphony*, to be heard that afternoon, in celebration of the 250th anniversary of the opening of the Sheldonian Theatre, would prove him worthy of all the honours Oxford could confer.

The performance was given by the Oxford Bach Choir and conducted by Hugh Allen.

At another ceremony on 25 June the honorary degree of D.C.L. was conferred by the Chancellor, the Marquess Curzon, on some of the war leaders, Marshal Joffre, Lord Haig, Earl Beatty, General Wilson, Herbert Hoover, and Lord Wemys. It was an imaginative kindness to relate Ralph's honour to the Sheldonian celebration. He would have felt less at home among Admirals and Generals.

[1] Reprinted as revised in 1953, in *National Music and other Essays*, Oxford University Press 1963.

[2] Dr. C. V. Wedgwood, the historian.

In July there was a Festival of three concerts at the R.C.M. Ralph's *Songs of Travel* came before a performance of George Butterworth's *Banks of Green Willow*, conducted by Adrian Boult: both works belonged to a world which must have seemed immeasurably far away.

Joining the teaching staff at the R.C.M. was the beginning of more than twenty years of work there. Ralph found it interesting though he said that he was not a good teacher. This was probably difficult for him to judge. One of his pupils, Elizabeth Maconchy, has written:

> . . . he had worked out his own salvation as a composer and he encouraged his pupils to do the same.[1]

But he had the good fortune to have many receptive young composers to teach, whose minds were ready for what his experience, knowledge, and love of his art had to give them.

Among his pupils in the first years were some, like himself, recently demobilized, Patrick Hadley and Ivor Gurney, that tragic young man whose return to music and poetry from the war in which he had suffered physical and spiritual mutilation was to be so brief. Armstrong Gibbs went to the R.C.M. in 1919 when he gave up school work and became a professional composer, and he worked with Ralph for a year. Others who came to him for composition lessons during the twenties were Dorothy Gow, Imogen Holst, Leonard Isaacs, Christopher le Fleming, Robin Milford, Jasper Rooper, Guy Warrack, Grace Williams, and Ian Whyte. Later, H. K. Andrews, Stanley Bate, Ina Boyle, and Ruth Gipps were also among his pupils. They became friends whose careers he watched with interest and pleasure. Sometimes he was called upon, too, to help them in their love affairs, to see parents and to try to persuade them that such and such a proposed marriage was not to be discouraged. He was always on the side of romance and so was prepared to brave such situations, and the young could rely on him to help and support with all the weight of his professorial authority.

During the spring term of 1920 the choral class tackled Gustav's *Hymn of Jesus* and gave a performance on 5 March, with piano accompaniment only, just three weeks before the composer conducted the first public performance at the Queen's Hall.

[1] *R.C.M. Magazine*, Easter Term 1959.

This work was dedicated to Ralph, and after hearing it he told the composer that he 'wanted to get up and embrace everyone and then get drunk'. It was an immediate success and, with *The Planets*, gave Gustav an established place in English music and in public estimation. This disturbed and alarmed him, but it was a recognition of his quality that delighted his friends. Ralph had been asked to write about him for *Music and Letters*, and two articles, the first with a drawing by Rothenstein, were published in the July and October numbers.

Besides his work at the R.C.M., Ralph was busy with rehearsals for the first Leith Hill Musical Festival since 1914. Tenors and basses had been demobilized and, instead of the eight choirs who had taken part six years before, there were twelve to be rehearsed in the main work, Handel's *L'Allegro ed Il Penseroso*. One of the choirs who had joined only in 1913, wrote:

> At the close of our Leith Hill Festival the Blackheath Choral Society feel that there was but one thing more needed and that was an opportunity of thanking you. We feel so strongly all that you have done for us, not only on April 27th and at the rehearsals in the winter, but in reviving the Music Festival at all. Gratitude is sometimes taken for granted: on the other hand it is a pleasure to express it and that must be our excuse for troubling you in this letter.
>
> Yours respectfully,
>
> [followed by twenty-three signatures.]

The concert ended with Parry's *Jerusalem*. At one of the R.C.M. concerts the previous summer it had been sung, and a note in the programme said 'the audience is invited to sing the second verse'. At Dorking this note has remained unchanged on the programme of every Leith Hill Festival concert since.

Steuart Wilson, also released from his war service, had been among the soloists in the Handel work at Leith Hill, and later in the year he gave the first performance of Ralph's *Four Hymns* for tenor solo and orchestra written for him before the war. This performance, at which Ralph was not present, took place at Cardiff, and was conducted by Julius Harrison; the L.S.O. had been playing the night before at some up-valley centre, and Steuart remembers 'we all drove in early morning to find the instrument van had not arrived by train, and didn't in fact arrive until half an hour before the concert! Elgar gave up his rehearsal and I had just a chance for the orchestra to look at the parts, but scarcely even a run-through.' The *Four Hymns* were repeated at the Three Choirs Festival at Worcester and in October at a concert at the Aeolian Hall. The words are by Jeremy Taylor, Isaac Watts, Richard Crashaw, and a translation from Greek made by Robert Bridges, originally for the Yattendon Hymnal, which had been included in the English Hymnal. This was the first time Ralph had made an anthology of poems to set: all are romantic poems of divine love and longing. Although a declared agnostic, he was able, all through his life, to set to music words in the accepted terms of Christian revelation as if they meant to him what they must have meant to George Herbert or to Bunyan. He had returned to *Pilgrim's Progress*, and was writing a one-act opera, *The Shepherds of the Delectable Mountains*, as well as the unaccompanied *Mass in G Minor* for Gustav and his Whitsuntide singers. He said cheerfully, 'There is no reason why an atheist could not write a good Mass.'

After the Leith Hill Festival of 1921 the long bondage of Hervey Fisher's illness ended. He died in May, so Ralph and Adeline were free to go home to Cheyne Walk and a more normal life. Returning to London was the utmost relief and his own study a sanctuary after the discomfort of the past two years in the makeshift of seaside lodgings.

They were back in London in time for the British Music Society's conference from 13–20 June. For this Ralph's Romance for Violin and Chamber Orchestra, *The Lark Ascending*, was played by Marie Hall, to whom it is dedicated, at the final concert of the conference. Ralph also took the Chair when 'British Music Abroad' was discussed in all its bearings.

During one of his war-time leaves, Ralph and Adeline had met Mrs. Ritchie and her daughter, Pegs, Chelsea neighbours and connexions of the Fishers. The daughter had been a V.A.D. with Clare Mackail (Campbell McInnes's sister-in-law), and before the war a student at the Slade.[1] Both girls were welcome visitors: they brought gaiety and liveliness back into a time that had been long darkened by Hervey's illness. They swept Ralph off to balls at the Slade, where he appeared in fancy dress, splendid as Bluebeard or fashionably oriental as a sheik. He also adventured with them to the Hammersmith Palais de Danse; he was a cheerful, if un-

[1] The Slade School of Fine Arts.

talented, dancer, his feet could never manage the rhythms he could write or conduct, but he loved parties, and rather liked dressing up.

It was at a party that he met Sibelius (who was to have conducted an R.C.M. performance of *En Saga*, though illness had in fact prevented him from doing so). Ralph had been leaving when Sibelius asked who he was. They had been introduced earlier but Sibelius was not familiar with the English pronunciation of the name. When he realized it was a fellow composer whose work he admired, he rushed down the stairs to waylay him in the hall. It was, however, rather a disappointing meeting for they failed, partly through shyness and partly because their only common language was inadequate French,[1] to make real contact with one another though they were both full of goodwill.

Another pleasure was becoming conductor of the Bach Choir. Ralph had been a member for about sixteen years and for some of this time he had served on the Committee. At a Committee meeting on 6 January 1921, Sir Hugh Allen's resignation as Musical Director was accepted, and on 9 March it was agreed that Mr. Adrian Boult should be offered the Directorship: 'failing Mr. Boult's acceptance thereof, to Dr. Vaughan Williams'. Mr. Boult was unable to accept and Dr. Vaughan Williams 'expressed his willingness to accept the position of Musical Director of the Bach Choir: provided that he might feel free to continue with the Handel Society for part of the next season, in the event of the latter not having found a suitable successor to himself in the meantime'. The Handel Society was an amateur choir and orchestra whose main object was the revival of Handel oratorios, though it also undertook new works and had some first performances to its credit. It had had a number of distinguished professional musicians as conductors, including Coleridge-Taylor, Henschel, and Norman O'Neill but, owing to the war, it had lapsed since 1915 until Ralph took charge on its re-birth in 1919: in 1921 Eugene Goossens succeeded him and Ralph was able to devote himself to the Bach Choir. After having been a member for so long he had a very good idea of what its capabilities and potentialities were. Hugh Allen had been ruthless in his auditions, clearing away

[1] Confirmed by a sentence in a letter from Adeline to Cordelia in 1948. 'Sib doesn't know enough English to write it—when R. met him he spoke French.'

members whose voices were not equal to their zeal and enforcing a sight-reading test. Ralph said that, as far as he was concerned, sight-reading was only one part of a sight test, and 'sight test' became a catch word when he was giving an audition to pretty sopranos or altos.

He was full of ideas about the works he wanted to conduct, and having an experienced choir with whom he could rehearse all the year offered scope which the small groups that made up the Leith Hill choir could not give him. His first concert, a programme of Bach cantatas, was given at the Central Hall, Westminster, on 14 December. Ralph was in his element. This was the music he loved most; the London Symphony Orchestra was led by his friend W. H. Reed, Harold Samuel was the pianist and Harold Darke the organist, and Steuart Wilson and Clive Carey were among the soloists. Among his friends in the choir were Bobby and Dorothy Longman, and, as it happened, quite a sprinkling of in-laws, as well as his brother Hervey with his wife Constance—they had married during the war. This mixture of professional musicians and good amateurs was to him one of the most enjoyable kinds of music making.

Meanwhile the *Pastoral Symphony* was in the final stages. The first performance took place on 26 January at the Queen's Hall with Adrian Boult conducting the Orchestra of the Royal Philharmonic Society.

Lucy Broadwood wrote on the 29th:

Thank you a million times for the gorgeously beautiful symphony you gave us on Thursday. I hope that some of our joy returned, reflected, to you, and that to have the 'Old Philharmonic' shouting and waving to you across the dour bust of Beethoven was a happy thing, and a funny thing too, for you. The one regret that I have is not to be, at such times, a young thing at a musical college—with young ears and enough training to understand the modern idiom. Now and then I find a new musical nut very hard to crack, and now and then I know that certain things which I apprehend with some effort were easily and absolutely understood by the younger listeners and those more accustomed to hearing quite new things. Now I am longing to quickly hear your splendid symphony again. The trumpet stirred me desperately—and how finely it was played. And surely the voice[1] was perfection? . . .

[1] Flora Mann was the soprano soloist.

The second performance of the *Pastoral Symphony*, on 17 February, was at the R.C.M.

Another letter which must have meant a great deal to Ralph came from one of his Cambridge friends, Crompton Llewelyn Davies:

Where are you and Adeline?—is there any chance of seeing you? You have been often in my thoughts. The other day I turned up a copy of *Sea Symphony* which you had given me and I thought of Leeds. And reading about *Pastoral Symphony* which, alas, I missed hearing, I have felt a sort of triumph in the work you have planned and carried out. And remembering walks and talks with you I fancy I can understand in some sort of way how promises have come true and high intentions been carried out. Of course, I know nothing about it and shouldn't be writing like this but the big things I think come when anyone—like Milton and Keats—is conscious of wanting to express something and sets himself to fit himself to do so—with the humanity to remain sensitive to everything around but the strength to assimilate it for the main purpose and at the same time to study and know all the means of expression. Forgive me for blundering on like this but I have been wanting to say something to you. . . .

There was another concert with the Bach Choir on 7 April, a mixed programme with the six-part motet *Christ is Risen Again* by Byrd, *St. Patrick's Prayer* (a Fantasia on Two Irish Hymn Melodies) by Charles Burke, one of Gustav's Morley College pupils, Gustav's own *Choral Hymns from the Rig Veda* (1st Group), and Dvořák's *Stabat Mater*.

An enthusiastic young friend, Diana Awdrey, who had enjoyed coming to the Leith Hill Festival, organized a festival at Stinchcombe in Gloucestershire. It had the same musical committee as Leith Hill, Adrian Boult, Lucy Broadwood, Dorothy Longman, and Ralph, and they chose music within the choirs' capacity from the Leith Hill programmes. For this first venture Ralph went to Stinchcombe to judge the competitions, to talk to the choirs and to launch this offspring of Leith Hill on its successful career. He came back from Stinchcombe for the final rehearsals of the Leith Hill Festival which had grown to such a size that it had had to be divided into three sections, and there were three concerts, on the Tuesday, Wednesday, and Friday of the last week in the month. Gustav judged competitions and at the Wednesday concert Adeline presented the banners and certificates.

Ralph had written two part songs, *It was a Lover and his Lass* and an arrangement of *Ca' the Yowes*, as well as a setting of *O vos omnes*, words from the service of Tenebrae for Maundy Thursday, a ceremony that he had heard at Westminster Cathedral and found deeply impressive; he was preparing these for the publisher, Curwen.

Also, in this busy spring he went to Holland to hear 'a big performance' of the *St. Matthew Passion*, which he was studying for the Bach Choir to give the following spring. He came away disappointed, for he found he disagreed with almost everything in the performance. While he was there he heard that Percy Grainger was also in Holland. He had become a brilliant pianist, and he travelled a great deal giving recitals. They had not seen much of each other since the early years of the century when Ralph had often gone to Mrs. Grainger's house with other young composers to spend evenings singing and criticizing each other's part songs. Now Mrs. Grainger had just died, and Percy, who had been devoted to his mother, felt very desolate. Ralph found out where he was staying and went to see him.

At the end of May Ralph and Adeline sailed for America where Ralph had been asked to conduct the first performance of the *Pastoral Symphony* in the U.S.A. with the Litchfield County Choral Union at Norfolk, Connecticut. The invitation came from a wealthy amateur of music, Carl Stoeckel, who had built the Music Shed where concerts were given 'to honour the memory of Robbins Battell, and with the object of presenting to the people of Litchfield County, choral and orchestral music in the highest forms'. In 1914 Sibelius had been a guest there and the Music Shed had been the scene of the first performance of his *Oceanides*. Since then many musicians had accepted invitations to these festivals. It was a delightful plan—all expenses would be paid and Ralph was to stay with the Stoeckels. He wrote to Gustav:

Plaza Hotel, New Yk.

I have seen (a) Niagara, (b) the Woolworth buildings and am most impressed by (b). I've come to the conclusion that the Works of Man terrify me more than the Works of God. I told myself all the time that N'ga was the most wonderful thing in the world—and so it is—especially when you get right under it—but I didn't once want to fall on my knees and confess my sins—whereas I can sit all day and look out of my windows (16 floors up) at the sky-scrapers. . . .

By the way, my millionaire has put us up at the swaggerest hotel in N.Y. Our landing was like a sort of very nice nightmare—we waited in dock in the ship for 3 hours to pass the immigration officer. Then we came down an impossibly steep gangway into a dusty shed out of which there gradually loomed (a) Stoeckel's secretary (a pretty young woman in blue), (b) W. H. Gray,[1] (c) Forsyth[2]—then as we moved off I heard 'Ralph' shouted out, and there outside were the Longmans! . . . we were whirled off in a taxi and up 16 floors in an elevator—to a *suite* of rooms with *2 bathrooms* with this wonderful view all over N.Y.—then whirled down again into a sort of Cathedral where we had supper (Chicken Salad—oh, the American food—it's beyond powers of expression.) Then at 11, just as we were going to bed, the great man and his wife appeared—very nice and simple. But I never want a patron—it's too wearing.

I've come to the conclusion that N.Y. is a good place but wants hustling badly—the buses are slow and stop wherever you like—Broadway is I believe easier to cross than High Street, Thaxted.

We had two rehearsals of 1 1/4 hours as yet. I think I shall need all I shall get. I've got two more. Many of the players are very good but the back desks of the fiddles are not v. good—and trombones have not much beef about them.

Just off to Norfolk, Conn., now. . . .

Give my love to all my pupils if you see them,

Love R. V. W.

The performance of the *Pastoral Symphony* on 7 June was excellent. Ralph enjoyed working with American musicians who, like the audience, gave him a warm welcome. He and Adeline stayed in the Stoeckels' white, colonial house, with its high pillared portico and lovely garden, where, besides other musicians there for the concerts, three pretty girls had been invited to amuse Ralph: one of them taught him to put ice cream in his coffee. He remembered her affectionately whenever he did this in after years. It was a useful idea for one who never liked his coffee too hot. Prepared by this for exotic gastronomic surprises he

[1] H. W. Gray. Head of Novello's American branch who published many R. V. W. works.

[2] Cecil Forsyth. 1870–1941. English composer and author of *Orchestration* and other books.

did not flinch when he thought he was being offered 'iced antelope' and was disappointed when it turned out to be iced canteloup.

Adeline wrote her account to her sister, Cordelia:

June 8th

The music festival ended yesterday: two evening concerts. The first the choirs and the second one orchestral works—Ralph started the concert with his *Pastoral*—it went very beautifully and he had a good voice for the end[1]—about 1500 people and more camped outside on the grass. All the composers had laurel wreaths and I find we are expected to carry this huge trophy back to England! We have been in this nice country nearly a week—very green and the house is painted white wood . . . Ralph has seen a wood chuck. . . .

The Stoeckels are very dear people—only we have to do just what Mr. Stoeckel plans for us and Ralph feels a little restive from a surfeit of kindness! . . . Mrs. Stoeckel is good company. She is the heiress of the estate here and this music festival is to honour the memory of her father. They live in the *ancien régime*, beautiful horses instead of motors, Swiss maids, an English gardener and an English parlour-maid! a very happy feeling in the house. Meals are too rich and wine flows all the time!

. . . We have seen some nice people here for the festival and now today we are going to visit another house in the *Berkshire Hills* and spend the night there with a friendly Miss Watson—keen on music—and on Monday Mr. Stoeckel takes us to Boston . . . we visit the Music Conservatoire. . . . The Longmans got here for the *Pastoral* last night. . . . I am *well* and so is Ralph. I don't know really what the audience made of the *Pastoral* but the feeling was as if they liked it. They were mostly country people and factory hands, all very well dressed—a few negroes—one doesn't see many here.

She wrote again from New York on 14 June:

Mr. Stoeckel loves sightseeing and the café life—lunch at 1 spreads out till 3 or 4. Ralph is feeling restive and says he now knows how Mozart and his contemporaries felt living under a patron . . . we ought to be home by June 26th.

Taken all round the visit had been a success. They had seen the white New England villages, Ralph had been excited by names familiar from the histories of the civil war and from Whitman's

[1] The soprano soloist is not named in the programme.

poems, as well as by the towers and chasms of New York. They had made new friends and experienced the generous and overwhelming hospitality of the New World.

They were home in time to go to a College performance of Ralph's one act opera. *The Shepherds of the Delectable Mountains*, which was given in the Parry Theatre in the presence of Queen Mary, on 11 July. Ralph had had what he described as a 'snob dream' in which he had been to tea with the King and Queen and, when he left, the Queen took him to the door, winked broadly, and murmured 'Thursday'. This was so vivid that being presented to her after the performance promised to be rather an anticlimax, but her presence banished any waking thought of lèse-majesté. She admired the scenery and costumes of the opera, but did not say anything to him about the music.

For the summer holidays they went to Wheatfield, Cordelia's house at Tetsworth between Oxford and the Chilterns, while Cordelia and her young son Adam were in France. They had left their dog, Julius Caesar, and a tame badger at home. Adeline described their arrival:

> Ralph has fallen in love with Wheatfield as I thought he would. Tell Ad. he thinks it is perfect. We arrived soon after 8.30—a magical evening and R. trundled on his bicycle, I with the chauffeuse. . . . After our sup. Holland came across from the barn and opened the yard door displaying the badger eating his porridge—a lovely sight, and Julius Caesar was very friendly and Ralph took a great fancy to him but is rather alarmed at the strange appearance of the badger.
>
> It is hot today—I write this at my bedroom window—R is below, happy at the piano. . . .

They enjoyed seeing the badger and Julius Caesar playing together, and Julius went with them on all their excursions. The only thing he didn't like was Ralph's playing, for he used to sit close beside him at the piano and howl with a strange mixture of anguish and delight with which some dogs react to music. Ralph loved the Chiltern country and had long solitary bicycle rides as well as making a twice-weekly shopping expedition for the household.

In October he was fifty, and Jane Joseph, Gustav's pupil and friend, had written a short part-song for a group of his friends to salute him on his birthday. It was a complete surprise: Ralph went out and collected the singers, led by Gustav, and swept them in for an improvised party and he probably showed them one of his birthday letters which had given him particular pleasure, a greeting from one of the Kensington Festival Choirs:

We wish you all health and happiness on your 50th birthday and hope you will live to see another 50.

From St. Agnes Mothers' Meeting singing class.

CHAPTER IX

1923–1930

By 1923 it was possible to see in perspective some of the changes that had taken place in musical life since the war. In those five years there had been many deaths, among them that of the last surviving member of a choir which had sung *Elijah* conducted by Mendelssohn in 1847. Caruso, that idol of the operatic world, Boito, Leoncavallo, Saint-Saëns, Humperdinck, and Debussy—who had not lived to see the Armistice—and in Ralph's own world, Max Bruch, Parry, and Gervase Elwes had died; while Busoni, Fauré, Puccini, and Stanford were in the last years of their lives. The tercentenary of William Byrd's death was being celebrated, as well as César Franck's centenary; music by Kodály and Bartók was discussed in articles in the musical journals, and a little of it was heard at London concerts. Rutland Boughton was having considerable success with performances of *The Immortal Hour* and *Bethlehem* in London, and his Glastonbury Festival continued the adventurous work begun before the war. *Hassan*, a play by James Elroy Flecker (a poet who had died in 1915, perhaps a parallel in literature to Butterworth in music), with incidental music by Delius, had started its successful run at His Majesty's Theatre. Schoenberg's *Pierrot Lunaire* bewildered London critics and concertgoers. The London Contemporary Music Centre of the British Music Society had in 1922 become the British National Section of the newly founded International Society for Contemporary Music.

Among British composers the names of Bax, Goossens, and Ireland were frequently to be found in concert programmes, and a first string quartet by William Walton had been heard and admired at a British Music Society concert. Hugh Allen, Walford Davies, Dan Godfrey, and Richard Terry had been knighted. The Carnegie Trust Awards were helping British composers by publishing their scores (Ralph acted as one of the adjudicators for the Trust's Publication Scheme for the years 1921, 1922, 1923, and 1924), as was the Patron's Fund by giving concerts and rehearsing the works of young or little-known musicians at the R.C.M. The British Broadcasting Company had been established in 1922—and by January 1924, Ernest Newman had launched a spirited attack on the quality of their music programmes. A number of musicians still earned their livings in theatres, most of which had a small orchestra to play incidental music and to entertain during intervals. Many other musicians found employment in cinemas, for films were still a silent and visual entertainment to which orchestra or pianist added appropriate sound.

A third edition of *Grove's Dictionary of Music and Musicians* was being prepared under the editorship of H. C. Colles: the British National Opera Company were performing operas by British composers. Musical life was vigorous and absorbing, set against a background of treaties, trade agreements, reparations, alliances, depressions, and political crises.

Ralph's own life was immensely full, and the most prominent of the interweaving strands that made it up were his work with the Bach Choir and the Leith Hill Festival, performances of his own music which were becoming more frequent and which he often conducted, and his writing. He loved the Bach Choir, and he drove the singers hard. As 1923 was the first year in which he conducted the *St. Matthew Passion*, it is likely that he spent much of the winter preparing for the performance. He was to conduct the work throughout the next thirty-five years, discovering the essence of the music of the composer he loved above all others.

His 'first performance' was on 7 March 1923, at Queen's Hall, followed by two more, one on 17 March at the Central Hall, Westminster, and the other on 22 March at the Central Hall, Bermondsey. It was after the first of these that Stanford wrote:

March 8th '23

My dear Vaughan Williams,

You will forgive me for sending a word of congratulations on last night's performance of the Bach. It was so dignified and pious (*not* 'pi') all through: the points were so exactly what J.S.B. meant. The only things I felt were the trumpet was out of the picture![1] and for me, the Jesus part was too emotionally sung. I remember the greatest in it, Stockhausen,[2] and the only moment when he was emotional was

[1] He used a trumpet, played very softly, to support the Ripieno choir.

[2] 1826–1906.

'Eli, Eli', which made it very thrilling. But that is only my own view with which you may or not agree. I say thank you very heartily, and, after all, my ancestor W.S.B.[1] was the father of doing it here at all.

Yours very sincerely,
C. V. Stanford

This letter was valued, because it was not only from a master to a former pupil but also from an earlier conductor of the Choir. As well as the *St. Matthew*, Ralph conducted four performances of the *St. John Passion* in March, with a small choir drawn from the Bach Choir, and he also prepared and rehearsed three Cantatas, which were main works in the Leith Hill Festival concerts. These were in mid-April; on 25 April he was again judging at the Stinchcombe Festival, supporting the second year's work that the Gloucestershire choirs had done, still following in the footsteps of Leith Hill in their choice of music.

So far as his own work was concerned he conducted the *London Symphony* on 17 February: and on 7 April, in a day of music for unaccompanied choirs, the Wolverhampton Musical Society, under their conductor Joseph Lewis, gave the first London performance of the *Mass in G Minor*. He had given the first performance with the City of Birmingham choir,[2] and R. R. Terry, Director of Music at Westminster Cathedral, had used it liturgically in the Cathedral during the spring.[3] Ralph was also engaged on his score for a ballet, *Old King Cole*, which he had written for the Cambridge Branch of the English Folk Dance Society, of which he was President, to produce as part of a Cambridge Music Festival in early June. The scenario written by Mrs. Edward Vulliamy linked the nursery rhyme with that East Anglian king whose daughter, Helena, married the Emperor Constantine. The music is both romantic and gay, and one of those who remember the performance says, 'Apt for its purpose, when eyes as well as ears were entertained in the beautiful setting of Nevile's Court of Trinity on a summer evening.'[4]

Mrs. Vulliamy herself took the part of Helena, and made many of the costumes which, like the two fantastic thrones for King Cole and his daughter, were designed by Mrs. Sydney Cockerell and her sister, Mrs. Kingsford. Choristers from St. John's College,

[1] William Sterndale Bennett, 1816–75. [2] 6 December, 1922.
[3] 12 March, 1923. [4] From Mrs. Vulliamy's recollections of the performance.

Morris and country dancers from the Cambridge branch of the E.F.D.S., and Elsie Avril the leading musician of the E.F.D.S. as the Third Fiddler, all took part. The producer, John Burnaby, had the resources of Trinity College at his command. Boris Ord conducted the Cambridge University Musical Society's Orchestra, led by Haydn Inwards, from a score which was in MS. and not available till just before the rehearsals, and was subject to last-minute alterations and additions by the composer.

The importance of *Old King Cole* in the tissue of the composer's work is that it made him consider his ideas about dance as partner of music, as *Hugh* had made him consider, practically, his ideas about opera. Dance was a subject that had floated across his horizon in his encounter with Diaghilev and Nijinsky, again with Isadora Duncan, and then in his friendship with Cecil Sharp, whose choreography for Granville Barker's production of *A Midsummer Night's Dream* in 1914 had shown him that there were other possibilities in the use of dancers for the stage than classical ballet.

Ralph's association with the Folk Song Society went back to the early years of the century. He had long been on the Committee, and had become one of the Vice-Presidents in 1921. The English Folk Dance Society was founded in 1911, after a series of unhappy disagreements about technique and presentation had divided Cecil Sharp's earliest apostles and exponents of the dance.[1] At the inaugural meeting Cecil Sharp moved 'that a Society, to be called the English Folk Dance Society, be established, having headquarters in London, with the object of preserving and promoting the practice of English folk dances in their traditional form.' The aims of this Society were

> . . . the instruction of members and others in folk dancing; the training of teachers and the granting of certificates of proficiency; the holding of dance meetings for members at which dancing shall be general and of meetings at which papers shall be read and discussed; the publication of literature dealing with folk dancing and kindred subjects; the foundation, organization and artistic control of local branches in London, the provinces and elsewhere; the supply of teachers and providing of lectures and displays to schools, colleges and other institutions; the technical and artistic supervision of the vacation schools of

[1] Ralph had appeared at a party during these years dressed as Mary Neal, the leader of the 'other camp', wearing a large notice 'Power before accuracy'.

Folk Song and Dance at Stratford-on-Avon, organized by the Governors of the Shakespeare Memorial Theatre.[1]

Ralph was one of the Committee appointed at this meeting, and he took part in the affairs of the Society, lectured at Vacation Schools before and after the war, conducted singing and joined the dancing, though whether he ever achieved 'the true traditional form' is unrecorded. He considered it of the first importance for the musical well-being of the country that this inheritance of song and dance should become a part of every child's life: it may have been due to his influence that, when Adeline's eldest brother, the historian H. A. L. Fisher, became President of the Board of Education from 1916–22, he decided to emphasize the musical side of teaching, and called upon Cecil Sharp for practical advice in bringing this about. This was in 1919, after Cecil Sharp and Maud Karpeles had made their collecting expeditions to the Appalachian Mountains and brought back from remote districts a magnificent harvest of songs and ballads which early settlers from Britain had taken with them and handed down by word of mouth to their descendants. Tunes and variants, long lost to living memory in their places of origin, survived there, and this re-discovery emphasized the great richness, variety, and beauty of folk music still extant.

In 1921 a week's festival at the Lyric Theatre, Hammersmith (sandwiched in during the phenomenally long run of *The Beggar's Opera*), brought new support both from critics and public. The Society needed every teacher and lecturer available to meet the urgent demand for classes and information to extend the curricula of training colleges and schools and to meet the need people felt for this kind of music. New arrangements were called for, piano accompaniments or choral settings; and because he knew and loved the music Ralph was adept at providing them. Folk music weaves in and out of his work all through his life, sometimes adapted for some particular occasion, sometimes growing into the fabric of orchestral writing. One such work, the suite, *English Folk Songs*, was written for the Royal Military School of Music at Kneller Hall. After the first performance on 4 July 1923, *The Musical Times*, reviewing it, commented, 'The good

[1] *Cecil Sharp*. A. H. Fox Strangways in collaboration with Maud Karpeles. (Oxford University Press 1933.) Second edition revised, 1955.

composer has the ordinary monger of light stuff so hopelessly beaten.' This had been one of the works he had been particularly happy to undertake, as he enjoyed working in a medium new to him. A military band was a change from an orchestra, and in his not-so-far-off army days he had heard enough of the 'ordinary monger's light stuff' to feel that a chance to play real tunes would be an agreeable and salutary experience for bandsmen.

The British National Opera Company opened their summer season at Covent Garden with Gustav's opera, *The Perfect Fool*, and, though the composer was in America, he was back before the end of the season (which had included Ethel Smyth's *Fête Galante* and *The Boatswain's Mate*), to hear it and his *Savitri*, in which the name part was sung by Dorothy Silk.

Ralph and Adeline had been abroad in the spring, reverting to their pre-war habit of travelling for a few weeks. They went to Venice, but Adeline was ill there, and, though she urged Ralph to go sightseeing without her, their few days never fulfilled the promise that arriving in the evening and being rowed in a gondola, from the station to their hotel seeing the lights on the Grand Canal and the beckoning mystery of the little side turnings, had seemed to offer. They went on to the Dolomites, where they finished their holiday in the mountain air that Adeline loved and found reviving.

During the late summer they took a furnished house which Armstrong Gibbs found for them at Danbury in Essex. It was next door to his own house, and he let Ralph use his piano 'whenever he wanted to try over the sound of some hair-raisingly discordant passage'.[1] Ralph had started to write *Sancta Civitas* and, as usual, he liked the mixture of quiet working hours and long walks during the early stages of a new work. 'Besides walks,' Armstrong Gibbs said, 'he used to enjoy coming out with us in the car as we wandered round the lanes of the peaceful Essex countryside and I well remember on one occasion confessing to him that I could not bear high moors and treeless spaces, and being greatly comforted to find that he, too, hated a landscape without trees.'

That autumn brought Ralph's and Adeline's twenty-sixth wedding anniversary, and his mother wrote on the eve of his fifty-first birthday:

[1] Letter to U. V. W., 1959.

My dear old Ralph,

Your birthday when you receive this—I can only say many, many happy returns and years of your and Adeline's life together—such a perfect one between you two and such a very dear son to me. This very ungrammatical sentence expresses what I have to say to you two dear children.

Ralph might have gone to Leipzig in the winter to hear his Mass sung at the Thomaskirche, Bach's church, on 16 November, but for some reason he did not, for the conductor's letter describing the performance and praising the work is evidence of absence.

The year ended with the Bach Choir's performance of Gustav's *Festival Te Deum* and *Ode to Death*. In this concert Ralph was able to give two performances of the *Ode* with Harold Samuel playing the Bach pianoforte concerto in E major between the two hearings. He felt that no new work could be assimilated in one performance, and he liked to separate two hearings with a classical work, so that the contrast could allow the new music to come freshly to the audience, already prepared by their first hearing, and enable them to give it full consideration. Three carols by Peter Warlock ended the programme with another first performance, and Ralph's *Pastoral Symphony* (by special request) made up the evening.

Gustav was delighted, and wrote: 'Are you willing to sign a contract to conduct every first performance I get during the next ten years or so? You are teaching those people to sing. Pray accept my blessing. . . .'

Ralph confessed: 'It was a tussle I admit—but from the first they loved it. I know of no other work which I shd. have dared to make a choir slog so at——'

This letter was written on New Year's Eve, and he was just off to Middlesbrough for an Eisteddfod. He was busy with rehearsals for the Philharmonic concert on 24 January, at which he conducted his newly-made orchestral version of *On Wenlock Edge*, sung by John Booth in place of John Coates who was ill. The *St. Matthew Passion* on 15 March, with the Bach Choir, followed, and on the 28th he conducted his *London Symphony* at the R.C.M., the day before Stanford's death. Stanford had only recently resigned from the Chair of Music at Cambridge, and in looking for a successor the Senate made it a condition that the new holder of the office should live in Cambridge, which gives colour to the story that in his later years Stanford would take a train to Cambridge, give his pupil—usually only one—a lesson in the station waiting-room, and return to London by the next train. Ralph's name was one of the few suggested but, whatever was for or against him as a candidate, he had no desire to live in Cambridge, for he enjoyed London too much. To everyone's satisfaction Charles Wood was appointed.

In April, Adrian Boult conducted the *Sea Symphony* with the Royal Choral Society, and Ralph repeated Gustav's *Festival Te Deum* at Leith Hill. On 13 May the Bach Choir sang the *B Minor Mass*—another first performance for Ralph, and approved by his predecessor Hugh Allen.

> It was a fine show you gave last night: never dull for a moment and how those people worked! The tone has improved out of all knowledge and the enthusiasm with which they sing pervades the audience too. *Et expecto* lifted me out of my seat.
>
> The performance was exhilarating and often astonishing—I never heard them double along as you made them in the *Osanna*. It's the first time I've ever known angels to be hustled. You ought to be very happy and considerably tired.

On 14 June Arnold Goldsbrough conducted a students' concert of Ralph's works at Morley College, which must have pleased him, as he had been associated so long with the musical life there. He was spending a fair amount of time with students that early summer, for the R.C.M. were rehearsing *Hugh the Drover*, as were the British National Opera Company, but there had been worries about the professional performance, as an undated letter to Mr. Curwen, the publisher, shows:

> I send 3 solos and 2 duets from 'Hugh'. I think your idea about the chorus ones is good. I suppose we must be careful that the total price of the separate songs is *more* than the complete opera—otherwise people might be tempted to buy the plums without the cake.
>
> I've had *nothing* in writing from the B.N.O.C. Have you?

Ralph had had a letter from Cecil Sharp at the end of May, thanking him for a copy of the suite, *English Folk Songs*, and saying that Hugh Allen had lent him a copy of the score of *Hugh the Drover*: 'Which I have found great fun to read . . . it is jolly difficult . . . but I have no doubt they will manage it all right. May I be there to hear it. . . .' but he died a month later, to the desolation of his friends, many of whom had come to share his love of English songs and dances and to realize, as Ralph did, how immense a debt all musicians owed to his life's work.

A performance of Ralph's *Pianoforte Suite* was included in a concert at the R.C.M. on 1 July. The first performances of *Hugh* followed on 4, 7, 9, and 11 July, with Trefor Jones[1] as Hugh and Keith Falkner[2] as the Constable. It was conducted by S. P. Waddington[3] and went with a swing: everyone, performers, audiences, and even the critics, enjoyed it.

The second scene of *Hugh* takes place in a village on May Day morning, and, because Ralph wanted the sound of bells chiming a tune as they do at Northleach in Gloucestershire (which was the sort of village in which he imagined the story to be set), and because he wanted a weathercock on the spire to catch the first rays of morning light as the mayers come back with flowering branches, preventing the escape of the lovers, he had liked the idea of the village church being part of the set. But he was greatly surprised when Queen Mary, who came to the performance, and to whom he was presented, asked him why hero and heroine had not used it to be married in before they set off for the open road. He couldn't think of an answer on the spur of the moment. Neither he nor Harold Child had thought of the church as being 'practicable'.

The B.N.O.C. performance of *Hugh* followed a few days later. It was at the end of their season and the opera was terrifyingly under-rehearsed and the singers all tired. Malcolm Sargent conducted and, Ralph said, 'saved it from disaster every few bars, and pulled the chestnuts out of the fire in a miraculous way'; afterwards, taking a call with cast and conductor, he found most of the R.C.M. chorus there too. Knowing the opera so well, they had come in at the last moment to help the professionals.

After that it was wonderful to leave London for some weeks, and Mary Fletcher, Dorothy Longman's sister, lent them her home at Oare. The day they arrived there Adeline wrote to her:

I can't say the hundredth part of how pleased we are to be here. Ralph went about saying 'I shall write *here*' only to discover another

[1] Welsh tenor well known in both opera and oratorio.
[2] Bass baritone, later Director of the Royal College of Music.
[3] 1869–1953. Composer and teacher.

place and to say again 'I shall write here' and he *is* writing—we do so love the garden following the lines of the lane—and the hedgerow trees and the house from every aspect . . . we lack nothing but sun.

Ralph had two works for strings in hand, a violin concerto for Jelly d'Aranyi, and a viola piece to add to the very limited repertory that existed for the instrument. He had taken a literary idea on which to build his musical thought in *The Lark Ascending* and had made the violin become both the bird's song and its flight, being, rather than illustrating, the poem from which the title was taken. So, in *Flos Campi*, words were the starting point, episodes from the *Song of Songs*. The viola with its capability of warmth and its glowing quality was the instrument he knew best, and he used it fully in the six sections that explore the sorrows, glories, splendours, and joys of the Shulamite, the King, and the shepherd lover. He added a wordless chorus of voices to the strings that accompany the solo. It is perhaps because this work is so passionate that the violin concerto, which is clear, cool, and formal in structure, seemed academic by comparison,[1] and was so called by the composer, though his audiences found it as unpedagogical as could be. Both works kept him busy through the autumn, though he probably went to Hereford for the Three Choirs Festival to hear Gustav's voice and violin songs (a combination he had been exploring too, setting Housman poems for soprano and violin).[2] His own *On Wenlock Edge* was included in the Chamber Concert at the Festival.

The Norwich Festival, lapsed since 1911, was revived this year, from 29 October until 1 November. Ralph shared one concert with E. J. Moeran, and conducted the *Sea Symphony*. After it was over, Queen Mary, who had been in the audience, sent for him. He was fetched from his dressing-room, protesting that he was not fit to be seen. 'Go and tell her my collar has collapsed completely,' he said to the messenger. 'She knows—come along.' He tried again, 'Tell her I'm an *awful* man—with seventeen wives.' He thought of *Hugh* and wondered what he had left undone this time. 'Oh, she knows all that,' and the messenger hustled him into the Royal presence, but this time it was for congratulations on the work and the performance.

After this he had four lectures to give in Birmingham for the

[1] *Concerto Accademico*, now known as *Concerto in D minor*.
[2] *Along the Field*, Oxford University Press 1954.

British Music Society during November and early December, and a Bach Choir concert on 18 December. This took place at the R.C.M. and was a memorial for Stanford. It was mostly of Stanford's own works, but there was also a Bach cantata and it ended with Purcell's 'Soul of the World'.

Besides his own work, Ralph was again involved in hymns, for a new hymn book, *Songs of Praise*, was being prepared by *The English Hymnal* team, he and Martin Shaw editing the music and Percy Dearmer the words. For this Ralph decided that no second-bests and no compromises should go in, and his net was cast even more widely than it had been for the first edition of *The English Hymnal*.[1]

In 1924 the Oxford University Press established a Music Department under the direction of Hubert Foss, who was himself a musician. He had imagination, a scholarly mind, great understanding and, when necessary, courage; so, though he was only twenty-five when his work as director of the music department started, he was very soon adviser to many musicians, encouraging young composers and being ready to help with any problem. As far as Ralph was concerned he found that 'ask Foss's advice'—'ask Foss to see it'—'ask Foss to play it over to me at Amen House' became almost daily sayings, and in him he found the ideal publisher. This happened at a good moment, for he was working tremendously hard, and it meant a great deal to have a publisher who accepted works as they were written and saw to the preparation of scores so that, if more performances followed a successful first one, the music was soon available and the original manuscripts had not to be used by conductors as they so often had been in the past. It was a great gain also to avoid a situation that could easily arise when the only score was being copied, or had been submitted to a publisher for consideration and so was unavailable for a conductor.

In answer to a letter from an old friend offering to finance publication of *The Shepherds of the Delectable Mountains*, Ralph wrote:

My dear McEwen,

I was so much touched by your suggestion about my *Shepherds*, both the fact of your offer and the way you made it. But I do not

[1] In this hymn book he acknowledges his own tunes straight away, whereas in the first edition of *The English Hymnal* his tunes had been given as 'Anon'. In the 1933 edition of *The English Hymnal*, however, he acknowledged authorship.

think I ought to accept it. For one thing I think it is quite possible that a publisher might accept it in the ordinary course of business—only I am too lazy and too busy to make the necessary effort to approach one. Also I feel that I ought to be able (if necessary) to do this myself out of the ill-gotten gains of such sins of my youth as *Linden Lea* which becomes every year more horribly popular. But this does not prevent my feeling most grateful to you for such a testimony of friendship and interest.

Yours very sincerely
R. Vaughan Williams

He wrote to him again in May to say:

. . . you may be glad to hear that your interest in the *Shepherds* has indirectly borne fruit—for it stirred me up to send it to the Oxford Press and they have accepted it.

With this started his long association with the Oxford University Press.

The nicest thing that spring was a recital given by Steuart Wilson on 27 March. *The Monthly Musical Record* said: 'Mr. Wilson devoted himself heart and soul to his friend's fine music.' It was a big programme, with the *Four Hymns*, *Wenlock*, and *Merciless Beauty*, his setting of three Chaucer Rondels, as well as new songs, two with words by Seamus O'Sullivan, three by Adeline's niece, Fredegond Shove,[1] three Shakespeare settings and three Whitman songs. These had at some time been shown to Ravel, perhaps on his visit to England during the previous autumn, and Ralph had got into difficulty translating the poems into French for him. When it came to the words 'on the frontiers to eyes impenetrable', he foundered, and explained '*là, où on laisse les bagages*'. Ravel took the point quickly. '*Frontiers*,' he said.

The year before, *On Wenlock Edge* had been chosen for the I.S.C.M. Festival at Salzburg, but it had been sung so badly by a foreigner that a rather pathetic notice appeared in *The Monthly Musical Record* and probably elsewhere: 'The B.M.S., 3 Berners Street, will be glad to receive subscriptions to the Festival Fund which has been opened in order to secure a British conductor for

[1] One of these, *Motion and Stillness*, has a dated MS.—1922. Fredegond was the daughter of Fred and Florence Maitland, married to Gerald Shove, the (Cambridge) economist.

the *Pastoral Symphony* and a British singer for *Merciless Beauty*. . . .' These were the only British works chosen that year for the I.S.C.M. Festival which was in two parts, the first at Prague, the second at Venice. Somehow the money was raised, and those two who most of all understood and loved Ralph's music, Adrian Boult and Steuart Wilson, undertook the tasks. Steuart's part was at Venice, and not until September, but the Festival at Prague was in early May and to that Ralph and Adeline decided to go. Ralph had had two Bach Choir concerts—the *Passion* in late February, and a mixed programme, as well as the Leith Hill Festival's three concerts, so he was feeling very much in the mood for a jaunt. 'Just off to the Freak Festival,' he wrote, while Adeline, suddenly aware that it would be a 'dress up' occasion, hurried off to Gorringes and provided herself with a tussore silk dress. They had been to Prague before when they had visited Ivor Gatty there, so they knew the city, but this time it was all rather splendid, very hot, and they had to go to a lot of entertainments. Ralph was sceptical about the effect of the *Pastoral Symphony* on the rest of the musicians—'Oh, they hated it,' he said, though the critic who was there on behalf of *The Musical Times* thought otherwise. However, what Ralph did like enormously was a performance of Janaček's opera, *The Cunning Little Vixen*. It was new, and had had its first performance only a few months earlier: delightfully sung and acted, it was an original and enchanting work and the one he enjoyed most in the Festival. Adeline wrote to Cordelia:

> We have had an orgy of music and splendid weather. We go off tomorrow to Salzburg in Austria nr. mountains. Went to dinner at the British Legation, wasn't as terrific as I feared. . . . R's Pastoral got a very good reception—R is being filmed this aft.

A strange and delightful story of his music had reached Ralph, just before they had gone abroad, from the Rev. Lancelot Bark:[1]

> The second Anglo-Catholic pilgrimage to the Holy Places in 1925 on which I was director of the music, included the Isle of Patmos. The leaders of our pilgrimage, Dr. Hutton, Dean of Winchester, the late Dr. Russell Wakefield, Bishop of Birmingham, and other eminent Churchmen, were eager to make our visit to Patmos the highlight of

[1] Now Canon Bark.

the tour. For that purpose they requested me to form the pilgrims, over 300 in number, into a vast choir to ascend the hill leading to the monastery, singing *Sine Nomine*.[1] I spread it out with interludes between the verses, and perhaps more by good luck than good management, the last verse was reached as we entered the Quadrangle of the monastery where it rang out and echoed magnificently around the building.

The Abbott, who appeared to be the choir director, was thrilled by it, and asked me, through our interpreter, what was the tune. I told him it was a modern tune by our most eminent English composer. He insisted on my giving him a copy of it, for which I was conducted to the Scriptorium and supplied with a vast sheet of vellum and an immense inkpot. I understood that he was going to adapt it to some Antiphon for use in their services. So *Sine Nomine* reached Patmos in 1925.

Ralph wrote:

. . . The next musical visitor to Patmos will probably collect my tune as a Greek folk song!

He was able to meet the pilgrim and hear more about this adventure. It gave him as much pleasure as a letter that came many years later from the Abbey at Monserrat telling him that they regularly sang his *Mass* there.

At the Leeds Festival Gustav's *Choral Symphony* had its first performance. Ralph was not entirely happy about it: he felt that the chorus had not understood it, and he reserved his judgement. His own work in the Festival was the, by now familiar, *Sea Symphony*, conducted by Hugh Allen. Delius's *Song of the High Hills* was also given, so the singers had had a varied and difficult lot of big works to rehearse. But, allowing for all this, he was unhappy, as he wanted to find Gustav's new work as glorious as he had found *The Hymn of Jesus*. He wrote a long letter in which he went into all the excellencies and disappointments, ending: '. . . I shall live in faith till I have heard it again several times and then I shall find out what a bloody fool I was not to see it all the first time.'[2] It was repeated three weeks later at a Philharmonic concert, on 29 October. In between, two days before Ralph's fifty-third birthday, Henry Wood conducted the first performance of *Flos*

[1] Ralph's tune to 'For all the Saints'.

[2] See *Heirs and Rebels*, pp. 60, 61, 62 (Oxford University Press, 1959).

Margaret Vaughan Williams at Leith Hill Place, 1917

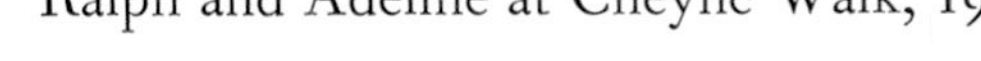

Ralph and Adeline at Cheyne Walk, 1917

1925

Campi, with Lionel Tertis as soloist. It bewildered a lot of people, but Ralph's chief pleasure was in Lionel's ravishing playing. He was also delighted to discover that the orchestra had nicknamed it 'Camp Flossie'. The first performance of the *Concerto Accademico* followed on 6 November at one of the Gerald Cooper concerts at the Aeolian Hall with Jelly d'Aranyi as soloist, and on 7 November the *London Symphony* was conducted by Henry Wood; rather a good month for any composer.

Gustav had found *Flos Campi* as unsatisfactory as Ralph had found the *Choral Symphony*, and he answered Ralph's letter:[1]

> . . . I couldn't get hold of Flos a bit and was therefore disappointed with it and me. But I'm not disappointed in Flos's composer, because he has not repeated himself. Therefore it is probably either an improvement or something that will lead to one. . . .

Gustav probably knew the two very different works that were occupying Ralph that winter. One was *Sancta Civitas*, now nearly finished, and the other, still only sketched, an opera with Synge's play, *Riders to the Sea*, as libretto. Ralph had talked about Synge's plays to Elizabeth Maconchy quite soon after she started lessons with him; and had told her that he had thought of setting *The Tinker's Wedding* as well as the tragic *Riders*. But he never got further than thinking about it.

In November Nicholas Gatty's opera *The Tempest* was staged at the R.C.M. and in December Ralph went to the Forest School in Sussex run by Margot Gatty and her husband, Hugh Parrington, for a performance of *The Taming of the Shrew*. He and Margot shared a desk in the viola section of the orchestra which played the incidental music, and Nicholas was one of the second violins. It must have been refreshingly like the pre-war days when he had taken part in their village concerts in Yorkshire of which Margot's memory was vivid. Ralph's enthusiasm 'was quite tremendous so that always old bow hairs would become broken and wave up and down as he bowed. Then, in a very vigorous section (his bow must have been a little short for him) he would bring it down so far to the point that it would slip *under* the bridge. This always sent darling Adeline in the front row into silent tears of amusement!'[2]

[1] See *Heirs and Rebels*, pp. 60, 61, 62 (Oxford University Press, 1959).
[2] Letter to U. V. W.

Queen Alexandra died that winter and at every concert in London funeral marches were added to the programme. With her died also the last elegance of the Edwardian age; this little, deaf, enamelled princess, with an aura of parma violets, sables, spotted veils, and pale gloves, whose epithalamium was written by Tennyson, had lived almost to the General Strike, which was already casting its shadow on England.

In a winter of unhappy political troubles, hunger marches, and means tests, music was thriving. At Dorking the Leith Hill Festival Committee discussed the possibility of building a hall for their concerts, which would also house any other local activities and provide a sprung floor for dances and a stage for operatic and dramatic performances. Smaller halls for other local activities were also planned. Following the Bach Choir's performance of the *B Minor Mass* in February, the Towns Division of the Leith Hill Festival sang the *Credo*, *Sanctus*, *Benedictus*, *Agnus Dei*, and *Dona Nobis Pacem* from the same work in April. This was something Ralph had wanted them to achieve for many years, and he felt that a choir capable of such music was worthy of a hall that would allow them to undertake big works unhampered by the cramped conditions and discomforts with which they had had to contend up to then.

H. A. L. Fisher was Warden of New College, so it was natural for Ralph and Adeline to stay with him and his wife when they went to Oxford. They were there in February for early rehearsals of *Sancta Civitas* as well as for the first performance which took place during the Heather Festival of Music, from 6 May to the 10th. This was during the turmoil of the General Strike, which was fortunate for Ralph for he was deeply troubled by the political situation and he was in doubt as to what part, if any, he should take when the strike happened. As it was, his work filled the foreground of his days and he was absorbed by the final rehearsals and the performance at which Hugh Allen conducted and Arthur Cranmer was the soloist. He said later in life that of all his choral works *Sancta Civitas* was the one he liked best, and there is no doubt that it epitomizes much of his thought, belief, and imagination. He took the words from the Authorized Version and Tavener's Bible, the solemn and visionary splendours of the language of Revelation that describes the fall of Babylon and the new heaven and the new earth. The great armies are slain, the angel standing in the sun summons the fowls of the air to devour the carrion, and the holy city descends 'as a bride adorned for her husband' where the glory and the honour of the nations are brought into the eternal light of rejoicing. Through the haze of alleluias at the end, the time of fulfilment and the time when all that has happened in the vision has not yet happened in reality meet for a moment, as a single voice promises, 'Behold I come quickly, I am the bright and the morning star. Surely I come quickly.' The voices of the chorus answer 'Even so come, Lord.'

There are moments in this work that touch other points in Ralph's music—the contraltos from the semi-chorus whose words 'and I saw a pure river of the water of life, and on either side of the river was there the tree of life, and the leaves of the tree were for the healing of the nations' are sister voices to those in the last movement of the *Sea Symphony* with their question 'Wherefore, unsatisfied soul? Whither O mocking life?' as well as to the cup bearer and to the branch bearer of the yet unwritten *Pilgrim's Progress*, who bring comfort to the Pilgrim after he has fought Apollyon: 'In the midst of that fair city flows the river of the water of life, clear as crystal . . . take thou the leaves of the tree of life. . . .' The images of the river and the tree come from many mythologies: the holy city is not only the new Jerusalem 'whose gardens and whose gallant walks continually are green', which Ralph always saw as the landscape of Van Eyck's *Adoration of the Lamb*, but also the dream in which Plato believed man must trust to give sense and reason, proportion and truth to daily life: for the quotation in Greek on the first page of the score comes from the *Phaedo*. Ralph's own copy in F. J. Church's translation, is heavily marked.

> A man of sense will not insist that things are exactly as I have described them. But I think he will believe that something of the kind is true of the soul and her habitations, seeing that she is shown to be immortal, and that it is worth while to stake everything on this belief. The venture is a fair one and he must charm his doubts with spells like these.

While he was beginning *Sancta Civitas* Ralph wrote his article on *The Letter and the Spirit*,[1] in it he summed up what he believed, both then and for the rest of his life:

[1] *Music and Letters*, 1920. Reprinted in *National Music*. Oxford University Press, 1963.

Before going any further may we take it that the object of all art is to obtain a partial revelation of that which is beyond human senses and human faculties—of that in fact which is spiritual? And that the means we employ to induce this revelation are those very senses and faculties themselves? The human, visible, audible and intelligible media which artists (of all kinds) use, are symbols not of other visible and audible things but of what lies beyond sense and knowledge.

He conducted the second performance of *Sancta Civitas* himself during the four-day Festival with which the Bach Choir celebrated its Jubilee in June—originally planned for May but postponed because of the General Strike. Of the four concerts the first two were all Bach, chorales, cantatas, motets, concertos, piano, violin, and organ solos. The final one was a performance of the *B Minor Mass*, their second that year, which meant that there was more rehearsal time for the less familiar works. The third concert began with the Brahms *Academic Festival Overture* and ended with Parry's *Blest Pair of Sirens*. Between these, Walford Davies's *Solemn Melody*, Brahms's *Alto Rhapsody* and Stanford's *Irish Rhapsody*, filled the second half. *Sancta Civitas* followed the Overture.

Dr. Straube, the Cantor of the Thomaskirche, Leipzig, was among the audience at the concerts. After the week was over, Ralph sent the choir 'a message from the Director':

As I shall not have an opportunity of meeting many of the members of the Bach Choir before next season, I want to tell them of my admiration of the manner in which they carried out an arduous four days' festival.

There was present throughout that 'inner fire' (to quote Dr. Straube), that enthusiasm and devotion which are of more value than any amount of technique.

Particularly I wish to thank the Choir for their fine performance of my 'Sancta Civitas' and I want to tell members that I am aware that this performance was the result of much more than our weekly practices.

The performance of the Mass was to my mind a worthy climax to a week of splendid singing.

After a summer holiday, this time in Surrey, Ralph and Adeline went to Worcester for the Three Choirs Festival, where Ralph conducted his *Pastoral Symphony*. As with so many works, the acoustics of a cathedral contribute some special quality, and the romantic, rose-coloured interior of Worcester Cathedral was a setting that gave a new dimension to the symphony. Ten days later he conducted it again at the Queen's Hall at a Promenade Concert.

In September too, R. O. Morris's appointment as Principal of the Curtis Musical Institute was announced, and at the end of the month he and Emmie left 13 Cheyne Walk, where they had been sharing the house with Ralph and Adeline, for Philadelphia. With them went a very young man, Herbert Sumsion,[1] who had accepted a position in the same Institute as an organ teacher.

All the Fisher sisters were prolific correspondents, and Emmie's almost daily letters to Adeline during the two years she was away have fragments in them which refer to the letters she had received from Cheyne Walk and give some picture of life there which is otherwise unrecorded. She gave, as well as her views on America, a full and detailed description of almost every meal she prepared and of trifling everyday doings, establishing as best she could, with the Atlantic between them, the domestic world she and Adeline had shared so long. She wrote of George Trevelyan coming to tea with Ralph, who wore white heather in his buttonhole, of a visit to Napier Miles at King's Weston, and of a letter from Ralph which had given special pleasure:

> Tell R. that it smells divinely of tobacco—getting less now alas—but . . . it was like seeing him. I like to think of him listening to the 2 LO,[2] upstairs in your room, I expect.

The winter was full of trouble about 2 LO. First there were rumours that Chappells were going to sell the Queen's Hall, then that the Queen's Hall Orchestra was to be disbanded because the broadcast concerts were reducing audiences. Beecham said that all musicians should leave the country because broadcasting was ruining musical art, and the papers remarked severely that 'it is the duty of all musicians to inform themselves as fully as possible as to the rights and wrongs of both sides'.

Ralph and Adeline spent Christmas at Leith Hill Place where life was far less pleasant than it had been before the war. Meggie was ill and unhappy. In her youth she had refused several proposals of marriage, to her mother's great distress. Ralph said she

[1] Later Organist of Gloucester Cathedral.
[2] The London Broadcasting Station.

had read too many bad novels and expected what he described as 'Hallelujah spasms' of which, he said, she was not capable. He said his own view of marriage was realistic, and he often propounded a plan by which the Government should arrange for all bachelors and spinsters who had not found their own partners by the time they were twenty-five to be married compulsorily, as he thought that most people could settle down fairly happily with most other people, and that if a marriage didn't give all that it promised it was possible and desirable to be thankful for what it did give. He continued to encourage and further any romances he came across and urged all his, by now large, collection of honorary nieces to marry, in a cheerful gather-ye-rosebuds spirit. He and Meggie, the sad text of these sermons, worked together for the Festival, but in everything else they were out of touch with each other. She was, he felt, fast following Aunt Sophy's eccentric example, refusing to eat properly, dressing badly, and growing narrow in her outlook and sympathies. It had even become a major triumph when she was persuaded to wear the stockings Adeline gave her for Christmas. But Ralph's mother remained alert, interested, and full of zest for life.

Back in London after Christmas, they were involved in a folk dance soirée (Emmie's description) and Ralph had an attack of food poisoning; pork at the R.C.M., lunch on a train, and delicatessen at Fredegond Shove's home in Cambridge were all suspect. But it was soon over and he was reported to have enjoyed chestnut pudding a week later, a sign that he was truly restored to health in time to attend a banquet at the College on 23 February, presided over by the Prince of Wales, in whose honour there followed a variety show, written and put on by professors and students. Ralph and Gustav sat together and enjoyed the brilliance, wit, and wickedness far more than the guest of honour was able to do: the grand finale which brought the house down was 'Mary had a little lamb' sung by the entire cast to the tune of Walford Davies's *Solemn Melody*.

Ralph had at this time become rather fat, for though the army had made him most elegantly thin, a less active life, and a great addiction to pies, cakes, buns, and puddings had put weight on his large bones: a photograph taken in Prague in 1925 shows him as a much solider person. The slim Ralph had gone for ever. He was not entirely sedentary, for at some time after the war he had reverted to his old habit of going for short walking holidays with friends. He often went with Dorothy and Bobby Longman and sometimes Fanny Farrer[1] made a fourth in the party. She and Mrs. Tatham had been Joint Hon. Secretaries of the Leith Hill Festival from Meggie's retirement in 1921 until 1923, after which she had done the work alone. She was a brilliant organizer and for many years smoothed out all the troubles that arose in the Festival weeks, collecting soloists who had gone to the wrong stations, finding lost instruments, soothing agitated choir members, planning the elaborate seating arrangements for performers and in every way taking burdens from Ralph's shoulders with competence and grace.

The usual plan for these holidays was a twelve or fifteen mile walk a day, time to enjoy the country with stops to revive Ralph, for though he loved walking he tired easily. The flat feet, about which his mother had worried in childhood and his C.O. in the Ambulance unit during the war, had not been improved by long route marches in army boots, but his fatigue was quickly overcome by a rest and a glass of beer or a good farmhouse tea. The walks were usually in Wiltshire or Dorset, parts of the world Ralph loved: the green roads and open skies of the Great Plain with its summer flowers, thymey smells, and an infinity of larks rising above the bleached grass and the pale coloured chalk country were very much to his taste.

Once, when they had walked up the Wylye Valley to where it was joined by the Till stream, along a green ox-way known as Stapleford Road, and had crossed the plain to Chitterne, a valley village with magnificent beech trees, they arrived so late that they went to the police-station to ask where they could find beds and breakfasts. They were sent to different cottages. When Ralph knocked at the door to which he had been directed, a young woman opened it and said he might stay if he would be very quiet and only whisper: her brother was a farm worker, she explained as she cooked eggs and bacon, and had to go to work very early, so he went to bed at dark and must have his sleep. But as Ralph sat down to eat, the lamplight fell on his face, and she looked at him, asked if he was Mr. Williams, and taking a photograph from the chimney-piece asked excitedly if he was in it. It was an ambulance snapshot and indeed he was in it. 'I must wake my

[1] Hon. Dame Frances Farrer.

brother,' she said, but he had already awakened, had heard Ralph's voice, and came rushing downstairs to greet his fellow soldier. There was more tea, and again more tea, and they sat up talking for most of the night, happy in the extraordinary chance that had brought them together.

There were other mild adventures during these walks—grudging innkeepers who suggested bread and cheese, and suddenly found they had jugged hare and XXX beer; encounters with keepers, talks with passers-by. One remark Ralph remembered with pleasure was that of the cottager who offered him fat bacon for supper, saying: 'I could get up at three in the morning to eat fat bacon.'

It was still almost the world Borrow had known, certainly not much changed since Hudson had written *A Shepherd's Life*. Many of the villages had little communication with the outside world beyond market day at the nearest town. Green roads, deep lanes, and footpaths took walkers into countryside where farms were rarely mechanized, and stooks were still the graceful tented shapes of Samuel Palmer's landscapes.

At some time during this summer, and for a day or two in many following years, Ralph visited the Music Camp which Bernard Robinson had founded. He liked living as simply as possible, sharing the few necessary tasks and spending all day singing and playing. And there were few summers when he was not involved with E.F.D.S. vacation courses, lecturing or conducting the singing. He arrived at a hotel in Exeter once, to take part in a summer school, so dusty after his bicycle ride that he was refused admission until Maud Karpeles and Henry Nevinson vouched for his respectability. And on another occasion Maud Karpeles was amused to find him reading *Vogue* in the hotel lounge. He was absorbed in the study of fashion, a subject which she had not realized interested him very much indeed.

Before a holiday in Surrey where the Morrises, home for the summer from Philadelphia, joined them, there was the Bach Choir's Summer Concert. This had given Ralph quite a lot of work to prepare, for they sang Handel's *Saul*, and there is a programme note which reveals, to anyone acquainted with his editing of scores for performances-in-special-circumstances, what must have been involved—many strips of MS. paper fixed to the printed parts, not always quite straight, much pencil marking, the result of many hours of work—not to mention the unsticking and rubbing-out which had to be done before the music was sent back to the publishers.

The original orchestration of 'Saul' is as follows:—

Flutes, Oboes, Bassoons, Trumpets, Trombones, Timpani, Carillons, Organ, Cembalo and Strings.

For the present performance the following instruments have been added:

Clarinets—these reinforce the oboes which in Handel's time were much louder and coarser instruments than those now in use: the Clarinets also double some of the very high trumpet notes. Double Bassoon added to the Bassoon parts in the loud passages for greater power.

Bass Tuba to supply the correct notes which Handel gave to the Bass Trombone and which the modern instrument does not possess.

But the greatest pleasure Ralph had from this concert was giving the first public performance of Gustav's setting for soprano and women's chorus of Robert Bridges's poem *The Elegy on a Lady whom Grief for the Death of her Betrothed killed. Assemble all ye maidens* is music of winter and grief, flowering in snow, and one of his friend's works that Ralph loved best. As was his custom with first performances, he gave it twice in the programme.

At the Three Choirs Festival Ralph conducted both the *Pastoral Symphony* and *The Shepherds*. He was not able to go to Norwich, where Henry Wood conducted the *London Symphony*, for early in October Adeline had a fall and broke her thigh so badly that she was encased in plaster from chest to toes. Realizing this would mean long inactivity she had her bed brought down to the drawing-room and settled there with a nurse to look after her. Emmie heard from Cordelia that 'Ralph's one terror seems to be of all the family coming in and making suggestions and thrusting gadgets on A'. But in spite of the plaster cocoon she managed to write letters and she had her hair cut short. There were visitors and books, Thornton Wilder's *The Bridge of San Luis Rey* and Virginia Woolf's *To the Lighthouse* among them: this re-creation of Leslie Stephen's household must have brought back many memories for her of Uncle Leslie's house and of her cousin, Stella.

Meanwhile Ralph conducted *Flos Campi*, judged choirs for the London Labour Choral Union, attended the first meeting of the Cecil Sharp Memorial Fund under the chairmanship of H. A. L. Fisher, and went to a touching and lovely performance of *Pelléas* at the College, with Mabel Ritchie[1] as a perfect Mélisande, as well as spending some time with Gustav, when *Egdon Heath* was being tried over on the piano.

He spent a night at Oxford and came home with a bad cold. It was a cold, foggy winter, bad gales came after Christmas followed by high tides and flooding. The Thames rose alarmingly, Chelsea became dangerous, the cellars at the Tate were said to be ten feet deep in water, and pictures were damaged, some irretrievably. People were reported drowned in Lambeth, so the Morrises in Philadelphia were anxious for every crumb of news. The only dramatic event at 13 Cheyne Walk was Ralph's rescue from the basement of their cat Henry, who was believed to have gone in search of a mouse and had nearly lost his life in the flood.

The Bach Choir's spring concert was early in the year, and besides the Bach Cantata, *Dearest Jesu*, and the *Sea Symphony*, there were two works by young composers in the programme, Robin Milford's *Double Fugue for Orchestra* and Gerald Finzi's *Concerto for Small Orchestra and Violin Solo*, the soloist being Sybil Eaton. This was the beginning of an important friendship with Gerald Finzi which lasted until the younger man's death. In February, *Egdon Heath* had its first London performance at a Philharmonic concert, and after his disappointment with the *Choral Symphony* Ralph was happy to be able to write to Gustav: 'I've come to the conclusion E. H. is beautiful—bless you therefore.'

The Bach Choir sang the *St. John Passion* on 24 March, and after that Ralph had only one more concert with the Choir, for he had resigned at a Committee Meeting in February. It was one of the things he minded giving up most of all, for his years as Musical Director had given him immense satisfaction. The final concert with the Choir was at the R.C.M., when Schweitzer joined them to play the organ, and, having ended the concert with *Blest Pair of Sirens*, Ralph said good-bye. It was almost unbearable, but knowing that his successor would be either Gustav or Adrian made it a little better than it might otherwise have been. The

[1] Margaret Ritchie.

reason for his resignation was simply that he and Adeline had come to the conclusion that they must leave the tall house in Cheyne Walk, at any rate temporarily, and find somewhere to live that would be easier for her. A London flat was a possibility, but she longed for the country, so they determined to spend a summer near Dorking and look for a house. It was near enough to London for Ralph to continue teaching, but he felt that he must forgo the Bach Choir rehearsals and all the extra journeys they would have entailed.

R. O. Morris's niece, Honorine Williamson, had come to help Adeline in the house: this was arranged to give Honorine herself some practical experience for she had just left a Domestic Science school. She settled into the household as a much loved niece, friend, and ally for the next twelve years.

In the winter of 1927–28 Ralph wrote a *Te Deum* commissioned for the enthronement of the Archbishop of Canterbury, and corrected the proofs of the *Oxford Book of Carols* which he had edited with Martin Shaw.

By the spring, Adeline was learning to walk again. Gustav, on a walking tour in Shropshire, wrote a long letter to her to cheer up her convalescence, telling her among other things:

> although it is, strictly speaking, off the point, I think it worth mentioning that the rate collector at Ludlow is Mr. Tantrums—which like most other details of life is improbable. . . .

He wrote again at Whitsun:

> We are singing His (we mean *Our*) Mass[1] from time to time and have discovered that He wrote it for this Cathedral.

The folding picture card with its ten views of Canterbury is signed by all the Whitsuntide Singers.

In the summer Ralph and Adeline took The Old Barn near Holmbury St. Mary for a few weeks. Ralph was writing several different things, finishing his opera, beginning a masque, and, as the main task, preparing one of three works he intended as presents for the three Divisions of the Leith Hill choirs for their Jubilee. He said he had started to write his *Benedicite* after reading Prescott's *Conquest of Mexico*, which had greatly excited him,

[1] *Mass in G minor*. R. V. W. dedicated to Gustav Holst and his Whitsuntide Singers.

though it had little bearing on the words he was setting. Adeline, in a letter, said that it sounded very fierce.

Gustav came to spend a day with them and got lost between the bus stop and their house, so Ralph drew maps for the other visitors and his directions in the margin started, 'You get off the bus at the photographs of the cows' which Adeline explained as meaning Wotton Manor Farm.[1] They had a car which Honorine drove, so they were able to go to Bosham for the day 'to get a whiff of seaweed' before they went back to London for Three Choirs rehearsals.

Sir Herbert Brewer had died in the spring and the 'young Mr. Sumsion', who had sailed to America with the Morrises, was appointed to succeed him as organist of Gloucester Cathedral. He had married an American girl, a romance Emmie Morris had watched with interest and reported to Adeline in her letters. He came home to a difficult programme, for Honegger's *King David*, Kodály's *Psalmus Hungaricus*, and Gustav's *Two Psalms* were added to the usual classics: the Festival was a success and Sumsion's succession was approved.

The Morrises had also come home for good: things at the Curtis Institute had not worked out as they had hoped and R.O. had resigned. They too spent the summer near Dorking and were thinking of taking a house of their own in London. Ralph and Adeline had taken a house in Dorking, its chief merit being that they were given a key to the neighbouring Glory Woods. Before they moved Ralph wrote to Gustav:

13 Cheyne Walk.
(The Best address)

Dear Gustav . . . we will see what we can fix up when we get to Dorking where our perfectly appalling address will be

Glorydene
St Paul's Road
Dorking
!
?
!!

We go to Littlehampton for a week tomorrow and to Dorking on the 29th.

[1] Even after the frame with its picture of stolid prize-winning milkers had disappeared Ralph called that bus stop the-Photographs-of-the-Cows; presumably he had so often waited there that he had become fond of the champions.

I enjoyed Gloucester v. much and Willy[1] was really inspired—I also shared bottles of beer with Elgar but, I fear, rather pained him by saying that in my opinion the Reformation was indirectly responsible for the 3 choirs festival, since if we had kept the celibacy of the clergy we shd. not have to have provided for their widows but only their orphans.

Yrs R. V. W.

When Pegs Ritchie had qualified and started to practise medicine, Ralph and Adeline had become her patients, so, during the time when Adeline was in plaster and while she was convalescing, they had seen a great deal of her. And it is from a letter to her written from Glorydene thanking her 'for the lovely blue tie' that Ralph's visit to Malines, to hear the Cathedral choir sing his Mass, can be dated, for he goes on: 'I had a grand time in Malines—the ecclesiastics understand food and drink and smoke. I will tell you all about it when we meet.' Assuming the tie to be a birthday present, he must have gone to Belgium some time during early October, for he was always prompt in writing thank-you letters. Half a page of a letter from Adeline to Cordelia tells a little more of this agreeable visit.

They found the Carillon player—a celebrated man of 70 with 2 pupils—the Canon wdn't let R climb quite to the top for the parapet was blown away by a shell and he said it was very dizzy work. The view was misty—so it was chiefly the excitement of the bells which made the climb worthwhile. The Canon was educated in England at Oxford, a man about 60 and he and 2 sisters live very comfortably in a dark old fashioned house in a courtyard—He was in business and became a priest after the war—his people are well known publishers. There was a little Polish monk staying in the house—Ralph found him delightfully simple—he liked the organist very much. (Canon Derain has a brother living in Dorking)

He enjoyed both his crossings—nothing could have been more successful.

Adeline's letters are very often the chief source of information about everyday events. She wrote almost daily to Emmie if they were separated, frequently to Cordelia, and among the letters to her friends there are a number to Rosamond Carr. Rosamond knew many of the musicians who came to the Cheyne Walk

[1] W. H. Reed.

household and she soon became a friend of the family. She was a little older than Honorine but near enough in age and interests to be asked to go with her to theatres and concerts, and when she left London and plunged into various jobs Adeline kept her in touch with all their doings. It is from letters to her that all sorts of fragments come that fill in the background of Ralph's life.

They left Glorydene after Christmas. Adeline wrote from The Brown House, Canford Cliffs, Dorset, in January:

Here we have been for 10 days wrapped in icy fog. That is over and the sun is out today—and there is a chance of Ralph shaking off his pre-Xmas cold! . . .

and again:

With Emmie and Morris gone I don't think we shall stay on at Cheyne—its day is over.

From the same address Ralph wrote to Pegs:

I have to be in London on Thursday and there's a Phil. concert that night. Will you come with me? We will dine first . . . and afterwards we would paint the town red if we can find anywhere to paint it in. . . .

They were all in London again for rehearsals at the R.C.M. of Ralph's opera *Sir John in Love* which was the long delayed fruit of his weeks at Stratford with the Benson company in 1913: he wrote it entirely for his own enjoyment, but his preface goes directly to the objections which he felt might be made.

To write yet another opera about Falstaff at this time of day may seem the height of impertinence for one appears in so doing to be entering into competition with four great men—Shakespeare, Verdi, Nicolai and Holst.

With regard to Shakespeare, my only excuse is that he is fair game, like the Bible, and may be made use of nowadays even for advertisements of soap and razors. I hope that it may be possible to consider that even Verdi's masterpiece does not exhaust all the possibilities of Shakespeare's genius.

And I hope that I have treated Holst with the sincerest flattery not only imitating his choice of Falstaff as the subject of an opera but in imitating his use of English folk tunes in the texture of the music. The best I can hope will be that *Sir John in Love* may be considered as a sequel to his brilliant *Boar's Head.* There remains Nicolai's *Merry Wives* which in my opinion is the most successful of all Falstaff operas; my excuse in this case must be that there is hardly any Shakespeare in his libretto.

My chief object in *Sir John in Love* has been to fit this wonderful comedy with, I trust, not unpleasant music. In the matter of folk tunes, they only appear occasionally and their *titles* have no dramatic relevancy (except possibly in the case of 'John, come kiss me now'.) When a particular folk tune appeared to me the fitting accompaniment to a situation, I have used it. When I could not find a suitable folk tune, I have made shift to make up something of my own. I therefore offer no apology for the occasional use of folk songs to enhance the dramatic point. If the result is successful I feel justified; if not, no amount of 'originality' will save the situation. However, the point is a small one since out of a total of 120 minutes music, the folk tunes occupy less than 15.

The text is taken almost entirely from the *Merry Wives*, with the addition of lyrics from Elizabethan poets. A few unimportant remarks (e.g. 'Here comes Master Ford') are my own.

This high-spirited note suggests all the fun he had with the disreputable crazy gang, Pistol, Bardolph, and Nym, some of whom romp through both parts of Henry IV and Henry V as well as this play, and the other eccentrics who lived in Windsor, lovelorn Slender, ubiquitous Mistress Quickly, Dr. Caius, Sir Hugh Evans, and all the citizens, servants, friends, and gossips attendant on the households of Ford and Page: but it hardly suggests the romantic freshness that the music has laid on the story. There is one moment of anguish when Ford's jealousy blazes painfully across the gaiety and make believe, not unlike a similar jealousy in the last act of *Figaro*; otherwise the play is gentle and the lyrics give the story points of repose. The love music for Falstaff, swanning gorgeously towards the ladies of his choice, is characteristically different from the music for Anne and Fenton. Slender's failure to get beyond the first line of a poem to Anne and Dr. Caius's imported 'Vrai dieu d'amours' add to each character's wholeness. At the end, after all the teasings and pinchings under Herne the Hunter's oak, after Anne's ruse to marry the man of her own choosing, returning with him through the moonlit forest while all the young people sing Ben Jonson's words 'See the chariot at hand here of love', it is Falstaff who has the last word:

Whether men do laugh or weep,
Whether they do wake or sleep,
Whether they die young or old,
Whether they feel heat or cold,
There is underneath the sun,
Nothing in true earnest done.

The opera was finished during the winter and the first performance was conducted by Malcolm Sargent at the R.C.M. in March. A letter from Dorothy Longman, thanking Ralph for tickets, ends with a first night vignette—

Adeline was holding such a reception last night that I couldn't get near, but please give her my love——

It was perhaps a misfortune for Ralph's operas to start with student performances for, however good they may have been, there was a danger that the general public might assume that the operas were works suitable only for amateurs. All his life and through the times of his greatest success as a writer of symphonies Ralph longed for his operas to be taken more seriously and to be given professional performances. Had they been, he might well have written more for the stage, which always fascinated him.

Having just had this performance of his own work, he was deeply interested by Donald Tovey's opera, *The Bride of Dionysus*, with a libretto by Bob Trevelyan,[1] which, with many other friends of both composer and poet, he went up to Edinburgh to see in April. In July he was discussing the possibilities of opera on tour: after a long meeting with Rutland Boughton he and Gustav produced a memorandum for a projected Welsh Festival which Rutland hoped to start, but which did not materialize.

After you left, Holst and I had a long conversation which is summarized in the enclosed suggestions which I send to you in case they are of any use to you—

Memorandum and suggestions for opera scheme by G. H. and R. V. W.

[1] R. C. Trevelyan.

1938

Ursula Wood, 1938

A. *No splash.* e.g. Mountain Ash Festival to start with—the opening performance to be on the same scale as what we propose to continue with. Also, *under the same circumstances.* A show by a small company intended for co-operative hall should not be judged by the critics under the circumstances of a London Theatre; therefore the invited 'Press' show should take place in the provinces at one of the co-operative halls.

B. Performances, though small in scale should be as nearly perfect as possible in *quality.* Therefore we do not advise operas which audiences may have seen on a large scale with all the glitter and tinsel of a large crowd and showy costumes etc. There must be no feeling of makeshift e.g. 2 men and a boy to represent a whole regiment of soldiers. The operas must be chosen with regard to this.

C. We suggest that under a good Director, local *amateur* effort might be enlisted in each town visited, to walk on and represent crowds etc. or even where possible, to help in the chorus.

D. We suggest everything on a small scale to start with—no orchestra but only a piano (N.B. a good piano should be bought and carried round, not to depend on the local piano). A company of about 20—everyone willing to take a hand at everything. e.g. the principal soprano of Monday would walk on on Tuesday, help mend the costumes on Wednesday and be noises off on Thursday—but every one of these artists must be first rate and hard working.

E. We suggest as two quite separate propositions that 'The Immortal Hour' is a good opera to start with and R. B.[1] would be the best Director—and to avoid any suspicion that R. B. was made Director and then chose his own work, the work should be selected first and R. B. then invited by a Committee to direct *it* and incidentally any other operas in the repertoire.

F. We suggest a repertoire of not more than 3 operas—besides 'The Immortal Hour' we suggest Gluck's 'Orpheus', Mozart's 'Cosi Fan Tutte', Verdi's 'Rigoletto' (Also Stanford's 'Shamus O'Brien' and Holst's 'Golden Goose Ballet'—these last 2 added by R. V. W. since conversation with Holst.)

G. We think it a mistake to pose as 'British' opera. British opera is at present very naturally suspect; it will we are sure have to be introduced in small doses.

The idea of a soprano who is also an able needlewoman comes like an echo of the famous Benson story of a telegram to a

[1] Rutland Boughton.

theatrical agency asking for 'an actor who is a fast bowler' to play Laertes.

Between his own opera and Tovey's, Ralph had put on the largest works Leith Hill Festival had yet attempted—for the villages Purcell's *King Arthur* (which he had heard at Cambridge and loved as much as *The Faery Queen*); Haydn's *Seasons*, for the Towns and, for Division I, Parry's *Job*. On May Day he had a letter from Lady Farrer, President of the Festival since it began, sending him a cheque for the score and parts of *Job*, 'it is from the *whole* L.H.M.F. . . . all your friends and devoted followers asking you to take this little offering with their thanks and faithful affection.'

In June he conducted a concert at St. Margaret's, Westminster, for the Bach Cantata Club, and on 23 June he was present to see Maud Karpeles lay the foundation stone for the building that was to become Cecil Sharp House. Then the final preparations for leaving Cheyne Walk were made, and a tenancy agreement signed giving them a lease of a house at Dorking, Chote Ghar, a name they quickly changed to The White Gates.

The house stands in a lane leading out of the main Guildford road with fields at the other end. It has a garden with flowering trees, an orchard, and tennis court: on the north side it meets the fields which slope to a little valley where a stream, overhung by alders, runs into a millpond. Beyond it, across another field, the railway lies at the foot of the Downs, the wooded, southern slope of Ranmore. Looking east, the ridge rises, beyond the town and the fine Victorian spire that gives an air to the otherwise poor architecture of St. Martin's Church, to Box Hill and the sweeping curve of Downs that continues into Kent. Westward, the ground slopes to the stream below a gentle line of hillside and copse, while a drove road cuts across the nearest field. It is a landscape inevitably composed by the lie of the land and the use man has made of it, gate, hedge, and haystack making up a foreground serene, spacious, and traditional.[1] The house itself had been built for summer occupation soon after the war. It has no architectural merit, being one big, galleried room surrounded by a corridor which in turn is surrounded by little rooms, those at the two

[1] Or so they did when Ralph and Adeline took the house, for houses built on the other side of the lane have now obscured the view, and both tennis court and field are built over.

south ends of the house having embryonic turrets at the corners, circular bays opening diagonally into the square rooms. From the outside they look most odd: inside they are pleasant additions, for with windows and window seats all round they caught any sun there was and were excellent sitting places. Ralph's study, facing west and south, had a french window opening into the garden, and one of these 'bulges' as he called it. In this he had a large kitchen table on which music accumulated, as it did on the window seat: under the tables boxes of manuscripts, music paper, and various odds and ends lay in confusion between tidyings up. Here he installed his little upright piano, wall bookcases brought from Cheyne Walk, a writing desk, and a huge arm-chair, as well as a lot of pictures, reproductions of Italian paintings that he liked, and two quiet landscapes by Ivor Gatty. The big room, known as the hall, held the huge grand piano, arm-chairs, and, at one end, the dining-table. There were some books, but most of them were in shelves in a gallery that ran round the room about ten feet above the floor, and provided a tremendous amount of storage space for anything not in immediate use. A loft over the garage was used to lodge ancient trunks and wooden boxes where Ralph kept band parts acquired for the Festival, as well as some gardening tools, apple racks, and cat baskets. It was a splendid house to spread themselves in, for there were endless places to keep things which then very quickly got lost.

Settling in was saddened by the news of Lucy Broadwood's death in August: she had been a friend for so long, an admired colleague, and an adviser in Ralph's work with folk songs.

In October there was a week-long Delius Festival which drew musicians to London, and Ralph realized just how much more bother it was going to be, however excellent the train service, for him to enjoy from Dorking the musical life he had had for the past thirty years. He loved the country for walks, expeditions, and bicycling—but to go back and live in it, which he had not done since he left Cambridge, was a very different matter. He had long felt himself essentially a Londoner, and he never ceased to miss the town life, the pleasure of wandering into the Tate Gallery for an hour, the river in front of his window, and most of all the Bach Choir rehearsals. Luckily he had many friends in London who were only too glad to have him to stay for a night after a concert, but this, though agreeable, was not at all the same thing as living there himself. But he accepted the new life, and tried not to regret the old.

Encouraged by Honorine, who had moved with them, Ralph had started to play tennis again, sometimes singles with her, sometimes doubles, when his brother Hervey came over from Leith Hill Place, or Honorine's friends were available to make up a four. His long legs and long arms compensated for lack of speed, and he enjoyed playing. He took his fair share of rolling, cutting, and marking the court: Mademoiselle's teaching of how to draw straight lines on paper seemed to have extended to drawing straight lines on grass. He also started to ride, a large enough, strong enough horse having been found in the local stables, and to his surprise he found he enjoyed this too, so long as his mount had a calm disposition and no inclination to gallop without the rider's permission, seldom given.

A pleasure that winter was reading Martin Shaw's autobiography, *Up to Now*, which had appeared that year and which both Ralph and Adeline found entirely delightful: they did not get on quite so easily with Robert Bridges's *Testament of Beauty*. Other books published that year which they read were *High Wind in Jamaica*, by Richard Hughes, Robert Graves's *Goodbye to all that*, and Lord David Cecil's Life of Cowper, *The Stricken Deer*.

Ralph had a great deal of work to do. The new works for the Leith Hill Festival Jubilee were being rehearsed, and he had been writing, among other things, a cello work for Casals who often stayed with Bob and Bessie Trevelyan at whose house Ralph must have met him many times. Casals played the *Fantasia on Sussex Folk Tunes* at a Philharmonic concert on 13 March, conducted by John Barbirolli, a concert at which Arthur Bliss presented Ralph with the Society's Gold Medal. It was not an altogether happy performance for neither he nor Casals was satisfied with the Fantasia. Ralph withdrew it and planned to rewrite it at some time, for he thought it had 'capabilities'. He was far happier at the next Philharmonic concert when Gustav was given the Gold Medal after Jelly d'Aranyi and Adila Fachiri had played his new *Double Concerto*.

The *Hymn Tune Prelude on Gibbons' Song 13* was written for Harriet Cohen whose playing he particularly admired. Three letters from composer to performer carry the story from the beginning to the eve of performance—they are all undated but the middle one was postmarked January 1930.

This is very sweet of you. *One* is finished, but I think one alone wd. be no use to you—the other is only howling in the air and has not been harnessed yet. But if you like I will send the one to you—I think you will probably hate it—and *you must be honest about it*

(1928 or 9)

Jan 1930

Alas—the other prelude won't boil I'm so sorry. Perhaps when I am in a calm mood later on and not scoring against time it will materialize

(postmark 7 Jan. 1930)

Dear Harriet

I know you will play it beautifully—no not too quick; and calm but with subconscious emotion—I *shd* love to hear you play it 1st—but my only day in London is Wed—at the R.C.M. Busy morning to night.

But I will come to the concert if I may.

(1930)

In May there was *Sir John in Love* at Oxford, with Malcolm Sargent conducting. Ralph and Adeline, Morris and Emmie stayed with the Fishers at New College. Gustav was in the audience, and Ralph made a speech from the stage on the last night. He dedicated the opera to S. P. Waddington, who had been a friend for many years and who had conducted the R.C.M. performance of *Hugh*.

The twenty-first Leith Hill Musical Festival was a week of rejoicing at the beginning of May. The new hall was not yet finished so the concerts still had to be at the Drill Hall which had succeeded the fire station as a concert room. Ralph's three new works were dedicated to the choirs who first sang them. Besides the Prescott-inspired *Benedicite* (a setting of the Prayer Book version of the Canticle with a poem by John Austin, the *Song of the Three Holy Children*) which he had written for the Town choirs, he gave *Three Choral Hymns* by Miles Coverdale[1] to Division I and a setting of the Hundredth Psalm to Division II. For Children's Day, a fairly recent addition to the Festival, he wrote three songs for which Fanny Farrer had written the verses.

[1] Adapted from German texts, two being by Martin Luther.

The programmes for each concert gave the names of the players in the orchestra, both amateur and professional, among them were Miss Bidder and Miss Lasker—Biddy and Vally—from the staff of St. Paul's Girls' School, both of whom had often played through new works in piano arrangement for Ralph, Dorothy Longman, and many local musicians, as well as young professionals who later became well known, many of whom continued to come year after year to make the Festival a reunion of friends as well as a musical occasion.

There was an unsigned note in the programme for each concert, ending:

> . . . and finally we have been blessed as we all know beyond anything we can record or even realise in our Conductor, Dr. Vaughan Williams, who has been ours from first to last, who has never missed a practice, a rehearsal or a Festival, and of whom a village chorus member once remarked—'He draws out of you what you know isn't there.' Could any Conductor desire, or be given, a greater tribute?

This was a year of tributes: the Worshipful Company of Musicians gave Ralph the Walter Cobbett Medal for services to the art of chamber music, and on 22 July at Swansea the University of Wales gave him the degree of *Doctor in Musica honoris causa*. When the Director of Music, Sir H. Walford Davies, introduced him he said:

> I am to present Dr. Vaughan Williams, by birth Welsh and English, a veritable British Composer, who speaks his own language to the enrichment of the world's music. . . .

CHAPTER X

1930–1934

Ralph started to write *Job* in 1927. Geoffrey Keynes had devised a dance scenario from Blake's illustrations to the book of Job and the whole undertaking became in a way a family affair, for the designs for scenes and dresses were done by Gwen Raverat, one of the Darwin cousins (as was Geoffrey Keynes's wife). When Ralph was invited to write the music the intention had been for Diaghilev to do the choreography, but he found the whole idea 'too English'—he and Ralph were never to work together. (By the time Diaghilev saw the Blake pictures and the stage models the music was already started, for the dramatic possibilities of the story had fired Ralph's imagination.) Ralph must have read and re-read *Job* in the Authorized Version of the Bible, for the splendour of the seventeenth-century English impressed its rhythm on the music. Years later he set words 'Then the Lord answered Job out of the whirlwind' to the tune he had written for the Galliard of the Sons of the Morning and they fitted with only the slightest of alteration. In the music of the masque the characters and scenes are clearly differentiated, the spacious heavens, the violence of hell, a Satan whose

> form had not yet lost
> all her original brightness nor appeared
> less than Archangel ruined, and the excess
> of glory obscured. . . .

the slithery and mocking saxophone that speaks for the Comforters and the fierce tunes for plague, pestilence, famine, and battle live between two pastoral landscapes, that of the beginning when Job is as yet untried and of the end when all he had lost is restored and blessed.

Ralph had insisted that it should be called 'A masque for dancing' rather than a ballet. Many difficulties of every kind arose during the time he was writing, and the consequent delays led to the decision to produce the music as an orchestral suite, to be heard first at the Norwich Festival. As a result, Ralph allowed himself to use a larger orchestra than he might have done for a stage work, as he did not have to think of the limitations of a theatre's orchestra pit. He had a wonderful time writing, really letting himself go, for he enjoyed thinking in terms of a large orchestra. Soon after he had completed the score it seemed that the Camargo Society was interested—Ninette de Valois and Lilian Baylis had seen the model sets and the scenario and realized their possibilities. On 31 July Ralph wrote to Vally Lasker:

. . . A pfte solo version of *Job* is wanted for rehearsing the dancers. Wd you feel inclined to undertake it? Something simple and practical —I know it can't be all got in but something that will give the essentials. I can't spare the full score—but I think it wd. be all right to do it off the pfte duet copy.

Ralph's mother, then eighty-seven, wrote excitedly about going to Norwich for the Festival in October (she was planning a holiday in Cornwall to follow) and the Keyneses, Gwen Raverat, and of course Gustav were in the audience when on 23 October Ralph conducted the Queen's Hall Orchestra in the first performance. He dedicated *Job* to his friend, ally and champion, Adrian Boult, though Adrian did not discover it until he came to conduct the work himself, and opening the score at his first rehearsal found his own name on the page.

Adeline's letters to Rosamond Carr gave an account of the first performance:

Herewith *The Times*—you see how less than lukewarm is Colles on *Job*, but I heard a rehearsal and know that I like it so I am not impressed. The Press were very unfavourable. . . . Capell in Daily Mail seemed to get it best—the programme was ill designed—the Janaček[1] very savage and noisy and *Job* came at the end, and already everyone was thinking of lunch as the time schedule had been worked out all wrong.

After Norwich Ralph went home to Dorking but he and Adeline spent November in London. On the 6th she wrote:

Our great event is over—*Sea Symphony* last night—it was fine. . . . Adrian Boult must be overworking he is nothing but a black streak

[1] Glagolitic Mass, translated by Rosa Newmarch, 1926.

in a white waistcoat—alarming—he is making a wonderful orchestra.[1] R fell in love with the drum—his deep notes. R goes to hear the Planets with Fanny tonight, tomorrow 'The Jealous Wife' at the Old Vic with Pegs. Also he is busy with the Morris Concert.

The concert of works by R. O. Morris was something on which Ralph had set his heart. He felt that R.O.'s diffidence obscured the real value of his music behind his reputation as a teacher and scholar, so he concentrated on making the evening a success to the last details, for Adeline wrote: 'We think Adila and Jelly must have some flowers'[2]: she told Rosamond Carr about it after they had gone home to Dorking:

We have been back 5 days after a most delightful and exciting London season. The climax was the Morris concert—lovely. We feel so satisfied—we were so happy about the music itself—the hall was almost brimming over—afterwards there was a party at the Edwin Fishers'[3] new house . . . you can guess how Uncle R. went 'all in' and when after having run the gamut of every delicacy and drink he came upon smoked salmon and began all over again. He was very anxious about the concert—looked a wreck.

Morris was angelic, a surprise to us all! It was most warming to my heart to see him on the platform bowing to the outburst of shouts and clapping—a real ovation, not a sham one at all—how well one knows the difference! Dorothy [Longman] gave a lovely tea party for us . . . just the perfect party, I did enjoy it all and so did R. Only he is glad to be in the country again and I see it is best to live amongst the cabbages and have an orgy now and then. . . .

When Ralph was in London he ordered some of his Christmas presents at Lamley's bookshop. He had a copy of A. P. Herbert's *Water Gipsies* posted to his mother. He had bought a copy as well for himself, which he started reading on the train—when he arrived home he rushed to the telephone to tell his sister to intercept the parcel for he realized that it was a book that would qualify as 'horrid' in the Leith Hill Place idiom. He and Adeline enjoyed it very much.

Ralph was preparing for the second performance of *Job*

[1] B.B.C. Orchestra.

[2] Adila Fachiri and Jelly d'Aranyi who played the Concerto in G minor for Violin and Orchestra and the Concerto for two violins and string orchestra.

[3] Youngest brother of Adeline and Emmie Morris.

which he conducted for a broadcast in February and at the same time was rehearsing the special performance of the *St. Matthew Passion* he had so long wanted the Leith Hill choirs to give, but which had been impossible in the Drill Hall. The Dorking Halls were at last finished and ready for the choirs to take possession. In this performance he wanted all three divisions to join together: it was to be an additional concert—as well as, not instead of, the Festival. It was planned for the end of March with a lecture on the music to be given in February with illustrations sung by the Dorking Oriana and the Dorking Madrigal choirs.

In January his sister Meggie had died and it was the wish of all her friends among the Committee and the choirs that this performance should be given as a memorial for her. Ralph accepted their wishes and concentrated on the music. By now the choirs had sung so many Bach cantatas that they were familiar with the idiom, and they caught Ralph's idea of the drama of the work—one listener who was at the performance wrote 'We went to the Dorking St. Matthew last night under R. V. W.—really amazing, the villagers sang as if they had known it all their life . . .'[1] For this occasion the choir was enormous, drawn from all three divisions of the Festival, nearly eight hundred singers taking part; so, though the new Hall was large, there was room for only five hundred people as audience. The soloists were Dorothy Silk, Astra Desmond, Steuart Wilson, Eric Greene, Arthur Cranmer and Keith Falkner, with Isidore Schwiller leading the orchestra. All were friends and colleagues on whom Ralph could depend absolutely. The memory that remained most vivid was the singing of the unaccompanied chorale 'Be near me Lord when dying' which he had rehearsed over and over again till he made the choir achieve a real pianissimo, a wonderful sound when so many voices were able to achieve the tiny crescendo like a sigh, a stillness of the world holding its breath before the Evangelist's awe-stricken—'and the veil of the temple was rent . . .'.

After this the choirs were let off lightly at the Festival, where no big choral works were attempted and the orchestra gave the major part of the concerts.

One of his summer occupations is recorded in a letter to Vally Lasker.

[1] Susan Lushington to Gilmour Jenkins.

I am vaguely thinking of taking up the viola again—have you got any idea of where my viola is?

Vally had already prepared the rehearsal score of *Job* which the dancers had been using for rehearsal. The Camargo Society realized that the venture would be expensive, but Geoffrey Keynes, his brother Maynard the economist, and Thomas Dunhill undertook the initial expenses. Constant Lambert made a reduced score so that the band could be accommodated in a theatre pit, and the venture went forward. Of all the people who wanted to see the Masque on the stage Ralph was the most impatient. There were some difficult situations, for he and Ninette de Valois, the choreographer, had different ideas on some points and Ralph was not asked to the early rehearsals nor allowed to go to them when he asked whether he might. Adeline told the story to Rosamond Carr.

R came back at 5 yesterday—he has had a glorious time at King's Weston[1] and is all the better for it. On his way through London he heard there was a rehearsal going on without music—so he went and found a few angels counting their bars and Job practising how to look like the Blake in a corner and a very nice young God on his throne (but God is to be called 'Job's spiritual self' on the programme!) Ninette appeared very tired—R. ventured to say 'you know this dance must have instruments carried by the dancers?'. She knew nothing of this but said 'I am sure you will be satisfied'. He was also surprised that she had not found out how large the angels' wings were to be and of what shape—so was at sea about the dance—R has gone up again today and I am sure he will do a lot to help things—but aren't they fools not to consult him from the first—for the stage is such a real thing to him and every bit of the music has its dramatic meaning. He finds they have got one picture out of sequence. . . .

A few days later, the story continued:

We had an exciting aftn. on Friday. Hon. and I went to full rehearsal of *Job*.

Of course a mixture as to costumes—but God had his mask on and the scenery looked beautiful—such a noble flock of painted sheep and Mrs. Job[2] was a joy to me—she realised her part like an actress—that is the trouble, the lack of dramatic sense in the dancing, and the smallness of the number of dancers—to me the music sounded lovely

[1] Staying with Napier Miles.

[2] Marjorie Stewart.

and made for dancing—not only the dancing that Ninette had invented. Still it's wonderful that she has managed it at all. Satan is a fine vigorous specimen and very handsome.[1]

'I understand that Blake intended Satan to be a handsome man?' he asked Ralph

'Certainly, a *very* handsome man'

He is to be painted green tonight. We saw him in loose trousers and a sort of Breton fisherman's cap. . . .

There is an extra rehearsal this morning and R has gone to it. He comes back for tea—and starts off again in his evening clothes to take Pegs's mother.[2]

These performances on 5 and 6 July at the Cambridge Theatre were given in Constant Lambert's rescored version. Three weeks later, during the Ninth Annual Festival of the International Society for Contemporary Music, the company gave a third performance at Oxford, where Ralph went to see it, but Adeline did not see a performance until September when the Cambridge Theatre production took its place in the repertoire of the Vic–Wells Ballet. Adeline wrote to Rosamond Carr:

Look out for a press picture of Uncle R. between Ninette clothed with bouquet and a naked Satan. We had a fine afternoon in our box. Orchestra cd. have been better, dancing much better, scenes mostly lovely. R. in London today, *Job* being shipped to the U.S.A.[3]

After this tour *Job* was regularly in the Vic–Wells programme, with Anton Dolin dancing unforgettably as the very handsome green Satan.

Besides all these excitements Ralph and Adeline had been driven by Honorine down to Chichester to hear Gustav's Whitsuntide Singers and Ralph had made some solitary expeditions on his bicycle 'a few cheeses in his pocket and means to be out till tea'.

Besides Honorine, a young nephew of Adeline's, Bob de Ropp, made The White Gates his headquarters for some years, and the house became tremendously full when Ralph's mother with her maid and her little dog, Joy, all arrived to stay after Ralph had

[1] Anton Dolin. [2] Mrs. Ritchie.

[3] An independent American production was also staged. Photographs were sent to Ralph and he greatly regretted that he had not been able to see this other interpretation of his score.

returned from Gloucester. It was Herbert Sumsion's second Three Choirs Festival there, and Alice, his pretty American wife, was already showing her talent for hospitality and the organizing ability which made her able to find rooms, last minute tickets, or anything else visitors to the Festival needed. Bernard Shaw was there. Ralph never thought highly of him as a music critic for he found him didactic and disagreed with most of his opinions. So Alice won his heart entirely when he and Shaw were both her guests at luncheon:

'You were late for the concert this morning, Mr. Shaw,' said Alice.

'Yes,' said G. B. S., unrepentant. 'And if it had been in Russia the orchestra would have stopped playing and said "Good morning, Comrade Shaw", before they started at the beginning again.'

'Good gracious,' said Alice. 'What a time the concert would take if they did that for everyone who came in late.'

And G. B. S. had nothing to say.

R. O. Morris and Emmie were there and Gustav for his *Choral Fantasia*, a first performance which had 'the worst press notices he had ever had'[1] but which Ralph found moving.

Besides writing, rehearsing the Leith Hill Choirs, teaching at the R.C.M. and attending the meetings of various committees of which he was a member—particularly those of the E.F.D.S.—Ralph had some gaieties during the winter, for he went to parties and theatres and even a thé dansant.

On 18 December at a celebration of the fiftieth anniversary of the foundation of University College, Liverpool, Ralph was given a degree of Doctor of Laws, *honoris causa*, and the public orator, presenting him to the Chancellor, Lord Derby, said:

In music, as in other arts, we have our innovators: who believe that to be original it is necessary to be difficult. Austere and self-denying, they pursue a strenuous and unlovely Muse along uncharted ways, and panting amateurs toil after them in vain. Ralph Vaughan Williams worships at the shrine of a less athletic beauty. His melodies and harmonies are not less original for being comprehensible. He is no mere imitator. He is the author of many works, songs and symphonies, choral works and operas, and they are all unmistakably his own. But his novelty is based in antiquity; growing freely, though rooted in the past. He is a scholar as well as an artist, a learned, though never a

[1] *Gustav Holst* by Imogen Holst. Oxford University Press, 1938.

pedantic, musician, he has refreshed our memory by his study of the early music of our country, folk song and the formal compositions of the masters created when delight in ordered sound was common among us. He has woven the old colours into new patterns.

On Christmas Day Rosamond Carr went to the White Gates—Ralph read the *Christmas Carol* aloud between tea and supper. On Boxing Day he left for Cardiff and from there he went to a Welsh mining village to conduct *Toward the Unknown Region* and the *Four Hymns*. The concert was in one of the distressed areas where times were desperately hard, but the singing was magnificent and the hospitality touching in its generosity. He sat up late talking music over cups of incredibly strong tea. When he came back, the E.F.D.S. Christmas School had started and he went to London each morning to take the singing.

On New Year's Day Gustav came to Dorking to spend the day with Ralph who was battling with a new symphony, and on 6 January, two days before Gustav sailed for America, they had another field day with Vally and Biddy translating Ralph's manuscript into sound.

His own story of the genesis of his Fourth Symphony was that he had read an account of one of the 'Freak Festivals' in which a symphony, he couldn't remember who had written it, was described in some detail. Like the myth of Beethoven and *Fidelio*, his breakfast-time reaction was an immediate '*il faut que je compose cela*'. So, without any philosophical, prophetic, or political germ, No. 4 took its life from a paragraph in *The Times*.

It has often been said that this work is related to the period in which it was written, and, though this must be true to some extent of any work by any composer who does not cut himself off from contemporary life, no one seems to have observed how far more closely it is related to the character of the man who wrote it. The towering furies of which he was capable, his fire, pride and strength are all revealed and so are his imagination and lyricism. He was experimenting with purely musical ideas; no sea or city, no essence of the country was at the heart of this score and what emerged has something in common with one of Rembrandt's self portraits in middle age.

Besides the symphony and intermittent work on *Riders to the Sea* which he had also discussed with Gustav, Ralph had made a Cantata, *In Windsor Forest*, from *Sir John in Love* for the Leith

Hill Festival (though the first performance had actually taken place in Windsor on 9 November 1931). He was beginning to feel that this might be the only chance for his operatic music to be heard, and that all people wanted was 'the plums and no cake'.

He did not go to the Kensington Festival in March—probably one of his heavy colds prevented him from being there to help by judging or conducting as he usually did—but he kept a letter from some of the competitors, the choir that had written to him for his fiftieth birthday and who remained devoted.

> We, the Mothers of St. Agnes Mothers Meeting, want to thank you very much indeed for your kind messages and to tell you how dreadfully we missed you on Thursday night. There were lots of us there, nearly forty, and it was a lovely evening. The other gentleman was nice, but we did miss you. We hope you will soon be quite well, and shall look forward to seeing you next year.
>
> Your grateful friends
> The Mothers

Much of the summer was spent in work on a series of lectures, for he had accepted an invitation to spend the autumn term at Bryn Mawr, Pennsylvania, where he was to give the Mary Flexner lectures. For his theme he took National Music in its widest sense and he used the opportunity to develop and crystallize into precise and definite shape many inter-related ideas about music which he had not, until then, put into writing.

Gustav returned from the United States at the beginning of June and in September both he and Ralph conducted at Worcester where the *Hymn of Jesus* was part of the programme in which Ralph's *Magnificat* for contralto, women's chorus, and orchestra had its first performance. It honoured a promise made at Gloucester a year earlier. Steuart Wilson had said, 'It is not quite nice that young unmarried women like Elsie Suddaby should always be singing *Magnificats*'. Astra Desmond, who was there, said to Ralph, 'I'm a married woman with four children, so why don't you write one for me?' He said he would.

He told Gustav that he was trying to 'get the smugness out of it'. He felt that daily liturgical usage had hidden the emotion of the words, and he was pleased when his brother said, 'You see it as a picture by Fra Angelico'. Later he explained that he thought of the flute as the disembodied, visiting spirit and the alto solo as the voice of a girl yielding to her lover for the first time.

A few days after leaving Worcester he set out for America. It was ten years since his first visit and this time Adeline stayed at home. He wrote to Maud Karpeles:

> Here I am on the last day of my sea voyage—I find I'm a *good sailor*—the waves were said to be bigger than they've been for 2 years—and I went to the look-out place high up and watched the ship plunging—it was superb—the sun came out occasionally and the huge rollers all blue and green and white were magnificent. Otherwise very comfortable but very dull. . . .

> College Inn,
> Bryn Mawr. Penna.
>
> Dear Gustav,
>
> Why didn't you tell me that Una[1] is here?—I only found out by accident—she is the Light of my Eyes and the Joy of my Heart and my Guardian Angel and has taught me the techniques of shopping and gave me a delicious supper all cooked by herself.
>
> I had a splendid 2 days with the Davisons[2]—they were both so nice—and while in Boston I went to i) a football match and ii) Boston Symph. Orch; both suffer I think from being too much organised. Tonight I shall hear Phila. Orch. and on Monday N.Y. Orch.
>
> I am feeling very happy here and everyone is v. hospitable—I went to a music store in Phila. yesterday and was introduced to the Manager—it was just like a chapter out of Martin Chuzzlewit.

Archie Davison[2] introduced him to Koussevitzky after the Boston Symphony Orchestra's concert, and when Ralph was asked which of his own works he would like to hear the orchestra play the answer was—'With that string section I would like to hear the *Tallis Fantasia*'—so he did, and almost the entire orchestra stayed to listen to the rehearsals, instead of making their usual escape and leaving the string players to it.

There was one time-difference in living in the United States which caught him out on several occasions—when a train was due to arrive at 6.30 he supposed that he would arrive suitably for a meal with his hosts, only to find they had eaten at 5.30. By bedtime he was desperate and when offered whisky he had

[1] Una Lucas—one time head girl of St. Paul's Girls' School.
[2] Archibald Davison, 1883–1959, American musicologist.

to ask for a biscuit to go with it. The next time he went for a visit he had a large meal on the train, arriving at 6.30 to be met with the words 'We kept back the dinner for you——'

He found the Bryn Mawr students' choir, directed by Ernest Willoughby, and Horace Alwyne's piano playing provided admirable illustrations to the nine talks the Mary Flexner Lectureship required, and he enjoyed rehearsing with them. The staff and students were delightful; they looked after him, amused him, and comforted him in the homesickness which gradually beset him, for suddenly the two months seemed as long to him as they were feeling to Adeline, in Dorking, and he began to count the days till he could return home.

He was near the end of his stay when he met Gustav's brother.

I've met Ernest Cossart[1] at last—it was all perfect—he was playing in Phila. and asked Una and me to dine and come on to the show.

We picked up again at once after 30 years and reminisced as hard as we could—then we went on to the show—a very good amusing play—and he was absolutely perfect in it—funnily, *on the stage* he kept on reminding me of you.

Just before leaving he wrote to Maud Karpeles again:

I am for the moment in N.Y. staying surrounded by luxury at the expense of some old friends. I had a wonderful experience at the top of the 'Empire State', first, sunset over the river and all the skyscrapers suddenly lighting up, then all the street lights came out and the moon. New York looked more classically and tragically beautiful than ever. I've got time here next week to talk to the E.F.D.S.—I thought it was going to be a cosy little affair and now I find they've invited all the musicians of N.Y. and I've got to talk for 3/4 of an hour! too bad. . . .

I start home on Dec. 3rd and v. glad I shall be though I've had a good time here.

He was home for Christmas and home in time to conduct his *Fantasia on Christmas Carols* at St. Paul's Girls' School with Gustav, who had taken up the trombone again, playing in the orchestra; in time, too, to conduct as usual at the annual Albert Hall entertainment given by the English Folk Dance and Song Society who had recently elected him their President.

[1] Stage name of Emil von Holst.

While he was still at Cheyne Walk, in 1926, Ralph had written two movements of a piano concerto and put them away till he could think of the right ending. Before the move to Dorking, when his study, like the sea, had given up its dead, this work floated to the surface, and in 1930 he had written the last movement—with some 'temporary stopping'. As usual, the music staff at St. Paul's came to his aid and played it through for him. But it was 1933 before the first performance, given on 1 February by Harriet Cohen, with Adrian Boult conducting the B.B.C. orchestra. Though Ralph did not love the piano, and did not easily think pianistically, he said that while he wrote his concerto he had the Busoni transcriptions of Bach very much in mind, for that was the way he wanted to write for the piano. Here was another puzzle for the critics—Frank Howes wrote:

> Vaughan Williams has a way of disconcerting his admirers with every new work of any size—there could be no more reassuring sign of artistic vigour and mental growth.

From the *Pastoral Symphony* onwards it was to be like this—no sooner did his hearers think they had summed up their composer than he, like Tam Lin in the ballad, changed from fire to water, from beast to bird, from air to flesh.

The Stinchcombe Musical Festival had become much larger and had grown from six to eleven choirs during the twelve years of its existence. Diana Awdrey, still organizing secretary and inspiration of the affair, asked Ralph to come and conduct for them. She sent him the programme, with her invitation—or command—and he answered:

> What a wonderful and complete programme! Does Herbert[1] really want me to conduct *Requiem*[2] *and Saul*?[3] Also 3.30–4.30 is rather short shrift for the *Requiem* which takes 45 minutes to *sing through*. Also couldn't we achieve just one little double bass? What a lot of 'alsos'? I know however how things are and won't complain! It will be lovely to come down again. I will come by the 8.15 Padd. if I may.
>
> Love from Uncle Ralph.

The Leith Hill Festival was at the end of April, and in May Ralph and Adeline decided to buy The White Gates where so

[1] Herbert Howells, Festival Conductor.

[2] Brahms Requiem.

[3] Handel.

far they had been tenants. They were also able to buy the adjoining field on which they planned to build a bungalow for Ralph's mother who felt happy with Adeline to whom she had always been devoted. Hervey and Constance were now living at Leith Hill Place.

The house was so full that Ralph moved from his study to the garage room where he worked at his symphony. He played tennis[1] and enjoyed haymaking until nearly the end of June. On the 27th he came home late after a day in London, it was a lovely moonlit night and he walked home taking the short cut through the field where the path runs beside a stream. No sooner had he left the lighted road than clouds covered the moon and he went too near the edge of the path, slipped and fell into the water. It was only a two-foot drop, but he hurt his ankle, and lost his hat. He managed to crawl home; he found he could not put any weight on his foot without excruciating pain, and the next day X-rays showed that he had cracked the fibula in two places. He spent the next few weeks in splints, and then hobbling with the aid of a crutch.

He realized that he was not going to be able to work upstairs for some time and he decided to spend his leisure in learning to play the clarinet. He advertised for a teacher, the advertisement was answered by a Miss E. Darbishire whose visit he awaited with some trepidation, for her letter had been rather severe. At the appointed time a lovely young girl arrived at his bedside, looking like the incarnation of spring. He discovered that she was a singer though she also played the clarinet. She was a good teacher but, sad to say, her pupil turned out to be untalented for the instrument in spite of the practising she forced him to do, for she was a firm disciplinarian. She and her sister were soon accepted as friends, and out of his lesson times were gay and frequent visitors. At the end of July Adeline was writing to Rosamond Carr about their building plans, adding sadly: 'Ralph blows his clarinet but gets no-way.' However his ankle was sufficiently better for him to be walking with a crutch in early August, and by the 31st he was able to conduct the *Pastoral Symphony* at a Prom. He went to Hereford where he stayed with the Bulmers for the Three Choirs Festival where he was greatly

[1] Ralph told Cedric Glover that he had played singles with Tovey who won: date of this match unknown.

cosseted. Everything was more enjoyable as the weather was wonderful. He conducted the *Three Choral Hymns* and *The Shepherds of the Delectable Mountains*.

Adeline wrote to him there, 'Don't be anx. I so trust the Sheps. will shine out as it ought to do', but this performance convinced him that it was a stage work and 'didn't do' at a concert.

On 9 September he went to the wedding of Barbara Lawrence who had been the Hon. Assistant Secretary of the Leith Hill Festival for the past four years. She married another neighbour Taffy[1] Gordon Clark and for her wedding present Ralph wrote an organ piece, *Passacaglia for the bride on B.G.C.* He enjoyed the reception afterwards and described her younger sister Naomi 'wandering about the garden in her bridesmaid's dress with a champagne bottle in her hand looking like a bacchante'.

They had given up the idea of building a bungalow in the garden and instead they were having an annexe added and various alterations made to the house. Adeline managed to write to Rosamond Carr from the midst of turmoil:

> We are having the devil's own work in trying to get the house ready for builders—for R and I are pledged to go to the sea with his mother on 12th . . . builders said to be coming on 18th and we go to Constance's[2] flat straight from Eastbourne for 6 weeks or till we can get in here again—I've never tried such a complicated pack before—beds and furniture to flat and putting away here.

They came back for a few hours on 16 September for the wedding of Gerald Finzi. He had been known to Ralph as a composer since the Carnegie Trust published his *Severn Rhapsody* in 1924 and they had met him when he was R. O. Morris's pupil for a short time. They knew he was unhappy in London, where he taught at the Royal Academy of Music, so, whenever they went away from Dorking, he had the use of The White Gates where he stayed and worked. He had often brought Joy Black and her sister to see them, and Ralph enjoyed playing tennis with these two tall and beautiful girls. Both he and Adeline had become very fond of Gerald, they admired his music, his great knowledge of English poetry, and his love of the countryside,

[1] Who later became Judge Gordon Clark, alias Cyril Hare, author of many detective stories.

[2] Hervey Vaughan Williams's wife.

and Joy with her many talents seemed a perfect companion for him. So they welcomed the idea of the wedding as one they could wholeheartedly approve. On their side, the 'young people' as Ralph always called them, felt that 'Uncle Ralph and Aunt Adeline' were the friends they would like to have at their marriage. They did not know how amused Ralph and Adeline were when Joy, given her marriage lines by the Registrar, said matter-of-factly that she would put it away with her dog licence. They all sat among the dust sheets for coffee and cakes, then went their respective ways. But Ralph and Adeline were greatly touched when two little maple trees arrived for the garden as a present from the young marrieds to the long married.

They spent October and November in London; and Ralph made several journeys to see how the building operations at The White Gates were getting on; by Christmas the house was habitable again, though the additions were not yet completed. In February they stayed in London again because there was a performance of *Job*, and Ralph had another broadcast to conduct. Gustav, who had not been really well for a long time, was in a nursing home, and this was a good opportunity to visit him.

At the beginning of March, Ralph was among the many musicians who went to Worcester for Elgar's Memorial Service.

> .... joining Steuart and Agnes Nicholls on the journey ... R loves Agnes Nicholls and was delighted to find that Steuart does too—their conversation (S & AN's) was largely on suet and its uses—both very good cooks. R. liked the Worcester Service tho' it was overlong. He missed the 'special' back, went to the wrong station, but by so doing had tea with the Sumsions, got home at 9.[1]

Strangely enough Ralph had been preparing *Gerontius* for the Leith Hill Festival before Elgar died. He had long wanted the choir to learn what he considered one of the century's most important choral works and, excitingly, arrangements had been made for the performance to be broadcast on the National programme.

Ralph asked W. H. Reed, who had been associated with

[1] Adeline to Cordelia.

Elgar at the Three Choirs, to lead, while Isidore Schwiller gladly took second place for this occasion. Steuart Wilson, Astra Desmond, and Harold Williams were the soloists, Elgar's daughter was among the audience and both she and Hugh Allen wrote warmly. But perhaps the most interesting letters came from two performers W. H. Reed and Steuart:

I feel I must write to you to express my feelings about the splendid performance of *The Dream of Gerontius* at the Leith Hill Festival.

I thought it was truly remarkable that a choir, composed as it is of separate units from the various towns, should produce such a marvellous ensemble when massed as they were for the Festival.

The entrance of the semi-chorus in the first Kyrie was most moving —remote and with such a lovely shade of tone—the sound stole upon one's senses as from another world.

The intonation was so good,—it was surely an achievement to have kept the pitch so well throughout a long and trying work, especially in all the softer passages and those calling for 'mezza voce' and restrained singing.

I feel too that I must congratulate you personally, if I may presume to do so, upon getting a sensitive and well balanced rendering, and for imbuing it with that spirituality one always felt when Sir Edward himself conducted.

I must say I was completely uplifted from beginning to end, and I felt that as long as his works are handled and given in the way that you and your splendid choir gave *The Dream*, so sure am I that these works will live.

I have to thank you too for giving me the opportunity to take part in a memorable performance.

Love from
Willie H. Reed.

Steuart wrote:

I didn't have time to discuss with you how marvellous the Choirs were in *Gerontius*. I think it was the best possible [proof] of Ruskin's dictum that music ought to be the art of saying what you feel deeply in the strongest and clearest way. I so often hear a 'bigger' performance in quantitative standards, but never a more feeling one in qualitative standards. It was a marvel of freshness of appreciation too. It's easy for us war-horses to key ourselves up with *technical* means to reproduce our first enthusiasms, but chorus singers haven't got these means, so when you hear something you know that it means that they are feeling it at *that* moment.

The worst of these high water marks is that one doesn't know what to do next——

Just before the Festival Ralph, who seems to have taken on some of Gustav's work at St. Paul's Girls' School, wrote to him in the nursing home:

March 17th

I am so glad we went yesterday. It was all Adeline's doing, she suddenly said 'Let's go' so we telephoned for the old Dorking taxi and set off for London.

Rose Morse was superb—she really is a genuine lieder singer (only of course she doesn't wobble or sing out of tune, which I understand is a fatal defect in a lieder singer). She made me understand the songs[1] for the first time and now I love them.

I'm still not quite there with the canons.[2] Vally was wonderful and played splendidly, so did Biddy but Vally has got more dash in her playing though not so sure.

As regards your title 'Brook Green'[3] I'm not so sure—won't it suggest a descriptive piece?

Tomorrow is Tertis and your viola piece[4]—I hope my wireless will not go wrong.

While Ralph was absorbed in the Festival, Gustav had decided that, as diet and rest had not affected a cure, he would accept the risk of a major operation: if it succeeded he would be able to do all that he wanted, and the alternative of a minor operation and restrictions on everything for the rest of his life was not to be considered. He rested, saw his friends, listened to music and tried to build up his strength for the operation, but his heart was not strong enough for the ordeal, and he died on 25 May.

His death meant loss for very many people; beyond his immediate circle of friends there were those to whom he had given music by his teaching, as well as by his writing. Although Ralph had to some extent been prepared for the possibility of his death, he had not tried to imagine what life would be like without his friendship.

[1] Gustav's settings of Humbert Wolfe poems.

[2] Canons in Three Keys: Settings of Mediaeval Latin Lyrics translated by Helen Waddell.

[3] *Brook Green Suite* for strings.

[4] *Lyric Movement* for Viola and Small Orchestra.

Writing to Isobel and Imogen, he said:

> My only thought is now which ever way I turn, what are we to do without him—everything seems to have turned back to him—what would Gustav think or advise or do——

The funeral service at Chichester Cathedral was on Midsummer day; Gustav's Whitsuntide Singers sang, as they had so often done before, his music and Ralph's and music by Weelkes, near to whose memorial his ashes were buried.

CHAPTER XI

1934–1939

Soon after Gustav's funeral Ralph spent a day walking in Sussex. The weather was hot and eventually he reached the coast and bathed. He cut his foot on a piece of broken glass or a sharp stone and, though it seemed slight damage at the time, it did not heal, and before long he had a poisoned abscess—unfortunately it was on the leg he had broken the year before. He wrote to Maud Karpeles:

> . . . I am sitting up for the 1st time for a 4tnight. Its perfectly absurd because I am feeling perfectly well—but I have not been allowed to move for fear of the poison spreading. I am so glad the school went well and I will come to Wargrave (wherever that may be) on Sept. 16th.
>
> . . . Poor Austria—I wonder what is going to happen—this looks like the break up of everything with Mussolini thundering at the door—the funny thing is that it seems to be our pacifist party in England who are crying out for us to intervene!
>
> Running Set is the one at the Proms (if the world is still there) on Sept. 27th.

A little later he wrote to her again:

> It's awful—but there is just a chance I may not be able to come on the 16th. I had to have the wretched thing opened up again about a week ago and though all goes v. well yet he won't promise any date at which I shall be moveable—tho' personally I think it is quite safe for I *shall* be well.
>
> Now shall I write a screed for you to read if I'm not there—or is that no use?—and anyway *what* am I to write about—*do* help me—I've not an idea in my head—don't say 'what you like' that's no use to me——

He was in bed for eight weeks. He was not in the mood for writing, and the physical limitations of a bed table made working on any big score out of the question, but, when he was offered a commission to set some verses, *The Pilgrim Pavement* by an

American writer, he accepted. He did not like commissions, but he thought that it might be good discipline to have to do this, and finish it in time for a winter performance in New York, so he struggled with what turned out to be uncongenial material. Later he tried to withdraw it, but was unable to do so.

One of the occasions he was very sad to miss was the Abinger Pageant for which E. M. Forster had written the programme notes and the narrator's speeches for a scenario provided by Anne Farrer and Tom Harrison who was also the producer. It began with the Farrers' shepherd, who really was called Damon, driving his flock of sheep across the scene. Ralph had composed and arranged the music, which included a tune he loved (and used again in his *First Nowell*)[1] *Angelus ad Virginem* and his own *O how amiable* which was later published and is dedicated to Fanny Farrer. It was wretched to have to give up his part in the pageant for he had been able to conduct only a few early rehearsals, and David Moule Evans conducted the performances in mid-July.

It was the summer in which John Christie gave the first Festival at Glyndebourne, a two-week season of *Figaro* and *Cosi fan Tutte*, but Ralph was not able to go, nor was he well in time for the Three Choirs Festival, which, without Elgar and without Gustav, who had become a familiar figure during the last few years, was a bereft occasion.

He wrote to Vally Lasker on 20 September:

> I find SPGS (and nothing else) in my diary for Wed. 26th—wd. you write a card and tell me what time I said I wd. be there and what I am to do when I arrive?

The day after this nebulous engagement he was able to conduct at a Prom, very largely devoted to his own works. He made a romantic appearance on the platform, leaning on a stick, and he had to sit to conduct both the *London Symphony* and the 'quodlibet' which he had made of English dance tunes for *The Running Set* and to which it had been danced at the E.F.D.S. Albert Hall performance in the winter. The audience enjoyed the high spirits and completely danceable music, for Ralph conducted dance music in such a way that it was hard to sit still. He followed this with a fine performance of his *London Symphony*, but he could not help wondering whether the 'great ovation'

[1] 1958.

reported by the papers was for his music or for the fact that he was very lame and obviously having difficulty in getting off the rostrum, and was a tribute to a sporting effort.

Friends and colleagues of Gustav's from St. Paul's Girls' School continued to lend their skill and time to Ralph's needs—would Vally arrange his 'Orchestra and pfte concerto for pfte?' would she 'spare ½ an hour to go through alterations in the symphony?' and how wonderful of Nora and Vally to have remembered his birthday.

In November he and Adeline stayed in London for one of what they called their 'seasons' at the Eversleigh Court Hotel in Cromwell Road. The reason for this visit was the first performance of Ralph's viola suite, written for Lionel Tertis and played by him at the Courtauld–Sargent concerts on 12 and 13 November, with the London Philharmonic Orchestra conducted by Malcolm Sargent. It was a work he had found difficult to write; a year earlier he had written to Peter Montgomery—'my viola suite is not finished—I do not know if it ever will be'—but it had materialized at last.

That winter Ralph was given the John Clementi Collard Life Fellowship—a single award held previously only by Sir Edward Elgar and given '*honoris causa* for outstanding services to British music'. John Barbirolli was conducting operas at Sadler's Wells: Robert Helpmann had a great success dancing Satan in *Job*; there were the first performances of William Walton's unfinished symphony; and *A Boy was Born* by Benjamin Britten, then aged twenty-one, was published. But on the continent there were sinister portents; the November number of *The Music Review* reported an attack on Paul Hindemith in *Die Musik* and commented: 'The folly of confusing music and politics is not only childish, it is tragic. Dr. Furtwängler whose word carries some weight in musical matters in Germany has published a protest against the application of political standards in the world of art.' It was still officially a time of peace, at any rate in England, but elsewhere a time that was beginning to make demands of heroism.

Early in 1935 Ralph's Bryn Mawr lectures were published under the title of *National Music*. He said that all his 'friends and relations' who had been quite calm when he wrote symphonies and operas suddenly became excited and sent each other postcards saying 'Ralph has written a book' and treated him with great respect because of it. Though this amused him, he was pleased by the reviews in both the English and the American papers, but he wrote to Imogen Holst:

> Thank you very much for your nice letter. Those lectures are only what I have been spouting for the last 20 years—now they've appeared in print I shall never be able to spout them again.

There was a story he liked to tell of a friend who said to him how much she had enjoyed a lecture he'd given—'I love it,' she said, 'and I nearly know it by heart.' But the fact was that, however often 'the lecture' was given, some new idea was added, some new thought or illustration came into its substance. It was perennial only in the same way that a plant is; recognizable as the familiar growth but with fresh flowers every year.

At the Albert Hall the E.F.D.S. festival on 5 January ended with several hundred performers dancing Sir Roger de Coverley. Ralph and Arnold Foster conducted the evening's music, and it was not unknown for Ralph to hand his baton to the other conductor or to Maud Karpeles and to slip off the platform to join in the general dancing for the last ten minutes. For the evening ended with one of the easier dances—usually *Sellenger's Round*, the other name for which is 'the beginning of the world' as it is said to be the tune to which the stars danced on the morning of the creation. These festivities were usually followed by a party, where Ralph was counted on to tell stories and Maud Karpeles to sing a ballad, her favourite being an extremely long one called *The Bloody Gardener* which everyone enjoyed and no one more than the singer.

Morley College had planned to build an extension, for it had long outgrown its premises; but the years of depression had made it impossible to find the means. In 1935 the Board of Education and the London County Council agreed at last that a building project postponed in 1931 might proceed, and the music department, staff, and students, as well as many other musicians, decided that the small hall already planned should be equipped as a music room as a memorial to Holst, the kind of memorial they believed he would have approved. Ralph was the Chairman of the Committee formed to raise the necessary money. He was very active, attending meetings, writing letters to the Press and to private people who might help, and sending leaflets all over the world. He also helped to organise recitals to raise funds. The Holst memorial concert on 26 January, conducted by Arnold Foster, was a spur to all concerned. Ralph's share in the work went on for many months, though most of the letter writing was concentrated in the beginning of the year.

He was busy too with the final preparations for the first performance of his fourth symphony. In the programme note he said that it was begun in 1931 and completed in 1934. With him the word 'completed' had an entirely fluid meaning for changes were made in details throughout the next thirty years. This was his first work without Gustav beside him all the way, and he felt the loss of that loving and critical mind more deeply than ever. Arnold Bax, to whom he dedicated the symphony, gave advice—at his suggestion some bars were omitted—and R. O. Morris was able to help with details. But the greatest ally was Adrian Boult, from whose rehearsals with the B.B.C. orchestra he learned that he had written what he intended to write, and that it came off.

Ralph and Adeline, Honorine and Rosamond Carr stayed at Eversleigh Court, Ralph flitting between rehearsals in London and festival rehearsals at Dorking, and filling up the intervals with gadding. He heard Walton's symphony, a performance of *Savitri* at the R.C.M., *The Travelling Companion* at Sadler's Wells, he took Rosamond and Honorine to see *Escape Me Never*, and went off on his own to a Chinese play. Of the symphony, Adeline wrote to her sister Cordelia:

> The symphony is emerging—and now I couldn't bear you *not* to hear it!—last week I thought I cdn't bear anyone to hear it! It was wonderful to get the 1st movement going this morning. It's powerful—I ought to have had more faith.

Many composers had come to rehearsals and all sorts of rumours were about. Arthur Benjamin reported, 'I met Willy Walton on my way to the Hall and he said—having been to rehearsals—that we were going to hear the greatest symphony since Beethoven'. On 10 April it was an exciting performance, excitedly received. Back at the hotel, hungry as he always was after concerts, Ralph had some supper, and said that Adrian had *created* the second movement—he himself had not known how it should go, but Adrian had. They all went to bed exhausted. The next day the papers were full of the symphony, praise, dismay, surprise, admiration, and more dismay. Then letters started coming, from strangers, from friends, the best of all from Adrian himself:

I think you saw what we all felt about the symphony—if there was inspiration about the performance it was the *work* that put it there. And if I got the bit between my teeth it was simply because the music made us feel like that. You know I feel that it is all very well for conductors to have their readings when works have taken their place in the repertory. While they are new it *really* is his business to absorb the composer's mind as much as possible—his own will emerge later—in fact, all too soon usually. And though it is harder perhaps (difficult anyway), I feel there is no excuse for a conductor, who at a first performance causes a composer to say 'very interesting, perhaps, but not my work'. In R.C.M. days we spent most of our time on conducting accompaniments—I always used to say it was easy to do symphonies. So don't worry if I ask too many questions—the thing will shake down after a performance or two—and then you may cease to recognise it!

Patrick Hadley and Balfour Gardiner shared a postcard—half each—from Montmajour, and Balfour Gardiner wrote: 'Paddy declares it has knocked Europe sideways.'

Back at Dorking Adeline wrote to Rosamond Carr:

Yesterday we went to the Delius ceremony at Limpsfield[1] such a lovely day—the first—such buttercups. Limpsfield would have been nice on any day but it was seething with cars and sightseers—our car pulled up in a shady lane where I was left—I saw quite enough. Beecham spoke very well. We brought a tea basket with us and had it when we got clear. R. goes to Cambridge and Bristol this week.

George V's Silver Jubilee was celebrated all over the country. Ralph had conducted singing out of doors at the Dorking rejoicings and part of a concert at the Albert Hall arranged by Walford Davies, who had succeeded Elgar as Master of the King's Musick. On 17 May Ralph had a letter from Buckingham Palace which worried him considerably.

Private & Confidential

Dear Dr. Vaughan Williams,

By command of the King I write to say that it would give His Majesty much pleasure to confer upon you the Order of Merit in the

[1] Delius was buried at Limpsfield as he had wished, since burial in his garden in France was not possible. He died at Grez-sur-Loing 10 June 1934.

Birthday Honours Gazette, in recognition of the distinguished contribution which you have made to the music of our time.

I shall be much obliged if you will kindly let me know at your earliest convenience whether this proposal is agreeable to you.

Yours sincerely,

Clive Wigram.

Ralph had been offered other honours, but he had not felt able to accept them, he preferred to be 'plain Mr.—Dr. if you prefer it' but the O.M. was another matter. This order, of which there are only twenty-four holders at any one time, was instituted by Edward VII in 1902.

After some thought and long discussion with Adeline, who said to her sister 'it's the only recognition I could bear for him', Ralph accepted, and his name appeared in the Birthday Honours List. The announcement was followed by many letters of congratulation. To his friend and publisher Hubert Foss he wrote:

One word of thanks for your letter—the good wishes of friends is the best part of all this business.

To his old friend Bobby Longman—who had written the other way round, saying it was the O.M. to be congratulated in making him a member:

I've already said 'thank you' but I want to say so again.

You know all the secrets of my heart—so I won't be sham-modest to you. But this sort of thing makes one wake up at night thinking of one's sins.

On the day of the investiture Ralph dressed at the R.C.M. and went to the Palace with Hugh Allen who was appointed G.C.V.O. Adeline wrote 'R. was conspicuous at Buck. Pal. by his plain outfit—which is now allowed—evening dress coat, white waistcoat, plain cloth breeches and court shoes. We had a dress rehearsal and he looked very fine——'[1]

The Farrers gave a party to celebrate the O.M.—there was a crown for Ralph, music, and feasting, with many of his friends and singers from the choirs.

He had reached what must have seemed the peak of his life. His music was widely known, his fellow musicians knew he was a

[1] To Rosamond Carr.

man to whom they could turn when authority was needed in any cause; he had many friends, a comfortable income augmented now by royalties, and, except for a liability to catch cold, his health was excellent. Most important, he had an unending flow of musical thought and invention. His work absorbed him and, because he taught and conducted and went to as many concerts as possible, he had the constant stimulation of exploring the works of other composers, including those of his own students.

His life at home was shared with a wife devoted to him, whose interest in his music had grown deeper, more critical and more helpful through the years. She was able to discuss technical problems with him and he respected her judgements.

In spite of her arthritis, Adeline was still able to go about in their car, driven by Honorine. She often preferred to go to rehearsals rather than to performances, especially if the performances were broadcast and she could listen at home. With the help of a crutch she was still able to walk in the garden. She was very thin; the cool beauty of her youth had changed to gaunt and austere age. Her back was straight, her head beautifully set on her shoulders, and her heavy eyelids in their deep sockets lifted to show pale blue eyes where amusement could flash or fury blaze, though she usually looked at the world with gentle irony. Pain had taught her stillness and she had a quality of heroic endurance that could be intimidating. Though she could melt into friendliness there were tremendous barriers of reserve that froze between her and people she did not like. She was devoted to Ralph's mother who, with her maid and her little dog, spent most of the year at The White Gates, and who still looked on her son and daughter-in-law as her 'dear children'.

During the spring and summer Ralph was immersed in his 'Skelton oratorio'. He enjoyed himself with the words, for he found the short lines were apt for tunes. There were two chief characters in his scheme, Drunken Alice and Jane Scroop, both to be sung by a mezzo soprano, and by choosing this voice Ralph was able to suggest both the sottish old client at Elinor Rumming's tavern and the very young girl at her convent school, mourning the death of her pet sparrow in an elegy of liturgy and nursery rhyme. Skelton as the source of a text for his music had been suggested to Ralph by Elgar and his friend Colonel Isaacs at one of the Three Choirs Festivals. Colonel Isaacs had suggested a short poem (which he did set, but years later[1]) but Elgar said that an oratorio on Elinor Rumming would be more fun.

On 20 June Adeline wrote to Cordelia:

Ralph has just rough-finished his work for Norwich 1936 and is revising his symp., for Oxford Press is thinking of engraving it.

Besides the Skelton settings he had two other big works in hand. One was his comic opera *The Poisoned Kiss*. He had thought that one of Richard Garnett's short stories, 'The Poison Maid', had the makings of a light opera and in 1927 he had asked Cecil Sharp's sister Evelyn, later the wife of Henry Nevinson,[2] to write a libretto. She took the story more portentously than Ralph had intended, 'too much of the triumph of love,' he said, rather depressed: but some of her subsidiary characters were excellent inventions and her lyrics were thoroughly settable. It was a gay work, with a proper hero and heroine; a sub-plot for an older near-villain, the heroine's father, and an Empress-student-of-magic, the hero's mother. There was a sub-sub-plot for their attendants and of course a soubrette maid and a valet-courier who could have been great-great-great-grand-niece and nephew of Susanna and Figaro: the last scene promised a mass marriage for all of the characters. The music belongs to the world of operetta, demanding polished singing and accomplished acting from pretty women and handsome men.

His other work belonged to a very different mood. The picture of Europe was a dark one. The Dictators were declaring their aims and intentions. Though Mussolini had drained the Pontine marshes and caused Italian trains to run to time, cleared the slums of Rome and built splendid stations and blocks of modern flats for the workers, his threats in other directions were clear enough. More horribly, the Nazis were dividing the world between Aryans and Jews in hysterical discrimination against some of their greatest citizens. Musicians, artists, writers, scientists, doctors, and people in every walk of life were suddenly dispossessed. The great exodus began, and racial and political refugees poured into England and America to the enrichment of both, for they brought the wealth of their talents and the

[1] Prayer to the Father of Heaven. 1948.

[2] 1856–1941. War Correspondent, essayist, humanist: a friend of Ralph's (through the E.F.D.S. in whose work he was deeply interested). He was the father of the painter C. R. W. Nevinson.

generosity of their belief that these two nations stood for the freedom of the human spirit.

Among the poems by Whitman which Ralph had set to music before the First World War was the *Dirge for two Veterans*. This became the starting point for a new work in which he used two more poems both of which, *Beat, beat drums* and *Reconciliation*, came from Whitman's experiences during the American Civil War. To these Ralph added sentences from the Bible and from a speech by John Bright. All were linked by a soprano voice whose repeated, imploring '*Dona Nobis Pacem*' gave the cantata its name.

In spite of the darkness covering the land, some international occasions were still possible. The International Folk Dance Festival at the Albert Hall in July brought to London teams of dancers in brilliant and decorative national costumes; and, to everyone's happy surprise, the I.S.C.M.[1] Festival took place at Prague as planned. At the Three Choirs Festival Ralph conducted *Sancta Civitas*—some passages in the ten-year-old work seemed to have a terrible appositeness:

> The kings of the earth and their armies were gathered together to make war against him that sat upon the horse and against his army and were slain. And all the fowls were filled with their flesh. . . .

Less than a month later, on 3 October, the war between Italy and Abyssinia began.

When George V died in January 1936, Adeline wrote to Cordelia:

> You may chance to hear R's setting of these lines tonight—I don't know where they are to be fitted in—Walford Davies asked him to write something last Thursday—at first R said he couldn't then a few hours later he found these lines from *Samson Agonistes* and in 24 hours it was done—Sat. morning they were engraved and Walford rang up last night to say he had rehearsed the chorus and it would be done some time tonight—O how I hope it will sound all right—I believe it will—and aren't the words good and right?

> Nothing is here for tears, nothing to wail
> Nothing but well and fair
> And what may quiet us in a death so noble.[2]

[1] International Society for Contemporary Music.
[2] Words adapted from *Samson Agonistes*.

Because of the King's death almost every woman in London wore black. Ralph said that the country should stay in perpetual mourning as all the pretty girls looked so admirable in their dark plumage, and the less beautiful looked better than usual.

Both Ralph's fourth symphony and *Job* were among the works played to European music critics who had been invited to England by the British Council; they were also given an Elgar concert and were taken to Oxford and Cambridge. Ralph was having his usual busy spring with the Leith Hill Festival, and as soon as it was over he dashed to Cambridge for the final rehearsals of *The Poisoned Kiss*. He enjoyed himself very much both there, where it had a week's run, and afterwards at Sadler's Wells on 18 May at the invitation of Lilian Baylis. The critics found the libretto laboured but praised the music. Unlike his other operas, it uses spoken dialogue, but his singers were able to manage this beautifully, and Ralph hoped that it would 'catch on'. But it has never had a fully professional performance.

He had been making still more revisions in the *London Symphony*, involving new cuts in the Epilogue; the revised version was tried out at a concert given by the First Orchestra at the R.C.M. conducted by Constant Lambert. The Huddersfield choir was preparing *Dona Nobis Pacem*, and Ralph went there for a rehearsal on his way to Hereford for the Three Choirs Festival. Adeline wrote to him:

> It was heavenly to have yours—1) from the train on way to Hudders,—and by 2nd post yours from Hereford. I feel so certain about Dona *itself*—but remembering the Leeds choir singing Gustav's Keats I do expect that they are not sensitive to words or pp. . . .
>
> I'm so glad you have such a lovely view and I'm sure all is gay—look upon it as a holiday as much as you can and be easy in your mind about all here.

He had only one short new work for the Festival that year, *Two Hymn Tune Preludes*, for small orchestra, but he conducted his *Pastoral Symphony* and *Viola Suite* as well. As soon as he had finished at Hereford he had to be in London for a Prom. devoted to his works on 14 September. Imogen Holst had a letter just after it:

> How dear of you to send me that message—they played magnificently. I hope the book goes well. I have been thinking of two things

Gustav once said to me. I don't know if he ever wrote them to anybody—I hope he did for they ought to be recorded.

1) about Aristocracy in Art—art is not for all but only for the chosen few—but the only way to find the few is to bring art to everyone—then the artists have a sort of magic signal by which they recognise each other in the crowd—he put it much better than that—but that is the gist.
2) that the artist is born again and starts again with every fresh work——

This was certainly true for Ralph, and when on 25 September the first performance of his *Five Tudor Portraits* took place at St. Andrew's Hall, Norwich, some of the audience were much surprised. Ralph conducted and the soloists were Astra Desmond and Roy Henderson. The elderly Countess of Albemarle sat in the front row getting pinker and pinker in the face and, when the pink turned to purple, Astra Desmond, thinking she was going to have a heart attack, was about to lean down from the platform and offer smelling salts. But before this aid could be given she rose to her feet, said 'Disgusting' loudly and clearly, and marched out of the hall. When Ralph was told about it afterwards he said it certainly showed that the choirs' diction was good, and added reflectively, 'A pity she didn't read the lines I didn't set. . . .'

A week later Ralph was in Huddersfield to hear Albert Coates conduct the first performance of *Dona Nobis Pacem*. The soprano's cry for peace gave the work a topical overtone that it has never lost.

The work was broadcast, and among those who heard it and wrote to Ralph to praise it was Ernest Rhys, the old Welsh poet. He had spent most of his life working for Dent's the publishers for whom he originated and edited The Everyman Library which made the great literature of the world available in shilling volumes. His was a specially interesting letter for he wrote not only about *Dona Nobis Pacem* but also about Whitman whom he had visited as a young man.

It was a difficult winter at The White Gates, for Adeline had fallen and broken her left arm early in October, and throughout the autumn Ralph's mother had seemed to be fading away. She had survived many illnesses which had seemed likely to be her last, but this time even Adeline had come to the conclusion that she would die. At the beginning of December Hervey's wife,

Constance, was found injured and unconscious just outside the gate of Leith Hill Place having been knocked down by a bicycle —she died on 3 December, and Hervey came to stay at The White Gates to be with his mother. Seeing her son's distress, Margaret rallied and, to everyone's amazement, determined that she must get well so that she could go back to Leith Hill Place and look after his household. It took many weeks to achieve, but she did it, though it was not until the end of May that Adeline wrote, 'The miracle has happened—R's mother has gone off waving her hand and smiling—I can believe her living on and on with the Great H [Hervey]—only he mustn't be the first to die—no, perhaps I'm wrong—I can see her living on alone in her old home having outlived us all.'[1]

On 27 January Adrian Boult with the B.B.C. chorus and orchestra gave the first London performance of the *Five Tudor Portraits*. *The Times* critic wrote:

> Since the appearance in 1935 of the severest of his orchestral works, the symphony in F minor [publications] have included such diverse things as the comic opera *The Poisoned Kiss* and the dramatic fantasy *Riders to the Sea*—which we have not yet heard. These and other works have created the impression that while Vaughan Williams' tone of voice is recognisable among living composers, one never knows what he will be at next. The voice may be used for good converse on any subject that comes his way.

This was natural to Ralph, for he was absorbed in each work as it came along, whether it was something he wanted to do, or something he was asked to do; just at that time he was in fact asked to write a number of works, including the *Flourish for a Coronation*, conducted by Beecham on 1 April, and the *Te Deum*, commissioned for the Coronation in May. He wrote the *Flourish* for a tremendous orchestra, determined that as he was asked to give it as a contribution to the festivities, at least as many orchestral players as possible should be paid for their part.

He went to the Coronation wearing the academic robe he had inherited from Alan Gray. He already possessed his 'O.M. court shoes'—and his large velvet hat had come with the robe which had

a cunning pocket for sandwiches . . . he said the sight was splendid, he would not have missed it . . . sorry you didn't hear the *Te Deum*; it

[1] To Rosamond Carr.

was good R said, it fitted in with the procession as the King and Queen came out during it—R. was much too interested to feel hungry.[1]

Before this they had had a happy festival at Dorking, with Parry's *Judith*, a concert version of *Carmen*, and, most fun of all, *The Blue Danube* arranged for singers. As Bobby Longman had once said:

To me, and I believe to a large proportion of singers, the Festival week is the happiest and best in the year—Thank God, thank you, thank Fanny and thank music.

There was a revival of *Hugh the Drover* at Sadler's Wells and the Whitsuntide Singers chose St. Albans that year, where Ralph joined Bobby and Dorothy Longman for the week-end. Then at the end of May he and Honorine were guests of the C. in C. Portsmouth—Adeline's brother Sir William Fisher—for the Coronation Review.

There was the getting off of R. and Hon. for the Naval Review. car 8.15 a.m. to London, train to Portsmouth—then back the same way arriving home at 4.30 a.m. with rain tumbling down and birds singing. They had a lovely time—plenty of pets for R. and wonderful hospitality, they returned brown from the day at sea.[1]

They went on enjoying themselves, Ralph was at Cambridge examining and staying with Edward Dent for two days, then, on 1 June:

Today we've had a great expedition to Wheatfield—over the Chilterns—R with all his maps. R and I love Wheatfield where we spent some summers and it's lovely to find a place that does not change—home by 8.[2]

The happiness did not last for Adeline. William Fisher became ill—so much work had fallen on him during the coronation celebrations.

She wrote to Cordelia:

You know as I do doctors are limited in their powers—the only hope is in the nature itself and the will to live. How we would give

[1] A. V. W. to Rosamond Carr.

[2] A. V. W. to Rosamond Carr. (1) May 28, 1937; (2) June 1, 1937.

our strength to keep him . . . we must all hold together all the closer . . . I get on with my packing for . . . I can then be free to move at a moment's notice. . . .

He died on 24 June and Adeline felt her world diminish.

In July Honorine drove her and Ralph to Gloucester for the preliminary choir rehearsals for the Festival. When he went in September to conduct *Dona Nobis Pacem* in the cathedral and the overture and one of the songs from *The Poisoned Kiss* at the Shire Hall, Ralph met Kodály who was there as a guest conductor.

Dona Nobis Pacem was sung at the Leeds Festival too, this time conducted by Malcolm Sargent who also conducted *Riders to the Sea* at the R.C.M. in December. But when the music was heard, Maurya's words, 'No man at all can be living for ever, and we must be satisfied' must have sounded like an epitaph for Ralph's mother. She had died on 20 November, ninety-five years old, a widow since she was thirty-three. Her life had bridged so many changes, so much history, and she had watched it all with alert and informed interest. Frances Cornford remembered her[1] 'walking with her stern profile and her lace cap, moving even when quite elderly like a young woman and with a kind of free dignified grace, of which I am quite sure she was unaware and which gave her carriage its especial quality——' She belonged to a very different world from Ralph's—Frances Cornford, observing from a family vantage point, saw the 'deeply evangelical austerity against which Ralph revolted with passion' as well as the serenity, hospitality, and grace of her life. She had been an ideally suitable mother for him, and there had been a lifelong mutual affection and respect between them which made a bridge even where understanding was lacking.

Another death that winter was that of Ivor Gurney. He had been born and brought up in Gloucester, where he was a cathedral chorister, and he had come to London as a scholar at the R.C.M. looking like a young Schubert. Wounded, gassed, and shell-shocked in the war, he had returned to the College afterwards until his health broke down entirely. The rest of his life was spent in mental hospitals, though he was still able to write and compose at times. Among the poems written in those years some lines blaze among the rambling and repetitive pages, and from them, as well as from his songs, the scope of his lost talent can be

[1] *R.C.M. Magazine*. Easter 1959.

guessed. Once, during the early years of his confinement, he escaped and came to Cheyne Walk, imploring Ralph not to send him back to hospital, for he minded lack of freedom more than anything. But the search for him would have made anything Ralph could do unavailing, though he felt like a murderer when he telephoned to say that Gurney was with him. Throughout all the years in hospital, Ralph and sometimes Adeline visited him, wrote to him and sent him books and maps which he loved. Ralph helped whenever there was any question of getting works published or performed. Marion Scott, another musician, was his good angel, and Herbert Howells a most constant friend, while Gerald Finzi, who had never met him, became his champion. The nursing staff grew very fond of this gentle and melancholy patient, and did all in their power to make his life tolerable—which it could never be without freedom, and that had become an impossible hope. The January 1938 number of *Music and Letters* had articles by Marion Scott, Sir John Squire, Walter de la Mare, Edmund Blunden, Herbert Howells, and Ralph written in his honour. The proof copy was brought to him just before his death on 26 December.

At this time Ralph was preparing music for another pageant, which E. M. Forster had written. They shared a passionate dislike of the ribbon development and the shoddy building that was encroaching on the countryside. They worked together to prepare the pageant for the Dorking and Leith Hill Preservation Society. Ralph was also starting another symphony—using music that had been accumulating for a full scale opera on *The Pilgrim's Progress*, which he felt he would never finish. He was going through one of those dark patches when he felt he would never write again: there are sentences in letters about 'having dried up'. But this followed a year of hard work, the growing apprehension about the political situation, the death of Gurney, which must have recalled the waste and desolation of the 1914 war, and his mother's death. He had also had to make a decision which brought international political problems into his own life. He had, during the previous summer, received an offer of the first award of the Shakespeare Prize, given by an anonymous Hamburg merchant, one of three prizes designed for annual award for work of conspicuous merit in music, literature, painting, sculpture, and architecture. It came to him through Professor

Fiedler, Professor of German and Fellow of Queen's College, Oxford, who wrote:

It would make me very happy if you would accept, and thereby make English music better known and appreciated in Germany.

Ralph wrote a summary of his thought:

I have never yet accepted a money prize though indeed I have never yet been offered one! and my first inclination is to refuse in spite of the great honour which this offer implies. But I feel that the honour is offered, not so much to me personally, as to the whole of English musical art. Therefore I must put personal questions on one side. Indeed this honour to English music is so unprecedented that I want to make sure that it is made only from a desire to recognise art and learning in this country.

Now, though I wish to avoid the personal side of the question, I feel bound to explain that I am strongly opposed to the present system of government in Germany, especially with regard to its treatment of artists and scholars.

I belong to more than one English society whose object is to combat all that the present German *régime* stands for.

Therefore am I the kind of person to whom a German University would wish to offer a prize?

I cannot accept this great honour without satisfying my own conscience that I shall not feel in any way hampered in the free expression of my own opinion in accepting it.

His formal acceptance is dated 16 August 1937.

Please forgive my delay in coming to a decision, but I feel that the great honour which the University of Hamburg asks me to accept is more than a personal matter, being in fact a gesture of recognition to the whole art of music in England through me as one of its representatives. Therefore I found it necessary to consult with others before deciding.

You have answered me that this honour is offered purely in the cause of art by a learned body to a member of the English musical profession; that it implies no political propaganda and that I shall feel free as an honourable man, if I accept, to hold and express any views on the general state of Germany which are allowable to any British citizen.

In these circumstances I have pleasure in cordially accepting the honour offered to me in your letter.

His acceptance was announced in the autumn, and there were congratulations. He wrote to Hubert Foss:

> Thank you very much, I thought I must accept, though honours from Germany are not what they were.

But by February 1939 Ralph's music was on Hitler's black list. Adeline wrote then to Rosamond Carr 'His music has been banned in Germany owing to his anti-Nazi propaganda. Pure moonshine of course—we haven't an idea of the reason except that his name appears on many Cttees etc.'

I must now come to my part in this story—I had seen *Job* in the 1932–33 season while I was a student at the Old Vic. Before this I had heard very little music and had not much enjoyed what I had heard. Visually *Job* was familiar for I knew the Blake illustrations, but the music was a new world, and I was completely overcome by it. For the next five years I thought of writing to the composer, though I never made any particular effort to hear any of his other works. This was partly because, after that glorious break away into a different world, I had returned to army life, in which I had been brought up and into which I married. My husband, Michael Wood, was at that time a Gunnery Instructor and our life was nomadic. By 1937 I had written a ballet scenario on the Ballad of Margaret and Clerk Saunders, and I screwed up enough courage to send it to Ralph at the R.C.M. where I had been told he could be found. His answer was disappointing:

> Dear Madam,
>
> Many thanks for your scenario. It seems to me more suitable for miming to accompany a recitation or singing of the ballad. However, I am sending it on to Mr. Kennedy of the E.F.D.S. to see what he thinks
>
> Yours faithfully

So, at Mr. Kennedy's invitation, I went to see him at Cecil Sharp House. He was interested, kind, and ready to persuade the composer—who would have nothing to do with Clerk Saunders. I suggested Spenser's *Epithalamion* as a possible alternative subject.

Douglas Kennedy wrote:

I have heard from Vaughan Williams and I have offered to make a dance scenario based on your scenario for Vaughan Williams to base his music on—this sounds as fantastic as the film world.

He quoted Ralph's letter:

At last I return the ballet scenario. It seems to me entirely dependent on what you as a choreographer can make of it . . . would you suggest a *reciter* to recite the necessary lines? This might be a new art form and interesting. I should love to do a ballet with you—though I warn you that I feel absolutely dried up at present and have the feeling that I shall never write another note of music.

This triangular correspondence went on through January and February, Douglas endlessly patient, I endlessly impatient, and Dr. Vaughan Williams difficult. At last I asked Douglas to suggest that the composer took me out to lunch, as the letters were enough to drive us all mad. My husband was stationed in the Isle of Wight then, but I came to London fairly often. So on 31 March we met. I do not know which of us was the more surprised. He had, it seemed, expected a sensible matron in sensible shoes; I had not expected him to wear a green pork-pie hat such as I had seen only on cavalry subalterns; nor had I, I think, expected someone so large and so beautiful. We went to a restaurant where the prices on the menu seemed enormous; I looked at his very ancient burberry and said that I hoped he didn't mind me asking, but I had always understood that composers lived in garrets, and Lyons would be perfectly all right for me. He promised that our luncheon would not cause him to starve for the rest of the month, so we started to enjoy ourselves. At that meeting we talked mostly about poetry—I told him I had been turned out of singing class because I couldn't sing and it was in *Linden Lea* that this was detected—which pleased him as much as the fact that I knew other Barnes poems. We drifted into a cinema to see the latest Disney Silly Symphony and we ended up sitting by the Serpentine and talking about madrigal poems.

A week later he sent me the two Bullen anthologies—this was followed by a long letter:

I meant to have written long ago, but I wanted to send you those Bullen books—the bookseller has only just sent them. . . . I do not dare undo the parcel because I should never be able to do it up again—so it goes as it is (I hope it is the books I meant!) . . . Then I wanted to send you a copy of 'The sky above the roof' (D'un Prison) but I've not got a copy of that—so the fates are against me.

I loved having your poems . . . the 2 1st verses of the Verlaine seem to me very good—v 3 I am not quite sure about 'seduction'—it seems prosaic—but that is perhaps because it has been spoilt by the daily press. Just as you don't like Bridegroom and Bride—in which I quite disagree with you. If we are to give up all beautiful words which are prostituted by the *Daily Mirror* our vocabulary will be very small. Think of

'the voice of the Bridegroom and the Bride shall be heard no more in thee'

I had a long journey to Liverpool and back the other day and thought a lot about *Epithalamion*—my ideas are crystallising—one thing I feel more and more certain the Bride and Bridegroom must not *dance*, they must move and mime (not too much) to a background of dancing—but I will write more when I have got it more fixed—or perhaps we shall meet—when?

Ralph's own spring was busy as usual, with Leith Hill rehearsals—*Dona Nobis Pacem* was one of the works that year—and visits to Cambridge for *Riders to the Sea*, Oxford for *Sancta Civitas* and *Benedicite*, and he came to London for the Music and Life Congress held by the Contemporary Music Society at which he spoke.

He also wrote to *The Times* in support of a work he had greatly admired:

Your unfavourable notice of a choral work by Willy Burkhard performed at a contemporary music concert at Queen's Hall last Friday prompts me to venture to express my opinion that we have here a remarkable, often beautiful and often deeply moving composition. It seemed to me that evening to stand out amid a waste of arid note-spinning as a genuine and deeply felt expression.

I ought perhaps to add in case my opinion should cause the composer to lose face among his fellow 'contemporary' musicians that he is fully as capable of inventing lacerating discords as any of them. But these discords come from a genuinely emotional impulse and not from a desire to outshine one's neighbour in hideosity.

I hope that one of our choral festivals will perform this work, having previously revised the present English translation.

He was making a liturgical setting of the Holy Communion, but this was interrupted by Henry Wood's request for a work for his Jubilee concert. 'He wants something for sixteen soloists,' he told me in a telephone talk, 'I've always wanted to set the Jessica and Lorenzo scene from the Merchant of Venice.' 'Eight Jessicas and eight Lorenzos?' I asked—'No, just a little bit for each voice,' and so the *Serenade to Music* was written.

Another business that occupied a good deal of time that summer was concerned with copyrights in folk music to which many committee meetings at Cecil Sharp House were devoted, and on which thorny subject there was a deep division of opinion among the members. Ralph did his best to bring them together although the opposing points of view were irreconcilable. Though he could be practical he found the argument tedious, and only a strict sense of duty kept him from resigning from the work.

He was worrying about his journey to Hamburg to receive the Shakespeare Prize. Just before he left, we spent an evening together when we saw the Ballet Jooss at the Old Vic. He loved their kind of dancing but their famous political ballet *The Green Table* was not an entertainment to put his heart at rest before his visit to Germany.

He left on 11 June with Professor Fiedler and his daughter Herma. I had a letter on the 14th about an opera he had seen, but the magic words in it were 'by the way, I copied out practically all of *Epithalamion* before I left England'.

On the 15th he received the prize in the Musik Halle where the Stadt Orchester, conducted by Eugen Jochum played the *Tallis Fantasia* and the *London Symphony*. There was also a large dinner, followed by many speeches. Ralph said that, the day before, he had visited Brahms's birthplace and that he had seen at Lubeck the organ played by Buxtehude and J. S. Bach and had realized anew what musicians all over the world owed to Germany, the land of musical giants. He was deeply conscious of the honour paid to English music whose representative he was that day and he had great pleasure in thanking the University of Hamburg both for the prize and for their cordial reception. The prize was rather in the nature of fairy gold, for he could not take it out of the country. When they first heard of it he and Adeline had thought of buying pictures or a splendid car or even diamonds but he could not have taken these out of Germany any more than the cash. Nor was he allowed to give it to the Quakers for relief work, so it had to be left in a bank.[1] When the ceremonies were over he was very glad to leave Germany where, by being very British and very formal, he had avoided giving the Nazi salute or saying Heil Hitler.

He told me about it when we met for a dance at Cecil Sharp House, and by this time we had begun to know about each other's home life. He told me about Adeline, Honorine, his family, his upbringing, the cats, and the garden as well as about the Pageant which was at that moment involving the household, Honorine as a performer, and Adeline, as well as all who helped in the house, as part of the audience at both performances. Ralph, after seeing a dress rehearsal, had left to go into retreat. In spite of 'having dried up, and being finished and never writing again', he was conscious of the stirrings of a symphony; in fact he had put a preliminary sketch for part of it into the pageant music as a try-out. Adeline wrote to him reassuringly:

> Even if compo. doesn't come the new scenes and the quiet will sow some seed.

The next day she reported the second proofs of the *Serenade* had come and the following day they were sent to him. 'I've skipped through, corrections seem to me to be all right—so glad you will take a day off and perhaps get in a visit to Salisbury as well.'

He wrote to me:

> I am on the Wiltshire downs—and the hermitage is succeeding I think—but I must confess that the other thing has taken precedence of Epithal . . . you know I can't do things unless I think I ought to be doing something else . . . I have been wonderful walks on the downs—they were perfect—sun, high wind and wonderful July field flowers—the kind I like best.

The flowers were all along the verges of the road when he walked into Salisbury after tea one day. He arrived hot and dusty and had dinner, then about nine he went to the Close and found Walter Alcock at home, busy with his model railway. It was

[1] He received a cheque after the Second World War.

quite late when he asked if Ralph would like to hear the organ in the cathedral. He played Bach while Ralph listened in the dark empty building.

It was a particularly beautiful summer, and the fine weather lasted till the Three Choirs Festival. Adeline wrote:

R is at Hereford and says he's enjoying himself—burnt his new grey trousers the 1st evening at the Hulls' backing into their electric fire, I sent him another pair.[1]

Once again it was *Dona Nobis Pacem* that he conducted while, as Mr. Churchill said, 'The whole state of the world is moving steadily to a crisis that cannot be long delayed'. On 29 September he conducted a serene performance of the *Pastoral Symphony*. In the days before the Henry Wood Jubilee Concert on 5 October, Mr. Chamberlain had returned from his third visit to Munich. But on that evening, in the *Serenade*, night in the garden at Belmont laid its balm of starry words and moonlit music on the audience gathered in the Queen's Hall to celebrate the man whose work had meant so much to musicians and public during the last fifty years.

Two days later Sir Henry wrote to Ralph about the *Serenade*:

We are so excited to hear from Columbia that they are going to record it. . .

What a charming little book Imogen has written about her father's life, finished it last night in bed.

Again accept my warmest and deepest thanks for the *Serenade*, it did raise my Jubilee concert out of the ordinary rut and lent real distinction to Part II. . . .

Imogen had sent a copy of her book to Ralph;[2] he had watched its growth and written a note at the beginning of it for her. He found it an admirable biography, a model of what such books should be, with all the indexes, chronologies, lists of works, and dates a reader could need: all matters about which he felt strongly, and he was happy to give it wholehearted praise.

Early in December Ralph's life was a whirlwind rush round the country.

[1] To Rosamond Carr.

[2] *Gustav Holst* by Imogen Holst. London. OUP. 1938

R came back so becolded from Newcastle he had to go to bed and I felt in some agony at letting him go this morning first for a long day's teaching, then a night train to Edinburgh—rehearsal for *Sea Symphony* tomorrow and concert. Tovey has to keep to his bed and asked R to come.[1]

It was a worthwhile journey, not only because he was delighted to be able to help his old friend in a difficulty, but because of the quality of the performance: he wrote:

My dear Donald F——

Thursday night was *electrifying*—even if we'd had six rehearsals together it would have been very good—as it was, it was *miraculous*. Roy Henderson called it the best performance he had ever heard, and he has heard a good many. Both your chorus and orchestra are so *musical*—and I know to whom they owe that.

The Dorking Committee for Refugees from Nazi oppression started work in December; Ralph was naturally one of the first people asked to join and he took a full share of work. He went to all the meetings, wrote many letters, raised money for particular cases, and visited frequently—usually once a week—the house which the Committee had acquired to lodge some of the refugees. Refugee work was centred at Bloomsbury House in London where both Maud Karpeles and I were helping. He wrote to Maud to thank her for her Christmas present; and asked, 'Have you met my Ursula who I believe was coming to you for refugee work?' We had indeed met, and we both enjoyed it when Ralph took us out for luncheon—he took me on to listen while he conducted singing for the E.F.D.S. Christmas vacation course, because he discovered that I did not know any folk songs and he had planned a programme of his favourites. He took me to the E.F.D.S. ball and the next evening to a party after the Albert Hall performance, in which everyone else there had been taking part. He was quickly settled into a huge sofa, with several beauties squashed in each side of him and became 'Uncle Ralph in tremendous form', telling stories and obviously feeling happy. It was apparent that everyone, men and women, loved him, and that immediately he arrived at a party it lit up and took on a glow because he was there enjoying himself. It was enchanting

[1] 7 Dec., Adeline to Rosamond Carr.

to feel this warmth and affection filling the room, emanating from him and surrounding him.

On 21 January the Menges Quartet, with two extra players, gave the first performance of his *Double Trio* at the Wigmore Hall. Adeline wrote to Rosamond Carr:

> I had a wonderful day in London yesterday—for a rehearsal at Wigmore of the double Trio—they played it finely and I liked it very much—it was written here, 1938. Then lunch at Eversleigh and back again to Wigmore where in the morning I had discovered the right place for myself. All the works, Dvořák, R's and Mendelssohn had their various beauty. Dorothy and Bobby were in the gallery and there was a reasonably good muster for a rainy Saturday aftn.

Ralph himself was dissatisfied with the work, though the players had liked it; he felt he had chosen the wrong medium, and that it should have been on a larger scale.

Though the symphony was still the background of his thought, Ralph was thinking of an opera about Belshazzar, and he asked me to type the libretto for him—'and to get to work and translate it into English—we will meet soon and talk about it.' This we did, in a milk bar before a concert. There we suddenly realized that we were being stared at from all the other tables. When we had gone in, the place had been empty so we had taken all the salt and pepper pots to stand for priests and dancing girls, courtiers and prophets, and then the place had filled up and the customers wanted salt and pepper. Somehow this project never got any further than that one conversation though a few sketches for the music, some of them from many years before, remain.

The very day that conscription was brought in Ralph had arranged a play-through of *Epithalamion* at Cecil Sharp House, the score, for string quartet, piano, and flute, had been copied and the parts made. Joseph Cooper was the pianist, Eve Kisch the flautist, and the quartet were four young players, Ruth Pearl, Irene Richards, Jean Stewart, and Vera Canning, who had recently formed themselves into the Leighton Quartet. Maud Karpeles met us, and she and I sat together while Ralph conducted the players, steering them through and correcting the inevitable discrepancies in their copies. At the end of the morning Ralph took us all out to lunch at Pagani's and, while we were eating our zabaglioni, Toscanini came in—we felt at the

Q

centre of the world of music and at the peak of happiness. The next day continued in the same way, for I went with Ralph to a rehearsal of *Hugh the Drover* at Sadler's Wells, then to hear the Tudor Singers rehearse.

All through the country people were filling sandbags, trying on gas masks, and listening to news bulletins. However, the London Music Festival went on, opening with a service at Westminster Abbey at which Ralph's *Festival Te Deum* was sung. He and Adeline had slipped away for a jaunt:

> We had 5 most lovely days—three nights at Cheltenham and 2 at Oxford—felt quite drunk with the spring beauty and the Cotswold country——[1]

On 13 May they were at Sadler's Wells for the double bill of *Hugh the Drover* and *Job*, where we all met, for my husband had just come back from three months in Jamaica, where he had been doing experimental work on rockets, and Ralph had sent us tickets.

Ralph's next amusement was a visit to Cambridge to see his 'clarinet professor'[2] sing Idamante in a performance of *Idomeneo*, and in June he went to Dublin to receive an Honorary Doctorate of Music at Trinity College. There was a dinner party afterwards, and the girl who sat next to him said in a delicious brogue, 'You composers are all so impotent.' 'Are WHAT?' said Ralph, ready to quote chapter and verse in defence of the honour of his profession. 'Ah! sure, it's impudent I mean,' she said, quailing before the light of battle in his eyes.

English translation was very much in his mind that summer. He had planned to conduct the Beethoven *Choral Symphony* at the next year's Leith Hill Festival: he wrote to Professor Fiedler, who had been his escort at Hamburg and with whom he had made friends.

> June 25th.
>
> Can you help me with a literary problem? I remember being told some years ago that when Schiller wrote his Ode '*An die Freude*' (9th symphony) he intended originally to put 'Freiheit' but the Freedom being in Germany as unpopular then as it appears to be now he was obliged to alter it to 'Freude'.
>
> Can you tell me anything about this and/or could you tell me of any books which I could consult?

[1] To Rosamond Carr. [2] Elizabeth Darbishire.

at the beginning where soloists & chorus
sing

Freude
Sing then
Joyous

Freude
sing then
Gladness

one can't say "Joy-oy" we usually
do "Sing then" — But one want
the idea of "Joy" yet for the
beginning — I think "Joyous gladness"
would do for the opening then
when the tune comes in one can

An example of R.V.W.'s handwriting.

If we could prove it, it would make the English version much easier since 'Freedom' is two syllables like 'Freiheit' and 'Joy' is only one syllable—also an ode to Freedom would be something much more inspiring then an ode to Joy.
Love to Herma.

July 3rd.
Thank you very much for your present. I have already dipped into it not only for 'Freude' but for other poems as well.

I fear I must give up my Freiheit idea—though that would have fitted all the verses that Beethoven employs. The difficulty occurs only right at the beginning where soloists and chorus sing

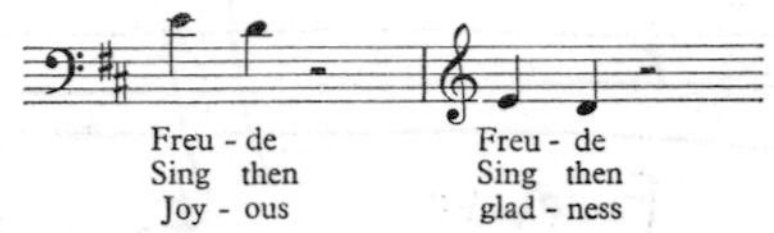

One can't say 'Joy-oy' we usually do 'sing then'—but one wants the idea of 'Joy' right from the beginning I think 'Joyous gladness' would do for the opening then when the tune comes in one can say 'Joy thou daughter' etc. . . .
Love to Herma.

In July Ralph and Honorine went to *Don Giovanni* at Glyndebourne, and the whole party from The White Gates came up for *Sir John in Love* at the R.C.M., a very lively performance with Denis Dowling splendid as Falstaff. Plans for *Epithalamion* were far enough advanced for the College wardrobe to have promised to lend clothes—'How many pairs of white tights?——' and for the cast to have been given rehearsal dates, when Ralph wrote to say Douglas Kennedy could not undertake it as he might be going to America:

I feel so sorry about it—not so much for my music which, if it is good, can wait its time and if it is bad had better not be heard, but for you and the whole thing. I liked the idea of you and me and Douglas all working together—if that cannot be achieved I do not feel inclined to push it. . . . It will be lovely seeing you at Hereford.

The Three Choirs Festival should have started on 3 September. Instead of being at Hereford, Ralph was at home listening to the Prime Minister's voice telling the country that we were at war.

CHAPTER XII

1939–1945

The beginning of the war made Ralph feel desperate for useful work. He immediately offered the use of his field to the District Council for allotments, reserving a patch for himself.

'We shall probably be living on potatoes next year—so I'm digging some of my field into a potato patch—it makes me nice and sleepy at night,' he wrote early in September. He had organized an air-raid shelter in the high bank between The White Gates garden and the next door to be shared by both households, and, when the fear of immediate air raids had decided the authorities to send as many children as possible out of the big towns, he and Adeline invited the daughter of his old friend and fellow soldier, Harry Steggles, to stay at Dorking. It wasn't a success, as Adeline wrote to Rosamond Carr. 'Our little girl evacuee, Myrtle Steggles, got homesick and ordered her parents to fetch her home—so that was done yesterday and we have to confess failure.' This was the normal pattern of events throughout the autumn. Children who had left their homes in orderly bus-loads or in crammed trains, excited, self-important, and pathetic, were slipping back to the cities, and homesickness in grown-ups as well as children raged through villages and remote country districts. Hospitality was turned to bewilderment, and dreams of rural peace and security dwindled when the reality was found to be without the amenities of fish and chip shops, cinemas and streets—everyone was ready to be brave, no one to be bored.

Ralph did many small local jobs. He helped with the collection of salvage: aluminium for aircraft, paper, rags, and junk of all sorts had suddenly become potential war material. So immense clearings-up diverted everyone and kept the dust carts busy. He also took on a war-savings round, and undertook even more work for the Dorking Refugee Committee, doing much to find work for people who wanted to stay in England and trying to get money, guarantees, introductions, and promises of jobs for those who wanted to go to America or Canada, writing, or dictating to Adeline, countless letters to anyone who might help. He was one of the small committee who worked to put into practice Myra Hess's idea of lunch-time concerts in the National Gallery, and he started lecture recitals at the White Horse Hotel in Dorking. He did anything anyone asked him to do that he felt might help in any way, and so, somehow, he got through the days. He wrote to me at the end of September:

Is it Herbert Fisher's *History of Europe* you are reading—magnificent but depressing—all good things men try to do perish . . . but nothing can destroy music—(a platitude. . . .)

On 1 November the B.B.C. orchestra, conducted by Adrian Boult, gave the first performance in England of his *Five Variants of Dives and Lazarus*, a short work commissioned by the British Council for the New York World Fair, which Adrian had conducted in America. It was broadcast from the Colston Hall, Bristol, where the B.B.C. orchestra were in exile. Ralph himself broadcast from London in November, gave away prizes at a school and did some lecturing; his College lessons had stopped for the term, but they started again in January and brought him to London every Monday of the Easter term.

He was also writing on 'Local Musicians' for the first number of *The Abinger Chronicle*, a thin little magazine invented and edited by Sylvia Sprigge, with Max Beerbohm (exiled from Italy to Surrey), E. M. Forster, Desmond MacCarthy, Oliver F. W. Lodge, Robert Trevelyan, and Ralph described as the chief contributors. The annual subscription was *6s.* and it gave great pleasure to its readers. Besides this he wrote a long article on Beethoven's *Choral Symphony*. The performance which he had planned for the 1940 Leith Hill Festival was obviously impossible, but, having the music fresh in his mind from the 'acting edition' he had prepared, this task helped to occupy the hours in which he did not feel able to write music. He also wrote scripts for broadcasts: *Making your Own Music* and *The Composer in Wartime*. None of us knew then what was in store for us in the way of destruction, but it seemed likely that the material means of music making, concert halls and even musical instruments might not survive, and the human voice might be the only thing left—so it was to song writing that he turned. In mid-November he wrote to me:

> Do you know the last 10 lines of P. Unbound?[1]

and on Boxing Day:

> Can you search Shelley for me for some lines to set—I want a series of war-time songs. I've done P. Unbound, last 9 lines (Song of Victory) and am thinking of the earlier lines 'Love from its . . . healing wings' (Song of Healing) I want some more—'Courage', 'Hope', etc., but they must be settable, e.g. next lines starting 'gentleness' *are quite unsettable*—can you find me some?

And the next day in another letter:

> By the way, in the Shelley you said you liked the line 'Neither to change nor falter nor repent'. My copy reads 'flatter' which I always thought poor—now I see the correct is 'falter'.

The correspondence went on: on 6 January:

> I've found more Shelley—Bridges 423[2] (1st verse only) so don't worry too much though I could do with one or two more.

I think I found words for Nos. II, V, and VI of what became *Six Choral Songs*, though I cannot be sure, for we both read a great deal of Shelley that winter, including the whole of the *Revolt of Islam*, and at some point Ralph explained how difficult he found it to read poetry without the ulterior interest of looking for settable poems—it was rather like his first glance round any church when sightseeing: 'lots of room for orchestra if I did the Passion here' or 'no room for players', before he started looking at the architecture.

On 13 January Ralph was at Oxford for a dinner to celebrate Hugh Allen's seventieth birthday; the war had not prevented a number of Hugh's friends from gathering to honour him and the menu shows that austerity had not yet set in.

By February Ralph saw that, although the *Choral Symphony* was too big a project for Leith Hill that year, some sort of Festival was possible for, though many members of choirs had been swept into war work that took them out of the district,

[1] *Prometheus Unbound*, Shelley. [2] *The Spirit of Man*.

other singers had, in a sort of general post, arrived in the district. He wrote to Isidore Schwiller:

Feb. 2nd. (1940)

We hope after all to be able to have a sort of Festival—the dates provisionally are March 9th and March 16th (both Saturday and both afternoon concerts). I can't say definitely yet so you must not keep the dates—but will you pencil them: but if that fails to materialise we shall have to restrict expenditure. Do you think that, in that case, the orchestra would be willing to come for a 'war-time' fee rather than not come at all?

The concerts did take place—*Elijah* and *Judas Maccabaeus* were the works, with a new Hon Secretary, Margery Cullen, in command, for Fanny Farrer had had to resign because of her full-time work for the Federation of Women's Institutes. It was about as difficult a beginning as any Hon. Secretary could have, for the Dorking Halls had been commandeered by the Meat Marketing Board, who yielded to Miss Cullen's pleas on behalf of Ralph and Lady Farrer only on condition that she was responsible, on behalf of the Festival Committee, for dismantling the equipment for storing meat, arranging the hall for the concerts and 'should an emergency arise' she had to be prepared to re-install the meat store machinery at twenty-four hours' notice. All this she valiantly undertook to do and, as the emergency did not arise, the concerts were held. Another happiness for Ralph and Adeline was Honorine's marriage to a young trumpeter, Bernard Brown, who had become a professional musician after leaving Cambridge, and was now a soldier stationed in London. Honorine had been part of their lives since the last year at Cheyne Walk—she had been like a daughter, bringing her young friends to the house, planning excursions, driving the car, and sharing in all the daily life, but they had both wanted marriage for her, feeling she should use her talent for life and happiness in a home of her own. So they rejoiced, and were particularly delighted because her husband was a musician and a man they had immediately liked and respected.

On 19 March Ralph conducted his *Mass in G minor* sung at St. Paul's Cathedral by a choir from the solo performers' section of the Incorporated Society of Musicians. The concert was given by permission of the Dean and Chapter to raise funds for distressed musicians. He took me with him, and I remember the blue spring evening—for it was already dusk inside the cathedral—the little lights for the singers, and Ralph wearing a cassock that did not meet although it was the largest they could find for him in the vestry.

Ralph was busy with his garden and allotment all through the spring, and when a few hens were added to the establishment their well-being became as great a concern as that of the cats. He wrote: 'I am also weeding and start haymaking today. No other job seems to come my way.' This was in June, a month made sad by the death of Dorothy Longman, one of their most loved friends; he wrote to Bobby of the happiness her life had given:

Perhaps there will be no more happiness or peace for any of us now and we must be thankful for what has been.

Only a few days later George Trevelyan wrote to Ralph of the death of Maurice Amos:

We had great days together in our youth, in the age of gold, didn't we? Now he escapes the iron age which we must shoulder.

This Ralph was doing very positively; he wrote to me:

I went and practised fire fighting the other day—they staged a *real* fire with lots of smoke and I had to crawl about on my stomach with an axe in one hand and the nozzle and a hosepipe in the other.

A few days later, he added reassuringly:

I am not fire fighting in the public sense—I only had a lesson on how to use the stirrup pump *in the house* in case of necessity.

There were lighter moments—a paperback edition of some of Edward Lear's writings had just been published.

I went and got Lear at once—it is a good book—but I wish they wd. not call them 'Limericks'. I feel sure he wd have hated the word—a Limerick is an indecent poem in the same metre as the Lear nonsense rhymes. I'd often thought of setting the Pobble, to music—it's one of the most mysteriously romantic poems I know. Have you read the prose nonsense story—it's superb—and I did not know it before.

In the same letter he says he has got 'Jeans',[1] and a little later:

> Have you read *The Discovery of Poetry* by Lyon, it is written for school boys but as far as I have got it seems good . . . it's no good shutting ones self up at present—things must come as they can—I can hardly bear to read the papers at the present.

Then when a young lad we both knew was reported missing after a naval battle:

> I fear the public rejoicing does little to mitigate the private grief. I always think that when we casually say 'the casualties were slight' that the loss of each individual is equally evil whether he is one of 10 or of 10,000—only the 10,000 stimulates our sluggish imagination. . . . I'm reading the best book I've struck about the F.U.[2]—Federal Europe by Mackay. I'm sure I didn't understand the Rimbaud poems when I read them—I heard the music on the wireless the other day and thought it good—but of course could not hear the words.[3]

His next letter was an invitation to come to Dorking to spend an afternoon at The White Gates. I had met Adeline only for moments, at the *Double Trio* concert and at Sadler's Wells, though I had seen Ralph often in London. He took me round the garden and showed me the path he had made. It was extraordinarily peaceful and the only reminder of the war was an immense trench all along the southern slope of Ranmore, a last ditch defence, he said, which made a great white scar on the green slope: and it was horrifying to realize that if it was ever used they would be on the enemy's side of it. Then the Beerbohms arrived for tea. They were very gay, and it was fantastic to realize that Ralph and Max had not met since their Charterhouse days. At first they talked about the people they had known there; the master whose wife died, and who went into mourning trousers, black instead of pea-green—and there were lots of Haig Brown stories—Ralph reproducing the aloof, faintly adenoidal and precise voice of their head master which Max recognized as exactly like. From the reconstructed moments it would have been possible to imagine they had both enjoyed themselves at Charterhouse—they had certainly both observed their masters with

[1] Sir James Jeans—probably *The Universe Around Us* or *The Mysterious Universe*.

[2] Federal Union.

[3] *Les Illuminations*, Benjamin Britten.

clear and satirical perception. Then there were music halls they remembered, and it seemed that Ralph had been able to slip into far more performances than anyone had supposed. Max knew very many songs, and sang them in a ghostly, rather cracked tenor voice, and Ralph's bass filled in the choruses, word perfect each time. They glowed over their memories of *The Follies* and they were delighted with each other. Lady Beerbohm had hair the colour of autumn bracken and she and Adeline talked together, Adeline finding out how they had settled down, and how they were managing to live without their books and possessions. When it was time to go, a car from Dorking came to take me to the station. The Beerbohms thought that both car and chauffeur belonged to me, and thanked me for the lift to their bus stop as if I had given them a delightful drive in a glass coach with outriders.

Ralph's next letter was about having the house fully sandbagged and a few days later the Battle of Britain had started. The curious thing was that, now the war was affecting our daily lives, we all went on doing as many as possible of the usual things. His next letter said they had spent six hours in their dug-out, and went on to talk about Proms which were in full swing at the Queen's Hall, and ended once again with a book, 'I am reading Roger Fry's life by Virginia Woolf—very good—all his doubts and difficulties remind me of many that I went through.'

He came to London to hear a rehearsal of the Shelley songs and so far London had been quiet enough. I was there too, staying with Maud Karpeles for a few days. After the rehearsal I saw Ralph off at Waterloo, and met some friends for tea. Almost at once an appalling raid started over London. However, his train was safe. But the Prom season ended abruptly, and on 2 September Honorine was killed in another raid on London. Adeline, who had written to Mary Fletcher just before her sister Dorothy Longman died, 'You encourage me to keep steady—how I hope I may—I often have a dread of failing Ralph if the test comes——' wrote to her again:

I was very touched at your writing and telling me that you have that happy recollection of our Honorine. She was a treasure to us, more and more dear as time went on—I cannot think of her fate without anguish—Ralph and I had such pleasure in her marriage—Ralph used to say 'every time we see her she is happier'—her husband is very unselfish and very gallant—my sister Cordelia has devoted herself to him and he is with her in London.

Emmie and Morris now moved to The White Gates, and settled in, adding their cats, Johnnie and Martha, to the establishment, where Foxy, a long-nosed, long-haired and affectionate grey had grown up with Pushkin, a brownish-tabby little female with pretty ways, a hard heart and an endless capacity for producing kittens. Other cats came and went—Ralph's favourite had been a stray called 'Whitey' who had come from no one knew where and, after some years, disappeared equally mysteriously; early in the war another stray, a large black tom called 'Belisha', moved in; one of them was usually in Ralph's study, sleeping on the windowsill, while he worked. When it was Ralph's turn to sleep there was sure to be a cat ready to settle on his lap as he sat in his big chair.

In October there was the delightful news that George Trevelyan had been appointed Master of Trinity—he wrote:

Dear V. W.

I cannot fail to answer you—your scrawl means more to me than any one of the 70 letters I got this morning, nice as many of them are. And anything about Trinity recalls those great days of ours in your Whewells Court room . . . they are gradually letting out academic anti-Fascists and anti Nazis—but too slowly.

Yrs. ever

G. M. T.

This referred to a matter very close to Ralph's interests. During the summer many refugees had been interned—in some cases they had been swept into detention camps at a few moments' notice, the only effective course in an emergency. The sorting out of 'friendly' and 'enemy' aliens had to take place afterwards and, because of lack of suitable accommodation, lack of understanding in camp staffs, and the slow process of tribunals, many people suffered greatly from conditions they had not expected to find in England. It was a wise decision to appoint Ralph as Chairman of the Home Office Committee for the Release of Interned Alien Musicians, and his judgement, knowledge, and experience enabled him to help his colleagues and fellow musicians, and gave him, at last, the kind of work he had wanted.

Among the musicians whose internment gave Ralph concern was a German composer, Robert Müller-Hartmann, whom he had met through Imogen Holst. He had come to Dorking with his wife and daughter to their friends the Hornsteins, whom Ralph already knew through the Dorking Refugee Committee on which Mrs. Hornstein also served. A warm friendship developed. Robert Müller-Hartmann spent much of his time after his release in the spring of 1941 at Dorking. Ralph came to respect his new neighbour's insight, scholarship, and wisdom particularly when he was in doubt or difficulty about works of his own.

He had already written to Müller-Hartmann in the first days of internment: 'May you again soon be free to work for the country of your adoption and for the cause we all have at heart.'

There were many other interned musicians on whose behalf he saw officials in Government departments, interviewed M.P.s and for whom he wrote letters urging suitable employment and help to emigrate. He was also able to bring back others who had been swept off to internment in Australia, or Canada, where my father,[1] who was working for the Ministry of Supply in Ottawa, was sometimes able to help him.

It had been a sad year; Adeline's brother, H. A. L. Fisher, had died, so had Donald Tovey, Dorothy Longman, and Honorine; few weeks passed without news of someone they knew being killed or wounded and they lamented again that other generation of young musicians lost twenty-five years before in the other war. When he wrote his motet, *Valiant for Truth*, all these friends were probably in his mind, though perhaps it was of Dorothy Longman he thought most, for her friendship and musicianship had been particularly precious to him. He wrote it in November, and recorded the date on a copy he sent to Bobby Longman when it was published, nearly a year later.

Ralph had taken to gardening with zeal and fury; he read books on the cultivation of vegetables, trenched, bastard trenched, weeded, hoed, and spent a fortune on seeds and bottles of liquid manure to supplement the natural product which he collected from the lane where cows passed up and down on their way to be milked and sometimes horses on their way to the fields for a day off. He hoed, raked, and talked very technically about this new craft, and he waited on his hens with a tenderness and

[1] Major-General Sir Robert Lock.

devotion to which they did not respond with the hoped-for lavishness of eggs. However, it all helped to use up his enormous energy.

Sometimes there were entertaining interludes. He went to Charterhouse for the opening of the new music school, and played the cuckoo with great distinction in a performance of *The Toy Symphony*, and in November he accepted an invitation to adjudicate at an Eisteddfod held by the 2nd Battalion Welsh Guards, stationed at West Byfleet. Rex Whistler was to judge the art section and Madame Clara Novello-Davies was invited to be President. She wrote a song for the occasion and sent it in plenty of time for rehearsal: but the entrants seemed more interested in the other works they were preparing and when Ralph came to spend the afternoon, he took them seriously and thoroughly through their music. As he finished talking to them, their Eisteddfod President emerged from the withdrawing room she had demanded in which to rest after lunch. Lieutenant Colonel Price, who was largely responsible for the idea and the planning of the day, remembered in tranquillity what must have been a shattering experience.

Behind the stage the curtains parted. We beheld Madame Clara now sheathed from head to foot in tight gold lamé, a wreath of gold leaves in her hair and carrying a baton of gold leaves presented to her, as we afterwards learned, by some long forgotten President of France. As she advanced to conduct her song, the ranks of the massed choirs in battle-dress parted in amazement. The train of her dress caught on a nail on the Pirbright floor, the music of her song had been placed upside down on the music stand and, the butterfly screw being loose, it gave under her as she appeared to lean on it for support and down she went in deep but involuntary obeisance to the audience. There was a quick recovery, a long speech about son Ivor[1] and away we went with her song. It was a fiasco. She tried it through twice and then, oblivious of Vaughan Williams at her feet, of the composition of her audience and indeed of the occasion, she rapped out 'You don't know it. Stand up!'—on and on we went and through and through the song. There seemed no hope of it ever ending. At last the Regimental Sergeant Major was rushed on to the stage to call for 'Three Cheers for Madame Clara Novello-Davies'; he just made himself heard above the din and that was that. Afterwards there were oysters and champagne.[2]

[1] Ivor Novello. [2] Letter to U. V. W.

When Ralph met Colonel Price again years later, they talked about that Eisteddfod and what fun it had been.

Ralph had been a fairly regular cinema goer. There had been an escapade at one of the Three Choirs Festivals when he met Myra Hess as they were both on their way to an evening concert. 'Do you want to hear this?' Ralph asked. 'No, not much,' said Myra. 'Well, let's go to the pictures instead,' said Ralph, and off they went, emerging just in time to join the cathedral audience, but remaining non-committal when asked what they had thought of the performance. He enjoyed films, though he maintained that the cinema had never been fantastic enough, and that no one had explored the possibilities of the medium. Disney, he said, had paved the way for an El Greco, who had not yet arisen, and he would have liked to work with Disney in a cartoon film. He was delighted when, in 1940, he was asked to write music for an exciting spy-adventure story, with an excellent cast, called *49th Parallel*—an ex-pupil of his, Muir Mathieson, was the director of music for London Films, and it was to his suggestion that Ralph owed this invitation. He was rather dismayed to find that he had to write very fast: the first lot of material was wanted almost at once, but his ideas flowed, and there was no limitation on the size or composition of the orchestra. He became fascinated too by the split-hair timings: a second of music meant *exactly* a second of music and this was quite a new frame to musical thought. He liked the people at the studio and he thoroughly enjoyed having a musical job to do.

He was also standing up against injustices. Alan Bush's music was banned by the B.B.C. in March, because he had signed 'The People's Convention'. Ralph heard of this and wrote to the Director General:

So far as I know Dr. Bush's political views, I am strongly opposed to them. Nevertheless I wish to protest against this victimisation of private opinion in the only way possible to me. You may remember that the British Broadcasting Corporation have lately done me the honour to commission from me a choral song. I now beg leave to withdraw my offer of this song to the British Broadcasting Corporation. I return the fee which was paid me and ask you to give directions that all manuscripts and materials of the song be returned to me. I will of course be responsible for the expenses incurred in its production.

In preparation for what remained of the Leith Hill Festival he took rehearsals wherever needed for the groups practising *The Messiah*. There was a good deal of local talent, both professional and amateur, on which he drew and he was also able to offer engagements to musicians from London.

The Messiah took a lot of organizing. The Dorking Halls were not available any longer but the Vicar and Churchwardens of St. Martin's generously came to the rescue and allowed the performance to take place in the church, where a string orchestra had to be fitted into the chancel. There could be no wind, for the organ pitch was wrong, so the music had to be arranged. The choir had to be crammed into inadequate space, but the audience was overflowing.

There was another performance a week later, after which he wrote to me:

Messiah went very well—but chorus No. 2. was not quite so good. I had tea and lunch with the orchestra and got through a lot of embracing.

Another letter from that time was written to Lord Kennet—who had written to ask advice on a possible musical career for his son, Wayland Young:

I apologise for the delay in answering—you sent your letter to my cousin Roland—it was forwarded twice to him and then on to me. Also, I wanted to think the whole thing over, which took some time. I fear my letter has developed into an essay—so I enclose [it] on separate sheets. I am delighted if I can do anything to help your son—both for our old friendship and for his sake.

I understand that when your son says he wants to go in for music he means first and foremost that he wants to be a composer.

I presume that he will have to earn his living; even if it is not absolutely necessary he will find it desirable. Now composing 'serious' music is very seldom a paying proposition, at all events in the early stages of one's career.

Very few of the Great Masters earned their living by their compositions—Bach was a schoolmaster and organist—Beethoven lived partly by giving pianoforte lessons and partly on a pension—Schubert and Mozart lived in miserable poverty and died early—Wagner was a conductor at the Dresden Opera till he was about 30 and sponged on his friends for the rest of his life—Brahms was approaching middle age before he was able to give up concert playing etc.

It may sound very egotistical, but I think it may help you if I tell you a little about myself. I am now making a good income by my compositions though they are not of the 'popular' order. But I did not achieve this till I was about 40 and it is quite precarious and may stop at any minute. So except for the fact that I was born with a very small silver spoon in my mouth I could not financially afford to devote my whole time to composition—from the age of about 20 to 30 I supplemented my income by playing the organ (very badly) and teaching and lecturing.

The upshot seems to be that a composer of serious music must, at the beginning of his career at all events, have some other means of livelihood—either musical, or technical, but alas, not often in the true sense of the word, or something outside music.

1) He can be an executant but to be a performer nowadays demands a very high standard: an ordinary student at the Royal College can do technical feats which 50 years ago would have been considered the province of a virtuoso. It is rather late at the age of 17 to start acquiring the necessary co-ordination of muscle and brain to achieve this. So I think the chances are against his being able to achieve sufficient professional skill as a performer. There are, of course, exceptions—Pugno,[1] I believe, started his professional career at 40, but he was already a skilled amateur pianist. A wind instrument, I think, is more possible but I do not know that to be an orchestra trombonist is an attractive career.

2) A school job—this requires more general musical knowledge and less special virtuosity, but the music master at a Public School is usually expected to be a competent organist. In a job like this I think that a general educational background like the history tripos would be a help.

3) He might become one of the young men at the B.B.C., but again unless he has special qualifications as a conductor or performer it is rather a dim job. One young friend of mine started as a conductor at a provincial B.B.C. He was very musical but I think not sufficiently technically skilled and now, as far as I can make out, he is acting as a sort of superior messenger boy at the B.B.C.

The snag about all musical jobs is that they involve a lot of unmusical work. On the one hand you do not get right away from the music in your working hours as you would do if you were a solicitor or a scientist. You have to spend a lot of time playing and conducting music you hate, teaching unwilling and unmusical people, pupils etc. This leaves you just as little leisure for real music as being in an office but, unlike being in an office you have 'music' of a sort in your

[1] Raoul Pugno. French pianist and composer. 1852–1914.

mind and in your ears all day long; therefore you do not come fresh to the music which is in your soul. People of very strong character can fight against this—Gustav Holst for some years earned his living as a trombone player in a dance band dressed up as a blue Hungarian, but it was a desperate struggle.

There is much then to be said for earning your living outside music and being a 'spare time' composer. On the other hand it is essential for a composer to be in touch with practical music—playing in an orchestra—singing in a chorus—conducting and teaching—doing all the odd jobs of arranging, orchestrating etc. by which composers eke out their livelihood; all this helps the composer to keep the necessary proportion between the world of facts and the world of dreams—Wagner I am sure, would not have achieved his mastery over the orchestra if he had not been for years conductor of the Dresden Opera; Brahms would have achieved a surer touch if he had not refused the post of conductor at Dusseldorf (?); Delius would perhaps have more backbone in his music if he had gone down into the arena and fought with beasts at Ephesus instead of living the life beautiful in a villa in France.

On the whole,—but with many doubts,—I vote for history—your son says that music will take up his whole time. By this I guess he means composing music. Now my advice to young composers is 'Don't.' I know by personal experience that the young composer thinks that what he is writing is what the world is waiting for—and I should not think much of him unless he did think so—but he also thinks that it must be done here and now and that tomorrow will be too late—not realising that if he studies and learns now the masterpiece will come later—and that at the age of 17 he has got all his life before him.

I think it was Smetana who as a young man realised this and set to work on an extensive study of the Great Masters. This study, it seems to me, can to a certain extent be combined with History lectures. Let him not despise the humble counterpoint exercise—not necessarily with a master. Let him one day look at a bit of Palestrina and try to write something if only a dozen bars that sound more or less like it. Let him look at the Bach inventions and then experiment on what we call 'bad Bach'. He should always have a miniature score in his pocket and look at it in trains and buses and hear as much music as possible. All this—it seems to me—can be spare time work. Your son raises the question of where to study after the war and queries Leipzig. I do not know the answer with regard to executive music though I believe that except for virtuoso training here is as good as anywhere and Heaven forfend that anyone should go to Germany and learn to make a noise like the German oboists, clarinettists or horn players. However, I do feel pretty certain that creative work must grow out of its native soil. My opinion is that the elements of composition can be taught better in this country, partly because less pedantically, than abroad. I think it is most important that the young composer should mature himself and find his direction in his own surroundings—*then* when he knows his own mind is the time to go to the foreign countries to compare fresh views, to broaden his outlook and to fructify his inspiration. Perhaps taking a sort of finishing course with some good foreign teacher always remembering the attitude of foreign to English musicians is unsympathetic, self-opinionated and pedantic. They believe that their tradition is the only one (this is specially true of the Viennese) and that anything that is not in accordance with that tradition is 'wrong' and arises from insular ignorance.

Almost all the British composers who have achieved anything have studied at home and only gone abroad when they were mature—Elgar, Holst, Parry, Bax, Walton. Stanford is an exception, but he was by no means a beginner when he went to study abroad and as a matter of fact he never quite recovered from Leipzig. On the other hand I have known many young composers with a genuine native invention who have gone to Germany or France in their most impressionable years and have come back speaking a musical language which can only be described as broken French or German. They have had their native qualities swamped and never recovered their personality.

This is especially true now when there is so much talk about 'new paths' in music. All these young composers do is to pick up a few shibboleths of the new language without understanding it, whereas if they were first thoroughly grounded in their native culture they would be able to assimilate anything that was worth while in these supposed new ideas into their own organism.

I am much elated to find that so many young people with the public school tradition are finding that music is a possible means of self expression. But we must remember—and you of course must know this as well as or better than I do—that one cannot *tell* whether a boy of 17 has the creative impulse or not. At this age they are bitten by music and naturally they burn to 'do it too'. They write out pages of Sibelius, Hindemith or Delius and imagine they are composing. This is an inevitable stage in artistic development, even among great artists—sometimes the personality emerges, sometimes it does not—sometimes the flicker of invention disappears when they eat of the fruit of the tree of knowledge—so we must be prepared for disappointments.[1]

[1] He had written another such letter to his young cousin Peter Montgomery in the early 'thirties. Though the general advice is much the same this is the fuller document with ten years' more experience.

This was one sort of good advice. He wrote to a girl he had met while staying with Steuart and Mary Wilson with another sort of wisdom:

My dear Myfanwy,

What splendid news and how romantic to be engaged by cable. I wish you could also be married by cable—this long dreary waiting will be terrible for you both. But *directly* he comes home don't wait a moment—middle age creeps on even when you are as young as you are and passion declines—so take your love at its height and damn the consequences. Your Charles will be a lucky man to have such a young and pretty wife—but I expect you are lucky too because from what I know of your character you would not love anyone who was not first rate. . . .

A third letter from this year was a lament written to Hubert Foss on his retirement from the Oxford Press. For years The White Gates synonym for letter-writing had been 'doing our dear Foss'. Adeline would ask, 'When would you like to do dear Foss?' or Ralph would say, 'dear Foss, after tea,' and they would settle down to answer all the letters, Ralph with a pile of them on his knees, Adeline in her tall wheeled chair with a stiff board and writing paper on her knee—her hands were bent with arthritis and her hold on the pen looked precarious, but she would write at great speed and her flowing hand was legible as well as distinctive. As each letter was answered Ralph threw it on the floor, and when the whole lot lay around his feet in a heap he would start on the ones that were not answers. He wrote a few himself and these he usually tackled before breakfast; both Myfanwy's letter and this valediction to Foss are in his own writing.

Dear Foss,

This is sad news indeed, how shall we get on without you? I did not realise how much I counted on you—'Ask Foss's advice'—'Ask Foss to see to it' or 'I'll ask Foss to play it over to me at Amen House' ——But perhaps it is not all over as regards all that and anyway it is a selfish and unofficial way of looking at things and I ought to think only of how grateful we all are for all you have done for music and incidentally for musicians. . . .

. . . I always admired the way you took an interest in even the humblest of music makings, choral competitions, school music etc. realising the profound truth that without this foundation the Elgars and Waltons can't exist.

Well good luck to you in any new ventures and congratulations to those who get you for a co-operator——

The *49th Parallel* recordings were most exciting—the London Symphony Orchestra, led by George Stratton, enjoyed themselves, the tunes seemed to fit well to the film sequences, Ralph did not appear to be at all nervous, he was prepared to cut, enlarge, alter, adapt—in fact he had begun to realize that, as he said later, you could use the same music for a landscape, a car crash, or a love scene; it would sound different if it looked different. But there seemed to be very little that needed changing, except for the short Austrian folk song he had put in for Glynis Johns to sing in the Hutterite settlement. She was very young, very frightened of the orchestra, and quite unable to sing it in the key in which it had been written—sing it as you like, said Ralph, and I'll change the key. But it was no good, so eventually George Stratton more or less played it into her ear, and she managed a husky hum, while Muir Mathieson whistled the second verse—and so after a delay of an hour or so the half minute was recorded. We saw the film in the autumn and it had a great success. Ralph was asked to write music for another one to be called *Coastal Command* as well as a short film for the National Trust—*The People's Land.*

Besides this he had written a quartet planned in such a way that it could be played by almost any combination of instruments as well as by the conventional two violins, viola, and cello. He realized that unusual combinations of instrumentalists might find themselves working and lodging in the same place, and that it would be agreeable for them to have a work they could tackle—he called this set of variations on Welsh hymn tunes *Household Music*. The excellent first performance was given by the Blech String Quartet during the autumn.

So far the raids had not been too serious at Dorking—the nearest bomb, Adeline wrote to Cordelia, had upset one of the Morris's cats, while Ralph had thought the noise was 'the cats scrapping', but they were in constant worry about their friends in London.

Ralph's first New Year task was entirely delightful. On 17 January, at the fourth concert of the season, the Royal Philharmonic Society had engaged Myra Hess to play and Ralph was invited to present her with the Society's Gold Medal. She wrote to him next day.

Dearest V. W.

I am still aglow from Saturday and I can never never thank you enough for your sweetness to me—As a Dutch friend of mine would say 'it was a great emotion'. Knowing that you do not love such functions my appreciation of your goodness in coming is deeper than I can ever express.

It is very lovely and gratifying to have the medal but the way you presented it to me will be one of my most heart warming memories.

Bless you 1942 times!

Yours devotedly,

Myra.

Ralph was working on the *St. Matthew Passion* once more, making an abridged version, arranging the score for strings and organ, and taking rehearsals of any choir members and any singers the war had brought to Dorking—the Refugee hostel contributed, among others, a lady tenor and the vicar and churchwardens of St. Martin's again offered Ralph the use of the church. Among his soloists were Arthur Cranmer, who was a magnificently moving Christus, and the soprano Elizabeth Darbishire, his one time clarinet professor. The performances were on two successive Saturdays, 21 and 28 March.

Music-making in London was reviving and, after a winter of raids, the long light evenings were full of hope and promise. *The Messiah* given by the Jacques Orchestra and the Bach Choir at Westminster Abbey was memorable for Kathleen Ferrier's singing;[1] the opera class at the R.C.M. gave a delightful performance of the three letter scenes from *The Merry Wives of Windsor*, Verdi's *Falstaff*, and Ralph's *Sir John in Love*, of which Ralph said he liked Nicolai's far the best; at Sadler's Wells Kurt Jooss produced the *Magic Flute* and the Sadler's Wells Ballet danced a version of *Comus*. The National Gallery continued with its daily lunchtime concerts; people were avid for music, and music which would never have been considered 'popular' before drew packed and attentive audiences. Chamber music was the food of the gods, the nourishment of the spirit, and people were already beginning to say 'after the war' and to look forward to a life in which con-

[1] Her first London appearance.

cert going would have an undreamed-of scope. Ralph was in London fairly often during that spring; he attended C.E.M.A.[1] meetings, Refugee Committees at the Home Office and, occasionally, when R. O. Morris was ill, took his composition pupils at the R.C.M. for he had long given up regular teaching there. He used to lunch or have an early dinner at a little basement club next to Oxford Circus tube station called the M.M. It was run by the cellist May Mukle, the membership fee was minute, the meals were cheap and the place was central, so there were always other musicians to be found having their meals there and Ralph enjoyed himself among friends.

As my husband had for some months been stationed at Cosham in charge of a great part of the anti-aircraft defences of Portsmouth and Southampton I had come back to our London flat and found work in the St. Marylebone Citizens Advice Bureau. It was particularly pleasant to have Jean Stewart as a neighbour in the flat below mine. We shared our fire-watching duties and very often our weekly meat ration. Ralph came to lunch or tea with either or both of us and he sometimes took us to our local pub, where our prestige soared because he bought us expensive drinks and where the barmaid became a devotee of his music. He had come to lunch with me on the day the telegram came with the news of Michael's death. Michael, who had only just gone back to Cosham after twenty-four hours' leave, had had a sudden heart attack and died within a few hours. In those days of war no death was totally unexpected, but a death like this from natural causes—though undoubtedly due to overwork—was a numbing shock, and Ralph's calm was more than comforting. He and Jean did everything, and he took me home with him to The White Gates. Adeline had a bed made for me in the hall—'I don't want you to feel far from us,' she said.

I stayed for a week, and Ralph took me to tea with his brother at Leith Hill Place, where the azaleas were in full flower.

It was a stabilizing week, but I had to consider the future, go home, give up my Citizens Advice Bureau work, which in those days was voluntary, and find a paid job. Before I could do this I was suddenly afflicted with great pain in my foot: after several weeks of being bandaged up with a supposed broken toe, an

[1] Council for the Encouragement of Music and the Arts, which later became the Arts Council.

X-ray disclosed a broken needle in my foot. After it had been taken out I was lame for several weeks. I went back to The White Gates, for Adeline wrote 'film work here is nearing a crisis—I leave all that to R. only wanting you to know how dearly I wd. like to have you here when you can.' It was then that I found I had become part of their lives as they of mine—Adeline was approachable because disaster and misadventure brought her warmest feelings to the surface. R. O. Morris, not long a widower, and I were also supposed to be at the same sort of stage of emotional convalescence. Morris taught me to play backgammon and, when my foot was better, took me for walks, while, best of all, Ralph to my infinite surprise suggested I should bring my writing into the study while he worked, and cleared a patch on one of his tables for me. I sat in the window seat, he at his desk, dashing to the piano every now and then, or stopping to say something about anything in the world, from weather for gardening to a curious technical point about film music or the story—this time an adventure about recovering a flag, the film being *Flemish Farm*—or cross-questioning me about what I was doing. So the summer settled into a time of content, and far more than seemed possible was salvaged. Adeline, writing to her sister Cordelia, said:

> There's nice rain for the garden—R is only troubled now that the hens are not getting enough amusement on a wet day—he failed to dig up worms for them—now we suggest crushing some crab shell——

The hens were a perpetual drag on Ralph's tender conscience—he visited them at least twice a day and, partly to make up for his dislike of them, he tried to see their better natures and worried over them if they were broody or ill. In another letter to Cordelia, Adeline told her:

> R. came in from his morning visit to the hens looking so distressed at finding Blondie very unwell she hasn't laid an egg for months but till today has eaten well tho' you'll remember she has a game leg. Brett [the gardener] is taking her to the vet and I expect a bill (like we had for a red hen a short time ago) 'anaesthesia for one fowl 3/6d.'

The ritual of cleaning was that on alternate Sundays Ralph or Morris would muck out the hen-house thoroughly: eventually it became my job, and whoever was supposed to be on duty came, clad in blue overalls and with a bucket of hot water, and made a few brief but encouraging remarks before retreating to pleasanter occupations.

On 29 June Harold Darke and the St. Michael Singers gave the first performance of *Valiant for Truth* in a programme that included Tudor motets, two works by Harold Darke and Haydn's *Te Deum*; the church was full. The Prom. season had started two days before and the concerts began at 6.30 so that they should be over before it was dark. The average attendance in the Albert Hall was 4,000 people each night.

Ralph's opening music for *49th Parallel* had been a broad and splendid tune which stood out against the dramatic mountain scenery of the Rockies, and he was now asked to turn it into a song. He wrote to Harold Child:

Here is the 49th Parallel tune with a nonsense verse attached to show the metre of suggested rhyme scheme.

To fit the tune we want something rather high falutin'—'noble and sentimental' either about Canada, or Freedom or Unity of Nations, 'parliament of man, the federation of the world'! I suggest 3 verses—

Now I have made a beast-ly tune,	A
You'll probably hate it	B
May be 'twill prove a precious boon	A
To you and me	C
When the fat cheques keep mounting up	D
We'll dine and sup	D
And bless that whose fate it was to earn so soon	A
Such L S D	C

This became *The New Commonwealth*—which turned out *not* to be one of the greatest L.S.D. earners of Ralph's works. Another task with the same intention, *noble et sentimentale*, was the setting of five war-time hymns with words by Canon Briggs, a colleague in hymn-book work and an old friend of Three Choirs Festivals, with whom he stayed during the Worcester meetings.

Two other friends associated with those Festivals died that summer, W. H. Reed and Dorothy Silk.

October was drawing near and Ralph, to his surprise, found that his birthday was to be celebrated very thoroughly—he said that one seemed to be a promising composer till one was seventy and then to become 'our veteran composer' overnight and to be ceremonially put on the shelf; but the shelf didn't materialize just then. There were broadcast concerts, a special National Gallery birthday concert, at which the Menges Quartet with the extra players gave a revised version of the *Double Trio*, and there was a first performance of a cycle of Shakespeare songs, *Let us garlands bring* by Gerald Finzi, of which he had already sent a copy to Ralph to whom they were dedicated. Gerald, who was working in the Ministry of War Transport, had no time for music other than for the little orchestra which he had founded at Newbury and which he conducted at weekends. He wrote about the songs:

—only one of these is new and the collection is put together as the only thing I can offer at present.

It is a beautiful song cycle, and Gerald's setting of '*Fear no more the heat o' the sun*'[1] one of the most perfect songs ever written, so Ralph thought it a noble present. After the concert the Finzis gave a lunch party, and Ralph enjoyed himself and quite forgot that he was supposed to have become venerable overnight. Gerald gave him, besides the songs, the very largest apple ever seen, which he took home with him.

Four days later he was in London again for the world première of *Coastal Command* at the Plaza Cinema. This was the work of the Crown Film Unit and the music was recorded by the R.A.F. orchestra, a band that had absorbed some of the finest musicians. Once again Muir Mathieson conducted and Ralph was very pleased with the result.

The birthday celebrations ended on 7 November when Ralph conducted the *Sea Symphony* and *Dona Nobis Pacem* at the Albert Hall—both works full of particular meaning for those days—it was hardly bearable to hear the baritone's voice:

And out of these a chant for the sailors of all nations,
Fitful like a surge.
Of sea captains young or old, and the mates, and of all intrepid sailors,
Of the few, very choice, taciturn, whom fate can never surprise nor death dismay. . . .

Perhaps in those days, when there was not enough sleep and not quite enough food, perpetual anxiety for other people and the

[1] Cymbeline.

possibility of one's own death at any moment, our senses were all sharpened, all meanings were heightened and people spoke to each other more openly than they might have done in a more placid time. So it seemed, anyway, from some of Ralph's birthday letters which had poured into the house and which he had been answering for a month. Ralph Wedgwood wrote:

I can believe that all this public fuss has its exasperating side for you, but at least it was a great pleasure to your friends to know that you were appreciated and to sun themselves in the reflected glory. Please give my love to Adeline. I hope your fame gives her unmixed pleasure—you will go on putting out your energy to the last—and may it be a long way off. The last Rembrandts were the best, the last Titians the most surprising—the arts often give to old age its finest moments, those which look forward over the edge of the world which surrounds them into the future. Go forward and prosper—what is 90 nowadays, and how much of life one can get into two decades.

There were voices from the past, S. P. Waddington, Nicholas Gatty, a cable from Campbell McInnes in Toronto, with memories of the first *Sea Symphony*, and greetings from Nora, Vally, and Biddy from St. Paul's Girls' School, an enchanting letter from Anne Gilchrist 'as one of the oldest if not the earliest members of the Folk Song Society'. One came from Sir Percy Buck:

I remember your first appearance at the Royal College, so I must be one of your oldest friends and having accomplished the three score years and ten myself would like to condole with you.

You ought to know that those of your own generation, so often carping and jealous, look on you—one and all of us—with equal affection and admiration. Your unflagging aim at all that is good and true, your ignoring of the academic, and your complete lack of self importance make us all love you very much.

Diana Montgomery-Massingberd conjured up another world:

When I think of you it is always with the background of summer days at L.H.P.[1]—currant bread or rather raisin bread in the dining room—at 11 o'c—Sarah at the tea table, the summer Quarendon apples at the further side of the K garden—a little boy making what I thought were lovely sounds out of his head on the pf. in the drawing room——

[1] Leith Hill Place.

George Trevelyan wrote from the Master's Lodge, Trinity:

I have been so delighted by the national outburst of feeling over your 70th birthday. Be sure your old and intimate friends feel it very deeply and with gratitude as a spark of light in these dark days. I never pass your old rooms in Whewells Ct without thinking of you and the old times there——

And Steuart Wilson, after writing about the *Sea Symphony* and *Dona Nobis Pacem* went on:

But do you know that you've left a more valuable thing to us of this generation than your music, and that's your personal character and your integrity and 'guts'. Your 'all this' won't mean anything in 100 years unless people can divine it in your music, but it has meant everything to us, that we could admire without reserve a man who could write such music and who could stand like a rock when he wanted to. Perhaps I should have put my own rock facing a little differently sometimes but what a thing it has been to have a rock in these days. That's the biggest service you have given to music in your generation—and in that respect we are all your pupils and should be your followers.

Perhaps one of the letters he liked best came from his new friend Robert Müller-Hartmann:

May I tell you for once how fortunate I think myself that I came to live in your Dorking, and how grateful I am for all the kindness you have shown to me . . . since I came to England I have studied your music with ever growing interest and joy and this has greatly helped me to change life in exile into an experience which I should not like to miss.

It was easier to thank the Oxford Press for their *Dictionary oj Quotations*, and Hervey for a pheasant than to answer letters which he loved to have but which made him feel uncomfortably sure that he could not be as good as all that.

Having survived the praise and the celebrations, and having plenty of time for the next film score, he returned to the symphony he had started in 1938, to his *St. Matthew Passion* rehearsals and to gardening. I spent Christmas at The White Gates, and found their quiet days by the fire, with lots of reading aloud, hot water bottles handed round to everyone after lunch, log fires, walks, and no break in the routine of working hours an admirable and happy pattern.

The symphony was sufficiently far advanced for a two-piano version to be played through on 31 January. Ralph had made a score for this, and Margery Cullen, the Festival's Hon. Secretary, with Ivy Herbert, another talented musician living near, undertook the task of deciphering and playing from the hieroglyphics which Ralph had provided. This play-through took place at Abinger Hall with an audience of three or four. Adeline was well enough to be driven over and we sat hearing the piano sketch the serenity of strings and the breadth and strength of the sounds to come. I had never heard this sort of thing before, and it was very hard to imagine how the music would sound orchestrally, but I watched Ralph's concentration and saw how much he was getting out of the play-through. When we got back to The White Gates, Adeline tripped in the doorway and twisted her foot; she was carried to bed, and the day ended depressingly for her and anxiously for Ralph, who was filled with doubts and worries about the symphony as well as distress for Adeline.

We were all fire watching in those days and Ralph used his duty nights to make a version of the *B minor Mass*, fitting the words of the English Liturgy to the music; he thought this would bring it into the range of village choirs who were frightened by the idea of singing Latin. He would work until he was sleepy, then lie fully dressed on his bed. If there was an alert, the fire-watcher's duty was to be ready to go out with his stirrup pump team and be ready to extinguish any fire. In the country it was fairly obvious that a 'plane was near, and any bombs or fire bombs were easy to locate—so Ralph kept his equipment at hand, tin helmet, bucket, pump, and torch, and wrestled with the problem of words and music until dawn, when he would walk round the garden before having a sleep. Even when he had been up most of the night, breakfast was still at half-past seven. He had his sleeps later, after lunch and after tea, when he would suddenly disappear in the middle of a sentence he was reading aloud, sink back into the depths of his big chair and go into a deep and tranquil slumber that refreshed and revived him.

The first orchestral play-through of the *Fifth Symphony* was at Maida Vale Studios on the morning of 25 May, and its quality was immediately apparent to the orchestra, the London Philharmonic, who played it so well that Ralph felt that it was what he had meant. The first performance, which he himself conducted, was on 24 June at a Promenade concert and the music seemed to many people to bring the peace and blessing for which they longed.

Next day the letters started to arrive, some of Ralph's friends delighted that 'he had returned to his earlier manner', some worried that he had—but the best was from Adrian Boult, for it told him just what he wanted to know:

> Everything seemed clear and well balanced and I thought the orchestra played finely: at the top of their form (which doesn't often happen nowadays). I thought too that first things seemed foremost all the time which is a great achievement in broadcasting and it must have reached most listeners faithfully. It isn't for one to judge compositions but Ann and I both feel that its serene loveliness is completely satisfying in these times and shows, as only music can, what we must work for when this madness is over. I look forward to another performance and to the privilege of doing it myself some time soon.

Earlier in the week Ralph had been doing what he could about one of the problems arising from 'this madness'. Michael Tippett had been training and conducting an orchestra of unemployed musicians at Morley College and, under the name of the 'South London Orchestra', they had worked together for some years, giving concerts which continued until 1940 when the College buildings were bombed. At this time the Director of Music at Morley College, Arnold Foster, left London, and Michael Tippett succeeded him, being the fourth successor to Gustav and, like his two predecessors, followed the tradition of music-making Holst had created. In spite of war-time difficulties, the dispersal of the South London Orchestra and the sudden reduction in the number of students in both choir and college orchestra owing to war conditions, he gradually gathered people together, had a sizeable choir, and found distinguished musicians to teach composition and musical appreciation among the refugees in the country. He gave concerts with exciting programmes in the Holst room at Morley, at the Wigmore Hall, and at the National Gallery, exploring works by Monteverdi, Purcell, and other classics, as well as giving first performances of modern works. He was in fact serving his profession, his art and his country to the best of his capacity. As a conscientious objector, however, he was directed to agricultural work, which he refused to accept. In June he was sentenced to three months' imprisonment. Ralph attended the tribunal and gave evidence:

I think Tippett's pacifist views entirely wrong, but I respect him very much for holding them so firmly. I think his compositions are very remarkable and form a distinct national asset and will increase the prestige of this country in the world. His teaching at Morley College is distinctly work of national importance to create a musical atmosphere at the College and elsewhere.

Adeline wrote an account of it to Cordelia the same evening:

R. had rather a tiring day going to Oxted—so many hours on the bus and they didn't succeed in getting Michael Tippett off—it couldn't well have been otherwise as the magistrate couldn't overrule the Tribunal wh. had ordered him to do farm work wh. he had refused and the case yesterday was accusing him of breaking the law unless he had some real excuse . . . he is a thorough going fanatic . . . and made an eloquent harangue. In the Daily Mail at first sight it looks as if R. had been sent to prison!

I had been extraordinarily fortunate in finding work as a secretary-receptionist to Paul Nathan, one of the admirable refugee doctors. My employer had been a famous children's specialist in Berlin who had re-qualified in Edinburgh and who was then practising in London. I had met him and his wife at concerts and parties and I found working for him was interesting, hard work, with gloriously elastic hours, for he perfectly understood that there were certain lunch-time concerts that could not be missed, while I was very glad to work extra time when there was need. This explains why I was able to be available so often for Ralph's London visits, and Adeline would know that I would be there to arrange his tie and to see that he was properly fed and was bundled into jerseys and a dry shirt before he went home after conducting. In one undated letter from her the P.S. says: 'You had better unpack R's bag.'

During the winter of 1942/43 Ralph had started work on a quartet. Jean Stewart, who had played in the Leith Hill Festival since she was a student, was now the viola of the Menges Quartet. She had urged Ralph to write a quartet for them and, she being one of his favourite honorary nieces as well as a very fine player, he had started the work but had achieved only two movements in time for her birthday in the spring. I had delivered these to her and her excitement and pleasure were equalled only when the second instalment arrived during the following winter. The importance of the viola part in each movement made it most specially Jean's present. This was the main work through the autumn months.

He wrote a passionate letter to support Dr. Moody the organist of Ripon Cathedral who, backed by the Royal College of Organists, was opposing his Dean and Chapter in the High Court because they proposed to do away with the settings of the Canticles on Sundays. Many musicians joined the battle and some of the clergy, including the Bishop, were on Dr. Moody's side—Ralph said:

It would be a terrible thing if the Cathedral Tradition were to disappear, and I hope very much that you will win your fight with the Dean and Chapter. These people do not seem to realise that music has also its nobilities and its indecencies. I wonder what they would say if it was suggested that a chapter from a pornographic novel should be substituted for the First Lesson? or that the Lord's Prayer should be re-written in the style of American journalism? And yet they permit, and even encourage, such indecencies in music for sake of 'bringing people to church'.

I admit, and I know you agree, that people should have a share in the service, but there is no more reason why they should join in the Anthem and Canticles than in the Absolution or the 'comfortable words'. And further, I think the idea of a choir service is a noble one, where the people come only to listen and to meditate. Would not a practical solution be to have a choir service every Sunday at 10 a.m. and 3 p.m. and a congregational at 11 a.m. and 6.30 p.m.?

We must beat this ecclesiastical totalitarianism somehow, but we can only do so by confining ourselves to what is really noble in our Cathedral repertory. You know of course as well as I do that many of our Canticles and Anthems are vicious, theatrical, mechanical, or intolerably smug. Unless we can root these out of our services we shall give the enemy cause to blaspheme.

Please make any use you like of this letter——

Ralph was always concerned with the problems facing musicians. He had become President of the Committee for the

Promotion of New Music[1] when it was formed in January 1943. It gave performances of new works. First-rate players rehearsed and performed them for no fees at all, and allowed composers to hear what they had written—a service of the first importance—and though Ralph called it the 'Society for the Prevention of Cruelty to New Music', and often found the discussions that followed performances very dull, he attended many of the concerts and gave the whole scheme wholehearted support.

In spite of air raids, which made Ralph unhappy at leaving home, he went to Oxford to conduct the London Philharmonic Orchestra in a performance of his *Fifth Symphony*, the *Running Set*, and *Greensleeves*, and he went to the National Gallery to hear his *Double Trio* on 18 February and to another concert on Shrove Tuesday. The performances of the *St. Matthew Passion* in St. Martin's Church, Dorking, were now a spring ceremony, and the church was always packed to overflowing. The Festival concert was a performance, also in the church, of Mendelssohn's *Hymn of Praise* and Ireland's *These Things Shall Be*.

Adeline wrote a postcard on 22 March after a particularly bad night of raids:

> I long to know how you are after last night—R. spent about 9 hours in trains yesterday going to Bedford and back—to listen to his symph. in the control box. On Friday he is pledged—against his firm resolve—to go to this lunch to Henry Wood. Tomorrow must be devoted to Richard II and perhaps an American to tea. . . .

Richard II was a B.B.C. commission for incidental music: it reminded him of the old Stratford days, and made him appreciate the luxury of choosing his own orchestra and not having to make do with what was there. Again, as with film music, he had to work to exact timing. This was one of the points he had made when writing an article on Film Music for the spring number of the *Royal College of Music Magazine* stressing the admirable discipline of timing, but deploring that the composer's share of the work was a final gloss rather than—as it should be—a factor as important in the story as the dialogue, and something that should be written in time for the actors to rehearse to. It was a splendid and idealistic idea of film making, but it never came about in any film in which Ralph was concerned.

[1] Later 'Society'.

Most of his difficulties that early summer followed the death of his brother Hervey. He had left Leith Hill Place to Ralph, although, when he had told Ralph that he intended to do so, Ralph had implored him not to. Hervey said then that Ralph could do as he pleased with it, but his it must be. After Hervey's death, Ralph spent a day by himself walking through the woods, looking at the farm, the cottages, the great kitchen garden and all the orchards, fields, and the woods in flower with azaleas and bluebells, asking himself whether he wanted to return to live there. He said to me: 'If I had to decide what trees were to be cut, what vegetables planted, what cows sold, I should lose all pleasure in the place—and if I ran the place properly I shouldn't have any time for my own work.' The next day he visited the offices of the National Trust and offered the house and land to them. Handing over was a long business. Decisions had to be made about many details, some pictures to be given to the Wedgwood Museum, others to be left in the house, old tenants to be secured in their tenancies and, as he was the owner for the time being, Ralph had to send in milk returns to the Ministry of Agriculture, for he had temporarily become a 'milk purveyor'. He and Adeline spent a few days staying in the house, living on a pre-war scale with butter, cream and fresh eggs, figs and nectarines, to support the work of sorting and choosing what to keep, what to sell, and what to give away, and to whom. There was a moment of excitement when a heavy iron box was discovered chained to a ring in the cellar floor: all sorts of marvellous ideas flashed through their minds as they waited for the lock to be forced—it contained one very bent fork. Ralph also discovered a pill box with what appeared to be one pill left in it which Adeline thought he was about to take, following the example of Aunt Sophy who had found one dose left in a bottle of ipecacuanha when clearing up a cupboard and had been heard to say 'a pity to waste a good emetic' as she swallowed it. Adeline seized the box and found that the pill was a pearl.

The sorting out was both amusing and melancholy. It was delightful to them both to discover china and glass to fill up gaps in their own and Cordelia's houses; and furniture that would be useful. Ralph took his father's bookcase, the table he had used when he worked in the library, and a Queen Anne secretaire—all for his Dorking study—and Adeline collected spoons and forks, black Wedgwood vases and some rugs. Loot and swag were words much bandied about, but the real treasures were, Ralph felt, inseparable from the house—particularly as, to their great delight, Randolph and Iris Wedgwood were to be the National Trust's tenants. After so many years when they had seen each other infrequently it was a great joy to Ralph to have Randolph as a neighbour, and it made all the letters, business with solicitors, accountants, National Trust officials, and bank managers worthwhile.

While all this was going on, the landings in Normandy were begun and flying bombs were devastating London and the south. Many children were sent away out of town and there was a second wave of evacuation. Because of this, my employer was less busy, and I spent the whole summer at Dorking, going up for short working days and coming back to the country in the evening, helping in the garden and going for walks with Morris or Ralph and sharing in the Leith Hill Place excitements.

Throughout the war the house had been full—at first, Cordelia's son brought his wife and baby daughter; later they moved to a house near by. Rosamond Carr with her adopted son, the children of Adeline's nephew Bob de Ropp, her niece, Ruth, and others came and went. From the summer of 1943, Ivy Herbert one of the players of the first run-through of the *Fifth Symphony*, and her friend Molly Potto, moved into the two annexe rooms, sharing lunch and dinner, but otherwise living their own busy lives in their domain, with music as the main link between the two households. R. O. Morris had one room, while Ralph and Adeline slept in a small sandbagged bedroom, into which a mattress for me was taken when life was thought to be dangerous. With one, and sometimes two, maids living in, looking after Adeline and doing part-time work for hospital or Red Cross, and a daily cook as well as a gardener too old for war work, Adeline managed her complicated housekeeping with apparent ease from her bed and her wheeled chair, arranging for shopping to be done and seeing to everyone's comfort.

For Ralph the year was busy with practical affairs, gardening and the oboe concerto which he was writing for Leon Goossens. The Proms made the only break, except for a visit from the Menges Quartet to play through Jean's quartet which they were rehearsing for a performance at the National Gallery on his birthday.

He had written 'price 1000 kisses' on the cover of Jean's score, just such a price as he had set on the *Hymn Tune Prelude* he wrote for Harriet Cohen, for one of his letters to her promises to claim his reward in full—his account keeping in such matters was gaily meticulous. Ralph came to London for the concert at which his quartet was played twice with a Haydn quartet between; afterwards there was a lunch party before he went back to Dorking. There was another performance of the quartet at a Boosey and Hawkes concert at the Wigmore Hall in November, and Ralph came to London for that as well as for a performance of *Dona Nobis Pacem* at Southwark Cathedral. He also came to the Old Vic to see *Peer Gynt* with Ralph Richardson as Peer and Sybil Thorndike as Asa. It was an exciting production and the Boyg, a shadow with an echo voice, gave him the idea for how the Apollyon scene in *Pilgrim's Progress* might be managed. He had said that the *Fifth Symphony* used themes from an unfinished opera—but the opera remained persistently alive, and every now and then he wrote a little more. He had used some of it for incidental music for a B.B.C. dramatisation in 1943.

The year ended with a carol concert at Cecil Sharp House which Ralph conducted, and a distribution of 'Leith Hill swag' as Christmas presents. We had had a strange year, flying bombs and perhaps the lowest ebb of comforts. There had been many deaths in the world of music. Henry Wood and Michael Calvocoressi, who had introduced Ralph to Ravel, were links with his youth, and Yvette Guilbert, whom he had admired and seen whenever he had the chance, Ethel Smyth, Carl Engel,[1] C. H. Kitson[2] had all been part of the musical landscape and were now musical history.

At home, gardening had been an all the year round occupation and Ralph's carrots had provided almost too many dishes. Many summer evenings had been spent in cutting them into presentable shapes, for they grew more and more mandrake-like, and Ralph thought they would demoralize the cook. Artichokes followed and leeks, then bonfires and heavy digging

[1] Carl Engel, 1893–1944, musicographer and author. Editor of the *Musical Quarterly*.

[2] C. H. Kitson, 1874–1944, theorist and teacher.

which Ralph insisted should be done properly. But meanwhile the war news was getting better, so that it looked as if, in the spring, there might be an end which we should all live to see.

The B.B.C. commissioned Ralph to write a *Thanksgiving* for this victory and he found it strange to be working on it though battles were continuing. He chose his texts carefully, and the narrator's voice was to speak with the awe of Henry V after Agincourt. There were other lines in his head as he wrote, the scenes of the night before the battle when Henry and Bates and Williams watched the dawn break, as doubtless many other English soldiers in Normandy had watched it—and spoke of rights and wrongs. Like Henry, Ralph felt that in this war the cause had been just, the quarrel honourable.

In a letter dated 8 September to Dr. Welch of the B.B.C. Ralph discussed other questions relating to the music for a thanksgiving service:

> I am glad to understand that you approve of the words of my Victory Anthem. May I venture to make one or two suggestions about the music for the rest of the service? I hope we shall have 'O God our help' and 'All people' and I hope the Old Hundredth will be sung in its proper version with the long notes at the beginning and end of each line. I would not mention this but for the fact that at St. Paul's Cathedral at a Thanksgiving service a few years ago the tune was sung in its square form—all minims. This caused me much dismay—nor would I mention the matter of hymns at all to you, but for something that happened, I am sure without your sanction, on the day of our invasion of Normandy. The hymn chosen after the 7.55 a.m. sermon on that day was not played through as usual but was sung with great pomp by a full choir and the hymn sung was 'Ein' feste Burg'. I could hardly believe my ears!

Adeline caught the cold that prostrated everyone in the house in turn and became very ill with pleurisy and pneumonia; she was well nursed, but there were several nights on which it did not seem likely that she would survive. On one of these, cows got through the fence into the garden and I was awakened by the noise—so was Ralph, and we put on coats and spent a wild half hour driving them back into the field and barricading the gap to keep them there till morning. It was a cold, cloudy night and we kept slipping into the holes that their hoofs had made in the soft earth, tumbling over old vegetable stumps and losing the sticks we were using to bang behind them shouting 'hup' and 'hurrup' and all the things that we had heard the cowman shout. Adeline was so relieved when Ralph returned triumphantly from this adventure that she seemed to start getting better, and in a few weeks she was fairly well again.

In March Ralph came to London for the day and we went to see the film of *Henry V*, which was topical as well as remote. The little striped tents of the armies were very unlike modern equipment but the talk was of Norman towns that were still daily in the news.

He went to Oxford two days later to conduct his oboe concerto with Leon Goossens and the Oxford Orchestral Society and, on Saturday of the same week, he conducted the *St. Matthew Passion* at Dorking. After this he wrote to thank the vicar, the Rev. L. Starey, for lending the church:

> Thank you very much for your letter. I breathe a sigh of relief when these occasions are over—when I think of all the enthusiasm and devotion to music of all 300 people—and then by a single act of carelessness I might bring it all to disaster it is rather overwhelming.

The Festival concert was on 28 April, and by then it was clear that the war in Europe must soon end. The next few days were almost a pause in life, waiting for this news, the sense of expectancy heightened by the spring weather. When at last V.E. day came, Adeline wrote to Cordelia:

> Dork. behaved very sedately yesterday—the church bells pealed at intervals, now and then a megaphone brayed outside the Star—and in the evening there were searchlights and fireworks and excited cries of children. I sat out under the lilac wh. is still full of scent and we had a young American for tea—Morris brought back news of London—great thunderstorm—Have you both—I mean Bernard and you—any plans for the weekend—you ought to hear our challenging cuckoos—or is the tumult in London too fascinating to leave?
>
> I wonder if R's *Thanksgiving* will be heard on Sunday—no word has come about it. He has been digging and now is at his comp—his *Pilgrim's Progress* is nearly finished.

Bernard Brown had drifted in to see Jean and me—and at dusk he played the long trumpet solo from the *Pastoral Symphony* on our roof garden. The melancholy, romantic sound faded over the roofs just as people started putting on lights at windows uncurtained after five and a half years of darkness. Bells that were to have been the signal for invasion rang for victory and it was hard to believe that the fighting in Europe had ended. On Sunday morning Ralph's *Thanksgiving for Victory* was broadcast; sunlight filled the garden: lilac, tulips, and young leaves were bright with dew. Adeline, Morris, Ralph, and I heard the broadcast together and we were all aware that it was easier to mourn than to rejoice.

CHAPTER XIII

1945–1951

Being at The White Gates so much I was able to see how Ralph managed to get through the immense amount of work he undertook. He was usually up by six in the morning and so he had an hour and a half of quiet time for music before breakfast. After breakfast he took his letters to read to Adeline and then he read *The Times*. By nine he was back in his study and there he stayed until lunch at half past twelve. The afternoon was a quiet time, a little reading aloud, a sleep, gardening, or a walk, then tea and more work in the study or sometimes more gardening or letter writing till supper time, a flexible feast adjusted to fit in with any broadcast to which they wanted to listen. If there was no music or no play they cared for, Ralph would read, sleep, and perhaps go back to the study for another hour before bedtime.

He was beginning another symphony, and he was working on music for yet another film, *Stricken Peninsula*. In addition to music he had a lot of business still over his brother's will and all the arrangements about Leith Hill Place. His work for refugees was lessening but by no means ended. For the English Folk Dance and Song Society's Committee there were meetings, library committees, and Editorial Boards to be attended; annual meetings of the English Hymnal Committee, concerts given by the Committee for the Promotion of New Music to hear, CEMA, British Council, and Surrey Education Committee meetings. Though he went only to those which he knew would produce some particular matter he should hear or speak about, it all took up a great deal of time. He took his responsibilities seriously but he avoided anything he thought inessential, so that finding a way through the maze of things he was asked to do was in itself quite a task.

When he came to London he usually contrived to combine work and pleasure, going on from a meeting to a concert or a film, but for some concerts or operas he felt justified in making a special expedition. One of these was the first performance of Britten's opera, *Peter Grimes*, at Sadler's Wells—and this led to re-reading Crabbe's poems. He managed to do a great deal of reading; both he and Adeline had, like many others, rediscovered and enjoyed Trollope's novels, they re-read much Dickens, George Eliot, and Hardy as well as anything new they could get. Penguin books, library books, borrowed books all streamed into the house, and there was always one book being read aloud.

During the early summer Ralph went to stay with Bruce and Elena Richmond near Salisbury. He was away only for one night but it was a refreshing change and he must have surprised them by his interest in gardening and his searching questions on fertilizers, for Adeline wrote 'he found a fine garden there—vegetables nourished on a rare guano which of course he is keen to get'.

On 31 July he conducted at a Promenade concert the first performance of the Suite he had made from the music of his *Flemish Farm* film. The suite had good notices but few performances; Ralph said of it that if you called anything 'a suite' it was damning it to extinction. Other Promenade concerts included the *Fifth Symphony* and the *Five Tudor Portraits*. On 14 September—for now we had the luxury of a Promenade season that was not curtailed because of darkening evenings—there was the first public performance of the *Thanksgiving for Victory*, conducted by Adrian Boult. This was a month after the end of the war in Japan, and the speaker's words, over the choirs murmuring 'a city not forsaken' spoke the hope one felt:

> And they shall build the old wastes, they shall raise up the former desolations, they shall repair the waste cities, the desolations of many generations.

A local performance followed—Adeline told Cordelia:

> R. took a rehearsal of his *Thanksgiving for Victory* in the Church yesterday—the vicar being the narrator: R found it very difficult to conduct.

All through the war I had been meeting friends of Ralph's—among those I had come to know best were Gerald and Joy Finzi. Gerald, working at the Ministry of War Transport, used to come to parties I gave and during the spring he brought one of the

Deputy Directors-General to the Ministry of War Transport, Sir Gilmour Jenkins. He was an amateur musician, a singer and conductor of a choir, and a great admirer of Ralph's and of Gerald's music. He soon became a friend of all the other frequenters of my parties—some of whom he had known in pre-war days when they had sung or played for the Music Club of which he had been the Secretary. Gerald was by this time most anxious to leave the Ministry to return to composing and, at his instigation, Ralph wrote a 'Dear Sir' letter to the Ministry which arrived on Gil's table—Gil had of course met Ralph before the war at Festivals and with Susan Lushington, so the answer to the letter Ralph had written to an imagined 'stuffy civil servant' was a delightful surprise, and the beginning of a close friendship.

Ralph was in London several times during October for National Gallery concerts, one of which celebrated his seventy-third birthday. Another, a few days later was 'to hear a Bartók 4^tte^ which he admired—at least what he could hear of it—he found himself next to Jean [Stewart] and Lorraine [du Val] and they persuaded him to go with them to lunch with the 4^tte^—somewhere near by—he seems to have launched some stories in French at lunch—the only others besides the 4^tte^ were Michael Tippett and the man who runs the concerts—the Gertlers, a good 4^tte^—Belgian with no English—then he was at the R.C.M. and managed to catch the good 5.30 having to run for it with Arnold Bax. . . .'[1]

He also saw both parts of *Henry IV* at the Old Vic in spite of having one of his frequent colds.

R. O. Morris had left The White Gates to share a London house with Hugo Anson, then Registrar at the R.C.M. This made life a little easier for Adeline who worried about Morris's delicate appetite, his colds and his cats who were difficult to please in their food and eccentric in their habits. She had not so far been able to walk since the day of the play-through of the *Fifth Symphony* at Abinger Hall, when she had hurt her foot, and her illness during the last winter of the war had weakened her considerably. When Ralph was out or away she would sometimes sit with her eyes closed, as if she felt she must reserve every atom of strength. But when people came to see her, or when Ralph was in the room, she would talk and listen and give no hint of feeling unwell. She

[1] Adeline to Cordelia.

had two chairs, one for the house and another in which she would be wheeled into the garden—occasionally she would go out in a car, being lifted in and out, but the exertion was almost too high a price to pay for the pleasure of seeing the country.

Ralph's first engagement in the next year was to lecture to sailors and Wrens at Morley College, for Inglis Gundry, one of his old pupils (who had during the war been music adviser to the Director of Education at the Admiralty). He spoke on Beethoven's Ninth Symphony, using for the first time the text he had prepared in 1939. About a hundred came and listened with serious intentness. Inglis Gundry organized the gramophone records for Ralph. It was an illuminating and exciting morning; Maud Karpeles and I were glad to be there, and we both wished we had been able to hear the lecture he had given the year before on the *St. Matthew Passion* to another such audience.

Sadler's Wells planned to put on *Sir John in Love*, the first professional production of the opera, and Ralph was 'full of ideas . . . to make it better'. Adeline wrote:

> R is deep in altering and adding to the parts of Sir John—the first orchestra try through next week. I forsee him living at Sadler's Wells and he will like that—Clive Carey is nice to work with.

He was also busy with *St. Matthew Passion* rehearsals; he managed to whisk up to Sadler's Wells as often as he was needed, enjoying rehearsals and sandwich meals in the bar with the cast, delighted by Anna Pollak's Mistress Ford, and generally enjoying the atmosphere of the theatre.

On 23 March at an afternoon concert at the Wigmore Hall Phyllis Sellick and Cyril Smith had given the first performance of his *Introduction and Fugue* for two pianos, and of course he was there.

He had started on the music for another film, *The Loves of Joanna Godden*, based on Sheila Kaye Smith's novel *Joanna Godden*. He was also working on his sixth symphony, but he had time to go to London to hear Inglis Gundry's opera, *The Partisans*, at St. Pancras Town Hall as well as to the Morley College performance of the Monteverdi *Vespers*. He also made a special visit to London to support Gerald Finzi in trying to prevent the conscription of music students.

Ralph now wanted Michael Mullinar to play over the new

symphony and he and his wife came to stay at Dorking for a July week-end. Ralph invited about twenty people to hear it. When they came, we sat in green twilight, for he had drawn the curtains of the gallery window against the late afternoon sunshine; Michael played the symphony twice to the small audience. After they had left, we had supper, then Michael played again.

Sometime while we had been listening there had been rain, and by now the evening was brilliant with evening light and the colour of everything in the room was intensified. Adeline's crimson Indian shawl, her face, the music paper on the piano were luminous points in the dusk. Michael played a song of his own, a setting of Waller's *Old Age*. Ralph sang it through, reading over his shoulder:

> The soul's dark cottage, battered and decayed
> Lets in new light through chinks that time hath made
> Stronger by weakness, wiser men become
> As they draw near to their eternal home.
> Leaving the old, both worlds at once they view
> That stand upon the threshold of the new.

Ralph started reading more poems, Waller and then Marvell—and then Michael played the symphony again, the scherzo clear as ice and the last movement leading out into space. He had an uncanny power of being able to suggest Ralph's orchestration and each of the many times he had played the work it had been with unflagging excitement and inspiration. Because of that day Ralph dedicated the symphony to him.

Ralph was at home most of the rest of the summer, though he went to see Steuart Wilson in hospital recovering cheerfully and reassuringly after an operation. And he took me to Glyndebourne where Britten's *Rape of Lucretia* was having its first performances. Besides telling Cordelia what we had for lunch, Adeline wrote:

> R. saw a curious thing in the garden—he was getting a cabbage for the hens—saw a snake slipping away and looking down there was a large, wounded toad on wh. the snake was feasting when R disturbed it. R saw the same thing when he was a little boy—he doesn't think it was an adder—too thick——
>
> Ralph and Ursula were home from Glyndebourne by 11. R was disappointed that he didn't see the other cast as he missed Ferrier—Pollak and Mabel Ritchie—he admired a great deal of it—the 2

figures who act as chorus and the music describing the ride. Today he is rehearsing the London Symph. and making his will!

The *London Symphony* was for a Prom on 21 July—when she wrote:

R's great day with London Symph—he was off at 8 for 10 o'c rehearsal—and will be back for 1 o'c lunch—then an afternoon sleep—dress and tea at 5, and off again by 6.2 and home at 10. I shall be glad when it is over as always—but he is in good fettle and really knows the *London Symph.* and the weather is much better than yesterday——[1]

The concert was broadcast and Adeline was able to hear it.

I went off to Switzerland for a holiday with Jean and two other friends, and Adeline wrote to me there in August:

We have had a quiet week—when haven't we—though it doesn't often feel quiet. R. forgets if he told you he is arranging his pfte concerto for 2 pianos (& orch) for Phyllis and Cyril to play on St. Cecilia's day in the Albert Hall (Nov 23?). We are now hoping to get Michael Mullinar to come next week for a week to work from R's sketch for time is short. . . .

. . . We are so relieved at finishing *Jude*[2] and are now comfortably reading the '4 Georges'.[3] I have been on my feet again with success and the rain has stopped.

Being able to stand again was tremendous progress, and cheered her more than anything else she could have done, for it seemed like independence though she still had to be helped into and out of her chair.

I came home to find a postcard from her 'Welcome—when shall we see you?' and was back in time for the *Sea Symphony* Prom and to hear the London rehearsals for the Hereford Festival—Gerald Finzi's *Dies Natalis* and Ralph's *Benedicite* were being rehearsed at the R.C.M. After a morning rehearsal of another work which had been destined for the 1939 Festival, George Dyson's *Quo Vadis*, Ralph took me to the film of *Ivan the Terrible*, which he told Adeline had some fine crowd scenes and the photography was beautiful though he found the story badly constructed. The next day, Adeline told Cordelia, 'He is on the razzle again, this time with Genia Hornstein to see *The Rape of L* at Sadler's Wells.'

[1] Adeline to Cordelia, 24 July 1946.

[2] *Jude the Obscure*, Thomas Hardy.

[3] Roger Fulford.

On 12 September Ralph conducted his *Fifth Symphony* at the Albert Hall, and on the 18th he conducted at a concert at the Dome at Brighton. After that he glued himself to his work on the film, and stayed at home for most of the autumn. During the summer Molly Potto and Ivy Herbert had moved into a home of their own in Dorking, so Ralph and Adeline had the house to themselves.

Ralph's birthday, his seventy-fourth, was not too publicly celebrated, but Dr. William Cole had the idea of doing 'an entirely R.V.W. service' at St. Martin's. He came in to tell Ralph about this idea and asked him if he had ever written a chant as only this was lacking. 'He said if I really wanted to please him would I do the Mornington chant. I thought no more about it but by 2nd post on Monday morning [a new] chant arrived, he must have written it on Sunday night and given it to the postman on Monday morning.'[1] Actually it was still hotter from the press, for Adeline, writing to Cordelia said, 'R very busy—writing a "chant" before break. for St. Martin's where they are doing the whole service on his birthday from his music——'

On 6 November Ralph conducted the *London Symphony* at the Albert Hall. It was a strange concert organized by *The Evening News*, rather long, and with Madame Suggia as the chief guest artist and Ralph conducting the *London Symphony*. Afterwards there was a party at the Dorchester; it was a very festive evening for there was a reception with many cocktails, and at dinner our champagne glasses were kept continually filled. Ralph was hungry and the cocktails had told on him. We sat at tables for twelve and on his other side was a pretty girl in a very full skirted dress. When it came to the cigar and cigarette stage of the evening Ralph had a cigar. He had not smoked all through the war: a niece had dared him to give up his pipe, and he had rashly said that he would though it had been a painful struggle. He had never reverted to it though he had very occasionally had a cigarette. Now the cigar was a sign of true release—but after so much champagne he found it rather hard to hold and finally it dropped under the frilled petticoats of his neighbour 'What *am* I to do?' he said, 'Let her burn alive or dive under her petticoats?' Luckily a waiter saved the situation. By then he felt the time had

[1] Letter from William Cole to U. V. W. 1963. The chant by R. V. W. is used regularly at this annual service on the Sunday nearest his birthday.

come to leave. We floated out; luckily everyone else was walking about three inches from the ground too, so our levitation was unnoticed. Adeline told Cordelia, 'R came home at 1 a.m. very gay'. and when he told her the story of the cigar and the petticoats he said, 'I feared my action might be misconstrued'.

Ralph had decided to form a choir to sing the *St. John Passion*. Before Christmas he wrote to the singers whose musicianship he trusted and whose voices were good enough to sing as a small group. There were about thirty people; he asked Ivy Herbert to be the Hon. Secretary—an office she handed on to Genia Hornstein after the first year. Ralph planned to have rehearsals at The White Gates and to sing the work, with a very small orchestra to accompany it, in the church. Besides this he was having a new set of parts made for the *St. Matthew Passion*; and photographic copies of his English version of the Mass in B minor had been prepared for the Festival, so that they should be ready for a run-through with the conductors of the choirs who would sing some of it in April. By the beginning of December he had finished his film music. 'Joanna is packed up and ready for posting to Ealing Studios—full score and reduced score. R feels such relief. . . .'[1]

Ernest Irving acknowledged its arrival:

Your letter arrived on Saturday morning producing somewhat the same effect upon me as the lady's millstone must have done on Abimelech. Never in the history of Ealing, or for that matter of the world, has the score been finished before the film, and I am carefully concealing it from the directors, who must not be approached from windward.

We have now received the score and have played it through from the sketch. It is the best music we have ever had here, and all the members of our little arcana were excited and delighted.

As the film is still incomplete it is of course quite impossible to express an opinion about the fitting of it but, in view of the latitude conceded by your instructions, I should think the necessary rearrangements will be possible without damaging the musical structure. If there should be anything sufficiently unmalleable as to demand actual reconstruction or new composition I shall ask you to be kind enough to take a look at the episode on the screen.

I note particularly and thoroughly agree, that in the time-space continuum you wish the time element to remain constant and adjustments made by extension or amputation, not by variation of velocity.

[1] Adeline to Cordelia.

I think if I may offer an opinion that the brooding music for Romney Marsh is most delicately sensitive and paints the exact picture of what I should hope to see on walking out from Appledore, at the same time cutting out the bungalows and pylons which, no doubt, frame the actual landscape.

I shall fit the sketch to the picture as soon as there is a cut copy to work on, and consult you about any alterations that I may have to suggest. Meanwhile thank you for a lovely musical job (not Job).

On Christmas Day Ralph wrote to Boris Ord at King's College, Cambridge, after he had listened to the Festival of Lessons and Carols——

Thank you very much for your letter which warmed my heart—I am so glad you are back at music again.

As regards an evening service—the atmosphere of smugness has so settled on those canticles that it seems almost impossible to lift the pall and get at the essence. I fear the service I wrote for Christ's Hospital will be no use to you.

Now it seems ungracious after your splendid letter to make a grouse—but I have meant to do this for years—indeed every Xmas but have never done it.

I deplore the almost entire absence of English carols in your King's College service. I think every English carol service ought to start with *God rest you Merry* and end with the *1st Noel*—then what about

The Lord at first
Virgin unspotted
Cherry Tree
Tomorrow shall be my dancing day
This is the truth
On Xmas night, and many more

I only find *London Waits*, *God rest you* (I think that is new this year) and *Holly & Ivy* (which I am glad to see is not now called French in your programme) among the traditional carols—a small proportion to my mind.

I spoke about this to . . . . last year and he did not know which were English and which were not!

Yrs with much gratitude
R. Vaughan Williams

The year had brought news of performances in America, Finland, Greece, and at the Graz Festival. Ralph had been given the honorary freedom of the Worshipful Company of Musicians, and his *Fifth Symphony*, which everyone had thought would be his last, had a successor almost finished. He was bubbling with new ideas, enjoying film music, starting the Dorking Bach Choir and, in spite of colds, fatigue after conducting and increasing trouble with hearing, he was full of energy. All through Adeline's letters to Cordelia there are references to comings and goings: young composers bringing work to show to Ralph, friends looking in on their way to somewhere else, Dorking friends for tea—the pattern continues unchanged—and in almost all the letters Cordelia is urged to come to spend the night, to stay for a week-end, or to come back with Ralph after a concert. She and Adeline enjoyed being together but, when Cordelia's other ties kept her from The White Gates, these daily letters between the sisters kept them in close touch, with scraps of news, the weather, the garden, the jam making, or even details of meals. Accounts of letters from relations or mutual friends were discussed, so Adeline's life was filled with a family life beyond the comings and goings of her own home.

Hugh Allen, Nicholas Gatty, Thomas Dunhill, and Granville Bantock had all died during the year. The first two had both been close friends in important parts of Ralph's life: but he had seen less of them lately and it was as if they were still absent only in a fortuitous or geographical sense. He was almost always too busy with people and things that were near to miss those who were not. Perhaps Gustav was the only exception, the one friend he never ceased to miss.

The *St. John* rehearsals went well; Ralph, as Adeline said, 'didn't spare them or himself'. Besides the music he was showing the choir the drama. His own picture of the work was so vivid, the singers so interested, and Margery Cullen's patience so tireless as she played for each practice, that he was very happy about the venture.

Sadler's Wells planned to do *The Shepherds of the Delectable Mountains*, so Ralph was summoned to rehearsals early in February. The staging was more elaborate than he liked, for he always believed more in lighting than in scenery, but he was glad to see it and to hear it again. It was a busy month for him, with the mixture of *Shepherds*, *St. John*, and *St. Matthew* rehearsals, and sending out appeals.

This spring the Leith Hill Musical Festival will rise like a phoenix from its ashes. Should we not mark the occasion by performances of especial excellence? But to achieve this we must have first-rate performers and long and careful rehearsal.

All this will cost money. Fees and expenses have nearly doubled since the war, and if we want good results we must expect to have to spend at least £1500 on the competitions and five concerts, including that healthy offspring of the Festival, the performance of Bach's Passion. Of this sum we cannot expect to receive more than £500 by the sale of tickets and by church collections. We have just over £300 in the bank and we hope for a grant of £40 from the Carnegie Trust. The rest must be met by our friends and well wishers.

The Festival was, of course, already planned—rehearsals had been going forward all the winter—and Ralph was perfectly sure that the money would come from somewhere. *St. John* was his private indulgence, and he was going to pay for it himself. The performance was on Ash Wednesday, the day after the *Shepherds*, and it was good enough for him to decide that he would give another performance the following spring, for which he was already planning to re-arrange the orchestral seating.

The Dorking Halls were still not ready to use for the *Passion* so he arranged to give two performances, one at Epsom and one at Redhill. He liked to have the local choir boys to sing the *Ripieno* part, but the Epsom boys that year were very tiresome.

'The dirty look' that alarmed Bernard [Brown] was aimed at a cheeky little choir boy who didn't stand up—it took effect! R doesn't mean to have these boys again—there was no one to keep them in order. R thought Lizzie[1] especially lovely—also Bernard's playing . . . his worry was the small mistakes that he felt he cd. have dealt with . . . and the chorus got into a difficulty—R too—He is getting over his fatigue and has gone to have his hair cut.[2]

He had a rehearsal at Redhill a week later, a long Sunday afternoon with the choirs, and the performance on the Wednesday after. This was excellent, and Ralph was far less worried and, so, far less tired than he had been after Epsom. Some recordings had been made of the Epsom performance, and when they came Ralph was able to hear how the work sounded to the audience and he was agreeably surprised.

[1] Elizabeth Darbishire.

[2] Letter from Adeline to Cordelia.

It was wonderful to be back in the Halls for the Festival in April. Children's Day had been dropped, as many of the teachers felt that competition was bad for their pupils, forgetting the value of what Walford Davies once described as 'pacing each other on the road to excellence'. But it kept a quiet day between the second and third concerts which was half a blessing, for it gave Ralph a rest physically, half a misery, for he was nervous about the Friday programme. His translation into English of the text of the *Mass in B minor*, from which the choirs were to sing the *Gloria*, *Gratias*, *Qui tollis*, *Cum Sancto Spiritu*, *Sanctus*, and *Dona Nobis*, was to be used for the first time and he was to conduct R. O. Morris's setting of *Corinna's Maying*. But the concert went as well as the two earlier ones. The *Mass* was an interesting experiment, the translation was proved to be thoroughly singable and Morris's *Corinna* was well liked. It had been a good Festival and, as the judges were the same as in 1939, a feeling of continuity prevailed.

After the Festival Ralph and Adeline battled their way through the orchestral accounts and Ralph cleared up his study, a job he always put off as long as possible but quite enjoyed doing when it came to the point. He was a ruthless tearer-up, and he would empty drawers and boxes on to the floor and dispose of letters, receipts and musical sketches he no longer needed until his enormous wastepaper basket was overflowing.

He came up to London to go to the exhibition of French tapestries; some of them, the very earliest and particularly the *Dame à la Licorne* series with its pale heroine and strawberry coloured backgrounds, gave him great pleasure, rather to his surprise for he did not care for tapestries of later date and he had been unaware of the existence of these early ones.

He was in a restless state, waiting for the orchestral rehearsal of his symphony. When I was next at Dorking Ralph had one of his moods for a long walk, so we went by bus to Mickleham, over the top of Box Hill tunnel and through the spring woods. He told me then how he had managed to keep going on route marches, when he got tired and felt he could not go on any longer, by promising himself to walk another hundred steps, then counting his hundred, then promising himself to walk another hundred—and by then he would find he could manage yet another hundred. By the time he had told me this I realized that his ankles were aching and he was getting himself along in just this way; so we sat on the grass for a long time and then found a good short-cut home.

Adeline had been ill again early in the spring and that anxiety, as well as the many rehearsals and recording sessions Ralph had had to fit in during the spring, had forced him to postpone the play-through of the revised score of his new symphony which Michael Mullinar had promised to undertake in March. It eventually took place on 5 June at the R.C.M. and Ralph invited some of his friends to come. R. O. Morris said in a letter to Adeline, 'the sustained vigour and originality of the musical idea is most imposing—truly astonishing to one who knows how incessantly Ralph has been labouring in one way and another since the war started'. After this day Ralph felt on much more solid ground, and able to think about a performance.

Jean Stewart had become engaged to a doctor, George Hadley, a fine amateur cellist. She took him to The White Gates to be introduced and Ralph immediately recruited him for the orchestra for the next Festival. Two days after the play-through, I went with Ralph to their wedding at Oxford. Ralph made the speech proposing their health, and it was full of wisdom, affection, and confidence. When Jean told him that she had to come back from her honeymoon in a week's time to play *Flos Campi* and she was afraid it might not be a very good performance, he said, 'My dear, you'll play it with half the technique and ten times the passion.'

We drove back in time for Ralph to go to a party at Leith Hill Place to celebrate the centenary of his grandfather's going to live there. He met many of his Wedgwood and Darwin cousins and was delighted at the way in which Iris had brought the house to life. It had never looked so beautiful, and he rejoiced to see familiar pieces of furniture and pictures he had always known looking so much at home in the newly decorated rooms.

The Royal Academy of Music chose *The Poisoned Kiss* for their end of term opera, and Ralph went to many of the rehearsals as well as a performance. He was glad to hear it again and as usual enjoyed being among young people and involved with anything to do with the stage. It was an early celebration of his seventy-fifth birthday and one he appreciated.

During the summer he was finishing scoring the symphony

and considering what to do with his *Double Trio* which had been put away since he had revised the original 1939 manuscript in 1942. He had never been satisfied with it as chamber music and he thought that it should perhaps have been an orchestral work. It became a *Partita* for string orchestra, with a new fourth movement. He asked Robert Müller-Hartmann to 'correct any mistakes before I send it to the copyist and also tell me of any places where you think I have made any error of judgment. . . .'

There were visits from Bob Trevelyan, bringing his translation of Catullus, and from Bobby Longman—'he looked so well—he and R showered compliments on each other,' Adeline told his sister-in-law, Mary Fletcher. Of other compliments showered on him that summer Ralph never knew. It was the first year of the Edinburgh Festival and 'as there was then no fixed policy about programmes each conductor was asked to say what he would like to play. Everyone included the V.W. Tallis. Bruno did it with the Vienna as his was the first programme to be received.'[1]

He had a Prom in August, and September started with the usual Three Choirs rehearsals at the R.C.M. It was a Gloucester Festival that year; he went off happily to stay with the Sumsions and to hear Christopher le Fleming's *Five Psalms*, Gerald Finzi's *Dies Natalis*, and his own *Magnificat*, and to conduct his *Fifth Symphony*, which was broadcast.

In September Ralph took the chair at a conference to inaugurate the International Folk Music Council which met at the Belgian Institute and Cecil Sharp House. After welcoming the delegates as President, he asked Steuart Wilson to take the chair for him; though he came to London for one meeting at which Steuart could not be present, a day on which he was obviously not feeling like being there, for he opened the proceedings by saying fiercely, 'Has anyone anything to say?—I hope not'. But the delegates were undaunted by this and said a number of things. Ralph was very glad when Steuart resumed his chair; so possibly were the delegates, for under Steuart's less severe rule some of the meetings were very entertaining. And Maud Karpeles, inventor of the Council as well as its Secretary, kept the many foreign visitors busy and happy.

[1] Letter from Herbert Wiseman to Maurice Jacobson: the others were Paul Paray (Colonne), Barbirolli (Hallé), Sargent (Liverpool), Susskind (Scottish National).

October 9th was the fiftieth anniversary of Ralph's and Adeline's marriage; he had found a small gold locket for her in London, plain enough he hoped for her to care to wear.

Birthday celebrations were piling up—a party at Cecil Sharp House on the tenth; on the eleventh a concert in the Dorking Halls given by the Croydon Philharmonic Society and the London Symphony Orchestra conducted by Alan Kirby, with Ena Mitchell, Astra Desmond, and Roy Henderson as soloists in the *Sea Symphony* and the *Tudor Portraits*; a party at the Dorking Halls on the 12th, with, at Ralph's special request, a conjuror—and a very brilliant one, who left everyone gasping when he produced a *6d.* postal order, which we had all seen Ralph sign, from the inside of a currant bun in a cardboard box that had not been moved from the table. The squiggly signature was unmistakeably authentic. There were presents, letters, a telegram from Sibelius, and broadcast concerts, with *Flos Campi*, *Sancta Civitas*, and the *Four Hymns*—Ralph's own choice—on 13 October. On the 15th he came to London again to conduct his *London Symphony* with the B.B.C. orchestra.

On 19 November Ralph presented the Royal Philharmonic Society's Gold Medal to William Walton after Frederick Riddle had played his viola concerto, conducted by Sir Thomas Beecham.

Ralph had been asked to write an anthem for the St. Cecilia's Day service at St. Sepulchre's church, Holborn, and he had decided to set some of the words of the book of *Job* to one of his *Job* tunes. He called it *The Voice out of the Whirlwind*. He felt it was not entirely a success but it was interesting to hear that the words fitted the tune as if he had had the rhythm of the prose at the back of his mind when he was writing the Masque.

Ralph's deafness was beginning to be a positive nuisance to him particularly at the extremes of the musical range. He wrote to Imogen Holst in November—just after this service:

> Thank you for your Heavenly Anthem—There are some more Donne sermons you might set—the one which was used as a prayer at the Cecilia service about Music in Heaven.
>
> Now, something else—I have long been worried about Gustav's double bass soli—(e.g. in particular, Saturn, P.F. [Perfect Fool], Egdon and end of Fugal Concerto)—they always seemed to me the one place where Gustav worked to a theory—the C.B. ought to sound

nice alone and therefore it did. But in practice unless you have a very large body of C.Bs they can hardly be heard and (this is the point of my letter) on the wireless they are to me *quite inaudible*—Please give Adrian and other conductors leave to add cellos and perhaps occasionally violas—I know it is not exactly the same sound—but what is the good of a sound which is not heard?

An orchestral rehearsal of the *Sixth Symphony* was arranged for 16 December at the Maida Vale Studio with Adrian Boult and the B.B.C. orchestra. Ralph was amazed and delighted to find that the players made sense of their parts at the first reading. Of Adrian's understanding he had had no doubt, but he had expected everyone to find it more difficult to play than they appeared to do. When he took the second run-through himself, he found it very hard to conduct. When Adrian followed him for a third play-through, Ralph started marking his score where he wanted to make changes. The small invited audience, many of whom had heard the piano play-through in June, were left excited but exhausted with concentration, some of them speculating about the 'meaning' of this work. Only the composer seemed completely untired, and after a solid lunch spent the afternoon at the Van Gogh exhibition at the Tate Gallery.

Earlier in the year Ernest Irving had written to ask Ralph to write music for the film about Scott's expedition to the South Pole. He was at first reluctant to commit so much time—but Irving was persuasive, and the idea of the strange world of ice and storm began to fascinate him. The film studio provided books, and *The Worst Journey in the World* joined *Jane Eyre*, *Pendennis*, *The Way of all Flesh*, and *Far from the Madding Crowd* as general reading. Pictures of the Scott expedition lay about the house and the work was begun. Ralph became more and more upset as he read about the inefficiencies of the organization; he despised heroism that risked lives unnecessarily, and such things as allowing five to travel on rations for four filled him with fury. Apart from this he was excited by the demands which the setting of the film made on his invention, to find musical equivalents for the physical sensations of ice, of wind blowing over the great, uninhabited desolation, of stubborn and impassable ridges of black and ice-covered rock, and to suggest man's endeavour to overcome the rigours of this bleak land and to match mortal spirit against elements. For light relief there were the penguins and the whales. There was to be music not only for the polar journey but also for the two women, Kathleen Scott and Oriana Wilson, so he had scope for many different kinds of tune. On the practical side he had had enough experience of work with the studios to make a number of provisos about the use of natural sounds and dialogue and how they were to be used in relation to his score. He had been angry about the choice of a Cornish carol in *Joanna Godden*—unlikely and unsuitable for Romney Marsh he thought. Had he been consulted he would have chosen *God rest you Merry* or *The First Nowell* as dramatically right. He did not want this sort of trouble to arise in the Scott film—and on behalf of the studio Irving gave large and comprehensive undertakings which were fully honoured. The film work, with consultations and visits to the studio to see the pictures, went on all through the year at irregular intervals, enlivened by letters from Ernest Irving, sometimes in verse, as one that came in answer to Ralph's suggestion for the use of voices singing wordlessly:

Una vox et praeterea nihil

I very much regret to state
Your scheme for treating No. 8.
Has pulled us up with quite a jerk
Because we fear it will not work.

Miss Mabel Ritchie's off-stage tune
Besides annoying Miss Lejeune[1]
Would cover, blur, confine and fog
Our most expensive dialogue.

Failure they meet and ruin black
Who mix two voices on one track.
Choose then a horn or cello, which
Have different timbres, weight and pitch.

Your programme would as you aver
Astound and shock the chronicler
But so, I must admit with pain
Did Casca, Crippen, Cromwell, Cain. . . .

However, Ralph persisted, and in the end converted Irving who in turn converted the authorities.

On one of his days at the studio his chauffeur, Beagley (who

[1] C. A. Lejeune at that time film critic of *The Observer*.

had been first groom then chauffeur at Leith Hill Place, and now, discharged from the Forces, had come to work at The White Gates), brought a story from the studios. He had been waiting for Ralph when a band of riders belonging to a historical film came along the road: one was having trouble with a lively horse—'O horse, dear horse, Woh! *Please* Woh—please, *please* Woh'. This gave Ralph great pleasure, and '*please* woh' came into family use.

About this time Hubert Foss wrote to ask Ralph for information about his musical education, Ralph answered:

> I am again in the film way (9 months does not seem to apply in this case—I'm more like a cat)—and so am rationing my visits to London—I'm sending you my 'musical influences' in a few days——

This was a chapter of musical autobiography he gave to Foss to draw on for material for a book he was writing on Ralph—but Foss included it in full.[1]

It was another long and cold winter: the *St. John* rehearsals were cheerful occasions in the big room at The White Gates with a huge fire to warm the singers, some of whom stayed on for coffee afterwards. 'We're beginning to know the work,' Ralph said, but he exhorted them to practise at home as well as at the weekly meetings. The performance on 7 February was followed by the *St. Matthew* a month later; this time, happily in the Dorking Halls. Everyone was delighted to be there again, and the meal for the orchestra in the smaller hall between rehearsal and performance had the feeling of a party.

As *The English Hymnal* were planning a Scottish supplement, Ralph asked me to write a hymn about St. Margaret. 'No hurry,' he said, so I took my time and looked her up—'sister of the Aethling, married to Malcolm King of Scotland, son to that Duncan murdered by Macbeth. . . .' When I arrived at Dorking a few days later, Ralph met me at the door: 'I hope you don't mind dreadfully, but I wrote the tune this morning—it's to the metre of *The Charge of the Light Brigade*.' To help he had left a nonsense verse in my room, a beautifully accented and slightly bawdy exposition of the stresses and metre his tune required.

He was writing another small work too, in preparation for the

[1] *Ralph Vaughan Williams*, by Hubert Foss: Harrap & Co. Ltd.; 1950. Reprinted as 'A Musical Autobiography' in *National Music*, Oxford University Press, 1963.

Parry centenary celebration at Oxford; for this he had chosen the poem by Skelton that Colonel Isaacs suggested he should set before Elgar had said that Elinor Rumming was the one for him. It was *Prayer to the Father of Heaven*, one that at first sight looked unsettable, but which had made him think of a tune—though there were many discussions about accentuation again, especially of the line: 'of all essentials the essential most perfite', which had to rhyme with 'might', 'night', and then 'delight'. It was a difficult and interesting poem to set, and it filled the gaps of time left between preparing for the Festival and the first performance of his *Sixth Symphony*.

Although the war was already three years behind us, living conditions were still complicated by rationing of food and clothing. Like many other families, Ralph and Adeline had been sent presents from abroad. A young Australian girl, Dorothy Wallis, who admired and knew a good deal of Ralph's music, used to send parcels of such luxuries as raisins, tins of butter, and home made cakes, a choice that showed splendid insight. From America a young clergyman who shared Ralph's love of William Barnes's poems sent a four-pound tin of boiled sweets at Christmas, while a young couple, Victor and Mary Shepherd, who had left England recently for South Africa, sent anything they knew to be difficult to get at home. Adeline wrote to thank them for a parcel of soap:

It is difficult to suggest anything better than what you have already chosen. We have a feeling that we must share 'austerity' to some extent with others, and Dorking is a much easier place to live in than London. We . . . have a certain amount of garden and can grow potatoes to help us a great part of the year. Fish is plentiful and there is always bread, cakes and oatmeal—of course the world is short of FATS—and milk—but apart from having to think more about food, and plan, so far we do not suffer—and my husband can even find braces in the town tho' they are not entirely elastic but will last some time. . . . Have you rice?—it would be nice to have a small quantity—and for jam have you quince or cape gooseberry? I remember both in the old days coming from S. Africa.

As to materials we mend and patch and so far we are all right, for I have a faithful maid who helps me—I am rather an infirm person and am looked after to an extent that makes me ashamed——

My husband is full of energy——

I wonder if you will hear a broadcast of his Partita for double string orchestra (3rd programme March 20th & 21st Adrian Boult). . . .

He and Adeline listened to the broadcast, so did Robert Müller-Hartmann who had helped him with it, copying, checking, and advising, and to whom it was dedicated. It came almost at the right moment to be a present on his naturalization, for Ralph wrote to him only a few weeks later to say: 'I feel it a great honour to claim you as a fellow citizen.'

Many people were looking forward to the *Sixth Symphony*. Morning and afternoon rehearsals at Maida Vale studios the first day were agreeably divided by lunch with R. O. Morris, who had been deeply impressed at the first run-through in December and was thoroughly convinced of the merit of this work, but discussed only technical details, which was exactly right for Ralph at that moment. The next morning rehearsal was easy, and we spent the rest of the day buying music and going to the Retrospective Exhibition of Paul Nash's pictures at the Tate Gallery. The Chairman of the Royal Philharmonic Society, Thomas Wood, gave a dinner party before the concert; pleasantly arranged as it was Ralph found it an ordeal, for before a first performance he was far too nervous to feel either sociable or hungry.

Ralph's programme notes for the symphony were, he said, severely practical, a map for the listener to use rather than a series of picture postcards. He was passionately anxious to discourage the critics from inventing 'meanings'. He would have liked to print Mendelssohn's saying that 'the meaning of music is too precise for words' on every concert programme at which his works were played. He could not stop the questions and, rightly or wrongly, he never allowed the idea that lay behind the last movement of this symphony to be known to the critics who speculated on its historical and philosophical origin. Yet, as silence followed the final whisper of the last notes, it seemed as if the whole audience must guess the riddle:

> And, like the baseless fabric of this vision,
> The cloud capp'd towers, the gorgeous palaces,
> The solemn temples, the great globe itself,
> Yea, all which it inherit, shall dissolve
> And, like this insubstantial pageant faded,
> Leave not a wrack behind. We are such stuff
> As dreams are made on, and our little life
> Is rounded with a sleep. . . .

We were at the Albert Hall again two nights later to hear *Sancta Civitas*. Rosamond Carr, who had been staying at Dorking, wrote in her diary that Ralph had complained, 'It's awful—people come up to me in the lavatory and say how much they liked my symphony.' For unless praise came from some fellow musician or some close friend he found it disconcerting. This had nothing to do with modesty or, as was sometimes suggested, humility, a quality which he detested in others and of which he had no trace. Perhaps it was partly shyness but it sprang also from a great dislike of discussing his work except with a very few of his friends.

It was a good summer for concerts: the Tudor Singers' Silver Jubilee on 30 April included the *Sanctus* and *Osanna* from Ralph's Mass as well as *The Souls of the Righteous*, a motet he had written for the dedication of the Battle of Britain chapel in 1947; and on 12 May the Parry Centenary was celebrated during the Oxford Festival of Music by a concert in the Sheldonian. Ralph's *Prayer to the Father of Heaven* followed Professor Westrup's oration: the Oxford Bach Choir, conducted by Thomas Armstrong, had worked hard at its difficulties till they had apparently disappeared and Ralph was very pleased with the performance.

The scenery Gwen Raverat had designed for *Job*, which followed the Blake drawings as faithfully as Geoffrey Keynes's scenario, had been lost when the Sadler's Wells Ballet Company had had to leave Holland at the outbreak of war in haste, confusion, and danger. Though the drawings were still available John Piper was asked for new designs. Where Gwen Raverat, Geoffrey Keynes, and Ralph had all thought in terms of Blake's vision, the Piper sets imposed another interpretation of Blake. The murkier colours and more sinister proportions did not please the composer—though the great advantage of the new production at Covent Garden was that the large orchestra pit allowed the original score to be used for the first time in a theatre. Adrian Boult conducted and Robert Helpmann was a splendidly evil Satan. Ralph was disappointed that so many of his stage directions were neglected—the sons and daughters had no feast at which to clash their wine cups, so the soft cymbal clashes were pointless; nor were their bodies brought in a shrouded, distant procession across the wide stage as the figures of War, Pestilence, and Famine haunted Job's dream—Ralph would have liked to be producer, designer and repetiteur himself. Even with these faults, it was an impressive production, and the choreography seemed to him better than he remembered from before the war. He went again on the 25th, as Adeline told Cordelia:

R. viewed Job from the tiers above the boxes—good for sound and he even heard the oboe which is a major difficulty with him. It wasn't a Rolls R evening—he went by 4.18 took Fanny [Farrer] to M.M. and he caught the 9.18 home. Programmes 6d., every seat filled even the slips. Today Betty Maconchy[1] is coming with *her* new symph.—so R will have an exacting afternoon, but he is very fond of her so she is welcome . . . here is Betty Mc and lunch—fried plaice and a stodgy pudding. . . .

Ralph's cousin, Roland Vaughan Williams, and his wife Grace had moved from High Ashes to Tanhurst and Adeline wrote to me:

2 Sundays without you seems most strange—on Friday R and I . . . drove to Tanhurst. R went over the well-remembered house and Roland sat in the car with me—a very happy visit—the view enchanting and the old Arab mare who has the free run of the garden put her head into the open door of the car adding to the charm of this lovely place—I like it so much more than Leith Hill Place.

I was at Dorking for much of the summer and there were long walks, visits to the cinema, and a musical party given by Yanya and Genia Hornstein for Robert Müller-Hartmann with his songs and piano music which Ralph was glad to have an opportunity of hearing. He and Ralph had seen a good deal of each other during the year as Müller-Hartmann had been making a German translation of *Sancta Civitas*; he used often to come in for an hour on Sunday mornings, walking down the hill and through the town to appear at the open french window of Ralph's study, when they would settle down to an hour of gossip and conversation which they both found enlivening.

As I had never been to a Three Choirs Festival, Adeline suggested that I should go to Worcester with Ralph. Ralph stayed with his old friends Canon and Mrs. Briggs, and I had a room in a house on the Green in which Thomas Tomkins had once lived. It was lovely weather, the Malvern Hills clear beyond the Severn, and there was a great air of festivity—I had only begun to

[1] Married to William LeFanu.

discover how much could go into a day. We spent our first morning at *The Kingdom*; Ralph conducted an exciting performance of *Job* in the afternoon—the sound of the music was quite different from that of Covent Garden in this stone building; a different resonance which suited the brass particularly. Then there were tea parties and Ralph swept the Briggs family off to the cinema with us. The next day we went to look for Wenlock Edge which Ralph had never seen. We went by Stokesay and Ludlow, but a long bank of low cloud hid Wenlock, though we saw the signpost 'to the Roman City of Uriconium'. After tea with the Briggs we went to drink sherry with the Headmaster of Kings School and his wife; this became a madrigal party, so Ralph joined the basses and sang for an hour. There was somehow still time for dinner before the evening concert, and after the concert the Sumsions had a party. The next morning I joined the Finzis for a dash round junk shops so that I should have something to take back to Adeline. Meanwhile Ralph was going through the score of *Tallis* which, with Kodály's *Missa Brevis*, made up the morning concert. After lunch we drove back through Gloucester and Birdlip, familiar country to us both, and then to Down Ampney where we stopped and where Ralph showed me the house where he was born and the dark, laurel-shadowed path that was his earliest recollection.

During the autumn he was still working on his Scott music; he had won his point about the use of voices to suggest desolation and icy winds, and he had already begun to think that he might later use the music for an Antarctic Symphony. However, it was *Pilgrim's Progress* that filled most of his days, and in early December it was played through to a few people at The Arts Council,[1] Ralph singing all the parts himself. He felt that it had not been a success. 'People were coldly polite,' he told Adeline, but he was philosophic about it—'It's not the sort of thing they expect for an opera anyway,' he said.

Early in the morning of 15 December Ralph telephoned to say they had just heard that Morris had died during the night, and Adeline wrote to me the next day.

> I like to think that dear Morris was 'spared' to come to your party[2] —he did not want to live into old age.

[1] Formerly C.E.M.A.

[2] He had come to one of my Wednesday parties a few days before he died.

He had written to her at the end of October:

> I hope you have managed to get out for a ride or two in the car, for it is one of those years when the autumn woods are going to give a gorgeous if melancholy display. Not that I find autumn particularly melancholy these days: it is the spring rather that saddens one, for it is no sooner come than it is gone—like the rest of us——

Morris died of a sudden heart attack—the elegant precision of his life extended to death. Ralph did not, as he had planned, go to the Philharmonic concert to hear Beecham conduct *In the Fen Country* that evening.

Scott of the Antarctic filled the Odeon cinema. Ralph did not go to the first showing, but we went one afternoon a day or two later; it was exciting, after having seen so many of the stills, seen some of the action without dialogue, and heard some of the music in all its stages, to see the whole film. Ralph still fulminated against the amateurish organization of the last stages of the expedition but he was pleased with his score. Directly the film ended, the cinema organ began to play as the lights went up—no break of silence was allowed, and the organist's choice of music was as inappropriate as it could be. The next day Ralph sent him a page of music, carrying on from the film, so as to allow the audience to recover without having another musical idiom hurled at them.

Early in the New Year Ralph started sitting for Epstein. This came about through Epstein's friend, the pianist Shula Doniach, who was an acquaintance of mine. She had told me that Epstein wanted to do a bust of Ralph; Adeline was pleased and Ralph submissive. She wrote to me:

> A lovely letter from E; 'I had not thought of a fee but of course you will want to keep the bronze—I will put the fee at 200 guineas' and then he suggests R's coming to the studio next Monday! I only have a little doubt so we haven't answered. R had rheumatic aches all over him yesterday, he asked for *your shawl*, and that and a bowl of bread and milk and hot bottles did wonders and today brek. in bed and temp down from 100 to normal.

He was up on the day appointed for she wrote again:

> Well—the first sitting went happily. Epstein seems to work with intense concentration—R imitates him beautifully—this suits R and

now that the work has started he is keen to get it finished—and he is off this morning—alas, by train—he returns at 2. Epstein says 6 sittings—and perhaps 1 or 2 more at the end. The studio is on the ground floor. There doesn't seem much comfort, the stove is allowed to go out—on the other hand R needn't keep still and could sit in his coat wh. I have urged his doing.

Ralph had been feeling creaky all that winter, and they discovered a delightful masseur—Adeline told Cordelia:

He is a cultivated man—about 55 and blind or nearly so—has been trained at St. Dunstans. R liked him at once and R said he talked to him all the time—he seems understanding and R will look forward to him coming twice a week which is all he can manage. . . . Mr. Collins has advised footbath with Epsom salts for R when his arches are tired—Beagley has bought a deep galvanised bath for them and Epsom salts—'commercial' as ordered—which Beagley says is for cattle! R slept well after his first treatment.

Ralph and Mr. Collins used to turn on the 'Evensong from Cathedrals' broadcast programmes during the massage sessions: when the music was to their taste they listened, but the rest of the programmes were punctuated by much laughter, and it appeared that they told each other stories, for Ralph would produce new ones prefaced by 'My masseur told me'—or he would say 'I must remember so and so to tell Collins'. He was also recommended to diet, less weight for his ankles would help, Dr. Clarke said.

I agree with you there is very little to be gained by it [Adeline wrote to Cordelia]. Still, I have got a guinea fowl and a boiling chicken wh. no one can say is not good for him—as he says—'I must eat something'. Dr. Clarke says in answer 'I know it's difficult in these times but eat less.' But I don't mean to let R take this too seriously.

He needed to be well for, besides his regular *St. John* and *St. Matthew* rehearsals, he had instituted Saturday practices 'for all who like to come'. He was as busy as usual—Robert Müller-Hartmann made such a good German translation of *Sancta Civitas* that now Ralph had asked him to translate *The Pilgrim's Progress*.

. . . There is no performance—alas—in view, but I think a German translation might possibly lead to a performance abroad. . . . A lot of words are straight out of Bunyan and I think there is an existing translation which might help you; and a lot is out of the Bible.

He went to the Dorking Operatic Society's performance of *The Gondoliers*, to the Royal Academy of Music's opera performance, and, in spite of a cold which had left him speechless, he shared an Albert Hall concert on 22 February with William Walton at which he included his *London Symphony*. A postcard from Adeline on the 24th said reassuringly, 'R's voice is almost right if only he doesn't wreck it tonight—he is in London recording.[1] He wanted to be there so all is well—a lovely day.'

He had to take a rehearsal for the *St. John Passion*, and to conduct the performance as well as taking a rehearsal for the *St. Matthew Passion* during the week.

Tom Harrison, who had produced both the Abinger Pageant and *England's Pleasant Land* before the war, was now working in Birmingham. He told Ralph that he was producing *Sir John in Love* for the Clarion Singers, an enterprising choir directed by Katherine Thomson, a musician whose family Ralph had known in Cambridge, and who was now married to a Professor at the University of Birmingham. Tom Harrison begged Ralph to come to the opera but, as it unfortunately clashed with the *St. Matthew* performance at Dorking, he determined to go to a rehearsal instead. He wanted me to go too, and Adeline wrote:

A few stray thoughts—R will ring you to clench plans—Beagley is taking him in the car to 7½[2] on Sunday morning, and R means to be at Padd. about 10.15. I think he is asking you to get his 3rd class return with yours . . . he will have chocolate, lozenges and petit beurre and aspirin—hot bottle and rug . . . R likes Famel Syrup and he does cough more easily—but alas he will have that Pash practice on Saturday——

It turned out that none of these medical provisions was needed. A comfortable hotel with huge bedroom fires—a luxury long forgotten in the south—welcomed us, and Ralph had an even warmer welcome from Mrs. Thomson, Tom Harrison, and Anthony Lewis, who was conducting, as well as from the singers. It was a musical and bubbling production and Ralph always loved rehearsals; he said he got far more feeling of the theatre

[1] At a recording of his *Sixth Symphony*.
[2] My address was 7½ Thayer Street, W.1.

from ordinary clothes and bare stages than from the finished performance. He went home much refreshed, for Adeline wrote, 'Birmingham is the place to recover in!'

He managed very well until the *St. Matthew*, but after that he felt so ill and miserable that he wrote to the choirs to tell them that they must continue to sing *The Passion* even if he had to give up conducting them. He hoped they would be prepared by this for his retirement. Having done this of course he felt much better, the weather changed and became almost summery, Harry Steggles arrived to visit him with a honeysuckle cutting for Adeline, and preparations for the Festival started. Ralph came to hear another of Inglis Gundry's operas in St. Pancras Town Hall just before Easter. He was quite well again, and fascinated by a new work he had undertaken. Arthur Trew and Christopher and Phyllis le Fleming had come to see him to ask if he would write something for the Rural Music Schools. They wanted a big work in which everyone, from beginners to experienced musicians, could play. Ralph planned a *Concerto Grosso*, with open strings for beginners and easy, middling difficult, and difficult parts for the rest, and he thoroughly enjoyed working it out.

Easter, and in consequence the Festival, was late that year. Ralph, who was usually opposed to the inclusion of his own music, had succumbed to the choirs' wish to put *A Sea Symphony* in the Friday concert; they sang magnificently and he enjoyed conducting it, with Ena Mitchell and Roy Henderson as soloists.

For some time Ralph had a secretary, Miss Bone, one day a week to write his letters, relieving Adeline who had been having trouble with her eyes. She still was a copious letter writer on her own account, but she read less and she seemed to be content to sit by the window or in the garden, ready to talk, but preferring to be silent.

At the end of May, Randolph and Iris gave a party at Leith Hill Place, the Azalea party, for the woods were in perfect blossom, and it pleased Ralph very much to see the garden full of people, the house more beautiful than it had been at any time he had known it, and Randolph and Iris happy to be living in it. To his great delight the old name by which the house was known in his grandfather's time—'Wedgwoods'—was in use again.

I had gay letters from Adeline while I was in Paris for a short holiday.

R is only perturbed at the Daily Mail today illustrating the newest stockings in Paris—black embroidered in white and white embroidered in black—he says how frightful if you come back in them.

Well, to come to lesser news, Oxford in pouring rain but good in all else but weather and No. 6. beautifully played[1] and Sheldonian packed and much excitement. He was rather tired—one such day after another—but he is now in the garden again in intervals of scoring, and there have been no interruptions. . . .

And two days later:

The weather close and warm here but sun doesn't shine. R has been out for derris for his broad beans . . . of course you will come on 18th and go to Margery. . . .

This was an invitation to a garden party at Margery Cullen's home—a very gay and friendly gathering which Ralph enjoyed enormously. It was followed by another celebration two days later when Cedric Glover took some of the people connected with the Leith Hill Festival to *Pelléas et Mélisande* at Covent Garden. It was one of Ralph's favourite operas, and though he said no other Mélisande he had seen was as touching as Mabel Ritchie, who had sung the part as a student in an R.C.M. performance, he enjoyed hearing it again. He held very passionate views about the snobbery of singing operas in any language but that of the country in which they were performed, for no opera libretto was so good as to be worth preserving with pedantic care. But he was ready to make an exception in this case.

He was enjoying the excursions that punctuated his work that summer. I went to Cornwall for two weeks, filming with the O.U.D.S.,—a mad venture, with Joy Finzi and her two sons. Gerald had wisely stayed at home. While I was there both Ralph and Adeline wrote to me. He had been to Cambridge for *King Arthur*, lunching at the Arts Theatre with Patrick Hadley:

I went to Cambridge yesterday—a perfect day and the country, especially the cornfields looking lovely. [Rosamond] Carr was my guest. The highlight of the show was Carr's friend Anne Keynes who

[1] By John Barbirolli and the Hallé Orchestra, 2 June, 1949.

ravished my heart in a filmy quite transparent tunic with sleeves attached to the wrists—when she lifted her arms it was most alluring—she also, by the way, sang charmingly—the singing and playing pretty good. . . . I am immersed in a new job which has to be finished soon—a Latin version of Sancta——

This was for a performance of *Sancta Civitas* in Italy[1] and Ralph enjoyed himself with Latin Bibles and jokes about the health of nations, 'Sanitas gentium'. Adeline wrote:

All well, such work going on over this Latin version of Sancta—a few more hours and off it goes to Curwen so that D.V. printing will begin on Monday—(iron pills to the rescue).

Other works, besides the *Concerto Grosso*, had been filling his mind. Many years ago he had planned an opera on Matthew Arnold's, *The Scholar Gipsy*. He later realized that what he really wanted to do was to set some of both *The Scholar Gipsy* and *Thyrsis* and he had started to sketch this two years earlier. There were a good many discussions about it during the summer; when he read the poems aloud they made us both cry, for they are poems that are not easy to read later than midsummer, as an almost unbearable nostalgia for the spring burdens one's heart. After using a speaker for his *Thanksgiving for Victory* he thought it would be interesting to try this again, but in a much smaller, almost chamber, work. He cut and re-cut the poems, 'cheating' he said, so that all his favourite lines should be in—and I re-typed the script almost every week.

Another interesting commission had come, through Fanny Farrer, now head of the Federation of Women's Institutes. She asked him for a work for women's voices for their National Singing Festival when they proposed to have a concert at the Albert Hall, in 1950. As this is an organization of countrywomen he thought immediately of folk songs, and he made a scheme grouping them in a pattern of seasons. Like the *Concerto Grosso* there were to be parts of varying difficulty so that the smaller, less practised choirs could rehearse the easy ones, while those who had members who were experienced musicians could sing the more difficult arrangements—and there were to be some of 'middling difficulty' for the rest. There were so many lovely

[1] Conducted by Josef Krips in Rome.

tunes, so many versions of each song, that he had an enjoyable time, bringing volume after volume of the *Folk Song Journal* down from the gallery and playing through the possibles while I was sent to the British Museum to look for variants of words. He was also writing a fantasia, with a terrific pianoforte part, for Michael Mullinar. In spite of all these concurrent works he had written to Ernest Irving in June:

I think it is about time I started thinking about the score of 'Sinfonia Antarctica', so could I have the scores and any sketches that you have, to look over.

The score of the film won a prize at Marianske Lazne—Ernest Irving wrote:

It seems harmless enough, being just a little diplom. which spells your name Williamsovi. There being no British representative present it was accepted on your behalf by the correspondent of the Daily Worker. As you are, of all men, indubitably a daily worker, I suppose you won't mind this. . . .

I have received about a hundred press notices of the award. . . . They are all on the same lines as this one from the *Manchester Guardian.*

I hope you are fit and well and full of notes——

Ralph answered:

I do not want the horrid little thing myself, so either keep it among your archives or put it in the waste paper basket; or ought we perhaps to return it, because the whole thing was so obviously a political ramp?

You did not enclose the cutting from the *Manchester Guardian*, but never mind, I daresay I can imagine it.

I cannot get on at all with the Scott symphony so it will have to wait a bit I expect.

Another small job he had done was to write the preface for the Prom. programme that season; it was called *First Performances*. He had been much upset by a *Times* notice after a Prom performance of his *Sixth Symphony* on 4 August, and he wrote to Frank Howes,[1] heading his letter 'confidential'.

I see in *The Times* that the notice of my symphony calls it 'The War Symphony'.

I dislike that implied connection very much. Of course there is

[1] *The Times* music critic.

nothing to prevent any writer from expressing his opinion to that effect in a notice, but it is quite a different thing, this reference to a supposed title, as if it were official on my part.

The Three Choirs Festival was at Hereford, and one of his principal interests was the first performance of Gerald Finzi's clarinet concerto in which Frederick Thurston was the soloist. Ralph conducted his *Pastoral Symphony* at an afternoon concert and afterwards we drove out to Weobley with the Finzis. It was a shining afternoon, apples glistening on the trees, the country quiet and fulfilled, summer moving into autumn. This was the part of the country where Ralph had collected carols and songs with Mrs. Leather forty years earlier; and the landscape was unchanged. Ralph found these few days in the West Country were refreshing and, in spite of having to conduct, Festivals always had a holiday feeling for him.

Although they saw a number of friends at The White Gates and liked to welcome them, everything was becoming more difficult for Adeline, her eyes troubled her and it was becoming an effort to have her chair wheeled out into the garden. She welcomed visitors, such as Ralph's old friend George McCleary who came with his daughter Fiona,—a former pupil—or Olive Heseltine, H. A. L. Fisher's sister-in-law who lived in a cottage in the woods near Abinger, or Evelyn Harvey, a member of the Dorking Bach Choir who used to bring her exquisitely arranged bunches of flowers, or older friends like Margot Gatty [Parrington]. While they were there she was alert and interested. Afterwards she would be exhausted, and it was clear that it was only with the utmost difficulty that she suppressed any indication of pain or of irritability at having to ask other people's aid for the simplest and smallest things. She found less pleasure in listening to broadcasts, unless they were of Ralph's music when she was as attentive and critical as ever. Her greatest pleasure was to have Cordelia with her, and she enjoyed hearing about the various children who had been in the house, Cordelia's grandchildren, Bob de Ropp's son and daughter and Rosamond Carr's Francis. When any of them came to stay she loved to hear them running about the house and 'happy voices from the garden'.

Ralph was at this time looking much less robust than he had done; he had weathered the war years and though the domestic tasks he had undertaken, carrying logs and coal, stoking the boiler, digging, carrying buckets of manure and heavy watering cans may have helped to bend his shoulders, they had had far less effect on him than one might have expected. But he sometimes looked devastatingly exhausted and very pale, though when he was enjoying himself he seemed to grow years younger.

A Canadian, friend-of-friends,[1] who visited them that September described the visit, seeing with fresh eyes what had become familiar to me.

This afternoon we had tea with Vaughan Williams and his wife and have come away feeling rather sad. Unfortunately because of Christopher's feeding we had to leave early, having spent little more than an hour with them—just when I felt some contact was being established. It makes me feel so humble and small to meet somebody like that who is great and simple—his success neither cheapening his greatness nor sophisticating his simplicity. But imagine him as a man of 75, tall but grown heavy, with a noble lion-like head and for all the heaviness of his features a lively open expression. We are in a large unkempt sitting room furnished with a concert grand and worn armchairs. Everywhere a litter of books and papers, and the gallery running around the room, looking like an unused gallery in a library, full of music bound in black serviceable bindings in negligent bookcases, and more heaped on chairs, not arranged but rather put there. An enormous tiger-like cat is asleep under the tea-table. V. W. comes in in slippers and a grey cardigan buttoned so that buttons and buttonholes do not coincide, and no collar on because the masseur has just left. Then two women bring in Mrs. V. W. in a chair—we had caught a glimpse of her in the garden apparently dozing over a book—a strong frail face, reminding me of the Fishers, very intelligent and with the quality of serenity that only seems to come after prolonged suffering. She is almost completely helpless with arthritis and her hands so fantastically crippled that they are no longer hands and you feel neither surprise nor repulsion. She has been, with gradual worsening, so crippled for 25 years; which explains the cold unlived-in feeling of the room, for she refuses to submit to the tyranny of nurses and many servants.

We find that she *is* a Fisher, and also a Coleridge; that he is a Darwin and a Wedgwood, and we talked a good deal about that. He tells us about Bernard Darwin, and about Karsh coming unbidden to photograph him, and how he became anxious when a green patina started

[1] George Whalley to Diana Haslam. Letter sent to U. V. W., 1959, at the suggestion of Robin Darwin.

to form on Epstein's bust of him and how he took it to Epstein to see what he should do. And he shows us a canvas of himself conducting painted by Robin Darwin aged 11—unmistakeably Robin's picture and unmistakeably V. W. conducting. But he is rather deaf and she looks so frail for all the clarity of her expression that I don't raise my voice enough and he misses some of the conversation. And just when we seem to be establishing some firm contact the car arrives and we have to leave, knowing that it must be almost an intolerable effort for them to meet strangers. But I haven't given you any impression of the vitality in both of them, and their sense of fun, and a simple charm as though they were nobody and their infirmities were nothing. And I have come away feeling small and petty thinking how little one has done compared with what he had done in 30 odd years—or with what Robin could paint at eleven.

The visit from Karsh had taken place earlier in the summer, 'the one really hot day', Ralph complained—for the photographer had bullied him, shrouded the hall in blankets, set up arc lights, sent Ralph to shave and put on a tie and required him to bring out all his jackets. Adeline was fascinated as Ralph's protests that he had work to do were brushed aside, and she was pleased too with the photographs when they came. Hearing that Mr. Karsh was going to see Sibelius, Ralph asked him to take the score of his *Sixth Symphony*, and he was pleased to have a note from Järvenpäa with Sibelius's commendation.

He was in London to hear Arthur Bliss's opera, *The Olympians*, at the beginning of October, then colds, coughs, and bad weather kept him at home for most of the month, but he was well for a concert on 6 November at which he conducted his *Sixth Symphony* and Arthur Bliss his own *Morning Heroes*. On 9 November William Cole conducted the *Sixth*, and Ralph his *Five Variants of Dives & Lazarus* and the *London Symphony* at the Dorking Halls, a performance 'given by friends of the Leith Hill Musical Festival to Dr. Ralph Vaughan Williams, O.M. as an expression of their affection and gratitude'. Ralph was happy with the *London*, while *No. 6.* was a tremendous effort, so he was glad to be able to enjoy hearing it, instead of having to battle with what he found the most difficult of all his own works to conduct.

It was lovely autumn weather, some leaves still on the trees. We went for a walk that Saturday, by field and path to Wotton Church, then back to Westcott and the bus; far enough to be a real walk, which Ralph loved, for, though he took most of his exercise gardening, he much preferred walking, specially if there was time to go farther than the 'standard walk' which he knew too well to find particularly interesting. He had ceased to like going alone, he said. This was partly because he tired more easily and if he had someone to talk to he did not notice fatigue so soon.

Another play-through was planned; he had written to ask Isidore Schwiller who had recently been ill:

> Would you undertake a small engagement of a private nature for me on November 20th? I am trying out[1] two new works of my own . . . for pianoforte solo, reciter, chorus and orchestra. The orchestra will be represented by a string quartet and pianoforte, and the chorus by eight of the Tudor Singers. Steuart Wilson will be the reciter, Mullinar pianist. Could you bring down a quartet? It would be very nice if you could. I leave the choice entirely to you, but it would be nice to have some of our Dorking (Festival) friends, and at all events I know you would not bring anyone who would not be welcome in our house. . . .
>
> . . . The performance is chiefly for my wife and myself, but I shall be asking a few friends from Dorking as well.

To Müller-Hartmann, one of the invited guests, he wrote:

> I am so glad you can come on the 20th.
>
> Do read *The Scholar Gypsy* and *Thyrsis*, which comes next to it in the book.
>
> As regards the 104th psalm you need not read that except for the pleasure of reading such magnificent language. My Fantasia is on the tune of the metrical version of the 104th Psalm in Sternhold & Hopkins and I only used one or two verses for the sake of giving the choir something to sing.

It was, as usual, exciting—Michael Mullinar thundering *The Old 104th*; Steuart reading Matthew Arnold, and the singers taking up the words: then sherry for everyone. After the performers had gone Adeline was exhausted and went to bed early. She reassured Cordelia, who had gone back to London after supper, in her letter next day,

> I am perfectly all right and we all slept well through a howling gale—then this morning it was lovely—R and I have had talks about

[1] The *Oxford Elegy* and *The Old 104th*.

the Elegy and we shall have many more while he is 'washing its face'. . . . R has to go in car to Kingston for a meeting—quite a good day, for as he says he doesn't feel like serious labour.

December brought news of the birth of a daughter to Bobby Longman and his second wife Lisette whose marriage had delighted Ralph and Adeline. Ralph wrote:

> Our fond love to you all three, and may the daughter be as beautiful as her mother, as virtuous as her father—Can one wish for anything better?

At the end of March I had another jaunt with Ralph, to Wolverhampton, where he went at the invitation of Percy Young for performances of *Riders to the Sea* and his *Mass*. Before the performance started the Mayor made a speech in praise of Ralph, who, not having heard any of it, joined in the loud applause. I leant across the Mayoress to tell him that it was for him and she, thinking he must be a zany, hurriedly changed places with me—a scuffle which we hoped covered his mistake. However, Clive Carey, sitting just behind, had a very pronounced twinkle in his eye. Both performances pleased Ralph and he enjoyed Dr. Young's dinner-party afterwards.

A Festival of Britain was planned to celebrate both the centenary of the Great Exhibition of 1851 and the country's recovery from the devastations and austerities of the war and the post-war years. Among other projects a new concert hall had long been thought of to replace the Queen's Hall. The new building, the Royal Festival Hall, was being built on the South Bank, a site unfamiliar for entertainments since the days of Vauxhall Gardens. Ralph, Sir George Dyson (then Director of the R.C.M.) and Benjamin Britten were music advisers to the South Bank Sub-Committee who were responsible for building the hall. One of the most important considerations was the type of organ to be installed and on this subject Ralph had very strong views. He disliked the specifications of the instrument to be built so much that, rather than that he should appear to be even nominally in favour of proposals with which he in fact disagreed, he resigned from his position as music adviser to the sub-Committee, as also did Sir George Dyson who was in full agreement with him.

He was in every way distressed about the rebuilding that was going on. It was not only that the main concert hall of London was being equipped with an organ which he felt was unsuitable to the English tradition of organ playing but that financial considerations seemed to come before all others in the rebuilding of the city. St. Paul's Cathedral stood in isolated dignity above ruins carpeted with wild flowers, every detail of proportion and design visible as it had not been since it was built: and he felt it was a chance that should be taken to preserve this spacious beauty and to rebuild the area only from Wren's original plan, and he looked with distaste as rebuilding started to cover the open spaces with what he considered inferior and unworthy architecture.

On 15 April I was back at Dorking after the death of my Uncle whom I had been away nursing. Ralph took me over to Roehampton to hear the run-through of his *Concerto Grosso*, with which he was really pleased. It had amused him to write for players at varying stages of proficiency and to make this exercise fit into his musical design.

The next concert excitement was the first performance of the *Folk Songs of the Four Seasons* by the massed choirs of the Federation of Women's Institutes. The Albert Hall was packed, and when the choirs rose to their feet it was strange to find that the audience seemed far fewer than the performers—mostly not young, mostly not good-looking, all in their best clothes, so unlike the uniform black or white of the usual choir. When they started to sing there was a freshness and sweetness in their voices that matched the songs, and beautified the singers. The difficult unaccompanied three-part arrangement of *The Unquiet Grave* was the one Ralph liked the best of all, and we felt infinite gratitude because these tunes had been preserved and were not lost with the deaths of the singers from whom they had been collected.

All through the year there had been plans and counter-plans about *Pilgrim's Progress*—delays of all sorts, confusion over the choice of a producer, and great despairs. On 27 July Adeline told Cordelia:

This afternoon R has a young conductor from Covent Garden to discuss Pils. Prog. (as R calls it). He has been suggested as a possibility as he is working for Covent Garden Opera. He is called Hancock. But will anything that's good happen now—we can but extract all the honey while we can—and your letters and the thought of you are something to nourish me.

She was visibly nourished by Ralph's presence, or perhaps she saved every scrap of strength for him, for when he was out of the room or away she withdrew almost entirely, sitting bowed in her chair, silent, eyes closed and drooping like a bird in a frozen winter night, reviving when he came in to talk and listen, though even then it often seemed an almost unendurable effort. He saw this clearly enough, but did not let her see that he was aware of it, so they both acted valiantly for each other most of the time. Ralph began to look much older, and there were times when it seemed as if neither of them would survive for much longer.

The vocal score of the opera was being photographed ready for rehearsal and Ralph had another small commission, to write music for a broadcast Sunday serial, Hardy's *Mayor of Casterbridge*—so this was one of the books he read aloud that summer.

Cordelia went to the Three Choirs London rehearsals. Adeline wrote to her:

> I am thinking of you at R.C.M. and hoping that R is getting through his rehearsal well. He had been going over the 6th every day for a long time calling it his 'Scouts good turn'.
>
> I shall want to hear how you like the Finzi.
>
> You will like to know that Dr. Clarke comforted R about my eyes—purely a 'condition'—the only thing to do was to use anything that I found comforting.

The 'Finzi' was Gerald's setting of Wordsworth's *Intimations of Immortality*, which was dedicated to Adeline. At the rehearsal an inspired misprint was found. At the foot of two pages of the vocal score there were the words 'Intimations of Immorality' and some of the publisher's minions obviously had to sit up all night pasting corrections into the copies for sale. Both this and Ralph's *Sixth* were on Tuesday; after his main work was over Ralph breathed a sigh of relief, and decided never to conduct *No. 6* again. *The Old 104th* had a dashing performance; Michael and he both acquitted themselves with great verve, and the *Hundredth Psalm* was plain sailing.

The first performance in London of the *Old 104th* took place at the Prom on 15 September, this time conducted by Malcolm Sargent, and again Michael Mullinar was the pianist.

During the early summer Bernard Shore had come to Dorking to discuss a plan he had for a National Festival of Schools Music to take place the following year, for which he wanted Ralph to write a choral work suited to the compass of young voices. Bernard agreed when Ralph suggested that I should be his librettist; he was a severe taskmaster: he had said at the beginning 'where there are difficulties it is the librettist's part to yield gracefully, to accommodate, to alter, to adapt, and generally to be tractable', so I knew my place exactly.

Ralph's seventy-eighth birthday was a quiet one, but there was one letter that gave him special pleasure. The Masque of Charterhouse had been revived that summer for the first time since 1935, and he had prepared an orchestral version of some of the music, including the *Carmen Carthusianum*, a tune of which he thought highly. He had taken Cordelia to the performance—her son Adam had also been at Charterhouse, so it was a place she knew well—and they both enjoyed it. Now the Headmaster wrote:

> The Head of the School has tactfully and hopefully reminded me that this nice fine day is your Birthday. I am taking the hint. We are having a half holiday in your honour and in gratitude for your recent generous service to Charterhouse.
>
> You may be sure that many young Carthusians are very grateful to you.

Ralph still had nightmares in which he found himself back at school, all freedom lost and, as he had never outgrown his feeling of being young, he was surprised to find himself in this legendary position of having a birthday worth a school half holiday. Once the surprise had subsided, gratification took its place.

The Rural Music Schools orchestra filled most of the Albert Hall on the afternoon of 18 November. In the *Concerto Grosso* beginners and middling ones, as well as the professionals, did all he wanted, and they had all delighted in working out the problems he had set them. Many of Ralph's friends came to the concert, and one of the most pleasant surprises for Ralph was meeting Mrs. Machray with whom he had been billeted at Bishop's Stortford in the first war. Her son and daughter were both playing in the concert so it was an affectionate reunion, Ralph asking for news of all the rest of the family and remembering with gratitude that oasis in the dreary months of ambulance training. After the concert we ended the day at Covent Garden where we saw *Tosca*.

The next week Ralph came to hear music by Anthony Scott—

a friend of the Finzis who had spent the war in the Royal Air Force and whose work Gerald admired. Ralph had met both Ruth and Tony Scott at Three Choirs Festivals and wanted to hear his music.

I was very glad to hear your work [he wrote at the end of November], and I think it is going to be extremely good, but please do not take my advice—it is always a mistake to take advice. What you have got to do is to see for yourself what you think of my suggestions. If you reject them then you will be all the stronger in your own opinion which will be all to the good. But never take anybody's opinion unless you find you entirely agree with it. After all, you know much more about the work than I do.

Please give my kind regards to your wife and I hope one day we shall meet again.

On 13 December Ralph came to London for a Royal Philharmonic Society concert at which the Hallé Orchestra was to play his *Sixth Symphony* in the presence of the Queen. Cordelia, Gil Jenkins, Ralph, and I had dinner together, and then Ralph left us for grander regions. Adeline, who listened to the broadcast, wrote to Cordelia next day of his account of the evening during which he had presented the Royal Philharmonic Society's Gold Medal to John Barbirolli and of what she herself had gathered from the broadcast.

R was home at 12.30—and told me of all as he drank his coffee.

The party was a crowded stand up affair and he was glad to leave it, not so Ursula I think! I heard applauding—the Sibelius very fine—R's voice a bit rigid—of course sitting with the Queen was a strain and he felt very tired—but he found her very nice and so much prettier than her photographs and she listened intelligently and her voice was easy to hear—he told her he was deaf. He says the one fault of the evening was that the duck was tough. Also he got into difficulty trying to open the Phil case and failing—he had given it open before and thought it sd. be given in the same way again—of course hopeless for him to try and do it himself. . . .

At the week-end Robert Müller-Hartmann died very suddenly. Ralph and I went to his funeral on a snowy morning. Ralph knew how much he would miss this wise, gentle musician, his friendship and the Sunday morning talks which had become something to which he looked forward. There was a carol concert in Dorking that afternoon, and the thought of Christmas seemed very strange after the cold graveside in the cemetery.

Rutland Boughton had written an angry letter to Ralph who had refused to sign a 'peace petition' knowing how spurious its origin was, though not doubting the honest intention in those who, like Rutland, believed it meant what they understood by Peace. Ralph answered:

Please forgive a typewritten letter, as otherwise I am rather illegible, and thank you for your letter.

My memory of our conversation is not quite the same as yours. As I remember it—just when we were going into a meeting of the Composers' Guild (I think) you met me and asked me in the most innocent manner, whether I was in favour of peace, to which I naturally replied 'Yes'. Then you asked me to sign a manifesto, but did not explain what the manifesto was. Luckily I had already been approached on the same subject and forewarned was forearmed. When I refused to sign you again said 'But surely you are in favour of peace'. Then the conversation had to stop.

I cannot help feeling that your approach to me in this matter was, to say the least of it, disingenuous, as I was almost tricked into signing something which you felt sure I should disapprove of if I knew all the facts.

As I say, luckily I did know the facts, because I had already been approached with a request to sign this bogus Russian 'peace' manifesto, which we most of us guessed at the time and now know through Russia's own newspapers, was simply a means to sow dissension and want of will among the Western Countries.

As I say, the Russians have by now admitted that this so-called 'peace' manifesto was designed to weaken the resistance to their nefarious designs of tyranny and imperialistic aggression.

I suppose that those who tried to get others to sign the manifesto adopted their method of technique from the Russians, who have shown at Lake Success that they have no regard for truth or justice but only for expediency in their own favour, with the result that they behave like selfish, dishonest and petulant children—e.g. when they refused to attend a meeting and then declared that the decision made there was invalid because they were not present. Or again, after talking all this hot air about 'peace' refused to sign a request to the forces in Korea to cease fire.

Their whole conduct would be comic if it were not so tragic.

If we have to negotiate with the Chinese it will indeed be a triumph of might over right.

As regards my Opera, might I ask you at all events to read the libretto before you criticise it or me for writing it, and as to what you accuse me of—i.e. 're-dressing an old theology', it seems to me that some of your ideas are a good deal more moribund than Bunyan's theology:—the old fashioned republicanism and Marxism which led direct to the appalling dictatorships of Hitler, Stalin and Mussolini, or your Rationalism, which dates from about 1880 and has entirely failed to solve any problems of the Universe.

You know how much I admire your energy, your honesty of purpose and your wish to give up everything for what you believe to be a good cause, but please do think whether it is not time, even now, to enlist under the banner of democracy and freedom rather than the dictatorship of Moscow.

It was a very quiet Christmas; Adeline was reading, her eyes a little better, Cecil Woodham Smith's *Life of Florence Nightingale*. 'What an age of frustration she was brought up in.' Ralph was scoring *The Sons of Light*, our joint cantata, and April, with so many details of the opera still undecided, seemed to be uncomfortably, excitingly, close. He was busy with rehearsals for both *Passion* performances, plans for the Festival and then, at last, there were conferences with the producer, Nevill Coghill, who had been chosen at last to do *Pilgrim's Progress*. He came down to Dorking with Michael Mullinar on 10 January, and they went through the whole opera, with an interval for lunch. Ralph sang some of the music, acted the parts and tried to explain his ideas about Apollyon as a shadow, or with darkness between tableaux —and a number of other details. Adeline enjoyed Michael thundering on the piano—though it was obviously an effort for her to keep afloat on the tremendous current of Ralph's activities. It was a time with few gleams of pleasure to break an atmosphere of strain—both seemed to be taxed beyond their physical powers and Ralph was doing an almost superhuman amount of work as the spring progressed.

The *St. John Passion* over, he felt better, and Adeline told Cordelia:

R has never got through a Pash. so well, and the next day he was quietly at work on his next job of scoring.

He also sat for his portrait for a Mrs. Page who, Adeline said, 'works quickly and won't stay for lunch'. Another spring sitting was described too—'Steuart's photographer[1] from *Vogue* here this morning taking pictures of R chiefly head and hands. He was without any fuss and worked hard. He's a great admirer of Mrs. Cameron and was thrilled with my old album . . . he was in-

At Leith Hill Festival 1951

terested in R's hands "to find such power in such sensitive hands".' The resulting photograph was a beauty, satisfying even Adeline who took a professionally critical view of portraits, and giving Ralph a great deal of amusement at appearing in *Vogue*, a magazine I always brought to Dorking so that he could advise on the fashions he preferred—'you should have this,' he would say, 'but never let me see you in that.' And he was always right.

[1] Norman Parkinson.

By mid-February the opera was beginning to move. Nevill Coghill had asked for Hal Burton as his designer, and Ralph joined them for a conference at Covent Garden. Ralph was very positive about some aspects of the staging, vague about others. His idea was that as much as possible should be done by lighting, and that the celestial beings should be radiant and undated. I do not recollect butter muslin being mentioned but his idea was for historical clothes for the real people, Bunyan, and Pilgrim, the neighbours, the By Ends couple, the woodcutter's boy, and the shepherds; a dazzling confusion of times and places for Vanity Fair (Lord Hate-Good as a Judge Jeffreys figure) while those for the people in the House Beautiful should be hieratic, as should those of the branch bearer and the cupbearer and the people of the Celestial City. This was a difficult proposition for Hal Burton who found himself working against time to prepare designs for the wardrobe department to make. If in the end some of them were unsatisfactory it was not surprising, for no time had been allowed for second thoughts. Leonard Hancock—for Ralph had insisted on a young conductor who would work right through the rehearsals, rather than a well known and busy star conductor who would come in at the end—knew his music thoroughly, and he understood from the first exactly what Ralph wanted. The chorus master, Douglas Robinson, had been a student at Huddersfield and had shared a score with Ralph at the final rehearsal of *Dona Nobis Pacem* there in 1936. He too was a fine musician and under his guidance the chorus had learned their music with intelligence and affection. Rehearsals were called in all sorts of odd places, from Holloway to the foyer and crush bar of the Opera House, and Ralph came to London very often.

At the end of February there was a revival of *Hugh the Drover* at Sadler's Wells which was an agreeable change; then, once the *St. Matthew Passion* was over on 3 March, Ralph was able to think of *Pilgrim* almost all the time.

The following week he went to Edinburgh, where the opera company were on tour, to have further rehearsals. Steuart and Mary Wilson were there too, so he was happy with them. He wrote to me:

All goes well here—a rehearsal this morning. I think L.H.[1] will be all right—he knows the score *well* (much better than I do!!) and is

[1] Leonard Hancock.

able to *listen* and evidently the orchestra likes playing under him. Not much pep yet but that is not what the rehearsal was for. We did Act 3. and then just ran through Act. 1. I'm pleased with Act. 3. Act 1 was hard to hear—my deafness seemed to get in the way. Steuart is doing me like a prince—he gave a lunch today to L. Hancock and his pretty little wife [Iris Kells] who is to be the woodcutter's boy. . . . Tonight is *Carmen* . . .—we meet on Sat.

By the beginning of April rehearsals in London were almost daily affairs. On the 10th he stayed on to hear *Katya Kabanova*—the first Janaček opera Ralph had seen since Prague days. We found it an added pleasure to see the stage now we knew the opera house from the other side, and Ralph was fascinated by the music; he had not known this opera before so it was a refreshing change from *Pilgrim* in every way. Another change for us both was going to hear a rehearsal of *The Sons of Light*, and this so very different music pleased him, though he apologized to Bernard Shore to whom it was dedicated, 'I can't write easy music, you know—I get excited, and then that's the end of its being easy.' The following week was appalling, with a long Sunday rehearsal for the Festival, morning rehearsals in London each day, and a dash back by car to afternoon rehearsals for the Festival concerts which he conducted in the evenings.

Ralph spent a restless week-end; he was glad when it was over and he could go back to the Opera House where on Monday the rehearsal was, 'all through, with orchestra' and on Tuesday 'all through with piano', Wednesday, the dress rehearsal and Friday the first night.

Ralph was terribly nervous before the performance—his tie would not tie, his sleeve links were recalcitrant, and he blazed with rage at a photographer who tried to intercept him in the Opera House on his way to his seat. Cordelia, Mary Wilson, Gil Jenkins, and I had to surround and protect him, and there were very few of his friends he wanted to see until it was over. Though I had experienced the prolonged agony before a first performance several times, here, knowing all the anxious moments, all the possibilities and impossibilities on one level, and yet being filled with the music on another level, I understood how fearful this culmination of years of intense work translating vision into music and drama must be for the composer, who is at the mercy of many non-musical factors for, if the production, the designs, or the lighting do not please it is more than probable that these will come before the music in critical appraisal. At this first performance, from the opening sounds of the great hymn tune, 'York', through the four acts, to the moment when the same tune closed Bunyan's dream, there seemed no question about the music. The spell and tension lifted as Ralph, holding the hand of the singer who had played Bunyan,[1] advanced to take a curtain call—the composer and his librettist. Then there was champagne in the crush bar and finally we were able to go and in the car Ralph said, 'They won't like it, they don't want an opera with no heroine and no love duets—and I don't care, it's what I meant, and there it is.' He was already looking forward to the next performance.

The next morning the papers were cool, respectful, and obviously disappointed, but before he had seen them Ralph wrote to Steuart to whose insistence he knew he owed the performance.

7.15 a.m.

My mind goes back 40 years—also on a musical occasion when I first met you and ever since then my music and any success I have had in it has been connected with you—and now comes the climax. I know that I owe last night to you (probably in face of strong opposition) and I do hope you do not feel that you have backed the wrong horse.

It was, everyone says, a splendid performance and I feel most grateful to everyone—and I have entirely lost my heart (not for the first time) to the woodcutter's lad.

My love to Mary. . . .

On Monday, 30 April, the performance of *Pilgrim* was broadcast; it went better on the stage that night and Ralph came home happy to think that Adeline had been able to hear it. She had tried to listen, but it was apparent that it had been too much for her; she was tired, and almost unable to speak. But by the next morning she was better again. Ralph came to London quite happily two days later to see a spirited performance of *Sir John in Love* given by the Peter Jones Operatic Society.

He did not go to the concert given to celebrate the opening of the Festival Hall; he was glad to have a few quiet days before *The Sons of Light*. He had been offered a box for this concert but he thought he would hear better if he sat on the platform—so chairs

[1] Inia te Wiata.

were arranged behind the orchestra. The mass of children gathered for this National Festival of Schools' Music was impressive, one African, startlingly dark among all the white blouses, white shirts and pink faces. The Albert Hall seen in reverse, looking towards the dark tiers of boxes from the lighted stage, was unfamiliar, and for the first time I could watch Adrian Boult's face instead of his back. Ralph, Adrian, and I stood together after the Cantata was over; then Ralph was holding my hand and bowing and I could see he had been pleased by the performance and that he was pleased with the work.

I did not go back to Dorking that evening, but he telephoned, as he did each morning, to tell me how Adeline was—she was in bed, very quiet, and not talking much, the doctor was coming every day. So when on the 10th Ralph said he was coming to London that afternoon I knew he must be happier about her.

I met him and we went to London University for him to take a rehearsal of *Toward the Unknown Region*, at which Charles Thornton Lofthouse had been working with his students' choral society. Ralph had not heard this work since the war and he thought he would like to take another look at it. The choir sang it well and their words were clear enough to follow without a score, which pleased Ralph. After the rehearsal we went to the M.M. club for tea, and made plans for Saturday. I saw him off at Waterloo. Soon after I had got home he telephoned to say that Adeline had died in the afternoon. Cordelia had come; would I come too?

Adeline had died with her women round her like a queen in a story. She had died while the fresh voices of the students sang

> Nor any path to follow,
> No map there, nor guide,
> Nor voice sounding nor touch of human hand . . .
> . . . all waits undreamed of in that region, that inaccessible land. . . .

When I went to her room next day, taking flowers from the garden, she looked as fragile as the body of a small bird. Her early beauty, her lively mind, her austere discipline, her tenderness and edged wit had dissolved and left no trace on the wrecked face that lay between hyacinths and jonquils on the pillow.

CHAPTER XIV

1951–1953

There is a lull after death in a house—stillness pervades every room and all usual activities are touched with strangeness. Adeline died just before Whitsun, and the week-end seemed infinitely long. But after the funeral at Brockenhurst, where she was buried with her parents, Ralph came home to a frenzy of activity. He wanted everything done at once; he tore up letters and photographs, cleared desks, distributed jewellery to her nieces, with Cordelia's guidance as to what would suit each best, answered letters, and attacked every problem with concentration and speed. When he asked me to manage his domestic affairs a few days later, we planned everything on the basis of my being at Dorking for half of each week, so that each of us had an independent life. He said then that he would not cancel any of his engagements, looking back was no good, so he might as well go on with everything normally. He did in fact go to hear the Kantrovitch Quartet play Robert Müller-Hartmann's posthumous quartet on 17 May and when Genia Hornstein thanked him for coming at such a time he said, 'I'm not going to be a hermit.' But there were moments when his courage ebbed, for he wrote to the Shepherds in South Africa, 'My wife died about a month ago, so now I am all alone.' He had been to the Festival of Britain concert at Dorking Halls on 21 May to hear the Surrey Federation of Women's Institutes sing his *Folk Songs of the Four Seasons*, and to London to hear Britten's *Spring Symphony* as well as to attend the re-opening of Cecil Sharp House by Princess Margaret and to hear the Royal Choral Society sing *A Sea Symphony*. On 16 June he conducted the Leith Hill Festival Choir in *Dona Nobis Pacem*.

He had been making alterations to *Pilgrim's Progress*, lengthening Act III, the Vanity Fair scene, and preparing the new version in time to be tried out on tour.

Though many of Ralph's friends had shown a lively interest in *Pilgrim's Progress*, the one who had the most constructive help to offer was Edward Dent.[1] He most strongly supported Ralph's conviction that it was opera for the stage, not a disguised oratorio. His professional attitude to its stage effectiveness was refreshing and, with Michael Mullinar playing the new additions, he and Ralph spent most of a day working at 'improvements' for the following season.

Among the minor characters originally included was Lord Lechery for whom he now wanted a song. I was instructed to search for one, but when I failed to find anything suitable Ralph said I had better write one; this I did, but when I brought it to show him I found that he had written one too. We decided to send unsigned typescripts of both to Steuart Wilson, and Ralph promised to set whichever one was chosen. I was very glad when Steuart gave my words the prize, though Ralph was slightly sad at losing.

He had been working all through the early summer since Adeline's death, so I suggested that it would be a good idea to have a holiday, particularly as the decorators were coming into the house. Ralph was surprised, for he had hardly been away since the war started, and then only for festivals or concerts. He said firmly that he was too old to travel, but that it might be pleasant to go to Kent and to see Romney Marsh. On the way to Hythe, we stopped at both Winchelsea and Rye. At Rye he insisted on climbing the church tower, where he stood with one foot on the low parapet to look at the wide view. It had been a horrible climb, I thought, up a ladder-like stair, but Ralph did it easily; he said the view would have made it worth going up a *really* difficult tower. We spent the next day exploring the marsh. The shingle banks of Dungeness were brilliant with clumps of flowers; we sat by the sea while he remembered the cold weeks he had spent there, at the gunnery school at Lydd, during the First World War.

Three days of mild sightseeing and reading *Lavengro* aloud in the evenings had made a refreshing change and when he went back to Dorking Ralph was ready to accept John Christie's invitation to go to Glyndebourne. Ralph made his usual joke, for he still persisted in his view that Glyndebourne was not sixteen times as good as well as sixteen times as expensive as Sadler's Wells,

[1] See *The Works of Ralph Vaughan Williams* by Michael Kennedy. London O.U.P. 1964. Appendix I under 1951, *The Pilgrim's Progress*, pp. 596–604.

'I always come to drink your hock, John.' But he enjoyed the opera, *Idomeneo*, as well as the dinner. He was ready for a very full week—with *Sir John in Love* done by the students at the Royal Academy and a journey to Leeds to see *Pilgrim's Progress* on tour.

The Three Choirs Festival that year was at Worcester. It was lovely weather; we stopped on the way at Dorchester and at Tewkesbury where we went round the Abbey, where one of the clergy, recognizing Ralph, showed us the organ with its sixteenth-, seventeenth- and eighteenth-century pipes, as well as a Raphael Madonna. We spent the Sunday before the concerts driving over to Malvern, Symonds Yat, and Tintern Abbey, where Ralph had not been since he was a small boy. It seemed to be a particularly gay festival that year; with the Finzis and the pretty red-haired Australian, Dorothy Wallis, who had sent many parcels to Dorking during the war, we went round the china works; Ralph thought it honourable to explain to our guide that he was a Wedgwood in case it might later be thought he had spied upon some secret process in this rival firm. But the guide acknowledged this statement with calm disdain—as if he had said he bought his cups from Woolworths.

Ralph did not conduct either his *Fifth Symphony* or *Sancta Civitas*, for which the Cathedral proved an ideal place with organ loft and galleries available for distant choirs, giving the effects which he intended and which were far more difficult to achieve in concert halls. Eric Greene sang the brief tenor solo most beautifully.

We came home by Stratford, as the Clarion Singers from Birmingham were giving performances there of *Sir John in Love*. Ralph enjoyed Tom Harrison's light-hearted production of *Sir John*, which was followed by a supper party given by the Quayles. Anthony Quayle, the director of the Festival Theatre, also gave us tickets for *Henry IV*, *Part I* for the following night.

This production of *Henry IV* had one amusing consequence for us, for we disagreed about the character of Hotspur, played by Michael Redgrave. Ralph said the only thing to do was to re-read the play. He started on it directly we got back to Dorking and when he had finished both parts of *Henry IV* he suggested that we read all the plays. We had both read them at one time or another, but never straight off—and it turned out to be an extraordinary experience. Ralph used an early nineteenth-century edition in ten volumes, and it took us a year. We both came to the conclusion, perhaps an obvious one, that the popular plays were the best, though we both had other favourites—of these Ralph's was *The Merry Wives of Windsor*.

Ralph had a quiet birthday; he was full of plans for the future. This included engagements to conduct the Hallé Orchestra in both Manchester and Sheffield the following spring. *Pilgrim* rehearsals started again, so he spent a good deal of time at Covent Garden. At one rehearsal someone in the chorus, hearing Lord Lechery's new song, asked who on earth Hylas was. 'Hercules's boy friend,' Ralph said with firm unconcern and the chorus all seemed surprised and amused that he should know about such things. He was amused by elegant little ballerinas counting most unlikely numbers like seventeen and a half before they crouched, wriggled or leapt as the doleful creatures of Apollyon's entourage, or clustered round Inia te Wiata (who played Bunyan), waiting for his part of the rehearsal. 'He had at least three of them sitting on each knee,' Ralph said enviously when he described it to a friend.

By degrees Ralph's life was changing; for so many years Adeline's presence and her immobility had been his magnetic north. All journeys had been short; he had planned exactly for how long he would be away at festivals, and all his absences had been as brief as possible. Now there was no need to hurry home to an empty house, though he realized this only gradually. He confessed that he had never ceased to miss London since they had left Cheyne Walk and at his suggestion I moved to a larger flat where he could have a room as a *pied à terre*.

He saw both the dress rehearsal and the first performance of *Billy Budd*, and he stayed with the Finzis to go to Wellesz's opera *L'Incognita* at Oxford; he went to *The Queen of Spades*, *Savitri* and *Hamlet* in London between rehearsals and broadcasts of his *Riders to the Sea*.

On 14 December the University of Bristol were to hold a convocation at which Honorary Degrees, including one on Ralph, were to be conferred by the Chancellor, Mr. Winston Churchill. It had seemed sensible and simple to go to Bristol by an early train but, unfortunately, the morning brought dense fog, the train was late in starting and, even when it emerged into clear weather, it ran so slowly that we arrived long after the ceremony had started. As Ralph was to receive the first Honorary Doctorate of Music ever given by the University, having already received a D.Litt in 1929, he had been put first on the list, but when he was not there the whole timetable had been moved forward and he arrived just in time to be last. Dr. Stanton presented him to the Chancellor, who was cherubically radiant in black and gold, with a glowing speech claiming him as 'our greatest English composer, and great musical ambassador'. After the ceremony there was a banquet; Ralph liked sweet wines so he did handsomely by the Bristol Cream, as well as everything else. I had thought he would be so agitated by his late arrival that the whole day would be ruined for him, but, except for his distress about the anxiety Dr. Stanton had suffered, he didn't mind; he simply enjoyed himself. After the lunch was over we went to visit his old friend Arnold Barter at Clifton. This was perhaps the happiest part of the day; they had been friends since early in the century when Barter had given one of the earliest performances of the *Sea Symphony*. Since then his musical society had done almost all Ralph's works, as well as many other adventurous programmes, and Ralph had been both his guest and his guest-conductor at various times. We were welcomed to a bright fire, a delicious tea, and our hosts, for Arnold shared a house with his brother, were glad to have him in their home again. On the way back Ralph slept contentedly in the train, and, when he woke at Paddington, said he must order some Bristol Cream at once.

Since the Wedgwoods had come to Leith Hill Place they had revived the custom of Ralph's grandparents, which had been followed by his aunt and his mother, of giving a Christmas party for everyone who worked on the estate. Ralph had memories of his mother asking their cook if Mrs.-so-and-so were coming, the answer being that complicated affirmative 'she didn't say as how she wasn't'. He was pleased to be invited to the party each year and Iris said everyone asked if 'Mr. Ralph' was coming, and considered him one of the principal attractions, as good as the conjuror or the film. For his part he enjoyed seeing the other guests, some of whom, like the Cook family, were descendants of people who had come to Leith Hill with his grandfather, and all of whom he had known for many years. The New Year started with this festivity, followed by a *St. John* rehearsal, the

E.F.D.S. Albert Hall entertainment and on 5 January Roy Douglas came to spend the day, working with him on *Antartica*.[1] Roy had been helping him for some years and had developed an unerring understanding of Ralph's calligraphy, which he translated into his own clear writing, as well as coming to play works through, advising on questionable points of instrumentation and bringing all his skill and musicianship to Ralph's help. *Antartica* had filled most of Ralph's working time through the past year, and he wanted to have a score of some sort ready to take to Manchester for John Barbirolli to look at in March. There was not much time, and a formidable number of engagements were gathering on the pages of his diary. He was at recording sessions for two days the following week when Adrian Boult was recording the *London Symphony*, and back at Dorking for a *St. John* rehearsal, for the Dorking Operatic Society's production of the *Yeomen of the Guard*, and a 'conductors' conference', the usual run-through of works for the Leith Hill Festival. The next few days in London were largely spent at Covent Garden, where he went to the dress rehearsal of *Wozzeck* and, as Cedric Glover's guest, to the performance. He did not enjoy the opera, though he was glad to have seen it and he knew Cedric well enough to be candid in his criticisms, as he was when he rejected his next invitation, to *Electra*, a few months later:

> Thank you so much for your invitation but I don't think I can face *Electra*. I remember being taken to it years ago by Bevis Ellis and I thought the opening bars were from the wrong opera and must be by Macfarren, and it sounded to me like that all the way through.

Roy Douglas played through *Antartica* again, this time at the Oxford University Press, when Arthur Bliss, Gerald Finzi, Edward Dent, and Ernest Irving, as well as Alan Frank, now head of the Music Department, came to hear it.

Walton's new opera, *Troilus and Cressida*, was produced at the Royal Opera House; Ralph found that he wanted to hear it more than once, so we saw it a second time. Another opera he saw during the winter was Nicolai's *Merry Wives of Windsor*, which was given a sparkling performance by students of University College, London.

[1] The Italian spelling was adopted when it was decided to call the work 'Sinfonia'.

The King's death on 6 February made a very sombre audience for *Pilgrim* on the first night of the revival on 12 February. In spite of entreaties, quoting the Old Vic staging of the Boyg in *Peer Gynt* and Covent Garden's own shadowy figure of the Countess in *The Queen of Spades*, Ralph had not been able to prevail on the authorities to scrap the large and ridiculous Apollyon which looked like a cross between an Assyrian figure and the Michelin tyre advertisement. Otherwise he felt the production had improved, although some of the staging still did not satisfy him. Musically, the added scenes gave the whole a much better balance, he felt his score was right and as good as he could make it.

As President of the Composers' Guild, Ralph, with Guy Warrack, the Chairman, signed a letter to *The Times* deploring the closing of the Crown Film Unit whose musical directors, Muir Mathieson and John Hollingsworth, had done so much for British composers by commissioning scores from them—in some cases providing a means of livelihood as an alternative to teaching, as well as securing distinguished scores for their productions.

Another project just then was a possible performance of the Spenser masque laid aside since the outbreak of war. Hubert Foss had plans for a performance at Hampton Court which should be televised. Ralph wrote, 'Ursula and I went to see a television show the other day in the studio—very interesting—but how a whole masque is to get into about 12 inches square passes my comprehension.' So there it was left for the time being; though the seed was sown, and Ralph looked for the score before we went to Manchester and left it ready for his return.

He had managed to have his annual 'flu between the *St. John Passion* and his engagement with the Hallé. He had promised to conduct two performances of the *Sea Symphony* in Manchester with the Hallé Choir, and in Sheffield with the Sheffield Philharmonic Chorus. Both had been admirably trained by Herbert Bardgett, and the soloists would be the same at both concerts, Isobel Baillie and Denis Dowling, both old friends, so the prospect was not too alarming. The concert began with Janet Craxton playing his *Oboe Concerto*; the *Sea Symphony* was in the second half. Afterwards in the artists' room he met a young music critic, Michael Kennedy and his wife, Eslyn, who came round to see John Barbirolli and to be introduced to Ralph. That was the beginning of a close friendship although Michael and Ralph had first corresponded in 1945. After the concert, John gave one of his splendid dinner-parties and Ralph, with a successful performance behind him, enjoyed it thoroughly.

It was very bleak on top of the pass when we drove to Sheffield, with no breath of spring yet showing on the high brown moor; but once over the hills and inside the City Hall there was plenty of life. One of the Hallé cellists was ill, and John Barbirolli apologized to Ralph; then his face suddenly lit up—'Would you mind if I played?' he asked. Ralph, remembering Kreisler at Gloucester in 1911, was enchanted at the idea and John sat at the first desk and played there for both rehearsal and concert.

We went to Cambridge a few days later to hear Arnold Foster's reduced score version of *The Sons of Light* which was sung by children from Cambridgeshire schools. There was also an exhibition of pictures by school children and Ralph complained bitterly of the free drawings and paintings. He considered it a great injustice to children to withhold the teaching of technique by which their imaginative ideas could be properly expressed; he felt that they should have at their service all the craft which they were capable of mastering.

At Dorking, he had his full rehearsal for the *St. Matthew Passion* performance on 27 March. He also gave a lecture at Downside Abbey where he stayed for a night and where he found silent meals in the refectory an interesting experience—one that he suggested for home use, but not with any great conviction.

After the Leith Hill Festival there was yet another trip to Manchester both to hear the *Sixth Symphony* at one of the Hallé concerts and to discuss *Antartica*. He had taken the score to John Barbirolli at his last visit and John had asked for the first performance for the following season; Ralph allowed it to be announced at this concert. The Barbirollis gave another dinner party, at which Kathleen Ferrier was also a guest. Ralph introduced her to Dubonnet, a drink she had not tried before, and there were jokes about 'Dubonnets over the border'. Though Ralph loved her singing he had met her only a few times, but at this party they became old friends in an evening.

Next day Ralph went to a Federal Union meeting in London at which he and Yehudi Menuhin spoke, and then there remained only one more engagement, a schools' concert at Dorking, before a holiday.

Although Ralph had said he was too old to travel ever again, he had acquired a new passport in the summer of 1951; his old one, like his bathing dress, had been lost during the war. Little by little, the idea of going abroad attracted him and, although the currency allowances for a year had dwindled to twenty-five pounds by 1952, he felt France would be a good beginning. He had never flown before, so that too was exciting, though unfortunately going down to land gave him a moment or two of earache.

We stayed in a hotel backing on to the gardens of the Palais Royal; we strolled about, looked at Notre Dame, and dined early, then spent the evening sitting in cafés. Ralph soon felt at home again in Paris, and he showed me the Hôtel du Portugal et l'Univers where he had lived when he studied with Ravel. We lunched and dined as cheaply as we could, walked everywhere, and after three days filled to the brim with sightseeing and sitting in cafés, we took the train to Chartres. The cathedral made less impact on Ralph than I had expected—he said he had heard too much about it—but he loved the fair which was going on in the town, and we wandered about in the warm May evening and sat and watched other people, idle and content.

Next day we went on to St. Malo, arriving late in the evening; porters gathered round when we asked the one who had taken our luggage for advice where to stay. They debated for some time before taking us to a small commercial hotel very near the station, which was just what we could afford. Summer seemed to have arrived overnight, so we spent the next morning on the beach, paddling and almost wanting to bathe, before we went on to Mont St. Michel. It was a dusty, stuffy, cheerful journey in a full bus. At last Ralph said, 'Look *now*'—and there, rising over the sea marshes was the outline of the Mont. He had not seen it since he was ten, but he had been waiting for the exact spot in the road where the Gothic vision would first appear. There were many people in the steep streets and in the party we joined to go round the buildings, but Ralph was far more conscious of his own memories than of the guide's discourse: we seemed to be going through the halls and chapels with his mother, Aunt Sophy, Hervey, Meggie, and a child of ten who was enthralled by architecture.

At last we came out into the airy cloisters at the top, where the walls were blurred with golden lichen, the sea light was dazzling and there was that summer sound of swifts, screaming as they circled above us. Later, sitting in a slip of garden, we both heard plainsong apparently coming from inside the walls. The building was deconsecrated long ago and had been used as a prison—now it was full of sightseers. So obviously the plainsong could not be true, and we came to the conclusion that the voice of the guide had been given some echo, some resonance, by the stone which had changed its quality and translated it back into music.

We dined on the terrace. As the sun sank, the shadow of the statue on the pinnacle of the mount stretched across the quicksands, across the bay, till it reached Avranches, miles away; the swifts flew lower, the smell of sea and marsh, of summer, of food cooking, of wine, all mingled and we sat and sat while Ralph talked of his memories of seventy years ago.

We had intended to stay for two nights, but Ralph prudently consulted the bus office because he had no faith in French timetables. He was absolutely right, for the summer schedule had started that morning and was quite different from the one on which our plans were based and which we had been told would be current for some weeks. So we took an afternoon bus to Dol, where we found an old-fashioned hotel where a wedding feast was in progress. Fascinated by the large numbers of empty bottles that were carried out every few minutes, Ralph ordered a quart of cider with his dinner and triumphantly drank it all. The swifts were still with us, and we walked on the battlements under lime trees until we came back to the square, and finished the day peacefully with glasses of Calvados. Before leaving next morning we explored Dol: a cathedral, some pleasant streets, with country shops where, as Ralph's summer hat had got several holes in it, he bought a new one made of greyish green straw, a proper haymaker's hat which suited him better than the old and shrunken pre-war panama which we left behind.

By now our money was very nearly gone. We saw as much as we could of Rouen, the cathedral, St. Maclou, and the outside of the prison where Joan of Arc had spent the last months of her life, and I was most thankful that Ralph did not want to climb the cathedral tower again. The worst moment was when he came dashing out of the gentlemen's lavatory in the square because he had not got the two francs needed. He had never had to pay before, and he was outraged particularly that this should happen at our poorest moment. There wasn't even enough money left for lunch—some of it had gone on repeated and ineffective repairs to a suitcase handle that fell off at awkward moments, usually when crossing from platform to platform, for we hadn't been able to afford porters since St. Malo. However, there was enough for coffee, a bar of chocolate and two apples; so we had the coffee at the station, tumbled thankfully into the train for which we had bought tickets in England and had our apples and chocolate there. One other passenger shared the carriage—he was very nice to us and did not appear to mind our rather grubby appearance or our odd meal. We talked all the way to Le Havre, and he told us fascinating stories of canonizations and of political scandals. He also said he would be met by a courier who would look after our luggage too, and put it on board for us. Finally Ralph asked if we might know his name—'My name's Hankey—and you?' '*Not* the composer?' he asked—'I do compose a bit,' said Ralph modestly—'and you are Lord Hankey?' Once in the boat we were solvent again, and invited him to join us for eggs and bacon, tea, bread and jam—very satisfying after our near-fast, and we had an amusing evening. He said what a pleasure it was for him to meet people involved in the arts, to which we replied the pleasure for us was to meet someone involved in history: we parted on this note of stately compliment.

Early in June George Dyson[1] brought Sir Gerald Kelly to see Ralph at Dorking. The R.C.M. wanted a portrait and, as Ralph could not think of any excuse for not being painted, he submitted. Sittings were arranged to begin at Sir Gerald's studio on 10 June where Ralph sat in a large chair on a small platform, and work started. It was fascinating to watch a painter at work, but Ralph, who could not see the canvas, nodded off to sleep, to Gerald's amusement, and had to be woken up every now and then and re-arranged in his original pose.

Between sittings there were two Oxford concerts—one on 14 June was the Oxford Orchestral Society's Jubilee. A note in the programme says:

> The works included . . . were chosen for their suitability to a solemn jubilee and because they are intimately connected with the

[1] Sir George Dyson, then Director of the Royal College of Music.

orchestra's tradition and those who created it. Some of them have appeared many times in the orchestra's programme and the English composers whose works are being played have all of them been associated in an intimate way with Oxford music——

Ralph conducted the *Serenade to Music*. A photograph taken after the concert shows him with the other conductors, Guy Warrack, Reginald Jacques, Sidney Watson, and Thomas Armstrong.

On 19 June, at Queen's College, Oxford, the Eglesfield Music Society and a chamber orchestra conducted by Bernard Rose gave the first performance of Ralph's *Oxford Elegy*. The other half of the concert was *Venus' Praise*, songs by Bruce Montgomery, and a concerto for string orchestra by Alan Rawsthorne. The effect of the *Elegy* was extraordinary; Steuart Wilson, the speaker, had tears running down his cheeks: he was mildly outraged that he should be weeping over a poem about Oxford. But they were enjoyable tears, luxuriously nostalgic, and we were still just on the safe side of summer.

> Soon will the swift midsummer pomps come on,
> Soon will the musk carnations break and swell,
> Soon shall we have gold-dusted snapdragon,
> Sweet william with his homely cottage smell
> And stocks in fragrant blow;
> Roses that down the alleys shine afar,
> And open, jasmine muffled lattices,
> And groups under the dreaming garden trees,
> And the full moon, and the white evening star.

We had them all, for we drove back with the Finzis to Ashmansworth to the evening scents of their garden, with jasmine fully out over their welcoming door.

Next day we went back to London for Desmond MacCarthy's memorial service at St. Martin in the Fields. Ralph sat next to Edward Dent and they read their service papers; both were deaf, both were untalented in the use of their hearing aids, and both spoke extremely clearly in penetrating whispers. They drifted into an animated discussion of the music each would prefer for his own memorial service. Oblivious of heads turning and of the enthralled attention of the congregation, they made fanciful and grandiose plans for their own obsequies—'But it wouldn't be any good,' Ralph concluded, 'because they're all things that would have to be properly rehearsed and no one ever bothers to rehearse for memorial services.' Before this theme could be fully developed the service began.

There had been talk of disbanding the Bournemouth Municipal Orchestra because of its cost: Ralph wrote to *The Bournemouth Daily Echo*:

A wise man once said that he would prefer to be Socrates discontented than a hog contented. The Town Council of Bournemouth evidently would like us to be contented. But contented with what? One of your councillors is reported to have said that of course we must spend money on necessities like the Health Service rather than on music. But is not music necessary for our spiritual health?

Have any of your councillors ever been into a school and perceived the exaltation created in the children's features when they sing good music? When they grow up this exaltation will die away and fade into the light of common day unless we see to it that this splendid vision of the ultimate realities is preserved for them.

It is this vision that I understand one of your councillors had the impertinence to describe as an expensive toy.

Up to the present, largely owing to its Symphony Orchestra, Bournemouth has been a civilised town. Are your Council prepared to let their names go down to posterity stigmatised with the disgrace of allowing the town, for whose welfare, spiritual as well as material, they are responsible, to lapse into barbarism?

It was a letter he enjoyed writing, a battle in which he was glad to take part.

Rutland Boughton had written to him again in terms that called for a strong reply: probably one of his attempts to get Ralph's signature for some new Peace manifesto:

This is really too bad! to accuse me of not being able to speak my mind because of my official position. To start with, I have no official position.

I am afraid I am now going to imitate St. Paul and 'speak as a fool'. I have always refused all honours and appointments which involved obligation to anyone in authority—(the O.M. involved no such obligations). My fault is probably that I have been always too much in opposition. When I was a boy at school I and another boy stood out as Radicals (as we were called then) against all the other boys. When I got to Cambridge in '93 I and a few friends read the Fabian tracts, and, in opposition to the majority of undergraduates, became socialists. (This was probably before you were born.)

The truth is I think that when I am with conservatives I become socialistic and when I am with socialists I become a true blue Tory.

Now the pendulum has swung right round and it is fashionable to be a socialist or 'Kremlinist'. (I will not defile what ought to be a fine name 'Communist' by calling the present creed by that name.) I have the courage to criticise and dissociate myself from the manifestations of what used to be a fine creed, and I am not afraid to have the finger of scorn pointed at me because I refuse to be taken in by all these bogus 'peace' moves which I think have even duped you.

Ever since I had a vote I have voted either Radical or Labour except once, after the last war when I was so disgusted by what I considered the mean trick of the Labour party in forcing an election.

I voted Labour in the last election though in my heart of hearts I wanted the Tories to get in, but the old spirit of opposition crept up and with all the country shouting for the Tories I determined to be on the other side; so I assure you my spirit remains what you call 'generous'. I believe in freedom and that is why I will not be bullied by Nazis, Fascists or Russians.

In July there was a concert of Ralph's music at Charterhouse. Looking at all those still anonymous faces I wondered who among them would emerge and return like this to hear his own music sung seventy years hence.

There was another glimpse of the past a few days later, for at Paddy Hadley's invitation Ralph was to lecture on East Anglian folk songs at the first King's Lynn Festival. We drove up through Essex, stopping at Saffron Walden, where Ralph used to practise the organ when his unit was stationed there, and by Ely, where we walked round the cathedral while Ralph described how he used to come over from Cambridge on Sundays to hear the choir. We arrived at Paddy's house at Heacham in time for a bathe before having dinner in the garden with Angus Morrison, our fellow guest. We drank Moselle while hundreds of shooting stars fell out of the sky, and the air was gentle and summery and smelt of lavender fields, now almost ready to be cut. There were more bathes, rehearsals, the Lanchester puppets, and concerts. Ralph's lecture was an afternoon affair: to illustrate it he had two young singers, one of Paddy's students from Caius and a schoolgirl from Lynn[1] who sang with absolute simplicity just as Ralph liked folk

[1] John Flower and Gillian Martin.

songs to be sung. The Queen Mother and Princess Margaret were in the audience, and Ralph was presented to them afterwards. He knew his subject well, and he had plenty to say about it; he spoke without much reference to his script but he was glad when his duty was done and he could be audience again and enjoy his *Fifth Symphony* which John Barbirolli conducted in St. Nicholas chapel where the angels in the roof were a constant pleasure to the sight.

As he had often done before, Ralph went to the Surrey Summer School for young musicians run by Norman and Violet Askew. This year it was at Claremont: and though it was sad to see the elegant rooms defaced with such school paraphernalia as ribstalls, the house allowed plenty of room for the young groups of musicians practising chamber music or orchestral works, and Ralph enjoyed meeting them at supper as well as listening to their playing and talking to them about music.

His own works included in the Proms came near the end of the season—*Five Tudor Portraits*, which Malcolm Sargent conducted, the *Fifth Symphony*, which Ralph conducted, and one new work which had kept him amused for some time early in the year. This was a *Romance for Harmonica and Orchestra* written for Larry Adler. The only mouth organ player Ralph had known previously was Harry Steggles, who had taken his instrument with him to the war. He remembered a little about how Harry had used it but he asked Larry Adler for full details. 'Write down everything it can do, and everything it can't do,' he said. This Larry did, and the sheet of foolscap with all the possibilities was propped up on his study desk for weeks while he worked all the can-dos into his tune. The result was gay and pastoral. Larry was delighted, especially as it made other composers ready to follow Ralph's lead and write music for him. But it made the critics nervous, for they felt less certain than ever of what Ralph was up to; his new ideas were more unpredictable than they had ever been and they did not know what to expect next.

The evening before the *Fifth Symphony* Prom we went to the little Mermaid Theatre that Bernard Miles had built in his garden in St. John's Wood to hear Kirsten Flagstad sing *Dido*, an opera which Ralph still loved as much as when he had taken part in it as a student.

Besides Prom rehearsals there were rehearsals at the R.C.M.

for the Three Choirs Festival, this year at Hereford. While we were there our most memorable day was one spent exploring the Black Mountains. Ralph wanted to see Llanthony again: he had been there long before, walking up through the hills. This time it had to be by car, a large old-fashioned Rolls-Royce, far too wide for the lanes, but we were lucky and did not meet any traffic—in fact we seemed to have the whole landscape to ourselves. When we got to Llanthony the country was dark, overcast by rain clouds with sudden streaks of silvery light, sinister and unfriendly, but very beautiful.

On our return to London, we attended the celebration at Westminster Abbey on 30 September of the centenary of Stanford's birth. After the service Ralph walked in a procession with the choir and clergy, followed by a few others, to the grave, where he laid a wreath on the stone. It was strange to think that Stanford had been only twenty years older than Ralph and to realize that a century is not very long though it can translate a man known in daily life into a character in musical history. We looked at Darwin's grave as we went out: Ralph spoke of him as Great Uncle Charles; a voice, a quality of movement, another well remembered figure still alive in the memory in spite of the reality of the dark stone, the formal epitaph.

As Hubert Foss was making plans for the production of our Spenser Masque Ralph decided to enlarge his original scheme in which there had been only one song. 'If there is a baritone he might as well do some more work,' he said, so to the original song—'Ah when will this long weary day have end?'—he added two more, a 'Love song of the birds' and 'Now welcome night'. There was a pianoforte run-through at the Fosses' house. Indeed that was a tremendous day, for we spent the afternoon with Arthur Benjamin who played—and sang—his opera *A Tale of Two Cities*, to Ralph, and we ended by seeing *The Seraglio* at Sadler's Wells.

On Sunday, 5 October, the eightieth birthday celebrations started with a rehearsal at Dorking for the concert there. On Monday Ralph was the guest of honour at a dinner given by the Incorporated Society of Musicians where very many of his friends had gathered to celebrate him, and where Herbert Howells spoke of his work in every branch of the composer's art. He found that it was dismaying to be so much applauded, interviewed, photographed, and surrounded; because of this, rehearsals were much more happy than concerts, for at them he could be comfortably a musician and listen to the music, instead of being acclaimed as an octogenarian, which he found odd anyway. But the Dorking concert was one of the most friendly of his festivities—the only shadow was that Steuart Wilson was in hospital and unable to be the speaker in *An Oxford Elegy*. Ralph asked Cecil Day Lewis to take his part, and Steuart started a birthday letter wrathfully: 'I wish I wasn't missing the party—I could wring my gall-bladder's neck and give it to Cecil Day Lewis to eat——' Cecil happily escaped this fate; he and his wife Jill[1] came to dine with us after rehearsal, as did Randolph and Iris Wedgwood, Cordelia Curle, Gil Jenkins, and others. The White Gates was full of celebration, tissue paper, greetings, telegrams, and champagne. The concert was given by members of the Leith Hill Festival choirs, with Isobel Baillie and Arthur Cranmer as soloists: Isidore Schwiller led the orchestra and conducting was shared between Adrian Boult and William Cole. *The Hundredth Psalm*, *An Oxford Elegy*, *Five Mystical Songs*, and *Benedicite* made a rejoicing programme, followed by a party in the Martineau Hall. Ernest Irving was there, unwell but undaunted in a bath chair, which Ralph wheeled from the concert into the party. It was a splendidly organized entertainment, all the guests were delighted to see each other, Ralph had his fill of embracings, and there was a conjurer to crown his pleasures in the day. Although his birthday was on a Sunday, the L.C.C. gave a party for him in the Festival Hall. It followed a concert of his own works chosen by himself—*Thanksgiving for Victory* (renamed *A Song of Thanksgiving*), the *Fifth Symphony*, *Flos Campi*, and *The Sons of Light*. Adrian conducted, and when Ralph took his calls at the end of the concert he looked surprised by the tremendous warmth of the greeting and of the applause. Upstairs a huge birthday cake waited for him, and the chairman of the L.C.C., Mr. Bayliss, led him to it, and made a speech. Ralph's thanks were briefly spoken, a joke about 'if music be the love of food'—and the party was soon going merrily, with more friends meeting each other and more kisses for Ralph.

Next day was devoted to letters; so many had come that there

[1] Daughter of Sir Michael Balcon with whom Ralph had become acquainted in film studios.

had not been time to read them—they were heartwarming. Rutland Boughton, all his political furies laid aside, wrote warmly and generously; Bobby and Lisette Longman, George McCleary, all affectionate and allowing themselves to say more than is usual to a man's face. John Ireland wrote:

> The position of esteem and affection in which you are held is entirely the result of merit, personality and artistic integrity. May there still be many happy returns of your birthday, and a still greater contribution by you to the fabric of creative musical art——

From a much newer friend, Gil Jenkins:

> It must always be a wonderful experience to know a great man, but it is more wonderful to find one who wears his greatness so simply, so modestly and so gracefully.

And from George Trevelyan:

> All England is rejoicing over your birthday, and you may be sure I do too. We have both achieved very much what we were respectively dreaming of at Seatoller in 1895. We have had fortunate lives in a very unfortunate age. We neither of us can move about much now, but if ever you find yourself in Cambridge do look me up. . . .

He had not been at the parties—Randolph, who had, took a different view of Ralph's age:

> It must have moved your heart to be so surrounded by love and enthusiasm. I know it moved me, and I felt proud to be there and to contribute my share to the good wishes and to the enthusiasm. You looked young and happy—and emotions like that bring you youth and happiness all through.

By the time all the presents were thanked for, all the telegrams and letters answered, it was time for the next celebration—a grand luncheon party at the Garrick Club given by Geoffrey Cumberlege and the Oxford Press. After that the whirl subsided—walks to look at the autumn woods, visits to the Wedgwoods at Leith Hill Place, a party given by the publishers of *Musica Britannica*, and a visit to see *Porgy and Bess*, were diluted by days of work.

In late November we went to Manchester again where John

Barbirolli and the Hallé Orchestra spent a day on preliminary rehearsals of *Sinfonia Antartica.* Roy Douglas was with us, and Michael and Eslyn Kennedy joined us for rehearsals. It sounded new and strange now we could listen undistracted by the action on the screen.

For many years I had given Christmas parties. This year Ralph suggested that it would be a good occasion on which to drink his birthday present champagne of which he had quite a store: so we did. *The Sunday Times* asked him to contribute to their 'Books of the Year' feature and the books he chose were *Times on the Thames*, by Eric de Maré, *Why Waterloo?*, by A. P. Herbert, the Penguin Edition of Cecil Day Lewis's *Poems*, and *Period Piece* by his cousin, Gwen Raverat. He read this with avidity and found he shared very many of her memories of relations common to them both, while the drawings of Darwin aunts and uncles were 'wonderfully like'.

The New Year started with Ralph's 'conductors' conference' when the Leith Hill Festival conductors came with a few members of their choirs to run through the works they were preparing. Two years earlier he had heard a broadcast of Haydn's *Imperial Mass* and had immediately telephoned to Margery Cullen to see if enough copies could be bought or hired for the choirs to sing it. Unfortunately, very few were available, but the publishers had agreed to print enough for the following season, so, suitably for Coronation year, this was one of the works he rehearsed.

Another Coronation celebration was the Arts Council's commission to ten composers for part songs, to produce a collection like the first Queen Elizabeth's *Triumphs of Oriana.* Each composer was free to choose his poet, and Ralph, having by this time, as he said, 'tamed' me, asked me to write his words. This work, seeing *Iolanthe* and hearing the L.S.O. play the *London Symphony* helped to occupy the days before *Antartica.* The evening before going up to Manchester Ralph asked me to marry him. We had been to hear John Barbirolli conduct *Tristan* at Covent Garden. Next morning we caught the breakfast train in a confusing whirl made up of last night's music, our decision to marry as soon as there was a chink between concerts, and the excitement and apprehension that belonged to all first performances. The Hallé Orchestra had had time to assimilate the work since their autumn rehearsal. Both morning and afternoon rehearsals were easy, and John Barbirolli appeared less exhausted by *Tristan* than we were.

There was a final rehearsal on the morning before the concert, and the afternoon seemed interminable. When at last it was time to go to the Free Trade Hall Ralph was besieged by reporters and photographers, and Peter Scott, son of the explorer, and his wife shared their attention. Flashlights made green spots appear to be floating all over the hall during the interval, when Ralph was at his most nervous. By now we were beginning to know the symphony and something of the cold, desolation and strength of that remote world must have entered the experience of each one present, so that it was almost a release when the siren voice, the wind machine and the lower strings merged into silence. The silence lasted a moment before the applause began, and Ralph had to dash downstairs to take his call. He and John beamed at each other, Mabel Ritchie emerged from the hiding place dedicated to 'voices off', applause went on and on, and the symphony was safely launched. It was fortunate for us that the Barbirolli dinner-parties took place at the Grand Hotel, where we were staying, for what with excitement and festivity, nervousness and banqueting, cocktails and wine, and not having been able to eat any lunch or tea, it was an inebriating evening, and nice not to have to do more than totter as far as the lift.

The second performance, next day, was far less strain, and the Chairman of the Hallé, Leonard Behrens, and his wife gave a party afterwards at which Ralph was relaxed and happy.

We returned to Dorking for the usual Saturday practice for the *St. Matthew*. On 20 January Ralph lectured about Holst at Morley College, and on the 21st there was an afternoon rehearsal of *Antartica* at the Festival Hall for the first London performance. A gay telegram from the Adlers waited in the artists' room: 'Dear Uncle Ralph, our love and best wishes for tonight we will be there of course trust this work can be adapted for harmonica—Eileen and Larry.' There were many of Ralph's friends in the Festival Hall; Ernest Irving, to whom the work was dedicated, was there in a wheel chair for both rehearsal and performance, sparkling with excitement, pleasure, and affection.

After the concert the Longmans gave a supper-party for Ralph, Bobby's sister Margaret, Jill and Cecil Day Lewis, Steuart Wilson, Nicholas Roughead, and I were their guests.

Bobby wrote to Ralph next day:

If there had been any speeches, which God forbid, I should have told you of my gratitude for our long friendship, for the abiding pleasure your tunes have given me and would have reminded you that almost exactly forty years ago (on 4th February 1913) you had supper with me to celebrate the first London performance of your 1st symphony as tonight we celebrate the first London performance of your 7th symphony.

The next day was devoted to papers, letters, and a broadcast of *Antartica*—and after that we had a little time, between Bach rehearsals, to make plans and to let a few friends know about them. My father said, 'What *am* I to call him? I can't call a *composer* by his christian name,' while Ralph said, 'What am I to call your father?—I can't possibly call a *General* "Bob"!'—so they continued to call each other 'you'.—When Ralph asked Margery Cullen to take the *St. Matthew* practice for him on the following Saturday none of the singers guessed that the 'other engagement' he had for 7 February was his own wedding.

After the wedding he wrote to Gil Jenkins who had been his best man:

You are certainly the best man there is—it seemed a shame for you to have to do all the clearing up—but you insisted. I didn't even give you a proper goodbye, it seemed to me that it was one of the best weddings I have ever been at.

We had managed to keep our plans quiet, nevertheless the news of it appeared next day in the *Sunday Express*, so reporters knocked at the door of The White Gates. None of them was allowed in; we were still busy trying to answer all the *Antartica* letters before the wedding ones started to arrive.

Gil came to sing in the *St. John Passion* that year for the first time. Besides being in the chorus he sang the part of Pilate. Ralph wrote to him:

. . . now I want to thank you for the strength of your presence both moral and physical which gave us our clearness of purpose: this was of course especially noticeable in the numerous bass choruses which are too often apt to be hurried or ragged and which it was *you* who kept so finely steady.

We had done some househunting, and looked at all sorts of possible and impossible places. Mary Carter, one of the musicians whom we had both known for years and who had played for Ralph at Dorking, as well as leading her own trio, told us that 'the house next door', 10 Hanover Terrace, Regent's Park, was empty. It had been rebuilt inside and now had central heating installed, it overlooked the lake in the park and it had a garden. It was exactly what we wanted, quiet, central, and beautiful, so we thanked Mary and her husband, for suggesting that we should be their neighbours and took the Crown Lease for twenty-one years. It gladdened my heart when Ralph said it seemed rather short, and asked if it could be extended when it expired. We felt immortal.

There was an exhibition of Mexican art at the Tate Gallery to which we went, though Ralph found it not very much to his taste—it did not give him anything like the excitement that reading the Prescott *Conquest of Mexico* had done. His diary for the weeks of March and April records concerts—broadcasts to which he listened—Grace Williams's *Sea Pictures* among them, and then in April the Festival for which Cordelia, Gil Jenkins, and the Finzis came to stay. The Surrey County Music Association, the Salvation Army band, and an evening at the Ballets Jooss were the last engagements before we left for a holiday in Italy.

We stayed first at Bergamo, then at Desenzano, where the fruit sellers' barrows were wreathed with orange and lemon branches like the borders of Ghirlandaio pictures. From there we went by boat to Sirmione and, though the town was full of holidaymakers, the Scaglieri castle with its water courtyards was quiet, cool, and deserted. The Italians all seemed to own Vespa motor scooters which Ralph immediately christened 'flying bidets'; they roared up and down the streets of Verona where we spent a few days, and of Padua where we stopped for some hours on our way to Venice. But trying to see Padua like this was not a very successful plan as everything closed for the afternoon: however we did manage to go to the Giotto chapel, only to find it filled with scaffolding and cameras. It was several years later that we accidentally saw the film that was being made of the frescoes.

Venice was perfect. We stayed in the annexe of a *pensione* on

Zattere, next door to Ruskin's lodgings, which was cool and airy, with big ships passing our window and a little café built out over the water almost on our doorstep—just right for our tea-time ices and midnight coffee. Ralph took entire charge of the plans for sightseeing—he read the guide books and worked out where we should go and when—he also looked up timetables. In fact he did all the difficult part. I kept the money in my bag, and peeled the oranges. The first fell to my lot because a handful of little paper notes blew into a canal one day and were recovered with great difficulty. This was a serious matter, when currency regulations were so strict and the amount allowed to the traveller was so small. The second of my responsibilities was important because Ralph liked oranges only if, and when, they presented no trouble to 'undo'.

We looked at pictures and churches and palaces: we went up the campanile, and all over St. Mark's, along galleries among the mosaics, for which we had been well prepared by the exhibition of Ravenna mosaics which we had seen in London. We found that, like tapestries and stained glass, the earlier they were the better we liked them. We stood by the bronze horses and Ralph, patting one firmly on the flank as if it was alive, said how strange it was to think Nero had seen them. We went to Torcello, with its two churches standing among the vines and fields of vegetables by the tamarisk edge of the water in deserted stillness. A wonderful lunch at the inn and sunset on the lagoon as we came home all added to the pleasure of the day, and accentuated the contrast with the crowded rios and the cheerful voices on the canals. We were lucky too to be in Venice on the day when the great banners were put up on the flagstaffs outside St. Mark's and all the vaporetti were off duty, so there were only gondolas on the canals, and for one day we saw Venice as the travellers of the past had known it.

On our way home we spent a day in Milan. We had by then just enough money left for either an opera *or* a dinner. Honour demanded that we should try for tickets at La Scala; only two were left in the gallery and the man at the booking office said we should see nothing from there. So, after a day spent mostly at the Brera, we felt justified in devoting our money to dinner, which we did.

We arrived home to find an immense pile of letters, and I suddenly realized I had done nothing about a dress for the

Coronation. We had missed the opening of the Royal Academy exhibition where Gerald Kelly's portrait of Ralph was attracting a good deal of attention but we had been sent an amusing cartoon of the picture in which Ralph glowered over the heads of the crowd saying, 'Why can't we all go home?' Gerald had indeed been rather angry with us for going away and had insisted on keeping Ralph's suit. We had had to send the car back to Dorking for more clothes, as we were convinced that Gerald was perfectly prepared for Ralph to go home in his shirt and pants, though he denied this later.

There were rehearsals of *Riders to the Sea* and *Hugh the Drover* at Sadler's Wells and, towards the end of May, rehearsals of the Coronation music in the Abbey, which was full of galleries, scaffolding, screens, and people as busy as bees working at all sorts of carpentry and upholstery. Ralph had written a very short anthem, *O Taste and See*, for the service and, remembering how long a time at the ceremony was spent in sitting, he had asked the Archbishop's permission to make an arrangement of the *Old Hundredth*, in which the congregation might join. This permission had been given, and his arrangement was finished before we went to Italy.

During the last week in May Ralph went to concerts at which a *Mass* by Robin Milford and a setting of the *Magnificat* by Gerald Finzi were performed. On 1 June we spent all day at the Festival Hall. Ralph was to conduct his *Tallis* and the Golden Age Singers were giving the first performance of *A Garland for the Queen*, as the group of new part-songs was called, sharing the concert with the Augmented Choir of the Cambridge Madrigal Society, with Anthony Lewis and Boris Ord as conductors for *The Vision of Britain* from Purcell's *King Arthur*, and madrigals from *The Triumphs of Oriana*. Gerald and Joy Finzi, and their sons, and Edmund Rubbra all came back to our flat to change. The concert left most of us uncertain about the success of the commissioned songs as a group; the Oriana madrigals had so much freshness, and the lovely, familiar music set too high a standard for the new ones to compete with.

We had to be in the Abbey for the Coronation by a very early hour next day; it was the strangest breakfast, at seven o'clock, with Ralph dressed once more in his tails, his white tie, and with his O.M. hidden under a tucked-in napkin, our chauffeur all ready for the road, while I, complete with necklace and earrings, was still in my dressing gown, because while it may be possible to eat breakfast in evening dress, it is unwise to cook in it. It was a chilly, rainy morning, and the crowds who had slept out to be sure of a place on the route looked miserable. In the Abbey all the druggett had vanished, blue and gold was everywhere under the lights, and there was a great feeling of expectancy. We were swept into a conscious partaking in history by a ceremonial as stately and serene as tradition and meticulous rehearsal and planning could make it.

There was much music and then we were all brought to our feet by the *Old Hundredth.* Ralph's direction in the score—'all available trumpets'—was fully honoured, and they blazed triumphantly the introduction to the tune. Everyone was singing, some few enthusiasts blundering into the verses that were not meant for them; three trumpets carried Ralph's descant tune magically through the great building over the unaccompanied voices of the choir. The boy's solo at the beginning of Ralph's anthem was a perfectly calculated dramatic effect; after so much richness of texture and grandeur, the unaccompanied treble voice held the listeners in its soaring tranquillity.

At the end of the long service, our block of seats was one of the last to be allowed to move, which gave Ralph time to go to the Peers' lavatory on our way, hoping to find at least some sign of superiority over the one up aloft which he had previously patronized. But it was, he discovered, an egalitarian arrangement and was not pure gold or wreathed in strawberry leaves as he had innocently expected.

Outside the Abbey it looked as if an enormous cast were assembling for *Iolanthe.* Peers, their robes hooked over their arms, were searching for peeresses, or gossiping with each other. We met a friend who had been with the Royal party, splendid in white satin and diamonds, so I gave her a deep curtsey, 'Bow, bow ye lower middle classes,' I said, but only Ralph knew what I was talking about. When we reached Westminster Hall nearly all the buns had gone—we shared a brioche and a glass of cup till our car arrived, then we drove back to Dorking, dazzled and full of history and far too sleepy to fulfil our intention of going out to see fireworks after supper.

The next day we were back in London for rehearsals of *Hugh the Drover* and the masque *Epithalamion*, now called *The Bridal Day*[1] which was interesting in rehearsal. Neither of us was happy about its performance on the screen, where dances that seemed spacious in a hall became a congested muddle, unrelated to the music. There was only one day of rehearsal in the studio with cameras, lighting, and costume, so it was too late for suggestions. The music was well sung and played, but we were embarrassed by the performance and both felt that television was not for us—and certainly not for this work which needed, we saw, a stage performance.

We stayed in London the following week, spending all day on Monday at Sadler's Wells. In the evening we went to the gala first night of Britten's opera *Gloriana*. Covent Garden *en fête* was enchanting—decorated with roses and carnations, the audience dressed up, even the gallery and slips seemed to be glittering with tiaras, the men wearing orders, and everyone festive. But it was quite the wrong sort of audience for any composer to have to face on the first night of a new work. The regular opera-going musical people were a small minority in that spectacular crowd. The reviews next day were such that Ralph felt bound to put forward a point of view none had suggested, so he wrote to *The Times*:

> I do not propose, after a single hearing, to appraise either the words or the music of *Gloriana*. The important thing to my mind, at the moment, is that, as far as I know, for the first time in history the Sovereign has commanded an opera by a composer of these islands for a great occasion. Those who cavil at the public expense involved should realise what such a gesture means to the prestige of our own music.

Hugh and *Riders to the Sea* followed at Sadler's Wells the same week. The next week we went to Manchester again, after a rehearsal for a broadcast performance of *An Oxford Elegy*, and when we came back we saw the revival of Rutland Boughton's *Immortal Hour*. Ralph wrote to him:

> It was a great pleasure to hear *The Immortal Hour* again: there are some lovely things in it, and you are not afraid of writing a tune. On the whole I like the first act better than the second except for the

[1] A title we took from the words in Spenser's other wedding poem—*Prothalamion*—'against the bridal day which was not long . . .'.

druid's song: and as to the luring song, it is like the Marseillaise or the National Anthem, 'hors de combat'.

I first heard it with you playing magnificently on the pianoforte years and years ago at Glastonbury when you gathered together a noble company of young enthusiasts. I so well remember that we took ourselves too seriously to be frightened of relaxing in the evening when Clive Carey and Johnstone Douglas used to improvise duets on two pianofortes which were slightly out of tune with each other and Fellowes was there with his new-found madrigals, and Bernard Shaw propounded truisms from Cherubini, imagining that he had discovered them himself; and Katie and Bee Larpent set up a restaurant which they called 'Cramalot' which rather shocked the more pure-minded of your audience.

Well, we were all young then, but I believe you remain young still.

We continued to go up and down to and from London. There were a good many decisions to be made about the new house, and one journey was made sadly to the memorial service for Hubert Foss, who died in June: an old friend whose work at the Oxford Press had done much for Ralph, and one of the people on whose judgement and wisdom he had relied.

That summer we saw a number of Ralph's old friends—Susan Richmond, whom he had known in Benson's company at Stratford, Bobby and Lisette Longman, James Friskin, who had played the timpani in *The Wasps* at Cambridge, now a member of the staff at the Juilliard School in U.S.A., and his wife, Rebecca Clarke, viola player, composer and one time member of the Palestrina Society; Rosamond Carr, George and Fiona McCleary and Harry Steggles all came to The White Gates, some to stay, some to spend an afternoon or evening with us, and we saw a number of Dorking friends as well. Gil came down one hot week-end: Ralph had asked him to make his London headquarters with us at Hanover Terrace and he was full of good counsel about the new house: he was staying with us when Randolph brought G. E. Moore and Oliver Strachey over for the afternoon. George Moore was absolutely fascinating, small, sharp-eyed, with a teasing pleasure in singing revivalist hymns. I looked at him, and Ralph and Randolph together and thought of the Log Book, and the cheerful notes in it about who was last down to breakfast, who bathed and what the day's subjects for discussion had been. They seemed to be on exactly the same terms of cheerful pleasure

About 1942, with Foxy

Down Ampney, 1948

Sirmione, 1953

Rehearsing at Buffalo, 1954

in each other's company as they had been in their Cambridge days and to be, each in his own different way, absolute charmers.

Ralph conducted his *London Symphony* at the Winter Gardens at Bournemouth. After the rehearsal we had seen Isidore Schwiller's son Ralph who played in the orchestra; he remarked that Ralph had asked the second violins to mark up a solo passage from p. to f. 'I've changed my ideas in forty years,' he said. On our way down we stayed at Balmer Lawn in the New Forest for a night, where we found a long path beside a stream for our evening walk. The next day we stopped at Brockenhurst for an hour. Ralph gave instructions to the sexton for the upkeep of the Fisher family grave and examined the recent inscription of Adeline's name. She had gone back to the place she had most loved, and to the people who had meant most to her, or so Ralph felt as he left her among the trees and birds and bells, a memory of a beautiful young creature to whom the New Forest had been home.

The first week in September brought the London rehearsals for the Three Choirs Festival, and an extra rehearsal, or run-through of a new work, to which he invited some friends. He wrote to Frank Howes:

> If you happen to be passing the R.C.M. on Thursday September 3rd at 2.45 p.m. you will find Roy Douglas, playing through a new tune by me, and David Willcocks, to see if he would like to do it at Worcester next year. I need hardly say that you would be welcome.
>
> The Press are not invited. [This was his usual postscript when he invited any of his friends among the critics to hear a play-through.]

The work was a new Christmas cantata. A year earlier he had told me that he thought there should be another Christmas work, and that it would be fun to write one. I said that I had compiled a programme of Christmas poems, using linking passages from the gospels, and I had put it away and forgotten about it. When I took it to Dorking, Ralph got out his own scenario and the two were almost identical. From this we built up the libretto for *Hodie*. We could neither of us find anything suitable for the three Kings. I urged the claims of Stephen Hawker's mysterious poem 'The Mystic Magi' but it didn't fit into the scheme, so I was told to 'write something'—and also to lengthen a small anonymous poem he liked. He had worked at this among all the events that had filled the last few months and Roy Douglas had been over to go through the sketches and later the more-or-less final draft. It had been written with the voices of Nancy Evans, Eric Greene, and Gordon Clinton in mind, so they were asked to come and hear Roy play and Ralph sing. Eric Greene said that *if* he was to be an archangel he might as well have a little more to sing. Ralph promised him another tune on the spot and a few weeks later, reading Veronica Wedgwood's book on *Seventeenth Century Literature*, he found William Drummond's 'Bright Portals of the Sky' which seemed very well suited to Gabriel-Eric, and which was approved by that archangel.

We stayed at Gloucester for most of the Festival week. Ralph conducted *Dona Nobis Pacem* and *Job*. Gerald Finzi, Herbert Howells, and Anthony Scott had works performed. On one of the afternoons when we did not go to a concert Ralph and I went to see Peter Scott's bird sanctuary at Slimbridge, and another day we called on Adeline's niece Ermengard at Brookthorpe. Then we drove back to Dorking to prepare for the move to our new home in London.

CHAPTER XV

1953–1955

As the removal vans were loaded with all we had decided to take to London Ralph sat on a rejected chair at a rejected table in the annexe arranging Christmas carols, calm at the centre of confusion. At the other end of the journey he undertook to arrange his books and music in the boxroom. It was long and narrow, our share of the space behind the central pediment of Hanover Terrace, and lined with book-shelves from the gallery at The White Gates; it made a wonderful place for storing reference books and music not in daily use. The work took Ralph several weeks, he spent an hour or so each day and by the end he knew exactly where to lay his hand on anything he wanted. We planned our garden that autumn, for the builders had left us an area of rubble in which three flowering trees survived, and before long we felt we had lived in the house for years. It fitted like a glove; with Gil on the top floor for his London part of the week and another friend, Frank Hollins, settled in the mews house.

Ralph was President of the Nottingham Oriana Choir, so when we went there to see a performance of *Hugh the Drover*, we started our visit at a very agreeable tea party at which he could meet 'all the Orianas'. *Hugh* was, as always, an opera which the amateurs and professionals seemed to enjoy equally, and the hospitable committee gave a party to which Benjamin Britten and Peter Pears, who had been giving a concert that evening, also came. They decided against accompanying us on a late night excursion to the Goose Fair on which Ralph insisted, but we joined forces next morning for what we all believed to be sightseeing connected with Robin Hood. But there were no outlaws that morning, only the Mayor and the Sheriff who took us over the Town Hall and Civic buildings.

The next day we went to Leeds for the Festival—we stayed near Knaresborough with the Parkinsons, who took us to rehearsals and concerts.

Josef Krips, for whose performance in Rome Ralph had translated *Sancta Civitas* into Latin, conducted it again, but in its original English form, with Bruce Boyce and Peter Pears as soloists and the London Symphony Orchestra and the Leeds Philharmonic Society. As we sat waiting for the concert to begin, Ralph remembered his earliest success, the concerts in which *Toward the Unknown Region* and the *Sea Symphony* had had their first performances, and said how nice it was not to be conducting this time, nor feeling nervous. Next day Dorothy Parkinson took us to Fountains Abbey. It was a perfect moment to go there, for the trees were golden, the grass very green and the great ruin, empty of sightseers, seemed so penetratingly alive that the centuries through which it had stood unused seemed irrelevant.

When we went home, Ralph conducted his *Serenade to Music* at the concert celebrating the L.P.O's twenty-first anniversary, and also celebrated his own birthday by going out to dinner after a day of presents and letters and telegrams. There was a first performance of Elizabeth Maconchy's *Proud Thames* at the Festival Hall, Harold Darke's Bach recitals at St. Michael's Cornhill, Bryan Drake's recital at the Wigmore Hall, dinner with the Longmans, lectures by Edward Dent and Reginald Thatcher, and visits from friends to see our new house, all pleasant adornments of London life. We saw Peggy Ashcroft and Michael Redgrave in *Antony and Cleopatra*, the Intimate Opera, and *Anna and the King of Siam* which was far less fun as a musical than as a book. Gil was a member of the Madrigal Society to which he went regularly and often took Ralph as a guest but in December Ralph was elected an Honorary Member of the Society by the Committee. 'Under the Society's regulations it was then only possible for the Committee to elect an Honorary Member for two years. In view of his eminence the Committee wished to appoint him an Honorary Member for life. Accordingly an Extraordinary meeting of the Society was held in January 1954, and the rules were altered to permit the General Meeting to appoint not more than two Honorary Members for life. R. V. W. was then appointed an Honorary Member for life. No other Honorary Member for life has so far been appointed.'[1] This was an honour he appreciated, and he enjoyed the Society's evenings.

In November we had the first of our Singeries. These became monthly meetings of our friends who liked singing madrigals;

[1] Letter from James G. Craufurd to Sir Gilmour Jenkins 1963.

we usually had from fifteen to twenty-five people and Ralph conducted except sometimes when he wanted to sing, when Gil took over for a short time. For two hours they sang Gibbons and Weelkes, Bennet and Mundy, Morley and Pilkington, Byrd and Wilbye. The repertoire grew, as Ralph usually ordered a few 'new ones' for each party, and he worked out a programme of twelve or fourteen madrigals each time. There was an interval for eating and drinking and conversation cut short each time by the conductor's anxiety to resume music—'You can gossip any time,' he said firmly, 'you are here to sing.'

We were allowed more licence at the Christmas party. The programme was almost entirely traditional English carols, of which Ralph said—and proved—we had so many of unmatchable beauty that it was unnecessary to drag in 'horrid little foreign tunes'. Exceptions were made for two that were not horrid, *In Dulci Jubilo* and *Es ist ein' Ros*. Everyone dressed in his or her best, and Christopher Finzi came in the afternoon to help us to make cup. We achieved a very good and festive brew by quadrupling the brandy in the recipe and omitting the soda water. Ralph said that from the conductor's point of view there was a noticeable difference in the singing before and after the interval.

We spent much of December at the Kingsway Hall where Adrian Boult and the London Philharmonic Orchestra were recording Ralph's symphonies for Decca. It was both tedious and exhilarating: tedious in the gaps and waits, the murky, greenish blue tipped-up seats, the rumble of trains passing under the hall and disorganizing the music, the cold weather and the sandwich meals: exhilarating in the concentration, the repetition of each passage, first live, then recorded, then live again, with hearing sharpened to take in every variation of clarity, balance, and tempo. It was a lesson in musical structure, as well as in professional concentration, to watch composer, conductor, and players listening critically to every detail of their work as it came back from the machine while the live sound was fresh in their ears.

We dashed around to hear new music, for, although Ralph had started a new symphony, he could not settle to work while the recording sessions filled so many days. We saw films and went to the opera, and just before Christmas we went down to a concert of Christmas music conducted by Gerald Finzi at Enbourne, near Newbury. Afterwards the Finzis gave us a small black kitten called Crispin. Foxy and Pushkin had both died a year or two before, and a long, erratic tabby, Zebedee, Pushkin's grandson, who had come to London with us, had escaped from our garden and had been found run over. So for a month we had been uncomfortably catless. Crispin was intelligent, amusing, and affectionate. He climbed on to Ralph's back, and loved to lie along his shoulders while he worked, descending on to the table from time to time to add his paw marks to the manuscript. A few months later his younger brother, Friskin, another little black, fuzzy bumble-bee of a kitten joined us, and he liked to sit inside Ralph's waistcoat, so that writing became a complicated manoeuvre. But Ralph liked being wrapped in cats as much as they liked sitting on him.

A new excitement came on to our horizon at the very end of the year. Ralph woke one morning saying, 'I've never been to Rome and we've never seen the Grand Canyon—what shall we do about it?' Rome seemed a good idea for our next holiday: by breakfast time we had settled on that plan, and by the afternoon we had the Canyon in sight, for Keith Falkner, then a professor of music at Cornell University, came to lunch. Ralph spoke of Colorado, and Keith suggested an American lecture tour—it seemed too pat, a wish too exactly granted, but it was a time when wishes came true. Before long Ralph, through Keith's good offices, was invited to be visiting professor at Cornell for the autumn term of 1954, and a lecture tour through the United States was designed to let us see the Pacific and the Grand Canyon.

While these dizzy plans were still in the air Dennis Arundell came to talk to Ralph about the performances of *Pilgrim's Progress* he was to produce for the Cambridge University Musical Society in February: they discussed it most thoroughly, and Ralph promised to come to the early rehearsals for both stage and orchestra. Early in January Boris Ord came to spend a morning and went through the score with him.

Ralph started the day a little later now; the half past seven breakfast of a lifetime had been replaced by early morning tea and half past eight breakfast. He worked from nine thirty till one, the afternoons were devoted to sleep, walks, and letter writing, then he worked again after tea, sometimes till dinner time. He had finished a tuba concerto for Philip Catelinet of the L.S.O. in time for the orchestra's golden jubilee concert in June. When we were having tea after Mr. Catelinet had played through the solo part to Ralph, Crispin got inside the tuba and sat there, an odd and vivid memory dating the work, for only a very medium-sized kitten is mute-size for a tuba.

The other work occupying Ralph was one of his rare chamber works, this time a sonata for violin and piano; it was a change for him to have to think in terms of two instruments after so many orchestral and choral works. He had also been revising another work for only two performers, his Housman songs for voice and violin. They had been sung and played by Joan Elwes and Marie Wilson but not published. After a performance—possibly a few performances—the music had been returned to Ralph and it came to light again only during the clearing up before the move. He sent it to Alan Frank at the Oxford Press and the songs were published.[1] A year later they were included in the Arts Council series of recitals and were sung also at an Aldeburgh Festival.

Our first expedition to Cambridge for rehearsals of *Pilgrim's Progress* was made during the cold beginning of February. Everyone in the town was carrying skates, and the wind seemed to come straight from Siberia. Some of the rehearsals were in Boris's big sitting-room with the round topped window high up in Gibbs Building looking down on The Backs, some in a school room, and all these early ones were dismaying. Coming back to our hotel after a particularly fearful one, when even Dennis Arundell's inexhaustible patience seemed to be near vanishing point, we stood for a moment by the river—and Ralph wondered whether a chilly death or a public disgrace was to be preferred. He chose the chance of disgrace. As the hotel had very kindly left coffee in our room, we felt better for a time, until we realised that it had been so strong that we were not going to get any sleep at all; then despair set in once more.

Among the pleasures of Cambridge, the greatest was that of seeing our friends. We visited the Trevelyans, Gwen Raverat and the G. E. Moores, passing Ralph's first lodgings in Magdalene Street on our way to their houses; and we saw Frances Cornford, restarting a friendship that came to mean a great deal to us all.

After such dismal beginnings the Cambridge performances of *Pilgrim's Progress* were radiant. John Noble had, besides a fine

[1] *Along the Field.*

voice, a touching and dedicated dignity as the Pilgrim, and the youth of most of the cast gave a special freshness to everything. '*This* is what I meant,' Ralph said. Dennis's patience, the musicianship of the young singers, the exuberant action in Vanity Fair set against dark curtains on the difficult, steep stage in the Guildhall, made up for any disappointments there had been in the professional production. Boris brought the choir and the large orchestra to a finely rehearsed ensemble, and Ralph's conception of Bunyan's dream was vindicated. Humphry Trevelyan, the Lord Hate-Good, wrote to me:

I do want you and V W to know what an immense success the *Pilgrim's Progress* has been. People in the University began to realise about Thursday that something great was going on in the Guildhall and they started flocking and going twice and three times and trying to go again and not being able to get in.

It was wonderful to hear how it was spoken of by everyone who had seen it—with a sort of quiet yet exalted enthusiasm; and it was wonderful to feel, as one of the cast, that one was taking part in a great and spiritual event, such as comes only rarely.

And Paddy Hadley told us about the last part of the week which we had to miss because Ralph had to be in Dorking for the *St. John*:

I've never known such unanimity about anything that's ever happened in Camb. as there has been about last week. I must say I fully share same. Did you hear that Boris slipped on some steps in King's and dislocated his shoulder? So that Allen Percival (one of the subconductors) stepped in Thurs, Fri and Sat. Mat., and acquitted himself with distinction. Boris operated the last perf. with his left hand. It was wonderful.

Michael and Eslyn Kennedy came with us for the first night. Gil, the Hornsteins, and many other friends came from far, and it greatly pleased Ralph that they had seen and heard this production.

It was a late Easter, the *Passion* was towards the end of March and the Festival was not until the last week in April. Ralph had given up his office of Festival conductor the year before, so now he went as guest conductor, a much less arduous position. With his retirement the veto on his own works ceased, and he conducted those which were included in the Festival; *Toward the Unknown Region*, the *Oboe Concerto* with Evelyn Rothwell as soloist, as well as a dashing performance of the *Five Tudor Portraits* with Astra Desmond and Hervey Alan.

It was still cold at the beginning of May when we went to Pulborough for a Teachers' training course, where Bernard Shore was teaching and where Ralph took a rehearsal—a week later we left on our way to Rome, and summer.

After boat and train it was wonderful to emerge into sunshine at Pisa, where we had time to see the Duomo and the baptistry—where a man was singing to the echoes—before continuing the journey to Florence. Perhaps of all the treasures there the most memorable were Donatello's *Singing Boys* and his old *Mary Magdalen*—'vieillesse felonne et fière'—and Ralph's much loved Medici Chapel with Michelangelo's *Night and Day*: but every hour, every place was filled with pleasures of recognition and delight.

Ralph had planned to show me Siena, and we found that a bus journey from Florence to Rome could be broken there. So we rolled through the timeless country, where there were women cutting grass with sickles, ox-drawn carts, and washing spread out to dry for, it seemed, a mile each side of every village, and where landscapes of flowers and corn, vines and lilac hills lay behind advertisements for stockings, tyres, and Coca-Cola. Against one of these an aged shepherdess with a spindle was leaning, and the ages met in this odd tableau.

From Siena a very creaky bus took us to San Giminiano, where Ralph and Adeline had stayed long ago. Ralph was searching for Pinturicchio and Ghirlandaio frescoes he remembered. We explored the narrow streets between the slender towers; an alsatian puppy that looked like Romulus's and Remus's wolf took charge of us and, like an animal in a fairy tale, led us to the monastery where the pictures were to be seen.

In Rome Ralph throve on long walks and chianti, on tiny cups of strong coffee, lemon water-ices on cassata, on the wild strawberries packed in figure-of-eight shaped baskets, and on sightseeing. His ankles hardly ever ached; he could dash about all day and sit up half the night watching the city's life, sleep at siesta time, and be up early.

The gardens of water and shadow at Tivoli, lunch in an open

air restaurant on the Appian way, tea as guests in a palazzo from which we watched people climbing to the top of the Palatine hill where a holy statue was to be seen, candles flickering along the outlines of domed roofs on Ascension evening, Ralph positively genuflecting before the Capitoline Venus, watched by the severely chaperoning statue of a Roman matron, are all clear memories. Then there was an encounter with Meredith Davies on the Spanish steps. We met again at a dinner party given by the Kennedy Cookes of the British Council, to which Jacques Ibert and his wife came late after a concert. He, Meredith, and Ralph sank into conversation about music.

We had hoped for orgies of Palestrina, but the Roman choirs were all rehearsing for a canonization and so there was nothing special to be heard. We did go to *La Traviata* and to the cinema, and there was just enough money left for a little shopping before leaving for home. Ralph had had the first part of his travel-wish.

We were home at the end of May, and on 3 June we heard Adrian Boult conduct *Five Tudor Portraits*, in which Norma Procter and William Parsons sang, and ten days later John Barbirolli conducted the first performance of the *Tuba Concerto* at the last of the four concerts celebrating the golden jubilee of the L.S.O.

The rest of the summer was rather quiet; Michael Mullinar and Fred Grinke played through Ralph's sonata, the Finzis came to stay for a concert of Gerald's music and we spent two nights play-going at Stratford on the way to Worcester for the Three Choirs preliminary rehearsal. We took some amusing Canadian cousins of mine sightseeing; and in return they took us out to dinner in great splendour, an occasion on which Ralph taught them the merits of green chartreuse. But most of the time he was working on sketches for his new symphony and preparing the lectures he would give in America. He also had to learn the score of *This Day*, or as he preferred it to be called, *Hodie*. It was, he found, remarkably hard to conduct, and at the R.C.M. rehearsals he began to wish he had not written such a complicated opening. For once he had allowed the vocal score to be printed before the first performance, and there was a joke at Worcester that year, for the assistant in the music shop was alleged to have said: 'We expect this day to arrive tomorrow.'

Ralph dedicated *Hodie* to Herbert Howells:

Dear Herbert,
I find that in this Cantata I have inadvertently cribbed a phrase from your beautiful *Hymnus Paradisi*. Your passage seems so germane to my context that I have decided to keep it. R. V. W.

To which Herbert answered:

My dear Ralph,
I have the score of *This Day* safely. Nothing has ever touched me more than its dedication—Bless you. Our love to you both. Affec. Herbert.

When it came to the point neither composer could remember or discover which phrase it was in either work.

Herbert himself had a first performance at the Festival of his *Missa Sabrinensis*, and with that, the *Hymn of Jesus*, the Haydn *Imperial Mass*, and Ralph's *Pastoral Symphony*, *Flos Campi*, and *Hodie*, all three of which he was to conduct, there were no jaunts round the country, though there were the usual cheerful between-and-after-concert parties. The concert which included *Hodie* was to be broadcast and there was a long break after the first half, which took rather less than its estimated time—*Hodie* was to come after the nine o'clock news. Ralph, with the three soloists, sat in the curtained-off artists' room, reading and re-reading the lugubrious tributes to virtue on eighteenth-century memorials. Ralph said afterwards it had felt like a night in a condemned cell, and it was such a relief to start that he was, after all, not frightened, even of the difficult opening chorus.

The B.B.C. planned to broadcast Ralph's violin sonata on his birthday while he would be in America, so Michael Mullinar and Fred Grinke came and played it again for a small party of friends before we left. Afterwards there was a letter from Arthur Bliss:

I must write and thank you both for giving us the chance to hear the new violin work. It was wonderful music, and I shall never forget the occasion. Bon voyage and don't let the Americans become too enthusiastic—though I hope Ralph will find time in California to visit the Berkeley branch of the University of California—I remember taking my huge class in 1939 bar by bar through Ralph's IVth symphony.

On the quay at Liverpool our luggage looked as if we were emigrating with all our possessions. We had to take summer and winter clothes as well as books, records, and music for Ralph's lectures, and much scoring paper for his symphony. Among our travelling companions we found Enid and Gerald Moore, which brightened the fearful prospect of eight days at sea.

At the end of the voyage we were awakened at four in the morning by the hoot of a passing tug—and there beyond the port-hole were the Manhattan skyscrapers against a pale yellow sky, rising out of the mist. 'You see what I mean about San Giminiano being like New York?' Ralph said.

Everyone had told us that the Immigration Department was terrible to visitors, but the officers who received us said that we must stay for Christmas and insisted on marking our papers with permission to remain in the United States till the New Year. The Customs officials were equally friendly. Keith Falkner and Donald Grout[1] had come from Cornell and were waiting on the quay. In an hour we were settled in a very grand hotel and in a few more minutes we were out of it, sightseeing, lunching, and later having tea with our friends the Langstaffs in their garden at Brooklyn. At dusk we met Keith and Donald at the Empire State Building, and from the top we watched the sunset colours fading over the water and all the city lights coming out in chains and garlands along the streets and in the towering buildings. From there we could see that New York is almost as much a water city as Venice—and Ralph said: 'I think this is the most beautiful city in the world.'

Next day we drove to Ithaca. After we were through the shacks and advertisements, the country was beautiful, little lakes, frame houses, rivers, and forests and the first azalea colouring of the Fall. This was all new country to Ralph and he loved it. It was very hot; when we stopped for petrol we also had milk shakes, and Ralph, who had never had them before, was delighted with their discovery, and drank them whenever possible all through our visit, usually pink ones.

At Cornell we were met by Christabel Falkner, who had arranged everything domestically. At the country club where we were to live we found our rooms equipped with everything we could possibly need, as everyone on the music staff of the

[1] The musicologist, and Professor of Music at Cornell.

University had lent something—cups and saucers, saucepans, glasses, and all the rest. Our refrigerator was full, and one of the rooms had a piano and a table ready for Ralph to use as a study. The next day he gave his first lecture. He had been very nervous, but the atmosphere was friendly and it took only a few minutes for him to feel easy with his audience. He had Donald Grout playing to illustrate the talk, so he had no qualms about that part of the performance. The second lecture followed two days later, and at a party after it we met all the music department and many other people from the University. Seven young composers came over from the Eastman School of Music at Rochester to hear this talk and, for the third, a hundred students drove the eighty miles from Rochester to hear him. These were the only lectures he had promised to give, but he enjoyed the audience so much that he suggested giving one more in November when we returned from our travels. Ralph had been offered an Honorary Doctorate of Music at McGill University if he would receive it in person but, try as we would, the dates for the lecture tour and for concerts already planned for November could not be juggled to make the journey to Montreal possible, so, very sadly, he had to refuse the honour.

Although we had been at Cornell for only ten days we felt thoroughly at home. Everyone had been welcoming and had taken us out to see the country, invited us to their homes, fetched us and taken us shopping in Ithaca, so we were sorry to be going away: Ralph was due to start his lecture tour at Toronto. Keith had planned to drive us there, but, as he was ill, Donald Grout took us instead. Boyd Neel, Dean of the Music Department, welcomed us, and after the lecture introduced a group of young composers who wanted to talk with Ralph. Old friends of his, Ettore Mazzolini and his wife were there too, and we had a delightful evening as Boyd's guests. While we were at Toronto Ralph was told that Arthur Benjamin's opera *A Tale of Two Cities* was being rehearsed there for a broadcast. It had won a prize in the Festival of Britain but had not been performed. Ralph immediately went to the rehearsal which he found impressive, and he was able to write to Arthur about it.

Coming back from Canada into the United States we had our passports checked, and the young man doing it saw that Ralph had been born at Down Ampney—'Why,' he said, 'I was stationed right there in that village in the war.' He had glowing memories of the country and of the people, and asked after many of them. Although Ralph explained that it was now eighty years since he had lived there, it was such a pleasure to the young man to find anyone who knew the village that he kept us talking, while the queue of motorists grew longer and longer. When we did part, with warm handshakes and mutual expressions of pleasure and esteem, we received many black looks—and many smiles.

We stayed for the week-end at Niagara where we did everything—dressed in oilskins, looking like an amateur lifeboat crew, we went under the falls and round them. Ralph had been issued with oilskins that were too small and he and Donald were almost paralysed with laughter when they appeared from the men's changing room, Ralph holding his trousers on as they didn't meet under his coat. This was not only funny but also inconvenient as it made the narrow catwalks very hard for him to negotiate. The sound of the water pounding down below the falls is exhausting, the sight terrifying, and the spray almost blinding. But above, the smooth *accelerando* as the river gets to the brink and slips over, glassily smooth, is hypnotic. We watched it all through a rainy afternoon until it was time for Donald to continue the course of instruction in American cocktails with which he was enlarging our horizons. There was a moon that night so we saw the whirlpool in its terrifying grandeur, which was more beautiful than the lighted Falls. When they were lit with white lights the brilliance and shadow had a Doré-like fantastic horror, the other colours were garish. Next day we tossed round the pool below in a tiny boat and walked about the town, idling through the day. We set off by six the following morning to catch a train from Buffalo to Detroit. Our next stop was the University of Michigan at Ann Arbor. We found it hard to get used to the huge size of these American universities. They had a story here that Robert Bridges was asked to come as visiting Professor: he was told that it would be enough if he walked across the campus once a day so that the students could see him; when he arrived he found it was seven miles across. We were met and driven everywhere by a gay and delightful musicologist, Louise Cuyler; on our first evening there was a concert of Ralph's music given by the School of Music: *On Wenlock Edge* and the *Four Hymns*, *In Windsor*

Forest and the *Serenade* gave Ralph great pleasure by the sensitive musicianship of the performances. Here we met Ross Lee Finney and his wife who invited us to dinner on our first evening and in whose house Ralph felt easy and at home. As the lecture was on his birthday the President of the University gave a dinner-party for him afterwards. We were beginning to feel the breadth of America, and as always the fascination of the Indian names like the Huron river, remembered from childhood reading. For some reason the lecture at Ann Arbor had not been as good as usual—at Chicago, our next stop, it was good; perhaps because we had so much enjoyed the Art Gallery, or the shopping, or the gay company of Molly Imlach from the British Consulate who looked after us all through the visit and saw us off for Bloomington. That was the shortest visit of all for we arrived in time for the lecture, and left early next morning to catch a train to St. Louis where we were to get the train for Los Angeles.

This three-day journey was most impressive. The landscape went on and on and on, and the occasional silver structures of an oil-well head, with its derricks and pipes, looked like the bones of a prehistoric monster, the only creature that would have seemed in scale with the immense expanse of the desert.

At Los Angeles we were met by the Dean of the Music Faculty and his wife, Dr. and Mrs. Moreman, and all through our stay the music department looked after us with loving hospitality. As we came west we had bought newspapers whenever the train stopped, and we had noticed that there was little European news—usually none at all. This made us realize how little we knew of America and how little they knew of us, so it was all the more touching and delighting to see the whole audience rise when Lukas Foss brought Ralph on to the platform to introduce him. Everything had been beautifully arranged, and the lecture was one of the best he had given: even though it was substantially the same lecture each time, the different audiences seemed to bring a different atmosphere and evoke a different response. He talked for over the usual hour; then the Roth String Quartet played his quartet in G minor and Walter Winger sang songs from *The Pilgrim's Progress*—and the students looked as if they would be prepared to stay for longer still.

Although it was only a fortnight since we had left Cornell, Ralph had given so many lectures and we had done so much travelling that a holiday seemed sensible. We could have gone on to San Francisco, but this would have meant more travelling and more sightseeing. Instead, we decided to go to Santa Barbara and have a complete rest. The music department of the University of California, Los Angeles, sent a car to fetch us, and we settled down for a week's holiday by the sea. It was romantic to wake to the sound of the waves and know it was the Pacific Ocean, remote and legendary, to see hibiscus flowers growing through the balcony and to watch humming birds at the flowers or the flock of pelicans with lumbering prehistoric flight turning seaward as we had breakfast. Ralph had brought some work with him, a small but amusing job of arranging Highland tunes, mostly from the Tolmie collection, for a choir in the Isle of Mull —they had been sent on from home, with a letter from his friend Eila Mackenzie who described how difficult it was to run a choir, as there were few men and usually the ones who were there could not read music.

At Santa Barbara we had an unexpected pleasure, for the music and drama students at the University were both rehearsing *Riders to the Sea* and each group was about to put on a special performance for a teachers' conference. Ralph thought that a double bill—play and then opera—would probably be a mistake, but he was delighted to be proved wrong. There was no orchestra, the only instrument being a piano, off stage. It was an exciting experience to see the play as Synge wrote it, and then to hear the same words set to music. A day or two later, Dr. Gillespie and Mr. Sytowski brought the cast of the opera to tea at our hotel.

For the last days at Santa Barbara we were joined by two cousins of mine. They were gay and decorative visitors in whose company we explored the town and tried the Californian wines, though we soon reverted to Bourbon. It seemed typical of the energetic kindness of the Americans that Ruth Vincent should drive the eighty miles from Los Angeles to fetch us away at the end of our holiday, arriving early enough in the morning to take us to lunch at the Huntingdon–Hartford Foundation. This is a village of little houses in a deep valley, where composers, writers or painters live as guests for any period up to six months to complete works that the normal pressure of life would prevent them finishing. But Ralph, though he was impressed by the

Rehearsing 'The Lark Ascending' with Frederick Grinke in Gloucester Cathedral, 1956

At Hanover Terrace, 1957

generosity of the scheme, said he himself would have found it impossible to work surrounded by others all in creative throes and undiluted by ordinary people.

The Vincents took us back to Los Angeles and to our train, the famous 'Santa Fe' which creaked and groaned and jerked all through the night; we might have grumbled less if we had realized at the time that we were being dragged up seven thousand feet. We arrived at the Grand Canyon early in the morning and stayed in the little hotel almost on its edge. Having reached this long-imagined place, I feared that Ralph's enthusiasm for doing everything would lead him to hire mules and ride down to the Colorado River which lay like a tiny stream at the bottom of the gorge. He got as far as inspecting the mules—'Not up to my weight', he said—and contented himself with walks along the edge of the chasm, bus trips and the contemplation of the two sunsets and one dawn that our visit covered. The extraordinary colours, the huge castellations, the magnitude of the scale were dismaying, but Ralph would stand on the brink of precipices. One thing that interested him very much was a short dance performance by Indians who worked at the hotel. It was designed for tourists and was fragmentary in content and perfunctory in execution; but there was one moment when a dancer, with legs bent and arms outstretched, almost became a bird, and suggested what lay behind the sketch.

We jolted back to Syracuse, with a few hours in Chicago which we spent at a cinema, to be met by Christabel Falkner and to hear about the wonderful performance given by Mitropoulos of Ralph's *Fourth Symphony* while we had been in the train. Our last weeks at Cornell were full of activity. Ralph wrote in the morning, saw pupils in the afternoons, going through their scores with them, and arranged to hear as much as he could of the university music—orchestra, choirs, anything and everything going on. Besides this we flew to Buffalo for rehearsals of the *London Symphony* which he was to conduct at Cornell with the Buffalo Orchestra. Dr. Krips came to the rehearsal and was an amused spectator of a scene when one of the trumpeters left his desk to photograph Ralph in action. Unfortunately for him, he chose a moment too near his cue, but he had the presence of mind to take photographs of Ralph, first with a look of dismay when the trumpet did not come in and then thundering his denunciation in a way well known at Dorking. When he received the photographs, Ralph was horrified—'*Do* I ever look like that?' I said, 'Yes—ask the L.H.M.F. Choir.'

Another piece of work he achieved was a re-writing of his lectures, preparing them for publication. He dictated and I typed—not very fast—but we managed to have the script complete for Donald Grout to read and criticize before we left. One evening Keith, accompanied by Christabel, shared a words and music recital with the poet Morris Bishop. At this Keith sang a new song which we had brought to America for him as a present. During the previous summer Ralph had read T. E. Lawrence's translation of *The Odyssey*. One day he had been reading that part of the fourth book that tells of Menelaus and Proteus at Pharos, ending:

> from the river of earth the west wind ever sings soft and thrillingly to re-animate the souls of men—there you will have Helen for yourself and will be deemed of the household of Zeus.

The same day I wrote some verse which I left on Ralph's table before I went out to work in the garden. When I came in the song was almost finished. This, like a very few other of his songs, was written in one day.

The concert with the Buffalo orchestra at Cornell was on 9 November. Ralph had received an invitation to give an organ recital at a church in Buffalo on that same evening but had declined, not mentioning the concert, but saying that he had not played the organ for more than fifty years. Back came a letter saying they were so sorry to learn that he was too infirm, and this time he explained that in any case he would not have been free to accept the engagement, as he was conducting that evening. He was oddly gratified, besides being amused, by the episode.

The Buffalo orchestra arrived, and the conducting was shared between Ralph and Robert Hull, who conducted the orchestral version of the *Songs of Travel* with Keith as soloist. When the music arrived the score was discovered to be Ralph's original manuscript with nearly an inch missing through wear and tear from the bottom of each worn page. Bob Hull also conducted the *Old 104th*, with John Kirkpatrick, also a member of the music department, as pianist; he, with the Cornell A Cappella Chorus and the Sage chapel choir, gave a dashing performance. After the interval Ralph conducted the *London Symphony*. I had dog-eared the pages of his score after the rehearsal, and had stuck a tab on the page where he had to turn back for a repeat. When the symphony was due to start, neither score nor the baton had been put out, but the librarian came on after Ralph and gave them to him. From my distant seat I saw with dismay that it was not Ralph's own copy. He did not notice and, as he had no marks on the first few pages, it was not until he was well into the first movement that he realized he had a new score, with sticky, unused pages and none of his marks. I felt the moment of his discovery almost as an electric shock and knew he was in a rage. He was so angry that he gave one of the best performances of his life, though he said afterwards that this in no way excused the librarian's inefficiency. The lost score turned up next day—shut inside the grand piano. By then the librarian had gone back to Buffalo with the orchestra. He then distinguished himself by sending Keith a 2nd flute part instead of the vocal score of *Sancta Civitas*, which was to be performed in Buffalo ten days later. This caused Dr. Krips to sit up all night to copy a flute part from the full score, cursing the publishers for not having sent it. Keith returned the flute part with a chilly message to the librarian that he was not a male alto; but in time everything was sorted out and everyone got everything right. At Cornell, Orrea Pernell, an old friend of Ralph's now living in the United States, played *The Lark Ascending*, and Helen Boatwright was soloist in Ralph's *Benedicite*. Ralph conducted the University Orchestra in *The Wasps Suite*, and the A Cappella Chorus sang his *Three Shakespeare Songs* conducted by Robert Hull. This was the first time Ralph had heard them since the original performance. They were so well sung at Cornell that he was very pleased with them—'I thought they were too difficult, but they aren't,' he said.

Unfortunately, snow had made flying impossible, so Christabel, Ralph and I went to Buffalo by train. Keith was already there and he met us. By now Ralph felt absolutely at home with the Buffalo orchestra; he started the concert by conducting *Tallis*. This was followed by the first performance of *Sancta Civitas* in the United States. It was a work which Dr. Krips knew well and the choir, trained by Hans Vigeland, sang as if they had known the music all their lives, and Keith was magnificent. Ralph said it was one of the best performances he had ever heard, and, as it was his own favourite of his choral works, he was very happy. At the party afterwards he and Dr. Krips and Mrs. Krips and I shook hands with five hundred citizens. By about the two hundredth Ralph hissed at me, 'We shan't get any champagne if this goes on much longer.' However, all was well; after the five hundredth introduction there was still plenty of champagne, and after six glasses of it he found the party as good as the concert. He was presented with the key of the city and there were speeches —a lovely one from Dr. Krips about Ralph, and another by Ralph about Dr. Krips, the audience and music in general. Then he had time to lose small pieces of his heart to many of the pretty citizenesses.

The weather had cleared, so we flew back to Cornell. Ralph was gay, but the rest of our party were silent. When we landed we were congratulated on being the only passengers who had not been sick and Ralph was the only passenger who had not noticed that it had been a horribly bumpy flight. We had only two more days left at Cornell. On the eve of Thanksgiving we gave an evening party for the music department and a few other friends. The next day—Thanksgiving—we spent with the Grouts—Keith and his elder daughter Julia were our fellow guests. The event of the day was a tremendous meal—the courses unrolled leisurely and amply from two till five. Margaret Grout, an exquisite cook, had made sure that we should have a Thanksgiving dinner of traditional perfection, and after the last cup of coffee Donald, at Ralph's request, played Bach for him.

Next day we left Cornell for New York with Keith and Christabel and even more luggage than we had brought. We had a glorious week at New York. We were the guests of Mr. Rudolf Bing, General Manager of the Metropolitan Opera House, at *Meistersinger*, and the Falkners came with us to Yale, where Ralph, to his great pleasure, received the Howland Prize—which Gustav had also received years before. We spent a day in the University, and Ralph lectured once more; the Dean of the School of Music, Luther Noss, and his wife gave a dinner-party in their beautiful old house, and the last official engagement was over. We were sad to part from Keith and Christabel, though we knew it would not be too long before we would meet them in England. Not only had they made this wonderful journey possible, but they had given us welcome, hospitality, and pleasure in all sorts of ways, and their imaginative kindness had touched every day of our visit.

Left on our own we stayed at a hotel recommended by Myra Hess. 'You friends of the Great Dame Hess?' said the liftman, and when we said we were he was delighted. We dashed about, seeing the Metropolitan Museum, going to a Philharmonic concert, a play, and several dinner parties. We went to *Aïda*, sitting once again in Mr. Bing's box. Ralph was so exasperated by applause breaking into the music that he turned to the offenders in the next box and hissed, 'Be quiet, uncivilized barbarians.' They did not dare to clap again, even at the end of the act, and Ralph felt guilty of behaviour unbecoming in a guest. Another evening we went to dinner with James and Rebecca Friskin, where William Schuman, then head of the Juilliard School, and his wife were fellow guests. After dinner, more musicians came to meet Ralph, among them his old pupil Peggy Glanville Hicks. Samuel Barber came over to talk to me, and said that he had always been grateful to Ralph whom he had met on one of his other visits to America. 'I showed him my setting of *Dover Beach*,' he said, 'and he liked it, and he encouraged me when no one believed in my music.' I was able to tell him that Ralph still admired it greatly. It was one of the poems he had once set himself, so he must have looked at it very critically.

The Howland Prize was a medal and a thousand dollars, so our days in New York were intoxicatingly rich. The money Ralph had made lecturing had provided us with travel and living expenses and plenty of comfort but this was luxury. Ralph whisked me off clothes shopping, we lived in taxis, and had little suppers about 1 a.m. almost every night. The *Queen Mary* seemed a very quiet refuge when we finally went on board. But the voyage turned out to be anything but quiet—for we had one of the worst crossings there had been for years. Julian Huxley was one of our fellow passengers, and he came to tell Ralph how well he remembered singing in the chorus when Hugh Allen conducted the first performance of the *Sea Symphony* at Oxford. He also told us about white tailed squirrels on the 'other side' of the Grand Canyon, and advised us to drink pink gin if the sea was rough. This was the best advice we had ever had for, in spite of storms, we never missed a meal. Another pleasant surprise was finding that Dorothy Pattinson, the producer of the R.A.M.

operas, was on board with her husband. Ralph liked the storms; he felt that we were able to feel as if we really were at sea when the waves were immense enough to dwarf even the *Queen Mary*. He remained well until we got into the calm of Southampton water; then he started to feel seasick, breakfasted on soda water and landed looking very wan indeed. We were met by my parents and Gil Jenkins at Southampton, the Boults at Waterloo, and Genia Hornstein at home. When she greeted us Ralph responded with a loving hug and the words, 'My dear, how wonderful to hear an English voice again.' Only when we all started to laugh did he realize that her voice is as emphatically and gloriously un-English, as excitably Russian, as the cyrillic form of her English writing.

So we were home for Christmas, for our carol party and the New Year, and we had seen Rome and the Grand Canyon in the year that had just ended.

The *Eighth Symphony* had been going well enough for Ralph to tell John Barbirolli of its existence. John had asked for a new work for the tenth Cheltenham Festival and although Ralph was not sure enough of its being ready, he said that if it was John should have it. It was ready enough for him to play it through to me in the middle of January, and later Roy Douglas came to play it to the usual 'committee' in April. Frank Howes's book on Ralph's music[1] had recently been published and when I invited him by telephone he said in a voice of horror—'He's not written *another* one?' I apologized for his fecundity, and Frank accepted my invitation. Ralph wrote to him after this:

> Thank you very much for your letter, and for coming to hear my new tune. As you say, though I do not accept yours, or anyone's advice blindly, I assure you it makes its effect. On the main point, however, I am not taking your advice. I feel the thing *is* a symphony and it is going to remain one. But a lot of your suggestions about detail I am going to think over hard, and probably adopt. However, I shall probably do nothing till I have let it 'mature in bond' for a bit.

A very few days later John and Evelyn Barbirolli came to dinner and Ralph gave the score to John to take home to read, which he did before leaving for Australia. He wrote just before they left to say he was 'greatly intrigued by it', and there, for the time being, it rested.

[1] *The Music of Ralph Vaughan Williams*, O.U.P. 1954.

The City of Birmingham Symphony Orchestra gave all Ralph's symphonies during the season, and we went up at the beginning of the year to hear the *Sea Symphony* and, on the way, to visit Gerald Finzi who was in hospital in Oxford. We found him under an enormous pile of scoring paper, which seemed to take up all the room on his bed; he was cheerful and we made plans for the Cheltenham Festival in July.

On 19 January Malcolm Sargent conducted the first London performance of *Hodie*; we went to several concerts and operas including Michael Tippett's *The Midsummer Marriage*. Ralph had now accepted his partial deafness as a natural part of life. We found that, except for plays he knew well, Shakespeare mostly, the theatre gave him very little pleasure; so we adapted our lives to this limitation and relied on operas and foreign films with English subtitles for entertainment—and often I went to plays while he went to the sort of new music programmes that consisted of several new works which I knew I should not enjoy and which Ralph thought he ought to hear. His companion for these ventures was usually Christopher Finzi.

At Dorking, the Leith Hill Festival celebrated its jubilee, and a little book was prepared during the winter with contributions from many of the people who had worked for its success. This was edited by Judge Gordon Clark who also wrote a record of some of the changes and chances through which the Festival had passed. Ralph added his *Reminiscences of Fifty Years*, and the whole made a 'Record of fifty years of music making in Surrey'. As the Festival competitions all start with sight reading, the choirs had long wanted a song with which they could sing themselves in before the dreaded 'sight test'. This seemed an appropriate joint contribution to the celebrations. So we made it.[1]

Ralph had heard the Salvation Army Staff Band, and had been much impressed by their playing, so, when they invited him to write a work for them, he liked the idea and accepted their invitation. His copy of Forsyth's book on orchestration lay open on his study table as he explored the possibilities of their instruments. When the work was finished and printed, we were invited to the Army Headquarters in Judd Street and delightfully entertained

[1] *Song for a Spring Festival*, printed by Oxford University Press for the exclusive use of Leith Hill Choirs.

after listening to it—the *Prelude on Three Welsh Hymn Tunes*. The work was recorded later in Ralph's presence at the Maida Vale studios.

Just after Christmas he was asked to advise about a performance of *The Bridal Day* to be given by students at the Chelsea College of Physical Education, now at Eastbourne. Peggie Cartwright, who taught there, was the inventive choreographer; she came to see Ralph to discuss the sort of dances he had in mind, and we went to a rehearsal early in the production where we met the producer, Miss Gough, and Mr. Davies, who was the pianist. At first, the choice of this work for a cast of girls seemed strange, but they were good actresses and at the dress rehearsal we realized we need have no qualms. Bacchus was robustly vinous, and the bridegroom, dressed as a grave, bearded young man, suggested a miniature by Oliver or Hilliard. Geoffrey Gilbert was the flautist and the Macgibbon Quartet, who had Jean Stewart as viola, made a link with the play-through before the war. Bernard and Olive Shore were among the audience, and Bernard, from the Ministry of Education, was delighted that the students had been so enterprising and so successful in their work. As the Cambridge performance had done for *Pilgrim*, this proved to Ralph that his romantic masque, using speaker, solo singer, chorus, dancers, and mimes, could make the effect he had intended as a work for the stage.

At the end of April we went down to Newquay. Ralph scarcely knew the north coast of Cornwall: we hoped to have a sunny, idle time but were not lucky with the weather, so we went sightseeing by all the available bus trips. The perfect expedition was on May Day when we went to Padstow to see the Hobby Horse. We hired a car, and arrived to find the town looking oddly familiar, and remembered:

> How each field turns a street, each street a park,
> Made green and trimm'd with trees! see how
> Devotion gives each house a bough
> A branch! each porch, each door, ere this
> An ark, a tabernacle is
> Made up of white-thorn neatly interwove
> As if here were those cooler shades of love.[1]

[1] Herrick, *Corinna's Maying*.

This was the traditional May Day. The conjuration of the hobby horse, the strange tune of death and resurrection, dancers in the streets, flowers in the men's hats, and the unselfconscious air of celebration, the music reaching back into centuries past and the dance perhaps even further, gave us a day of unforgettable spring ceremony.

Ralph had continued to be a supporter of the idea that Federalism was the only hope for the peace of the world so he accepted an invitation to be President of the Committee to arrange a concert—at which he agreed to conduct the *London Symphony*—in aid of the Federal Education and Research Trust. To Adrian Boult's exposition of its aims he added a note in the programme—'. . . a long and varied life has shown me that politically the world lacks a fresh vision of its own unity and that it is often for the artist to try to show the way.'

During the early summer the B.B.C. gave a series of recitals of English songs. The programmes were chosen by Leonard Isaacs, and the first concert was entirely devoted to songs by Ralph. The music was chosen from every part of his career and hearing them together one realized how striking a feature, from the earliest songs to the latest, was his ability to grasp each poet's individual speech and to make it an integral part of the tune. It was fortunate that Keith Falkner was in England and able to take part, sharing the solo work with Nancy Evans and Richard Lewis, Michael Mullinar, and the Hirsch Quartet.

We went to the whole series enjoying this panoramic view of one aspect of English music, and Ralph found it one of the most valuable and enlightened series of concerts he had ever attended.

Paddy Hadley had been in East Anglia during the severe floods of 1953, and from this experience he and Charles Cudworth had devised a cantata, *Fen and Flood*, showing how man's wit and resource stood against the powers of water on the low lying, fertile but dangerous East Anglian coast. Paddy had used *The Captain's Apprentice*, one of the tunes Ralph had collected at King's Lynn, and he had dedicated the work to Ralph. It was designed for the male voice choir of Caius College, Cambridge, and it was there it had its first performance during May week. After the performance Ralph asked Paddy if he might arrange it for S.A.T.B., for he felt it should have wider possibilities for performance than it could have as a work for male voices. Paddy enthusiastically permitted this.

Also in June we went to *Götterdämmerung* at Covent Garden—Ralph's prescription for enjoying any part of *The Ring* was 'a long sleep before, to prevent sleep during'. He said that he had come to the conclusion that once in every ten years or so was about the right interval for hearing *The Ring*. *Meistersinger* as often as possible, *Tristan* was special and I had better hear *Parsifal* once, although I should not like it. He had no intention of subjecting himself to it again.

This summer Ralph was awarded the Albert Medal of the Royal Society of Arts; he was the first musician to receive it, and Ralph Wedgwood wrote to him:

> I am sure that there will be very many who will be as delighted as I am to think that the honour has been so well bestowed.

At the end of July we went to the Cheltenham Festival. There was a lot of music Ralph wanted to hear, and he very much liked the atmosphere of this Festival. He would spend the morning at rehearsals and the afternoons either going out into the country round or meeting friends. After the concert everyone gathered in the Festival Club—another room in the Town Hall—where people could sit and talk as late as they pleased and where the bar did not shut inhospitably early. George Hannam-Clark, Ralph's old friend from the Benson Company, joined us, with the Kennedys and the Sumsions; there were evenings when everyone remembered their best stories—one reminiscence led to another, and George and Ralph added to each others' memories of long past scandals, improbable escapades, and songs from The Follies.

Earlier in the year Ralph had had a long letter from a girl who described herself as a gypsy, and wrote to him about a broadcast of *Job*. He asked if she knew any songs, or had any friends who were singers, and her answer gave enough encouragement for us to arrange to go to visit her. She had said, 'I have a version of the *Raggle Taggle Gypsies*, *oh*, and a mix up of *Blow the Wind Southerly* and *If I was a blackbird* which the old women cry over, but I don't sing every day. I can dance like a peacock but I like some port to get started on.' Frank Hollins offered to drive us down so our plans were made for an August week-end.

We found the place in the New Forest with some difficulty; it was a little strip of field in which an old fashioned gypsy caravan stood with a wooden shack beside it. A splendid horse looked over a gate, gold and silver bantams perched on the hazels bordering the grass and a huge yellow dog followed our hostess to meet us. Her husband was a painter, and they lived this pastoral life, idyllic in summer but rigorous in cold weather. We spent several hours on the version of the *Raggle Taggle Gypsies*, which had a long *cantilena* phrase, the gypsy's luring of the lady, after each verse. And we learned that she had invited all the other gypsies who might have songs to meet us in the pub by the Rufus stone at seven. A great number of people turned up and we crowded the bar. Ralph ordered drinks, brown ale for the men, port for the women, and after a little general conversation singing started; Ralph and Frank struggled with the tunes, I with the words, while a very sinister and rakish figure stood at my elbow, hissing into my ear and confusing the issue. It was exceedingly merry, but no tunes of any quality emerged from the evening, and after a while our hostess decided to dance. She had barely started when the landlord came in and said we were too noisy and disreputable a crowd, and we must leave. We were bundled out into the night, songless but amused; we picnicked on the heather in brilliant moonlight before we drove on to Lyndhurst for the night.

For the first time since the war Ralph decided to miss the Three Choirs Festival; we had taken tickets for a trip to Greece and were to leave at the beginning of September. Ralph had never been to Greece except for the months in Salonika during the war, and he felt that this would be a good time to go. We went with a Hellenic tour, a party of about thirty people who looked at each other with dismay and dislike when they assembled at Victoria Station and were still virtually strangers by Genoa. There we embarked, and the fact that the little ship was filled with new strangers immediately worked its compelling magic and our party found a friendly unity. We sailed between Scylla and Charybdis into an ocean full of flying fishes; then Ralph became afflicted with violent toothache. Everyone offered his nostrum, but nothing helped, and he suffered for twenty-four hours. We cabled to the British Council at Athens, and no sooner did we dock at Piraeus than we were whisked away to a fierce Athenian dentist who removed the tooth. Ralph had a large dinner and several whiskies, a good night's sleep, and next morning he felt well and able for anything. Our party was too large for one bus, but not enough for two, so six of us were given a Cadillac driven by a very tall Greek called Hercules. He took charge of us and, because we could go much faster than the bus, we had all sorts of delightful and unscheduled stops. The first day of sightseeing was impressive—Daphni, where Byzantine mosaics gaze down in mournful splendour, and where, as we all stood in the courtyard, a dark eyed Mercury loitering with other locals to look at the tourists came straight through the crowd to us and gave us each a branch of bay leaves—a touching welcome to the world of legend. Mycenae was all we had expected—the lion gate, the steep road, and the brooding ruins. It had the same air of menace that is so apparent at Corfe Castle, but, being open and no longer dominated by any great building, it was more bearable. Our great moment was when we asked what was the distant hill, with what looked like a fortress, to the south and Mr. Cook the archaeologist who was in charge of us all said briefly, 'Argos'. The magic of the sea light, the herb-scented air, the stories we had lived with all our lives had already made their impact—'I *am* glad we are here,' Ralph said. Our hotel room at Nauplia looked out on the little Turkish fort in the bay, and we breakfasted in sunshine, gazing at the green hill of Argos. From there we went to Epidaurus; the theatre delighted Ralph but he found details boring—one broken column much like another, so we decided to miss the ruins and sit on the terrace drinking iced beer. On our way Ralph said 'We should sacrifice a black cock to Aesculapius,' when a little black cock appeared and walked gravely beside us to the café. We saw the mighty stone fortress at Tiryns and in the afternoon we bathed. This was a triumph, for Ralph thought he had given up bathing—he had not been in the sea since 1934—but a new bathing dress had been acquired and the warm Aegean did the rest. We went to Corinth, Olympia, Patras, over the ferry to Rion and up through the mountains to Delphi, a drive of hair-raising corners and spreading views. We stopped to drink herb tea and eat honey cakes, bought for us as a present from the drivers, at a tiny inn under a plane tree where shepherds in pleated tunics sat playing checkers, and so on and on till we saw the great valley of olive trees that lies behind Itea and we reached Delphi. There we spent the whole of the next day. Eagles soared over the valley, the air was clear, and before the day grew too hot Ralph mounted a pony to go to the top of the hill. He and the pony looked at each other with foreboding, but we eventually got him on to the crate-like sidesaddle and the pony boy led him up the zigzag tracks to the highest part of the ruins. The rest of us climbed the hill on foot; when we met Ralph he was horseless. The ride had been, he said, 'extremely pericoloso' and he would prefer to walk down. The water from the Castalian spring is piped for a few yards to fall into a stone trough by the wayside where the passers-by stop to drink, cupping their hands under the pipe while the animals drink from the trough. We waited while a shawled peasant woman and her donkey, loaded with firewood, drank, and then we followed; it was the most beautiful water I have ever tasted even in that land of springs and wells. We joined some of the rest of our party at the little improvised café, and the waiter took a jug across to fill it for the glasses of water that accompany coffee. There were the treasures in the museum to see, and after dinner we went to a café with a terrace built out over the valley, where we danced with Greek soldiers in a long chain dance. Enormous stars hung in the night or fell like Semele's shower of gold while bagpipe music alternated with out-of-date gramophone records. 'I am glad we came,' Ralph said again.

There was no sphinx at Thebes when we passed the cross-roads there, and so came to Athens. Here we went sightseeing, took part in all the bathing excursions, saw *Hecuba* in the theatre of Herodias Atticus, and went to the Parthenon each evening at sunset. We went to Crete and spent a blazing morning at Knossos, which Ralph didn't like, 'a sort of second class railway station,' he said; but he did like the museum at Heraklion. Finally we sailed to Mikonos, arriving after midnight. A porter from the hotel met us and came up to Ralph, kissed him, and said, 'My son is at the Paris conservatoire; music is most wonderful.' Most of the party went to Delos next morning, but it was windy and the sea was rough so we spent an idle day sitting in cafés and exploring the little white streets of the town. Ralph bought, and learned to blow, a conch shell, which sounded like the ship's siren. Each time he blew passengers started up from the café tables clutching their bags, bundles, and baskets, only to subside laughing when they realized it was Ralph experimenting with his new musical instrument. When we were due to leave, the boat was late, so we sat on the quay; the new moon rose over Delos, its light reflected in the pale green water of the harbour among the caiques; the island grew dark blue and the white-washed village glimmered, the lights were lit and as darkness fell the boat came in and we climbed on board.

We had two more nights in Athens.

We met Frank Hollins in Venice and spent two days looking at some of our favourite places—'No need to do much this time,' Ralph said. 'We'll come back again another year.' Frank had left his car on the mainland, to which we crossed by ferry, and started our drive home.

Our last stop was at Solèsmes. Ralph had long wanted to hear the plainsong, but was not as greatly excited by it as he had expected. Our way back to St. Malo and the last car ferry of the summer went through Dol, where we were sad to see the Grande Bretagne Hotel had changed from the old fashioned inn we had stayed at two years earlier into a smart hotel—'That's what will happen to Mikonos and everywhere,' Ralph said gloomily. We spent our last francs on a bottle of Calvados at St. Malo before we embarked at sunset. We had had the best of everything, even the weather, for, after the blazing sunshine, the oleanders and morning-glories, sea light and olive trees of the ancient world, we had found the great forests of France touched by autumn, the beechwoods just golden and faintly melancholy, like the deserted rooms and unlighted windows of the chateaux they surrounded.

Our travels were not over, for Ralph had undertaken to conduct the *Serenade to Music* at Birmingham on 11 October before Rudolf Schwarz with the City of Birmingham Symphony Orchestra played his *Fourth Symphony*. We went home on the morning of Ralph's birthday in time to open, but not to answer, all his letters, and in time to go to the concert at the Festival Hall to hear Adrian conduct *Job*. Two days later we went to Ireland. Arnold Bax had died at Cork in 1953 and Harriet Cohen had arranged for a memorial lecture to be given at the University each year. Ralph, a Vice President of the Arnold Bax Society founded in the summer of 1955, had been asked by her to be the first lecturer. He was free to choose any subject, and he had chosen to talk about folk songs. The real theme of his talk was that almost all the good Irish (not Gaelic) folk songs were derived from the English pale. He had worked hard to get this talk ready and to collect the illustrations, and it was completed before we went to Birmingham. We flew to Dublin, where, as fog had delayed our start, we thought we might have missed the train. Gil Jenkins, then Permanent Secretary to the Ministry of Transport and Civil Aviation, had asked the airport and the railway people to look after us. We were dashed through all barriers, raced to the station by car where the train had been kept waiting, and to crown all, as there was a restaurant car strike, we were given aeroplane lunch trays and a bottle of wine. It was all most princely. At Cork we were met, looked after, taken sightseeing, and our three days there were filled to the brim. Ralph's lecture was one of his best variations on the perpetual theme of 'individual flowerings on a common stem'. He explored the likenesses between English tunes and tunes long held to be of native Irish origin, and there were moments when the audience looked as if they would like to lynch him as he calmly, with historical knowledge, musical scholarship, reference, and hypothesis, recaptured their long appropriated songs for England. He enjoyed himself and so, despite their outraged nationalist feelings, did the audience.

They enjoyed themselves far more than the next audience to whom he spoke—this was at a ceremony in honour of Martin Shaw's eightieth birthday at Ipswich in the church of St. Mary le Tower, at which some of Martin's own music was sung and Ralph gave an address. He was indeed offered the pulpit, but he preferred the chancel steps. As the talk was to be printed in the Diocesan magazine, he had prepared a script on the work Martin had done for church music, as composer, organist, and choir trainer. When it came to the point he delivered a much more fiery oration, practically a commination service on the basis of 'cursed be the congregations, choirmasters, and organists who do not listen to Martin'. The assembled congregation shrank in their seats, much as the ladies in the next box at the Metropolitan opera house had done, as Ralph warmed to his task and thundered on. Martin and Joan Shaw, at first surprised, were shaking with laughter, and the dignitaries of the Church among whom we sat in the Choir looked amazed.

He gave one more talk that year, at the invitation of Alan Bush who was running a Composers' Concourse. Ralph's subject was Parry and Stanford as teachers; he spoke of how he had seen them as a student, and how he looked back on them now, sixty years later. It was a heart searching task to prepare and one in which understanding held the balance between criticism and generosity in weighing the qualities of his masters.

Ralph was presented formally with the Royal Society of Arts medal, and at the meeting he found Robin Darwin, who looked after him and was throughout the proceedings the support and company he always liked to have on formal occasions. Otherwise the autumn was pleasantly full of opera going and other entertainments—one of these was a visit to the Classical theatre of China whose company's mime was superlative. A day or two after we had seen their performance, the musicians of the company came to call at Hanover Terrace, bringing gifts of flower prints. They had an interpreter and we talked about their music and our music, about their pictures, and, not for the first time, we blessed Arthur Waley's translations for making us aware of a little of the literary background of the arts in their country.

It was a long time since Ralph had done any film music, so he was pleased to be asked for a score for a short documentary. The plan involved Boris Ord to whom he wrote:

> I have been asked to do the music for a short film on the subject of Elizabethan England, and they want to introduce into it the choir of King's College. Do you think there is any chance? They want two items; the first they call 'choir in procession'—whatever that may mean—and secondly 'choir singing in stalls'—for which I would suggest, if the thing comes off, Smith's responses, which I think is the most lovely thing you do. The first entry would be a minute fifteen seconds, or less, and the second entry thirty seconds. If you think of it at all perhaps we could meet and discuss it. I believe British Transport Films, or whatever their name is, have already written to you.
>
> Beside writing to them would you also send me the enclosed card with yes or no crossed out?

The answer was yes, and Ralph went ahead with his plans, finding tunes to suit the pictures as well as inventing them. So the year ended with this agreeable work.

CHAPTER XVI

1956–1958

With the new year the Bach rehearsals started again, and Ralph had promised to conduct the *St. Matthew Passion* in Manchester with the Hallé Choir and Orchestra. January was a fairly easy month, the E.F.D.S. Albert Hall performance, a Singery, *Don Giovanni*, the *Magic Flute* and *Rigoletto* and *The Consul* by Menotti, the film of *Richard III*, a Macnaghten concert, Dr. Krips conducting *The Creation*, the Madrigal Society, and a Philharmonic concert, still left room for work. Ralph was glad when his film music was recorded and he could think about his Bach rehearsals and get on with a short work he was writing for chorus and organ on the strange words in the first chapter of *Ezekiel* which he called *A Vision of Aeroplanes*. He had also started to think about and make sketches for a new symphony.

We went to Manchester in February for the first choral rehearsal of the *Passion*. Ralph found the choirs rather a tough proposition, while they found some of his ideas difficult and unsympathetic; however, the long evening was battled through and both survived. John and the Hallé gave Ralph a nine-hour rehearsal of his new symphony before we went home, in time to go to some of the rehearsals for a broadcast performance of *Sir John in Love* which was to take place on the Sunday after the *St. John Passion* at Dorking. The Cambridge Opera Group were also rehearsing *Sir John in Love*. We had seen one rehearsal before Christmas and we had looked forward to the performance, but Ralph caught a cold at the second Manchester rehearsal and we had to abandon the expedition, which he hated doing. However, some of our friends went to see the opera and enjoyed it and gave us a full account, telling us just how good it had been. He was well again for a March Singery, and a concert of Gerald Finzi's music the day after the *St. Matthew* at Dorking, but his cold had never completely disappeared and he was not really well when we went to Manchester the following week. Long rehearsals in the

Town Hall in cold foggy weather did not help, but the performance had to be given and Ralph was both stubborn and tough and he enjoyed working with the Hallé who were great friends and splendid allies. The other particular delight in this performance was having a number of boys for the *Ripieno* Chorus who sang from the gallery, so that their music came from above and made a clear pattern lacing through the first chorale. As at Dorking, he used a trumpet to play their tune, a single line of support that gave an edge to the sound of the voices. It was a tremendous effort, for the choirs had not the long-standing, year-to-year familiarity with the music that Ralph was by now accustomed to, it was only a week since his other performance and he had a temperature. Nevertheless the result of all these extra responsibilities and unfamiliarities was a radiant performance, worth all that its preparation had involved. But we were both thankful to get home next day and Ralph retired to bed for a week.

Jill Day Lewis introduced a friend of hers, Simona Pakenham, to us and told us that Simona was writing a book about Ralph. We invited her to the next Singery: she was surprised to find that he was far less remote a person than she had expected. He loved to have pretty women about, and good looks added to intelligence absolutely won his heart. As most of our women friends had this fortunate double gift, and as he had a most unfair share of masculine charm which he well knew how to use, the attraction all round was mutual, gay, and osculatory. The tenors and basses naturally followed their conductor's example, so I was hardly surprised when she told me later, 'I had never seen so much kissing in my life as at that first Singery.'

One of the great delights for Ralph was the way so many of his old friends had come back into his life. Living in London made it much easier for him to see them, and old friends, former pupils, and some of his relations, notably Frances Cornford, came to stay or to call, gathering up threads from every part of his life and adding to the texture of the present. In some extraordinary way he managed to enjoy much sociability without shortening his working hours, which were to him, as they always had been, the most important part of each day. As Frances Cornford observed 'He would heave himself out of his big armchair in the drawing room (which like his own appearance was both noble and comfortable) and shamble away into his study next door. Here he would effortlessly enter his own kingdom. . .'[1]

The young opera group from Cambridge came to ask advice about their future. Most of them had left the University, or would do so at the end of the summer, and they passionately wanted to go on with operas. They were full of ideas and enthusiasm, and at that meeting the New Opera Company more or less constituted itself, with reckless schemes for the future and with Ralph as President.

At the end of April we went to Cheltenham to see a production of *The Poisoned Kiss* done by the boys of the Grammar School in the Hall of Cheltenham College. The music master, Mr. William Neve, had made an arrangement for piano and percussion and, in spite of losing four Empresses in succession because their voices had broken unexpectedly, he achieved a delightful performance. A lot of the dialogue had been cut, and some local and topical jokes had been added, with advantage. Ralph immediately said that we must get possession of the book and rewrite the dialogue. We discussed this on our way to Manchester where his *Eighth Symphony* was to have its first performance. At a very late stage in the composition of it I had been innocently guilty of causing an expensive addition to be made to the already large percussion group. Seeing that there was a performance of *Turandot*, an opera I had never heard, I suggested that we should go. The only tickets left were for the front row of the stalls and there we sat: Ralph was fascinated by the sound of the tuned gongs, so the moment the lights went up he lifted the curtain that hides the orchestra from the audience, and beckoned to the player. They spent the whole interval in conference. Next morning the gongs were added to the score, where a note says—'Gongs are not absolutely essential, but their inclusion is highly desirable.'

The rehearsals for the symphony were lively; the string players listened and watched critically while the wind and brass played the scherzo without them, and the rest of the orchestra returned the compliment by paying devoted attention to the strings for whom alone the Cavatina is written. The finale was remarkable visually for the way Joyce Aldous managed the tubular bells, with a cross hands movement which she had invented and carried

[1] *R.C.M. Magazine*, Easter 1959.

out with precise elegance that was a joy to see. The sounds Ralph had explored, the vibraphone, bells, and gongs, tended to attract too much attention and to obscure the real musical qualities of the symphony, particularly of the last movement, from both the critics and the public. At the concert we were besieged by reporters, and I had to invent a line about Ralph's music being his public life, and the rest his private life—but I didn't think of it in time to prevent a lot of nonsense about what he had eaten during the day appearing in far larger print than the account of the concert. John and the Hallé gave a splendid first performance. The dedication of the symphony was simply to John Barbirolli, but Ralph wrote on the manuscript 'for "Glorious John" '—there was no one more worthy to inherit Dryden's adjective.

Ignorance had made us oblivious of the Cup Final next day in which Manchester City were playing and which it was alleged would make it impossible for us to travel by train unless we had booked seats. When we heard about it, we hired a car and drove home. Simona Pakenham and Genia Hornstein had come to hear the symphony and Genia drove home with us. Simona braved the football supporters' train. We were glad we had not, for the drive across country was leisurely and agreeable. We stopped at Lichfield to see the cathedral and Dr. Johnson's house there, Ralph refused to climb all the stairs but Genia and I saw a picture of Erasmus Darwin, Ralph's great-great-grandfather, to whom he had an unmistakable likeness.[1]

The first performance of the *Eighth Symphony* in London was on 14 May. Many more of Ralph's friends were able to hear it, and once again he surprised them, which was as it should be. Afterwards Cedric Glover wrote to ask why Ralph could not let his audience have a score to look at before the performance, and Ralph answered:

> Thank you for your letter. You know I like being appreciated, and make no pretence about it! As regards printing the miniature score beforehand—I may tell you that a *lot* of alterations were made at the rehearsals.

At Whitsun we had the pleasure of a visit from the Beaux of London City,[2] who came to dance at Hanover Terrace in the

[1] The portrait in the National Portrait Gallery, by J. Wright, shows Dr. Darwin's hands, which might have been painted from Ralph's own.

[2] A London group of Morris dancers.

private road in front of the houses. Little by little neighbours and sightseers from the park gathered till there was a good audience. After they had finished, Ralph made an impassioned speech about Morris dancing to the crowd before we took the dancers in for drinks.

Another festivity was the wedding of Irmgard, the German girl who had cooked for us since we moved to London. Having no relations in England, she was married from our house. Ralph gave her away and we had a party afterwards. She was a charming sight in her long white dress; her bridegroom, a clarinettist in the Scots Guards band, was in uniform, and many of our friends who knew her and had enjoyed her cooking were there. Her successor, Edna Harling, a Salvation Army ex-bandswoman, who had given up the trombone for cookery, made the feast.

Harold Darke's fortieth anniversary as organist of St. Michael's, Cornhill, was celebrated with a concert for which George Dyson, Herbert Howells, Harold himself, and Ralph had written new works: Ralph's contribution, *A Vision of Aeroplanes*, had a fiendishly difficult organ part, played by John Birch to the admiration of his colleagues.

This year was the fiftieth anniversary of *The English Hymnal*. Ralph wrote an article, recorded a broadcast, and went to Addington Palace, against our doctor's advice, for he had slight phlebitis in his leg and was supposed to spend as much time as he could with his foot up. It was the consequence of a sudden desire to roll the lawn on a day too wet for mowing and it kept him immobile for most of July and prevented him from going to Nicola Darwin's wedding party. Nicola had sung for him in the *St. John Passion* several times and he had hoped to be at the wedding, not only for her sake but also to see her father, his cousin Bernard, whom he met rarely in later life but for whom he had great affection.

Cordelia was most anxious for her friend, the sculptor David McFall, to do a head of Ralph, who strenuously opposed the idea. Cordelia persisted, and eventually David was invited to come to the house. Ralph told him that he must do his work while he himself was working; so David arrived with a bucket of clay and a bust peg for the first sitting on 22 August. During the five days on which he came Ralph told me that he had worked harder than usual himself. 'I mustn't let the young man see me slacking,' he said. It was a perfect arrangement, for David caught the private face, known to very few people, of Ralph absorbed in work. The likeness is extraordinary: the grave beauty of the bronze captured the truth in strength and intimacy.

The best week of all that summer was that of the Gloucester Festival. A large party stayed at the King's School House, just behind the cathedral; the whole Finzi family were there, the organist of Worcester, David Willcocks, and of Hereford, Meredith Davies, Howard Ferguson, and Harold Brown, the Treasurer of the South Western Arts Association. It was like an end of term week at a glorified co-educational school, Ralph said. We had a wonderful Sunday when the Finzis drove us out to Chosen Hill[1] and Gerald described how he had been there as a young man on Christmas Eve at a party in the tiny house where the sexton lived and how they had all come out into the frosty midnight and heard bells ringing across Gloucestershire from beside the Severn to the hill villages of the Cotswolds. Gerald's Festival work, *In Terra Pax*, was a setting of a poem by Robert Bridges about such an experience. For us it was still summer, with roses in the tangled churchyard grass where the sexton's children were playing; blackberries in the hedges and the gold September light over the country we all knew and loved. Another expedition we four made was to see Rutland and Kathleen Boughton. After much wandering we found their house and sat and talked through the morning.

Howard Ferguson's *Amore Langueo*, Herbert Howells's *Hymnus Paradisi*, Gerald's *In Terra Pax*, and Ralph's *Hodie*, *Eighth Symphony* and *The Lark Ascending*, of which Fred Grinke gave a beautiful and serene performance, were in the programme. The choirs nearly fell out of their seats watching the timpani and percussion players in the last movement of *No. 8*. One night we came out of the concert to find rainy clouds carrying shadows of the floodlit cathedral, four towers standing mighty and mysterious in the sky above the real tower.

We had only three days at home before our holiday, and they were saddened by the news of Ralph Wedgwood's death. We had been to Leith Hill Place during the summer and the two Ralphs—Ralph and Randolph—had sat side by side still looking

[1] Churchdown.

recognizably like the Cambridge photograph, though Randolph was thinner and Ralph's tie less abundant. We were more than ever glad to remember this visit as well as many others and more glad of the years Randolph and Iris had spent at Leith Hill Place.

Ralph heard from George Trevelyan:

> Yesterday I heard of R. L. W's death—early this morning my wife died suddenly of a stroke after 53 years of happy married life. She was so ill that I cannot regret it. But I feel a mere shadow now—what days we have all had since 1893.

Ralph was sad for his two friends, Iris and George. The shadow of autumn fell on our lives too with this news, and I was glad that Ralph had a day's work, recording his *Eighth Symphony* with Adrian, to keep him busy before we left England.

He was ready for a holiday; he wanted to work, but to have a complete change, so we flew to Majorca. It had been a rainy summer, and the airport officials at Palma laughed as the passengers, all carrying umbrellas and mackintoshes, blinked at the sunlight. An hour later we were bathing in a warm sea.

Ralph had brought his scoring paper with him, so after bathing he usually spent the morning at work. After lunch, siesta and tea, we went for a walk or sat in the garden, and then he went back to write till dinner time. It was a pleasant holiday, very quiet, with a little sightseeing, and one memorable lunch party. Peggy Glanville Hicks telephoned one morning, which surprised us for we thought she was in America. But she was working with Robert Graves and a librettist on his novel, *Homer's Daughter*, from which she was going to make an opera, and this call was an invitation to luncheon. We met an enormous party for drinks in a café but the crowd gradually thinned out leaving about eight of us to go on to a restaurant. Robert was in favour of founding an oracle, and we asked if we could have part-time work as priest and priestess if we provided our own robes. Though neither he nor Ralph had been particularly happy at Charterhouse they talked about the school with nostalgic pleasure. Then Ralph praised the tune of Carmen Carthusianum and they both started singing. But a thunderstorm came on almost immediately, quenching the song and dampening the singers.

We had heard from Gerald Finzi since we came away telling

us that he was ill; only a few days later a special messenger brought letters from Joy and Gil telling us of his death. He had caught chickenpox from the children playing in the sexton's garden at Chosen and that, on top of a serious blood condition, had been fatal. Joy told us then that he had known for some years that he had not much longer to live, so this sudden death had its mercies, though it was hard to realize it then. We had arranged to be out all day, and we were glad to be on a remote hill-side, where a gallery cut into the rock with cool cave-like rooms behind gave us a view over much of the island. Swifts and swallows, on their way to Africa, were everywhere, swooping and soaring, perhaps the same birds that we had seen at Ashmansworth earlier in the summer. We remembered one concert that spring which we had been to with Gerald and Joy. When it was over and we were sitting in a café having supper, Ralph had said, 'Let's drive down to Ashmansworth tonight and see the dawn.'—and so we did, and heard the cuckoo in the pear tree before we went to bed by early daylight.

Ralph wrote a tribute for *The Times*, which he sent off that evening.

The other places we saw were a strange garden with water springing in little jets from Ali Baba jars under the lemon trees, a palace where we were told Queen Elizabeth had slept—it took a moment to remember there were other Queen Elizabeths—and of course Valldemosa, Chopin's piano, the little monastic apothecary's shop, and the view from the rooms in which George Sand and Chopin had stayed. We saw some dancers there, but they were less good than the student groups who came to entertain at our hotel. Ralph was very interested and talked to them about folk dancing, and disclosed that he was President of the English Folk Dance and Song Society. Next time they came their leader made a speech before they danced, 'One special we dedicate to you, the President of English Folk Dancers. It is a Fertility Dance.' We were also told of a group of dancers who had a man–woman and a devil, and whose dance is much like the Morris. We found the café where they practised and spent a morning watching them and drinking wine with them. The leader of the group was the man–woman, whose stiffened petticoats were supported by a crinoline frame, his dress was decorated with holy pictures in little framed medallions and he carried sweet herbs.

At our invitation the team came to dance at the hotel, but their ritual was too esoteric for most of the other visitors.

Ralph made good progress with the symphony but he was glad when the time came to go home to his piano. By then the summer was over, even in Majorca.

On 6 November we had the first meeting of his new R. V. W. Trust. Ralph had been one of the very small Committee of the Butterworth Trust since it was founded for the purpose of using the royalties from George's music to help musicians. Ralph wanted to spend some of his own money in the same way. Guided by Mr. A. B. Sturgess who had become his accountant in 1953, he had been going through the maze of difficulties that lies between the idea and the act of giving away money. Ralph's earnings were large, and increasing every year, which made him feel uncomfortable. He had always done what he could to help other musicians, but it was a sporadic giving and he wanted to find some regular means of doing more for music and less for the tax gatherers. So from this year all his income from his Performing Rights was made over to the Trust. He outlined his proposals to the Committee whom we had chosen very carefully, to represent every aspect of music making. They were Robert Armstrong, Bernard Brown, Edric Cundell, Gil Jenkins, Bernard Shore, Albert Sturgess, with special responsibility for guiding finance, Michael Tippett, and me, with Frank Thistleton as Secretary, bringing all the knowledge and experience he had gained as Secretary of The Musicians' Benevolent Fund to help us. We discussed our plans and allocated some of our funds. One of the things Ralph had long wanted was to give a concert of Gustav's lesser-known works. When the plans for the Trust were well advanced he had discussed this with Adrian, and the Festival Hall had been booked and the programme chosen. This was told to the Committee who were all in favour of the idea, though Ralph said he would not act so lavishly without advice and discussion in the future. He asked Gil to take on the Chairmanship, as he felt his own deafness was a handicap, and he also asked Sir Eric Edwards,[1] legal adviser to the Musicians' Benevolent Fund, to join the Committee. It was a very good beginning of a Trust that gave Ralph much satisfaction; money that came from music was being ploughed back to enrich the musical life of the country,

[1] Now Lord Chelmer.

to help small societies and festivals, to encourage concert givers to attempt works that needed more players and more rehearsal than they could normally afford, and to do as much as possible for composers and performers in any way that did not seem to be catered for by existing societies. It was wonderful to have money for all these things and a committee who knew something about each one of the applications and could advise and discuss the value of the work being done, for we determined never to give indiscriminately. He had waited a long time for this meeting, and he was full of gratitude to Mr. Sturgess to whose invention and planning were due both the structure and framework of the Trust.

The Holst concert had programme notes by Scott Goddard, Herbert Howells, and Edmund Rubbra: the programme had been most carefully chosen by Ralph and Adrian—*The Fugal Overture*, the choral ballet, *Morning of the Year*, *Ave Maria*, *Assemble all ye Maidens*, *Egdon Heath*, *Choral Fantasia*, *Ode to Death*, *Fugal Concerto*, and ballet music from *The Perfect Fool*—and the Festival Hall was half empty. It was sad to hear, afterwards, of the many people who, having read the press notices or heard about the concert from their friends, said they wished they had come: so much of the music had not been heard for far too long, for the period of denigration which often follows a composer's death had caused much of his music to be unplayed. This concert helped to dispel some misapprehensions and let people hear that they had been unwise enough to neglect music that was beautiful, individual, and strange.

Ralph had made an arrangement of the Bach Choral Prelude *Schmücke Dich* for cello solo and string orchestra for a concert at the end of December in honour of Casals's eightieth birthday. Anthony Pini was the soloist with the Collegium Musicum Londinii, led by Eli Goren, at the Friends' House on 28 December.

Since our visit to Rutland Boughton in September, the Russian suppression of the Hungarian uprising had shaken even so staunch a Communist as he had been. After all the arguments he had had with Ralph over many years, he wrote to say that he had left the party, stricken with despair for his beliefs of a lifetime. It was a noble letter, and a generous one, for he need not have so confided in Ralph, who answered, comforting him as best he could—

I feel much touched at your taking the trouble to explain your new position to me. It seems to me that all right-minded people are communists, as far as that word means that everything should be done eventually for the common good. But communism has got to mean now so much other than that, which I, for one, cannot subscribe to. Myself I see no reason why the Russian atrocities should prevent your remaining a communist in the ideal sense of the word. The Russians are a strange mixture of artistic ideals and barbarism, and the barbarians seem to come out on top, whether they call themselves Czarists, Karenskiists or Stalinists.

I hope we shall soon meet again——

Love to you both from us both——

The England of Elizabeth, the film produced by the British Transport Commission, for which Ralph had written music, turned out to be an agreeable, short film; but, delightful as it was to look at, the music was masked by the commentary, which was rather disappointing. Except for Bach rehearsals and our Singeries, we had a quiet spring, with a little opera going and a few concerts, for Ralph was immersed in his symphony as well as in making sketches for a brass band work. He had been asked to give away prizes at the brass band festival at the Albert Hall at the end of the previous year, and afterwards he said, 'I wish they'd ask me to write a test piece for them.' This wish came true, and he liked the scope it gave to explore further the range of less familiar instruments.

Having got through both *Passions* and all the winter weather I caught Asian influenza which was the winter's epidemic: Ralph did not, but we both enjoyed a few days at Brighton, the usual specific to cure any winter ills. While we were there we saw *Lysistrata*, which was as tonic as the sea air. In spite of his deafness, Ralph did not miss a word of it. We also spent one morning going to Rottingdean to see his prep. school. The Headmaster was surprised to be visited by an old boy who had left almost seventy years ago but he took us all over the building and Ralph found most of it recognizable. That afternoon as we sat on the beach, he dictated some of these memories and my hand was hard put to keeping up with his words. It seemed that if ever his musical invention ceased, or even if he should have a week or two when he could not write music, he could very well write his autobiography, and that this would be a good beginning. But when I suggested it he said, 'I've only lived in three houses so there's nothing much to write about.' I said that he had enjoyed reading Carl Nielsen's account of his early life, so other people might enjoy his. 'Oh, I don't know,' he said. 'You can do it for me.' So when we made our wills he said that if I did, it would discourage anyone else from writing about him. I protested that I couldn't write about music. 'Oh, Michael Kennedy will do that part very well,' he said. Michael and I both hoped it would be an autobiography.

In May we went to stay at Haddo House near Aberdeen for a performance of the *Sea Symphony*, which June Gordon conducted; the choir was local, but the orchestra was reinforced by musicians from London, who, with the two soloists, Jennifer Vyvyan and John Cameron, all stayed at the house. It was a tremendous party and great fun. It was a new part of the world to us and strange to find the early spring still lingering when in the south it was summer weather. We were shown, among other places, the ruins of the house where Byron's mother and father had spent their honeymoon dancing reels to keep warm. The *Sea Symphony* was preceded by a performance of Parry's *Blest Pair of Sirens*, which Ralph conducted. It was, he always said, his favourite English choral work, and the singers sang it as if it was theirs too.

Ralph had long felt that Robin Milford's music was unjustly neglected so at his instigation the R. V. W. Trust gave an all-Milford concert, for which the composer and his wife came to stay with us. Elizabeth Poston, writing to Ralph afterwards, said, 'Robin's tunes, like the water of the Greek springs, have a clarity and purity all their own, and this evening devoted to him showed this, and gave him pleasure in the excellence of the performances.'

After this we had an early holiday: Ralph said that I must see Austria, so we went first to Innsbruck, where we met his old friend Klara Kletschka. We went up mountains by cable car which I disliked extremely, and to the theatre which was gay and pretty; and we saw all the things one does see—at Zell-am-See we took the excursion bus up the Gross Glockner, where tiny flowers growing almost out of snow were the only pleasure in the icy wastes. Even Salzburg, with all its charms, could not keep my eyes from looking with longing towards the Brenner Pass, and pine trees were a dismal substitute for olives. We went on the Königsee in a silent electric boat. In mid-lake the pilot stopped, unpacked a flügel horn and played a halting phrase, which the mountain echo sent back, beautifully improved—'A good sound,' Ralph said. 'I shall put it into the symphony.' We stayed a few days in Munich and looked at pictures, the Altdorfer *Resurrection* in particular, and we saw the only opera for which we could get seats, *Palestrina* by Pfitzner, a very long and dreary affair, we thought. By now Ralph was not feeling well and for once we felt we had had an unsuccessful holiday. We agreed that for our next holiday we would go to Italy—or France—or Greece, and never go near mountains or pine forests again. We were glad to get home. It was just as well we did return, for Ralph was discovered to have acute anaemia and had to rest and take all sorts of pills. They worked magically, and the doctor, Ray Rowntree, who was by now a friend and a most welcome visitor—even if he ordered pills, or rest, or massage, or elastic stockings—pronounced a cure after a few days.

While we were away Ralph's friend Pegs married again and she brought her husband, Hugh Meredith, to dinner soon after we came home. Ralph was delighted for them both and full of congratulation and felicitation. Another visitor was Leopold Stokowski, whom we met at a lunch party at Amen House given by Mr. John Brown who had succeeded Geoffrey Cumberlege as Publisher of the Oxford Press. Later we heard his performance of Ralph's *Eighth Symphony*. Frances Cornford had become one of our regular visitors, and she was with us a good deal during the summer. Ralph let her off *The Trojans*, an opera he thought we ought to hear and which we did not enjoy. We were happier with the R.A.M.'s early celebration of Ralph's birthday, a performance of *The Poisoned Kiss*. We had succeeded in buying the copyright of the libretto, and, at Ralph's suggestion, I had spent much of the winter re-writing the dialogue, using rhymed couplets instead of prose passages. This version was used for the first time, and seemed an improvement. We saw both casts, and Michael and Eslyn Kennedy came to stay and to hear the opera with us.

Just after this Ralph went into the Middlesex Hospital for X-ray and other examinations—for, even apart from the short bout of anaemia, he had not been feeling really well all the summer and Ray Rowntree wanted to discover what was wrong. While he was there I was summoned to my parents, as my father had to have a major operation. Gil was at Hanover Terrace but busy at his Ministry, so I telephoned Genia Hornstein who, being the perfect friend, came at once. Ralph was due to come home next day, and I left, feeling certain that between them he would be in good hands. My father died after his operation and I came home till the funeral, as Ralph had several engagements which he could not miss and which I knew he did not want to undertake alone. One was a party in the Jerusalem Chamber at Westminster Abbey for an organists' conference at which William McKie particularly wanted him to be present and another was a performance of Arthur Benjamin's opera *A Tale of Two Cities*. We went to both dress rehearsal and first night, and Ralph was very pleased with the New Opera Company for putting it on. The dress rehearsal was very long and we were getting hungry when one of the 'aristos', bundled off-stage to the tumbrils, came and shared cold sausages with us—it was Gwynneth McCleary, daughter of Ralph's old friend, George.

By now we knew that Ralph would have to go into the Middlesex Hospital for a major operation, but we managed to organize the date so that he could go to the Prom to hear *Antartica*, and could have a clear fortnight for working on the new symphony. The hospital authorities were very kind, and I was allowed to stay with him till late and to come again in the early morning and stay till it was time for him to go to the operating theatre. Jean Stewart (whose husband, George Hadley, was a consultant at the hospital) fetched me early, so that I spent an hour with him, dopey and drowsy as he was before the operation. I saw him again in the late afternoon when the operation was over, which he did not believe, still drugged and very cross and complaining, 'they have left me lying about all day'. By morning it was a different story. My telephone rang at eight o'clock—'Are you all right? I've just kissed the night nurse good-bye, and where did you put my work?' The voice was Ralph at his most normal, and I knew in that instant that he would recover very quickly. He did very well indeed in hospital. The surgeon, who had obviously been boasting about him, was quite cross when he brought another doctor to see him and discovered him reading a green paperback instead of writing music, and the nurses, all of whom were 'pets' he said, were gay and kind.

This episode meant that we could not go to Worcester for the

Three Choirs Festival as we had intended, but it gave more time for work and provided a good reason for going nowhere except to convalesce happily at Ashmansworth where much of the symphony was written. We came back for the last night of the Proms, when his *Eighth Symphony* was played.

An enormous amount of celebration was being prepared for Ralph's eighty-fifth birthday, so he was anxious to get the new symphony well on the way before rehearsals for birthday concerts started. The first of these was of the choral version of *The Bridal Day* which he had made earlier in the year. The Spenserian stanzas fitted the dance tunes with little alteration to the music and it had not been difficult to turn it into a fresh work for chorus and orchestra; to differentiate it from the masque, Ralph went back to the title of the poem and called it *Epithalamion.*

The Classical Theatre of China, not the company we had seen before, advertised a short season, so we took seats for the first night, and once again were enchanted and amused—particularly by a most ingenious dragon or serpent which, carried by men dressed in black and almost invisible, wound its fiery way through the air—'That would be good for the *Ring*,' Ralph said. We took tickets for another performance but the company left in a political huff before their season had run a week.

At the invitation of the Royal Philharmonic Society, Ralph had chosen a programme of his own works for their concert on 9 October—the *Pastoral Symphony*, the orchestral version of *On Wenlock Edge* which John Barbirolli had revived the year before and recommended to him, and, as Adrian was to conduct, *Job.* Unfortunately Adrian was ill, so Basil Cameron nobly came back from Cornwall, where he had just arrived for a holiday, to rehearse and conduct the concert, which was a celebration in grand style. A greeting from the Festival Hall printed on the first page of the programme was addressed to Ralph:

> On behalf of your innumerable friends who have enjoyed performances of your works in this Hall: on behalf of the makers of music who have taken inspiration from your long service to the art; on behalf of the young people who, on the threshold of their musical adventures, have been helped by your kindliness and shrewdness of judgement and by your ever youthful interest in their caperings; on behalf of those who, though they may only live on the fringe of that creative world in which you are native nevertheless value the human

qualities which have given strength and purpose to your art—on behalf of all these and many more whose esteem can find no words, the Royal Festival Hall extends to you on your eighty-fifth birthday this tribute of affection and admiration.

It was Mr. Ernest Bean's[1] idea, also, to ask Cecil Day Lewis to write a poem, and Jill to speak it, as a special birthday present and, when all the more public part of the concert was over, to gather Ralph's friends together in the restaurant for a party. Among the guests it was particularly right that Ray Rowntree and the surgeon who had operated so successfully on Ralph should be there to take part in the rejoicings. Arthur Bliss made a speech, and Ralph, fearing that the evening was getting too emotional, made a light-hearted answer that made everyone laugh. People from every part of his life were there and once again the embracings and conversations made the evening into a celebration for everyone.

The Macnaghten concert on 11 October was almost all new works written as birthday presents to Ralph by ex-pupils and friends united in affection. It was an informally formal evening, the audience a gathering of familiar faces, and the music all new except for the group of madrigals with which the concert ended.

On Ralph's birthday we borrowed Jean and George Hadley's two elder daughters to open the front door and bring up the letters and telegrams; the eldest, Margaret, had written a piece for him, and she had a talk, composer to composer, after playing it through. The rest of the morning both children were kept scampering up and down with mountains of telegrams, sustained by a lot of cocktail sausages and orangeade which Edna, the trombonist cook, supplied at frequent intervals. Later, we went out to dinner and drank the health of the new symphony, and the as-yet-unwritten works that were beginning to take shape on the horizon.

Next day Dorking gave Ralph a party and a present. The present was a painting by John Nash; we had bought a landscape a year or two earlier, which Ralph had hung opposite his arm-chair in the study. The new one, a stormier scene, was one he had chosen from several that Margery Cullen had brought to the house.

[1] General Manager of the Festival Hall.

On 18 October the Composers' Guild held a birthday party for Ralph, who was their President, at Guy Warrack's house. They gave him two scores, the Tallis forty-part motet, and, to his delight, a facsimile score of the Bach *B minor Mass*. It was a very agreeable party and Ralph enjoyed meeting so many of his friends but he was longing to go home so that he could look at the *Mass* properly. It was the best of all his presents and gave him a great deal of pleasure. It was very beautiful, for the flowing writing with the slight irregularities of the drawn, not printed, lines, and the variety of thickness made by the strokes of the quill pen were personal and alive, while the marks of burns on the paper, the ring where a wet glass had stood on the page and the blots were intimate links with the composer's working day. The blots were extraordinarily like Ralph's own in their large size and in being rather badly mopped up; when I pointed this out he was enchanted to see it was true and was proved by the blots on his current manuscript.

On 27 October Ralph had the pleasure of hearing twenty-one brass bands playing his *Variations*. The Albert Hall was packed with the bands' supporters, and the volume of sound was stupendous. The bands played as if they enjoyed every note, and Ralph and I enjoyed ourselves also in the unfamiliar atmosphere, though *The Holy City*, which was also in the programme, was a grim experience.

The next day we went to Manchester for a Hallé concert devoted entirely to his works. It was their centenary year and Ralph had written a short *Flourish for Glorious John* for the opening concert of the season. Although it was not on the programme, they played it for him as an encore at the end of the concert, bringing a chair on to the stage where he had been summoned by applause.

In spite of these pleasant interruptions, Ralph was finishing his symphony. Early in November Roy Douglas came to spend the day; his clear judgement, his musicianship and his friendship became more important to Ralph as time went on and they worked together with concentration and content. At 5.30 we had 'the Committee' to hear it—Arthur Bliss, Frank Howes, Herbert Howells, Scott Goddard, Alan Frank, Gil, and, for the Royal Philharmonic Society who had asked whether they might give the first performance, Myers Foggin: Malcolm Sargent could not come, although he was to conduct it. There was a good deal of discussion afterwards, but Ralph deferred making any alterations till he had heard the orchestra.

He had been asked to unveil Epstein's bust of Blake in Westminster Abbey, but his leg was giving trouble again and he was unable to go out. Geoffrey Keynes (Ralph said 'worthier of the occasion') officiated in his place. By now we had discovered all sorts of means to make Ralph's odd weeks in bed more comfortable. Gil found a tilting table at which he could write, and a footrest that meant he could move into a chair for a few hours, usually for his meals. Then with a wireless, reading aloud, or having friends to tea or to have coffee with him after lunch or dinner, it was not too boring. During this particular spell of hibernation his cousin, Lucy Kempson, brought her niece and great niece, Rachel Kempson[1] and Vanessa Redgrave, to lunch, and Ralph was extremely happy surrounded by such a galaxy sitting on his bed and drinking coffee. As we had a Singery arranged for early December Ralph invited Rachel to come, Michael too if he was free. Ralph was up and about again for this, and they did come. This was our high water mark as far as the tenor section was concerned, and we were thought to be aiming very high indeed; we liked to think of Hotspur singing *The silver swan* and *When David heard* in our house.

A short job that came Ralph's way was the writing of some songs for a film. The Blake Centenary had suggested a film of Blake pictures, and music was needed for it. The film makers brought screen and machinery and ran the film through and showed Ralph the poems they would like him to set. At first he was not at all enthusiastic. He had always admired Blake as an artist, but he did not care greatly for his poems. However, he said he would see what he could do, stipulating that the songs should not include 'that horrible little lamb—a poem I *hate*'.[2]

He had nothing much to do after our carol party, so he considered the poems and decided that it would be interesting to set them for tenor and oboe; it was a match to dry tinder, for no sooner had he decided on the means than the tunes came tumbling out. He wrote nine songs in four days and one morning he said with rage, 'I was woken up by a tune for that *beastly* little lamb, and it's rather a good tune.' So he had to set the poem after all.

[1] Lady Redgrave. [2] 'Little lamb, who made thee?'

That day Jean Stewart brought her daughters to lunch. They had theirs with Edna, our cook-housekeeper, and I had provided some crackers for them. But Edna, who had a great sense of justice, gave each of us a cracker too. When we pulled them, a small pink, plastic lamb fell out of Ralph's. The songs were recorded in January by Wilfred Brown and Janet Craxton, the artists whom Ralph had chosen and to whom they were dedicated.

He was pleased by a letter from Rutland Boughton:

> It is curious how often your music throws me back to Dante: the finale of No. 6. sounds to me like an agnostic's Paradiso, and listening in to No. 4. last night it sounded at times as if you had outdone Virgil by positively rollicking on the verge of Hell. I hope you won't be annoyed by such allusions for as Goethe said, 'Music unites us by giving each man back to himself.'
>
> Have you a spare copy of the photo of Ursula and yourself published a while ago in one of the Sunday papers? I cut it out for a pin-up, but newsprint does not wear well; and you know your personality (as well as your music) has meant much to me from the time at the R.C.M. when you turned a criticism of Stanford's to my advantage. But as I get older I find that, not only Stanford but nearly all men and women are wiser and better than one's first estimate of them and that certainly applies *vastly* to you.

Ralph answered:

> I was so pleased to get your wonderful letter. I am ashamed to say I don't know my Dante—or my Virgil—well enough to be able to illustrate them in music, but it pleases me much that in your opinion I have built better than I know.
>
> I am sending you the photograph—I think it is good of me, and certainly gets much nearer to the real Ursula than any other photograph I have seen.
>
> I believe it is your birthday very soon, so please take these birthday greetings as applying to the exact day.
>
> I have discovered, as I expect you have, that as one gets older one seems to get younger.

The *Passion* rehearsals were starting again, but we had time for some amusements. One concert that Ralph liked was given by the London Schools Orchestra, conducted by Leslie Russell. The programme was chiefly of Ralph's own music, so it was exciting for the players to have the composer there and to meet him afterwards. But what Ralph enjoyed was the high standard of orchestral playing that school children could achieve: the technical mastery and artistry which they brought to music as difficult as his *Eighth Symphony* was astonishing and gladdening. Another rather special concert was given by the Pro Canto singers, a choir of blind singers trained by Eric Greene. The audience was conscious of doors that had been opened to a world of experience long denied to sightless people, enabling them to achieve a musical competence equal to that attained by other good amateurs. Eric's imagination and faith in his project had come to magnificent fruition, to which courage, hard work, and vision had all contributed: the sight of fingers tracing the Braille notation was the only reminder of difference from any other choir.

A Midsummer Night's Dream, Macnaghten concerts, Poulenc's *The Carmelites*—an opera which Ralph went to hear out of duty and disliked as much as he expected—and foreign films were our outside entertainment. Ralph spent an interesting morning at Maida Vale at the rehearsal of Michael Tippett's Second Symphony where he shared a score with the composer.

At a Croydon Philharmonic concert conducted by Myers Foggin, Ralph's S.A.T.B. arrangement of *Fen and Flood* shared the programme with the *Sea Symphony* and a *Choral Flourish* he had written for Alan Kirby. Paddy Hadley and his librettist Charles Cudworth were both there. The choir's performance was a justification of Ralph's faith that the introduction of women's voices had been well worth while, so all of them were pleased. The concert finished with a fine *Sea Symphony* and we drove back to London in an atmosphere of mutual esteem and affection.

In February we had one of the best performances of the *St. John Passion* Ralph had ever conducted; even he was satisfied with it. The choir knew it thoroughly, and the tiny orchestra was splendidly balanced; the players knew what he wanted, and he had carefully rehearsed those soloists who were new to his performance. The notice in the *Dorking Advertiser* spoke of it as a 'rewarding experience':

> The Dorking Bach Choir and a partly amateur orchestra responded magnificently to Dr. Vaughan Williams's direction. Every ounce of drama and all the musical riches of the score were drawn forth to give a performance at once scholarly and convincing. . . . Not often does one encounter such vibrant contrasts as those of the jeering 'Hail King'

and 'Let us not divide' with the eloquent poetry of 'Lie Still' and the chorales. Dr. Vaughan Williams's attention to detail, his clear grasp of the dramatic and musical structure, his balancing of the forces all made one feel that one was inside the mind and soul of Bach.

He was very tired after the concert, but tired in a way that led to a good night and no regrets. It was only after performances where something had gone wrong that fatigue caused sleeplessness and nightmare. Next day he was ready for a midday Bach concert, given by a group from Cambridge, and there were two other concerts that week, one at the R.A.M. and the other a Macnaghten concert for which Elizabeth Maconchy and her husband, William LeFanu, stayed with us to hear some of Gerald Finzi's songs. They were two of our most frequent visitors, and Ralph loved to have them and to hear what Betty was writing. At that time it was a very frivolous one-act opera for which I had written the libretto, and Ralph was full of suggestions for us both. He liked Betty's tunes and made her play through the new material each time she came, watching with great interest over its growth and development.

There were two performances of the *St. Matthew Passion* that year, the number of people who wanted to come and had failed to get tickets showed that it would be justifiable to make the experiment of a second performance. Ralph had invited Thomas Armstrong to conduct one of them, and they shared the rehearsals. Christopher Finzi and Noel Taylor between them arranged and set up tape recording machines, and took the whole performance on the evening when Ralph himself conducted. Once again he was pleased. He had a particularly good team of soloists[1] and, having had one performance already, the choir were extra well rehearsed. When he heard the play-back of the tapes a fortnight later he was satisfied. Being able to listen without taking part was a novel experience, and he was proud of the choir's singing. He was given the tape, and he had a record made of it for his own use. Everyone who took part was glad there was a permanent record of Ralph's interpretation but their hopes that it might be made generally available in a commercial record were never realized, as none of the gramophone companies was interested.[2]

[1] Eric Greene, Gordon Clinton, Pauline Brockless, Nancy Evans, Wilfred Brown and John Carol Case.

[2] It was, however, broadcast the following spring by the B.B.C.

Ruth Gipps, who had been one of Ralph's pupils at the R.C.M., brought her son to spend an afternoon with him. Lance, then ten, was a chorister at Westminster Abbey and writing a lot of music, some of which he brought to show Ralph. They spent an hour together going through his work and Ralph was impressed by the fact that one piece was written in twelve parts—the number of staves in his manuscript book.

Meanwhile we went to Sadler's Wells to hear Bartók's opera, *Bluebeard's Castle*; in spite of scenery which he thought confusing—'all those dog kennels'—Ralph found it exciting and beautiful. *William Tell*, the next week, was entertaining, if far too long. We went also to hear the opera which Joan Sharp and Arnold Foster had made on the story of the ballad *Lord Bateman* and which we had long known in manuscript. The Madrigal Society and a party for my birthday all helped him through the weeks before the *Ninth Symphony*. Roy Douglas had been correcting the band parts, and Ralph had decided to have a rehearsal nearly a fortnight before the concert, partly because he wanted to hear the work before the alarms and agitations of the first performance and partly to let the orchestra have extra rehearsal. He had not been very well since the *Passions*, very tired, and very apprehensive about the symphony, so they were difficult weeks to get through, though he worked as usual, writing *Three Vocalises* for Mabel Ritchie.

The special rehearsal was at St. Pancras Town Hall. The Symphony, dedicated to the Royal Philharmonic Society, was played through twice, and Ralph had invited a number of friends to hear it, as he always did to London plays-through. The balcony was full of these listeners but he sat near the conductor with Roy Douglas beside him.

It was what he had meant, but for some reason it was one of the most difficult of his works to get hold of. He was pleased by some of the things people said, some directly, some reported by others, some written; but the next ten days, the interval before the performance, seemed like a year. Gerald Kelly, who had been at the rehearsal, said to me, 'He is much more beautiful than he was—I must paint him again.' 'Oh dear,' Ralph grumbled, 'I can't go and sit still again and he doesn't like any of my ties.' However, this superficial objection was over-ridden and he promised one sitting after the symphony and before we went abroad.

He had corrected the proofs of the programme notes and had had his hair cut, so all was ready.

We were to sit in the Ceremonial Box and, as Ralph came in, the whole, packed audience rose—it had happened before during the last few years, but this time it was extraordinarily moving. Ralph himself was looking well, with his hair shiningly white and the kind of reserved dignity that applause caused in him, partly shyness, and partly diffidence. It was too long a journey from the box to the platform, so after the performance he took his calls where he was, and Malcolm, who appeared to have wings on his shoes, joined him to acknowledge the clapping and to share the flashing lights of the photographers. There was a party, but we were glad to get home to talk about the music by ourselves. Paddy Hadley, listening at his home, sent one of his most characteristic night telegrams—

Came over marvellously—the saxes and flugel contributed a strange unearthly magic to that wonderful score, fondest love Paddy.

This was neatly written out by Gil, who had been awakened at three in the morning by the telephone and had answered it, as he always did at night in case it might be about a crisis concerning his Ministry. He delivered it at breakfast and it was corroborated later by the Post Office. Ralph wrote to Anthony Scott a few days later:

Thank you so much for writing, and I won't pretend that I am not pleased that you like it. The Flugel man showed me at rehearsal that unless I allowed a minimum of vibrato, the tone would sound hard, rather like a bad horn. The valve trouble caused him to miss a few notes, but the trumpet, who was sitting next to him gallantly came to the rescue and played them for him: so that I, at all events, did not know anything had gone wrong.

Sancta Civitas was broadcast on Good Friday and Ralph wrote to Cedric Glover the same day as to Tony Scott:

Thank you so much for liking my new tune. *Sancta Civitas* was a very good performance also—the only fault, as usual, was with the balance and control who continued their bad habit of making everything into a harp concerto. I like it the best of my own choral works.

Directly Easter was over Roy Douglas came for a long conference on the score: Ralph gave the promised sitting to Gerald Kelly and then we flew to Naples.

It rained for much of the three days we spent there, so we went to museums and dined in little restaurants by the harbour and the Castel Ouovo. One morning was fine for a couple of hours, long enough for us to see Herculaneum. Through the good offices of the British consul we were allowed a first tier box at San Carlo—it was a concession for, not having brought evening clothes, we ought to have been out of sight in the fifth tier. The season was near its end and the opera we saw came from Sardinia, a rather dull and very long rigmarole about bandits, but the pleasure was the opera house itself looking much as it must have done to Nelson and the Hamiltons.

At last the sun came out, fortunately on the day we crossed to Ischia where we had taken one of the houses owned by the Waltons. They met us, drove us to Forio and installed us in the Villa Cristabella to unpack before we went to them for lunch. We had a view of a bay and the little town with a white chapel on the headland in front, a steep, wooded ridge behind, and from side windows we could see the mountain, covered with vineyards and chestnut woods. There was a garden with terraces everywhere, so that there was somewhere sheltered to sit which ever way the wind blew; and the house itself was rather like the little houses at Herculaneum. Everything had been done for us with imagination and practicality, there was food in the larder, and spring flowers in the sitting-room and bedroom. William was going to England so he very kindly lent Ralph his piano; about six men carried it up, and as they arrived a torrential storm broke. William commanded the situation, the piano was dried, the water was swept out of the room, and the men rewarded, everyone talked at once as the thunder rattled away over the bay. A few days later we had to borrow candles, and, when William came to see what had gone wrong with the electricity, he also brought a hot water bottle which we were very glad to have. There was a fireplace too and, though we were out whenever it was warm, it was nice to have a fire to sit by in the evenings while Ralph read aloud and I sewed. We read a great deal, and, having come to the end of our supplies, we bought and borrowed many paperbacks. One of these was Stanley Weyman's *Under the*

Red Robe, which Ralph loved reading. Lines like 'Foiled,—and by a woman!' were great fun, and we sat up till one to finish the story. We also re-read Aldous Huxley's *Brave New World* which had just been issued as a Penguin: so much that had seemed fantastic when it was first published was unpleasantly true or so nearly true that it was quite bloodcurdling, so we returned to *Lavengro*, Ralph's favourite novel, once again, and *The Heart of Midlothian*. We nearly blew ourselves up pouring paraffin on to the damp wood to achieve a blaze, and the little grate was usually surrounded by many sticks and logs put to dry. Ralph was glad to be right away and to put all thoughts of the symphony out of his mind. He was working at something very different. We had long wanted to write an opera together, and had at last achieved a story we liked. It was a mixture of two ballads, *Thomas the Rhymer* and *Tam Lin*. The hero, Thomas, having come back from a journey to find his Janet, is on the point of marrying her when the Elf Queen commands him to follow her. Janet's sisters try to persuade her to marry another young man but, with the help of an old woman whose own lover was taken from her long ago in the same way, she learns how to find Thomas, and eventually, as in *Tam Lin*, how to save him. We had plotted the action and found it fell into three acts. Some of the libretto was written, some was very much 'temporary stopping', for once Ralph started on the music he wrote very quickly, so we were both much happier with bad weather than we should have been otherwise.

There were some fine days when Sue Walton took us round the island or we made bus expeditions on our own. One day we took a steamer to Capri for the day and a boat to the Blue Grotto. Most people went by launch, and then disembarked into rowing boats, so there was a queue by the cave mouth. Our boatman, who had rowed the whole way, singing the *Isle of Capri* most of the time, for our operatic Italian did not permit long conversations and he didn't seem to know any other songs, was glad to rest till it was our turn to go in. The extraordinary electric-blue water and the reflections from it made the people in the other boats seem all the same neon colour. Their voices were intensified into a sound which seemed almost solid, and when Ralph, looking round, said 'My God', in a deep bass, it cut through them and produced a silence. They all turned, mesmerized, to hear what he would say. 'It's worse than Saint Peter's—let's go away.'

Lunch, a quiet afternoon in the deserted ruins of a Roman garden and the steamer journey home were all pleasant, but Ischia seemed far more beautiful to us.

For our last week we had hot weather, bathing and basking: the fireflies came, and the nights were full of their little, questing flames. We caught one and it sat on my hand switching itself on and off with an extraordinary brightness, illuminating every detail of rings and finger-nails, lines and graining of skin.

Back in Naples, we had time to see the Titians in the Capo di Monte to fulfil a promise made to Gerald Kelly: we were glad he had commanded us to go there. We spent a day driving through Sorrento and down the spectacular road to Amalfi.

We flew home again and had a day to unpack before we went to Nottingham for Ralph to receive a Doctorate of Music at the University. The same evening we went to a Jubilee celebration of the E.F.D.S. at Cecil Sharp House. Ralph had been President of the E.F.D.S. since the death of Lady Ampthill and he held their gold badge for services to folk music.

He was concerned with the Jubilee appeal for the Library. Based on Cecil Sharp's own collection of books and manuscripts it was to his mind a most important and valuable treasure of ethnological and musical books, sadly hampered by the lack of money from expanding and acquiring the material it should have. He gave the Director, Douglas Kennedy, his full support and they both hoped that so worthy a cause would get the necessary money to give the library an independent future. Ralph had used it himself during the spring in preparing a Penguin book of English Folk Songs which he was producing in partnership with A. L. Lloyd.

The holiday had done all we had hoped for Ralph. He felt well and was sunburnt and gay, ready for work and pleasure. We had a Singery, and an *English Hymnal* meeting, transferring it from the city to our dining-room, and best of all we went to *Don Carlos*. It was a dazzling production—'Covent Garden *can* do things well when they choose,' Ralph said, without much rancour. We went to *Tristan* too before the season ended.

Ralph said that, having seen so much of Italy, we ought to see England. One sunny June day he suggested that we should go to

Lincoln, so we packed a small suitcase and caught the next train. It was late afternoon when we arrived, and we strolled round the cathedral then and again at dusk, when the swifts, those companions of our summers, were flying low and the air was soft and smelt of newly cut grass. Next day we went inside the cathedral, and then hired a car and wandered across the fens to Tattershall and to Gunby where Ralph's cousin, Diana Montgomery-Massingberd[1] welcomed us, and Ralph said, 'Do you remember *Happy Days at Gunby*?'[2] He could see the players in the room, 'you stood here,' he said, and named them all, until the room was filled with that music of nearly seventy years ago as the two remaining musicians recalled it. When we left, we went on to Boston, Spalding, and Crowland, looking round the churches, wandering down the streets, enjoying the quiet expanse of green, the daisies and vetches, the rose-filled gardens and the serenity of the land.

We got to Peterborough in time to go into the cathedral for half an hour. We found that there was a folk dance evening going on in the Close and some of the dancers recognized Ralph and came to talk to him. We dined at the station hotel and came home comfortably, very pleased with this inspired idea of seeing England.

It was a pleasure to meet Josef Krips after a Festival Hall concert, to go to Cambridge to hear *Connemara*, a new work by Paddy Hadley and Charles Cudworth at the Caius May Week concert, and to have a visit from Percy and Ella Grainger whom we had visited when we were in the United States. Margery Cullen, laden with flowers and strawberries from her garden, came to tell Ralph about the Leith Hill Festival, the first he had ever missed, and George McCleary, Eugene Goossens, and Lionel Tertis were other visitors. Jack Langstaff, from Washington, came to stay: Ralph particularly liked the way he sang folk songs and had used his records often to illustrate lectures. So he asked him to sing at all sorts of odd moments, and *Sir Patrick Spens* was at least a twice-daily request. We went to his Wigmore Hall recital, and afterwards Gerald Moore, who had played for him, and Enid joined Gil and us for dinner in Soho.

We had been very much involved in a campaign to prevent the Nash Terraces in the Regent's Park from being demolished.

[1] She died in January 1964.

[2] Composed by R.V.W. 1892.

Now we were equally tangled in the affairs of the Sound Broadcasting Society. It had come into existence during the previous autumn when the first rumours of the cutting down of the Third Programme were circulating. Ralph was a Vice President and took part in a deputation to the B.B.C., other members of which were Sir Laurence Olivier, T. S. Eliot, Michael Tippett, and Peter Laslett—a Press conference had been called at our house at which they were to report. Erica Propper, Secretary of the Society, and I collected every chair we had, and packed them into our dining-room, and the Press, from *The Times* to *The Daily Worker*, *The Tatler* to *The New Statesman*, was represented, and the proceedings were reported in full. The only thing that marred the dignity of the occasion was Ralph's black eye. He had gone off to Sadler's Wells on his own to a meeting of the New Opera Company, and thought that, as I was safely at the dentist's, he would go home by tube rather than by the taxi on which he knew I should insist. He slipped on the escalator and arrived home with a bump on his head and a black eye. The doctor said it was not serious but 'let this be a warning'. He also said that Ralph could try raw beefsteak on it if he liked. Everyone was very sympathetic and it was generally assumed that he had been wounded defending the Third Programme from a detractor.

One evening we dined with the McKies at their house in Little Cloister, Westminster, and when it was dark we went across to the Abbey. William switched on a few lights so that the amazing architecture was revealed and accentuated, lit arch against darkness, vaulting and pillar suggested or outlined for us. While he played Bach we sat, or wandered about, listening. The Abbey becomes quite different at night, its silence has a benign and positive quality and the music intensified it. It was a parallel evening for Ralph to the one he had spent in Salisbury Cathedral with Walter Alcock playing to him—Bach and architecture and a summer night.

We went to Cheltenham for the Festival and enjoyed our few days there. Ralph as usual was avid for rehearsals as well as for concerts, and spent most of his time at the Town Hall, but we managed a few expeditions and the Barbirollis gave one of their late night dinner-parties, this time at the hotel on Cleeve Hill. The whole evening sky was lit by an extraordinary sunset smouldering and blazing in crimson and ultramarine clouds. Michael Kennedy thought it Wagnerian, Ralph was silent and bemused but once we reached the hotel the awe-inspiring effect vanished in the lively company of friends.

We had hoped to go to King's Lynn, where Lionel Tertis was to play *Flos Campi*, but unfortunately Ralph's phlebitis returned and he had to keep his foot up. Herbert Menges, who was to conduct, and Lionel came and spent an afternoon going through the score, and Erich Auerbach joined us for tea and took photographs of them all, playing, listening, or discussing.

Thomas the Rhymer was getting on well: the piano sketch nearly finished when Simona Pakenham and her husband Noel Iliff bicycled over from Kensington to ask Ralph to provide music for a script Simona had made from medieval mystery plays. It was a short, Christmas piece, and needed carol tunes and incidental music. It had to be ready by November for the singers to learn in time for a December matinée at Drury Lane in aid of St. Martin-in-the-Fields. Ralph liked Simona's choice of episodes and immediately started thinking about tunes to fit. They suggested that he should take part, and double God and the eldest shepherd, but he said he'd stick to the music, and he went to the boxroom for carol books to start on it at once. Collecting material and planning was work that fitted in very well with going to the New Opera Company's rehearsals and performances of Benjamin's *A Tale of Two Cities* and Ralph's *Sir John in Love*. We had been to piano rehearsals for *Sir John* in a large, depressing room near Edgware Road, and we knew the work almost as well as the performers, so it was as agreeable for us as for them to see it grow, improve, and change into a proper stage production.

Ralph had been asked to send a message to a school in Norfolk where one of the houses was to be called after him. He sent this:

To the boys and girls of the Primary School, Swaffham. I am very much pleased to think that one of your houses is to bear my name. I am myself a musician, and I believe that all the arts, and especially music, are necessary to a full life. The practical side of living of course is important, and this, I feel sure, is well taught in your school: such things teach you how to make your living. But music will enable you to see past facts to the very essence of things in a way which science cannot do. The arts are the means by which we can look through the magic casements and see what lies beyond.

The last performance of *Sir John* was on the first Saturday in August, and the Prom performance of his *Ninth Symphony* on the day after Bank Holiday. Ralph was interested to hear the symphony again now that the anxieties of its first appearance were over, and he was pleased with it. Once again most of the critics thought it was a re-hash of things he had done better before but a few people thought it was the beginning of something new in his work. So did Ralph himself and he was looking forward to Adrian's recording at the end of the month when they would work over it, section by section: this almost anatomical dissection was something from which he always felt he learned a great deal.

We planned to go away for September to work at the opera, as Ralph had completed the first piano score. His usual method was to produce a full score from the first piano sketch, then make another piano score from that full score, and re-score that. There were many changes on the way, and the last draft was usually very unlike the first; but it was from the first completed sketch that his ideas would take wing. I wanted to rewrite all the chorus part and we felt this could be done at the seaside, combining work with bathing and, we hoped, basking. We went to stay with Joy Finzi for a week, with the object, among other things, of exploring the Dorset coast for somewhere to stay.

Joy took us off in her van to all sorts of places, some we knew well, some not at all. We saw the Cerne giant, and Ralph sent postcards of him to Gil and Paddy, Frank Hollins and Michael Kennedy, with lighthearted improprieties on the back. We went to the country round Bridport, where we stayed in a tiny village inn one night. We found our seaside place and took rooms, then, as a heavy mist drove us inland, we telephoned to ask Sylvia Townsend Warner and Valentine Ackland if we might eat our picnic in their house, so sociabilities ensued. We saw Barnes's village, and drove through hills and valleys by deserted lanes, already faintly autumnal. One of our picnics was at Yarnbury castle, not far from Chitterne where Ralph, walking with the Longmans, had re-met his friend from the Ambulance years before. Another day we went to the White Horse ridge, drove along the track past Wayland Smith's cave and picnicked on the edge of a cornfield, walking over the head of the dragon-horse and seeing that spreading view of Berkshire and Oxfordshire at our feet. Ruth and Tony Scott were with us that day and we sat talking for half the afternoon. Another day, Anna Shuttleworth played Bach suites to Ralph on her cello, and one evening Joy drove us to Salisbury to see the cathedral floodlit. We had been told by Michael and Eslyn Kennedy at a performance of *Sir John in Love* that we must go one night. They had been spellbound by the beauty of the floodlighting and said it was something specially for Ralph who had always particularly loved that cathedral. We stopped to see Old Sarum on the way, another view for Ralph over to Stonehenge and across the Plain. When we got to Salisbury we saw the cathedral transformed to gold, and details that one had not noticed standing out, so that the design of the whole was even more noble than in daylight. A dazzled owl flapped in and out of the lights gilding the spire and, as the evening got darker, both the blue night sky and the golden building intensified in brilliance.

We had seen England in its most typical beauty of a cool, wet summer, with enough sunshine to ripen the corn and to fill the hedges and road verges with Ralph's favourite wild flowers, late summer's profusion of yellow and white and lilac colours.

We came home to a busy week. Michael Moores came to discuss the printing of Ralph's new synopsis and the revision of *Hugh the Drover*, and there were sittings with Gerald Kelly. In spite of all our wanderings, Ralph had done quite a lot of work on the Christmas play while we were at Ashmansworth. However, these busy days were not going to last long, and Ralph planned to finish the work for Simona before we left for Dorset.

Eddie Rosenbaum, Robert Müller-Hartmann's brother-in-law, had been one of the people we met unexpectedly in Ischia; now he telephoned to ask if he might bring Alexander Ben-Haim, a composer from Israel, to see Ralph. He had some music with him and the two shared the piano stool going through his work contented and absorbed, breaking off only for tea. That evening Ralph didn't want any dinner, but by bed time he was hungry and sat on his bed eating bananas and biscuits and making plans for going to Walthamstow for the recording of his *Ninth Symphony* next day. It was all very ordinary, usual and like many other nights had been and we did not guess that before dawn death, not sleep, would claim him.

APPENDIX I

Hugh the Drover

Bruce Richmond was staying at Leith Hill Place when Ralph came into the room where he was sitting and said, 'I want to set a prize fight to music—can you find someone to make a libretto for me?' Another writer on the staff of *The Times*, Harold Child, was suggested, introduced, and the work began.

Only one side of the correspondence remains, but from the temper of the letters it is clear that Ralph's article on *Librettos*, published in *The Vocalist* in 1902,[1] still expressed his thoughts: 'The duty of the words is to say just as much as the music has left unsaid and no more.' In that article he had also stated that the only suitable man to write a libretto was the composer. When it came to the point, he felt that his lack of stage experience and literary ability was too great. It is also probable that he was longing to gallop away with the music and the idea of more-or-less writing a play to begin with was too great a hindrance.

Those who know *Hugh the Drover* in its finished form will find it interesting to see how it developed: anyone who has ever worked with a composer will recognize the subordinate rôle the writer is forced to take, particularly when the initial idea comes from the musician. It is fascinating to see the visual quality of the ideas in Ralph's mind throughout the correspondence. His detailed commands about metre, and his absorption that almost turned requests into bullying, alternated with a fair amount of the best butter whenever the writer rebelled as he was adjured, cajoled, and carried along by the musician's enthusiasm. Only once was there obviously a mutiny, and the breach was mended before it became dangerous.

There are one or two episodes that are linked with personal experiences. The lavender seller and the ballad monger were both heard by Ralph in London. Eventually lavender had to be changed to primroses, as they had settled on a spring scene, but the cry comes into the *London Symphony* at which he was also

[1] Extract reprinted in *Heirs and Rebels*, 1959.

working during these years. The May song, starting off-stage and coming nearer, recalls a story told him by Hoppy Flack, a singer at Fowlmere[1] near Cambridge, from whom he collected it. When Hoppy was young he and his friends would go out each May eve, singing all through the short darkness and being given drinks at each house they visited. As time went on the singers became less enthusiastic, and finally only he and another elderly man kept up the custom. Hoppy's head was by then less good than it had been, or, there being only two of them, they drank more at each call. On their way he slipped and fell into a ditch, and his friend failed to pull him out of it. Not wishing to lose the money they were to be given as well as the refreshment, the friend went on. Hoppy lay there, listening to the May song, now near, now farther away, as the dawn was breaking and his friend went on singing from cottage to cottage till it was day. He told the story to Ralph so vividly that the memory of the magical stillness in that long ago summer night was transmuted into the music that begins the second act of the opera. By giving the May song to the villain, John the Butcher, Ralph saves him from being an altogether dislikeable character. This is perhaps the logical working out of what he says in his letter about 'a person capable of such beautiful songs and all that is implied by them'—for among the many country people he had met on collecting expeditions some of the singers had been toughs and, possibly, rogues as well, but had the sensitivity to cherish their music.

As is so often the case with Ralph's letters, almost all those written to Child are undated. It is probable that the correspondence starts in 1910. The letters from the Isle of Wight seem to belong to August of the next year—for his stay from the 7th to 20th was recorded in Mrs. Fisher's diary. Holst's notebooks give a date to the Italian ones, '1913 Xmas letters, R. V. W., Hotel Suisse, Ospedaletti, Ligure, Riviera, Italy'—though no letters to or from him survive for that time. The final postcard is postmarked 4 August, 1914. The order of the letters here, with these few exceptions, is conjectural.

The punctuation throughout is almost always dashes, invariably a sign of speed and enthusiasm in Ralph's writing. Some other stops have been added for clarity, otherwise the letters are unaltered.

[1] Modern spelling of Foulmire (cf. Walker's *British Atlas*, 1837).

(before July 1910) Hotel Latemar,
Karersee,
Botzen,
Tirol, Austria

Dear Mr. Child,

(I hope I spell your name right—I've never seen it written!) First I want to thank you very much for being so kind and sympathetic and apparently actually anxious to cooperate in this operatic venture.

Secondly to remind you that if our scheme ever comes to anything then it will never get past pen on paper, for I see *hardly any* chance of an opera by an English composer ever being produced, at all events in *our* lifetime—does this make any difference to your entering into the scheme?

Thirdly, this is the letter which I promised with my ideas on the particular kind of opera I had an idea we might cooperate in—please forgive the extreme length, I have a lot of nebulous ideas as to how an opera should be made which I have tried to work out on a small scale by myself—but have come to the conclusion that what I must try and do first is to get some practical knowledge of the stage (I have already found this to a very small extent in some incidental music to plays) and for this purpose I want to try my hand at an opera on more or less accepted lines and preferably a *comedy*, to be full of tunes, and lively, and one tune that will really *come off*. (I'm sorry for talking about myself such a lot but it is inevitable!)

This fitted in with another idea of mine which was to write a musical, what the Germans call 'Bauer Comedie'—only applied to English country life (real as far as possible—not sham)—something on the lines of Smetana's *Verkaufte Braut*[1]—for I have an idea for an opera written to *real* English words, with a certain amount of *real* English music and also a real English subject might just hit the right nail on the head.

As regards the form, *not* Wagnerian and not altogether Mozartian but more the Mozartian with some of his squareness taken away—perhaps a certain amount of the Charpentier-Puccini conversational methods thrown in—but it is all vague and I should like to fit in with your ideas.

Only I think the whole thing might be folk song-y in character, with a certain amount of real ballad stuff thrown in.

As to scenes I will put down some ideas I have which may possibly be useful *in case they happen to fit in with any ideas of yours*, otherwise please discard them absolutely.

1. Opening scene, a fair with all the paraphernalia—merry-go-round, cake stalls, shooting gallery, fat woman 'Show the life guardsman'—a ballad-monger, small boys with whistles, etc. etc. An

[1] *Bartered Bride.*

opening chorus and scena—(*not* a set chorus 'the chorus sing the praise of a good glass of beer') but ejaculations in fragments on a sort of symphonic basis, with lavender cries, people shouting out what they have to sell, etc. and the ballad seller singing bits of ballads—all leading up to a climax when a prize fight is announced—the village champion enters his name (scene between him and his young lady?) No challenger appears till at last a stranger rides (or walks up) (possibly a gypsy—see one of the opening chapters of Borrow's I Zincali)—I am not sure however whether it is in the nature of things for a gypsy to run off with a non-gypsy—which I suppose wd be the inevitable conclusion—perhaps the stranger might be some purely fanciful character? Defeat of the village champion—heroine feels relieved to transfer her affections to the stranger—disgust of the village hero.

2. Then would possibly follow a plot to down the stranger by the village hero and his boon companions—possibly a scene late at night in the village inn (or just outside it). The village hero and his friends go out at night intending to come back early in the morning to have their revenge—which is somehow triumphantly frustrated by the stranger who, when morning comes, rides (or perhaps drives in his little cart) off with the heroine before the whole village and the discomfited village hero.

   —But before this climax is reached I have an idea for another scene (which will I think fit in with the above) viz.

3. Early in the morning (still dark) the stranger comes in singing a ballad (see 'Sweet Europa" in Sharp's 'Folk Songs from Somerset') which brings the heroine to the window—there follows a scene in which they arrange to go off together (or whatever they *do* arrange.) This starts quietly and conversationally and gradually works up to a duet 'appassionata' in which the ballad tune (and possibly part of the words) has a large share—the stranger then goes off, the heroine shuts her window and the dawn gradually comes (empty stage). As soon as it is a little light the Mayers are heard in the far distance—coming back with their branches of May and singing—they gradually get nearer and nearer and fill the stage and the full light gradually comes——

But after all it is you who are to write the play, not me—these ideas are only to be taken for what they are worth. Or perhaps you want to write something quite different either

(*a*) all music,
(*b*) with dialogue,
(*c*) with melodrama,

perhaps a gay sort of comedy, like Cosi fan Tutte—with purely formal square-cut numbers,
or a purely fantastic opera,
or an English subject of quite a different nature, (e.g. The Mayor of Casterbridge.)

By the way, I have no objection to the structure being more or less formal and conventional—and I like duets, trios, quartets or even quintets—I think all opera has to be conventional (or perhaps I should say, not realistic.)

As regards the relationship of words and music—there are I think three grades,

1. Dry recitative, in which the pure facts are set forth,
2. 'arioso' or 'scena' in which the emotional growth of the drama can be set out,
3. Lyrical sections—which, dramatically, should be pure points of repose (corresponding to 'O Romeo, wherefore art thou Romeo.')

The story should not be told in lyrical moments and one must always remember that it is always difficult to take the logical meaning of a sentence in when it is sung.

Out of the way words and elaborate phraseology does not do in a lyric—because they are in themselves an attempt to supply the decorative element which the music is there to supply.

I think that is all—slow—long tableaux—or long dramatic pauses are always good, as the music takes a long time to speak, much longer than words by themselves—in fact, one wants purely musical effects in opera, just as one wants purely poetical effects in a drama.

I have put down all that occurs to me—but please don't consider any of it as of any importance.

I am here for about a month,

Yr very tr
R. Vaughan Williams.

13 Cheyne Walk,
S.W.1.
(Summer 1910.)

Dear Mr. Child,

I've at last read through your admirable scenario very thoroughly —it seems fine, it ought to turn into something just right and very good.

I want to make one or two criticisms—but I fully realise that both literally and dramatically I am a complete ignoramus and you are not —nevertheless I will put them down for what they are worth—only remember my suggestions may be impossible and are not in any way final. Well, first, generally:—

1. I should rather be more sympathetic with the English peasantry, the laugh all the way through is *at* the English people and *with* the Welshman.—Now what I want in the opera is that the English peasant shall not be looked on as a mere *clown* but a person capable of such beautiful songs (and all that is implied by them) as we now know of—but this need not alter the general tenor of the plot.
2. Don't think me captious—but I don't quite like the names.—but that is a small point—only they suggest to me the stage village a little.
3. Would it perhaps be better to make the heroine a real village girl —and not quite the status of a mayor's daughter, (cd. not the father be the village constable?)
4. Do you think there are too many side issues—e.g. the 2 maids and their two lovers; the plot of an opera *cannot* be too simple—but this we shall see later.
5. The period 1820 seems good, or even earlier—at all events it ought to be the right period for Annis to have a very pretty pair of buckled shoes to kick off in Act II.
6. Is the final climax quite strong enough? I shd. like it to end in more decisive triumph for the lovers—perhaps Blogg and his associates cd. have some further scheme of revenge connected with their Maying expedition which finally turns to their own confusion?

I'm afraid I've not done yet—but I have some more detailed suggestions (please don't accept any of them).

ACT I. Cd. the prize fight be made more the climax of the fair part of the business—the crowd might come on again (2nd time) in response to a definite summons on the part of a showman to come to see a fight—he having already got hold of Blogg and persuaded him to 'meet all comers'. (By the way, the crowd might go off 1st time following a procession of Morris Dancers (*not* dancing but processing to their dancing place.) I like the meeting of hero and heroine tremendously. I think we cd. arrange the prize fight *on*, cd. we not?—with a large crowd on chairs etc. to hide the fighters. (By the way I send you the Zincali with the passage marked on page 18.) *Note on the Zincali*—our *next* opera might be Lavengro— I've always had this in my mind but quite forgot to talk about it when we met.
In ACT II there are *3* lyric climaxes for the lovers—wd. it not be better to roll these into one—ending with the 'Drovers marriage'

ceremony, then the gradual dawn and arrival of the lovers—but I don't know.

—My keenness on yr scheme grows with every successive re-reading—send me any bits as you do them so that I can start thinking about them.

By the way on Sept. 1st[1] Wood is doing a folk song fantasia of mine, the *slow middle section* of which is a sort of study for what I shd. like my love scene, Act II, to be like. Thank you so much: I begin to see daylight in operatic regions.

Yrs v. tr.
R. Vaughan Williams.

13 Cheyne Walk,
(undated)

Dear Child,

No, it isn't that I feel uncomfortable except on a few points of detail.

But there are some problems and the chief one is this—your words at present suggest an absolutely formal and Mozartian setting with regular set numbers and the chorus standing around and having their chips-in at intervals—this is a very good way of doing things and one I have often wanted to try—but the two methods will not *mix* very well—and, for instance, the fair scene at the beginning would have to convert into the regular 'chorus sing the praise of a good glass of beer' sort of thing—which I don't mind in the least—only we must make up our minds from the start which it is to be—at least I *think* so—but in these matters I am infinitely bloominger-amateur than you. I should very much like to know what sort of music you imagined being set to it. How wd. it be to try a scene in prose, developing into something more lyrical and rhythmic (but not necessarily in cut and dried metres) as the situation demands? Another point is, I cannot quite see how the characters work out—but this is because I have only seen part of it—but we must avoid as far as possible any approach to the stage rustic—the lout grinning through a horse collar—don't you think so?

For example I'm not sure about Mary being queen of the May—the idea of the virtuous queen of the May is pure Ruskin, indeed I understand that the real queen of the May was usually the village prostitute. I shd. much like to have a talk about it, we shd. clear our mind tremendously—3-0 on Thursday would suit me admirably if I may come to you then.

[1] 1 September 1910. Work which was scrapped—conducted by Henry Wood at a Promenade Concert.

I feel the only thing to do really will be to get to work on it and I shall soon find out how it pans out.—But if you think I have got a cut and dried idea of what I want—you'll be disappointed—I feel hopelessly vague when confronted with facts—I believe the only way will be for you to write what you really like and then I see what I can do with it, and begin messing about.

Yours sincerely,
R. Vaughan Williams.

(Postcard post-marked 13. Jul. no year)

Cheyne Walk.

I am supposed to be writing something else but I find myself at odd moments thinking of bits of music for the scenes you sent me. It is all childishly simple—I hope you don't mind and I think the more or less formal style of the bit you sent me will do best. Have you done Hugh's 'Song of the road'?

13 Cheyne Walk,
S.W.1.

Dear Child,

I shd. think the drafts wd. do very well. I want something rather march-like in character I think (rather like my 'vagabond' song!)

I enclose a bit of music which I have thought of as a sort of theme for him when he mentions his name—it is quite bad and commonplace at present—but the rhythm is, I think, good.

R. V. W.

13 Cheyne Walk,
(undated)

My dear Child

And this just as I am beginning to enjoy myself and things are going to hum! I spent all yesterday afternoon and evening over Hugh's song and I think it's turning out very good, also the 'Linnet' song has got a very nice little tune. I'm most awfully distressed if I gave you a wrong impression by my letter—all I meant was that there was going to be no big bow-wow about my music—but just easy going stuff suitable (I hope) for a comic opera. Now don't let us put each other off just as things are beginning to go with a swing. I'm getting more and more excited about it every day. Send me some more as soon as ever you can as I shall soon have done all you have sent me.

Yours ever,
R. Vaughan Williams.

(No date. Ralph and Adeline were at Freshwater from 7–20 August 1911)

Samatt House,
Freshwater Bay,
Isle of Wight.

My dear Child

I think the opera is beginning to go swimmingly. I have sketched fully from Mary's ballad down to the end of Hugh's 1st song (sweet little linnet) and vaguely thought of a lot more, it is quite bad but that's my way of working. I think in spots and have to fill in with dummy material which gradually gets better. I've thrown all theories to the wind and am simply setting your text as it stands (nearly—of this more later). The result may be very good and original in form, I believe it will; or it may turn out scrappy—in that case we will have to recast it when finished. By the way, I am finding your words splendid to set. I didn't know before I started whether I shd. but I like them more and more, they run so easily and at the same time they are so full of real meat. It will be far the most distinguished comic opera libretto in existence; my only fear is (and I am quite serious over this) that my music, up to the present has by no means the same distinction. I find it very hard to be *light* and not banal at the same time.

Now one or two details:

(*a*) I have played old Harry with your rhymes in a few places. This will require much discussion.

(*b*) I have left out some lines in one or two places, this will require a little looking, too, because they make nonsense in their mutilated form.

(*c*) In some of your second verses the tune of the first does not fit—we must discuss whether you can alter your words or I can alter my tune.

(*d*) I wish you wd. put down in musical notation how you think Hugh's song of the road ought to go as regards rhythm.

♩ ♩ ♩ ♩. ♪ ♩
God save our gra - cious King

I've got the germ of rather a good tune for it, but it makes rather a gabble of some of the words—especially the 'horses hoofs', rather a jaw breaker to sing quickly. I feel I may have misunderstood entirely the rhythm of the song as you imagine it. I wish you wd. do this for *all* your lyrics—I don't promise to stick to your suggestions, but it would very likely give me ideas. Do you imagine the dialogue between Hugh and Mary *after* his song of the road to have *fast* or *slow* music? I've begun to think of rather nice slow music for it, but this wd. fit in equally well somewhere else.

(*e*) At present I don't feel quite happy about the devices between the last mentioned dialogue and the song and chorus etc. leading up to the fight. I have a feeling we might make the constable, led by Aunt Jane, come on the scene *at once* and the constable abuse Hugh as a vile seducer. Hugh offers to fight for Mary—the crowd *and* showman take up the idea and continue, as per script. But this is perhaps commonplace and the amateur's idea of stage effectiveness —and of course I can't tell anything till I see how the scene continues, probably it will all clear up then.

(*f*) I think I've thought of something for the catch 'a fight, a fight' and for the Boney song. By the way, this *must* be solo, the words are too good to be wasted on a chorus—(chorus might chip in). By the way, your final line in each verse of this song is in a different metre. Wd. it spoil it to make it all like the *last* verse?

(*g*) Cd. you put words to the enclosed tune—it's not a very good tune at present but will, I hope, mature in bond—but the rhythm will be exactly this. They sing it when they come on: 'Here come the Morris men' or something of that sort—they sing it twice, once alone, and then in combination with the 'Morris on' tune. (see enclosed) so either two verses are wanted or the same repeated.

(*h*) I have invented a new (small) character, a sort of turnkey who marches in front of the constable at his first entrance and says 'Make room for the Constable' in a ridiculous high tenor. We can either cut him out or develop him.

(*i*) I have extended the chorus part and given them extra words to say—these will have to be translated into English by you.

(*j*) There are several ejaculations for solo voices in the chorus parts —if there are going to be some minor characters in Act II then remarks might be allocated to them.

(*k*) There is a good deal of chorus work in Act I. I suggest the chorus shd. not be so important in Act II.

(*l*) I feel we want a sort of pause before the fight and a regular ensemble in slow time with everyone yelping their own particular screed—Mozart, of course, does this by making the characters repeat themselves ad nauseam, but we might do it by giving them lots to say or having sort of refrains which wd. be in repetition.

The sort of thing I mean is that they all stand still and say (only at great length)

Mary.	Don't fight he'll kill you.	
Hugh.	I fight only for you.	
John.	I'll kill the ruffian.	
Constable.	I bet my money on John.	
A. Jane.	O dear this is all very terrible.	
Chorus.	What fun.	All going on
Women.	Oh! I am frightened.	together

But don't do this unless it appeals to you. I have found it most satisfactory to follow your lead and I don't want to conventionalize it.

(*m*) How would it be to make a romantic ending to the whole thing. The cart with the two lovers in it making for the open country (seen in the distance) the chorus bidding their farewell all done in terms of a glorified version of Hugh's little drover tune.

Cart

chorus principals

chorus principals

orchestra

Yrs. R. V. W.

P.S. I am here till the end of the month. We must meet then and have a long discussion. I hope to have something to play to you.

P.P.S. On sleeping this letter over I find I have still more to say. The cast I propose is as follows

Mary (soprano)	Maggie Teyte
Jane (alto)	somebody like Rosina Brandram
Hugh	John Coates
John	Higley
Constable	Robert Radford

As there is a chance of not having Maggie Teyte wd. it be better *not* to make Mary into a *big* singing part so as to be able to secure somebody tolerably good looking and with a reasonably slim appearance. What do you think?

P.P.P.S. Do you think a sort of hornpipe tune with bangs at odd moments (rather like harlequinade music) wd. be good for the fight? If you don't care about the idea of the linnet song again it cd. be played on the orch. while he and Mary sing something else.

(No date: between
7 and 20 August 1911) Samatt House,

Dear Child

Thank you very much for your letter. I am sorry to hear that Mrs. Child has been so ill. It was too good of you to pay any attention to my stuff. I've finished all you sent me and want more. The worst of it is I'm inventing for 2nd act, which is awkward as I don't know what the 2nd act is to be about. I've been scheming out a duet for Hugh and Mary of rather a gayer character than in Act I. The scheme is as follows. They sing it as dawn begins slowly to get going (perhaps).

1st. Hugh sings a verse of the 'Linnet' song but rather extended and without the chirpy ending.
Mary answers with a parallel verse—then a sort of musical working out comes, and perhaps, the words to be a dialogue with occasional bits of duets—fairly slow and 'open airy'; ending soft.
—then Hugh says something about the dawn coming or 'let's get away to the open country' (supposing the dawn is not coming) or anything else you like.
Something of this kind, a sort of call.

Never mind about these notes exactly unless you happen to find it fitting anything; for I can make something different in the same character.
Mary answers parallel
4 bars of passion (slow)
Hugh's call and Mary's answer again, and a little more passion leading to a very quick and tremendously exciting short movement (but very 'open airy' with long vistas and distant hills) leading again to the 'linnet' tune, very big and loud, (but this need not affect you as the voices do *not sing it*, but sing something else together in great excitement). It dies down soft, the voices end, but the dawn goes on coming (birds singing etc.). Finally the whole ends up on a very high single note on the violins, held a long time—then (while the note is still held) is heard, in the far distance, the May day song, slow and mysterious.

Now please pay no attention to this unless it suggests anything you wd. like to do, or fits in with your scheme—if not we can

(*a*) scrap it
(*b*) use it elsewhere
(*c*) make it mean something different (music can always be made to 'mean' whatever you like)

By the way, I've written rather good stuff for the entry of the crowd and the fighting 'round', so don't alter the situation hurriedly or unadvisedly—on the other hand if you come to the conclusion that it had better be altered I don't think it will spoil my music much. I come back to 13 Cheyne Walk (illegible) Friday, I wd. like to have a long talk with you soon.

Yrs. R. V. W.

1 Feb 12
13 Cheyne Walk.

Dear Child

It was splendid to see your handwriting once more. I was getting so afraid the fount had stopped—it was good of you to go on when you were in such trouble. I do hope things are better with you now.

Now what I look forward to is the *second* act. I'm afraid of working out the whole seam over Act I, and having nothing left for Act II. I write out here a little tune[1] which I have had in my mind for some time. I've always connected it in my mind with the opening of 1st Act, and an auctioneer man shouting out 'going, going, gone; going, going, gone; worth twice the money, going, going, gone', or something of that sort, but you see, it would suit any sort of tag which people cd. repeat at intervals (e.g. something about Boney). But I feel it is important to have some refrain of the sort all through the opening scene to make the whole into a sort of Rondo—i.e. the refrain interspersed with various short episodes, such as lavender cries and so on, working up to a big noise then a pause in which the ballad seller's rather quavering voice is heard ('all the new ballads—all the new ballads and songs' etc.) greeted by rather a quiet slow chorus—then after a few false starts the ballad singer starts 'Tuesday morning' and is taken up by Mary. Does this appeal to you at all?

Yr.
R. Vaughan Williams.

13 Cheyne Walk,
S.W.1.

Dear Child

Could you come here one day *soon* and have a long talk over the opera—the 2nd Act is getting entirely out of hand—its grand opera of the worst description. I want to show it you and talk over many points. Could you ring me up. 6287 Western.

R. V. W.

Leith Hill Place,
Dorking.
(undated)

Dear Child

I hope my telegram didn't alarm you—but I suddenly found I was going to have a peaceful 4 days in which I hope to set to work on the opera—but I've really plenty to do with the rest of the first act if you haven't got the beginning part ready yet.

What I really write this about is that while I was brushing my hair

[1] This has been lost.

just before dinner tonight I had two ideas for Act II, one of which struck me as *very* brilliant and one rather brilliant.

The very brilliant one was that the soldiers should come in, as you suggested, at John's instigation to take Hugh off to gaol, that when the soldiers arrive the officer should recognise Hugh as the Welsh drover from whom he bought 3 horses a fortnight ago and has not yet paid for. (I am afraid this is against all Mr. Archer's principles,[1] because it keeps a secret from the audience—though it is a 'peripety'—do you think it too amateurish? Of course, it has one disadvantage from the operatic point of view, that it *absolutely* depends on the words being heard) and he proceeds to order his release and pay him the money on the spot. This provides a triumph for Hugh and discomfiting of John which we wanted. As a pendant to this do you think we might make the officer forcefully enlist John as a soldier (was there anything in the army corresponding to the press gang?)

John having been once more led off and Hugh proved a man of means, the constable begins to lick his boots and begs him to settle down and become his son-in-law. Hugh refuses and asks Mary to come off with him; she accepts, so after a short lecture to all concerned on the advantages of the open air life, (à la Feuersnot) he and Mary go off in their cart amid the general lamentation of the villagers. (i.e. a *soft* romantic open-airy ending and *not* rumbustious.) I dare say you've got something even better than all this by this time—so don't pay any attention.

My other *rather* brilliant idea is as follows—that the reason for Hugh and Mary deciding not to fly together, but to await events in the stocks, shall be *mental* and not physical—Mary says 'you are free, fly'—he says 'No, I'll wait here and claim you before them all'—this avoids the repetition of the situation of the first act. So Act II might altogether run,

John and friends come out of pub and blackguard Hugh,
Hugh left alone sings,
Mary looks out of the window and sings,
He calls to her and she comes down and unlocks him,
Long and passionate duet,
Mayers heard in the distance,
Hugh and Mary get back into the stocks,
Mayers enter, headed by John who serenades Mary,
Mary not there
Enter Constable,
General bustle,
Mary throws off cloak 'Here am I.'

[1] William Archer, translator of Ibsen.

By the way, you want a quick ensemble piece. How about this sort of rhythm?

or

or a quick patter

with slower things for the lovers to sing on the top. Or for a *slower* ensemble how about

It is better *musically* for a *non* recitative scene to keep a metre going regularly, more or less.
I've been wrestling with the new short scene before the entry of the showman and think I've got it right.

I'm making rather hay of some of your text—which it goes to my heart to do because it is so *frightfully* good.

Yrs.
R. V. W.

(Postcard post-marked
12.15 a.m. Chelsea S.W.
10 July 12.)
Many thanks for card.
I hope you are able to keep Hugh's entrance as it is, it is so good—and it seems to me that the facts almost explain themselves.
—I expect you are on to something 1st rate for the constable in Act II.
R. V. W.

Leith Hill Place.
Nr. Dorking,

June 1913
Dear Child

A good metre for a quick bustling ensemble might be

or

or

In the ensemble (if you put it in) I suggest the constable to start, A. Jane to take it up, and gradually everyone—and *meanwhile* Hugh and Mary to have a sort of whispering interlude of about 2 lines each.

'Will you remain true?'

'Yes I will stick to you always' etc.

Then for the last chorus (slow) I think 4 syllable lines best. Iambic, or possibly *slow* dactylic (brightest and best of the sons of the morning) but these are only suggestions.

R. V. W.

Hotel Tyrol, 27th July, 1913.
Innsbruck,
Tyrol.

Dear Child

I'm sorry I'm such a nuisance about the finale but it does not seem to me quite right yet. I don't know whether you will agree with me but I feel strongly that neither constable nor A. Jane nor chorus ought to even imagine the idea of *Mary and Hugh* going away *together*. As soon as the soldiers are gone two ideas present themselves to the mind of the constable. Either a) Hugh will now go *off alone*, or b) he may be persuaded to stop with her, take over the goodwill of John the Butcher's business and settle down in this 'salubrious town'.

Now I think this alteration of idea need not cause much alteration in the actual lines. My idea is as follows,

Soldiers go off—absolute silence for a few seconds—then the Const. goes up to Hugh and says to him

'Stop here and marry Mary.'

A. Jane follows him speaks to *Hugh*, not Mary, I think.

Chorus join in—(all this will involve very little change I think).

Then Hugh, aside to Mary in two *rather weighty* lines:

'Will you choose home comforts or me?'

Mary (rushing to his arms) 'Here is my home'.

Hugh 'Beloved' (or words to that effect).

Then Hugh turns to assembled company and says 'Friends, I do not like your town etc.'—As a lyrical finale to the speech I propose putting 'up at my side, as the drover wins his bride' *just* before they go off.

About the actual end I am again v. uncertain. I'm not sure that just the constable's 'stop her', then H. and M. heard off, then 'farewell' will not be better. Anyway I do not feel the chorus's last lines are quite formal enough—cd. they not be just a continuation of the ballad seller's 4 lines?—i.e. the *dramatist* speaking, not the chorus, *in person.*

In haste,
R. V. W.

P.S. I am back in a few days. Shall you be in London?

Hotel Suisse,
Ospedaletti-Ligure
Riviera,
Italy.

Dear Child

I send my version of the proposed cuts in Act I for your approval. I hope they don't make your words sound too illiterate—with these and one or two small cuts in other places we shall save 8 to 10 minutes which I hope will be enough.

It's beastly work this tampering—and there's some more for you to do!

I think the least trouble for you if I send them one by one.

(1) I send *two* now. (see music paper)[1]

(2) 8 lines for Mary (arioso) to take the place of 'I know not love.'

The above is my permanent address.

Yr.
R. V. W.

Single page—no date

Hotel Suisse,
Ospedaletti-Ligure,
Riviera,
Italy.

Dear Child

Many thanks for your letter. (I think I've got the idea for your little bit of Mary's you sent last time.)

[1] This has not survived.

Now for the next
4 lines of jubilation which can be sung by Mary or Hugh to fit in between, or with
'the cock has had its comb cut etc.' (after the fight) the tune is

to which various numbers of syllables could be fitted in—it is roughly in the 'Locksley Hall' metre.

[unsigned.]

(via Marseilles)

Hotel Suisse
Ospedaletti-Ligure,
Riviera,
Italy.

Dear Child

Those last two were splendid—specially John's. With regard to 'Joy O Joy' I find that it makes rather a gabble with so many syllables after all. Do you mind it running

Joy, Oh! Joy, I've fought for you and won you—
Joy, Oh! Joy, and you are free,
Love has blessed us, love has joined us
Me to you and you to me.

—But if that spoils it, the other could be put back.
Now for the next 2 (or rather 3) jobs.

1. Act II middle of duet, this is a rather difficult place, but I have not been satisfied with the run of the thing after 'Love has set me free'—it seemed as if it was going to swing on to the end, and then proved only to be a false start.—I think the fault was partly in the words (and I think you agreed with me) because Hugh starts saying 'Ah! no', and I don't quite like Mary, after saying she is free, announcing herself as a slave—now I think that a very small alteration (with a certain amount of repetition of words) wd. do the trick and enable me to make the music go along.
The words at present stand thus—and I have put in brackets the ones which I think require amending. But if you don't like the idea I can manage with it as it stands—and a very close relation of words and music perhaps will not matter.

Mary. Love that has set me free
I hear your call.
Nothing though it be
Oh! take my all.
Master of my poor heart
Take all I have
(Mine the blessed part
To be your slave.)

If you like them to alternate line by line—or Hugh to come in earlier I cd. manage it—but just as you like about that. A slight alteration with bracketed lines will do the trick for me all right.

Hugh. (No! No! in love no slaves no masters)
Love is free.
Then come my friend and lover, come with me.
Together.
The sky shall be—etc.

2. Act II. After discovery of Mary in the stocks—you will remember that I can cut a long speech of Mary's previous to 'here on my throne', but something is wanted here; partly to take the place of Mary's (cut) explanation and partly to continue the musical ensemble which now starts at 'Where's she gone to, where's my daughter'. I have patched up little bits of you with bits of me in the form of a quick dialogue which runs as follows,—you will see it is very bad, but perhaps you cd. do something better without too much upsetting my musical scheme, (you will see that there is no lyrical element in the voice parts—so there need be no syllabic correspondence between what I have written and what you will write—only we want short sentences).

(Mary throws off her cloak)

John. Mary!
Aunt Jane. My child.
Constable. My daughter.
Turnkey. Mary! Good God.
Chorus. Mary!
Constable (going up to Mary).
My daughter in the stocks 'fore all the town?
Mary (quietly)
Yes father!
Constable. How did you get here, Miss?
Mary. Of my own will.
Constable. Would you defy me?
Mary. Here I outface you and flaunt my pride,
Here in the stocks by this stranger's side.
Aunt Jane (to Mary)
Come away, come away.

Constable. Here, unlock her, (fumbling) where are the keys?
Turnkey. (fumbling) The keys!
Aunt Jane. The keys?
Constable. Where are my keys?
Mary. They're here!
(*all*) The keys.
Mary. Take them and set us free.
Chorus. Set them free, set them free.
Constable. Here, let her out,
But guard the spy my lads, stand well about.
(Mary is released, he seizes her by the arm)
Chorus. Let her be, let her be.
Constable. Come hussy!
Mary. Alone! no, no, (a struggle, she escapes and runs back to Hugh)
Here on my throne, I sit beside my king—

I enclose a sketch for the music of this.

3. Act II. In second verse of Mary's song 'see now the May' you have the line—

'No more a pool now, but a wave of the sea'

This refers to a remark about a pool earlier on, which we have cut—should we alter it?

Act II (right at the end)
I want two lines for Hugh and Mary to sing *off stage* after they have gone off.
—It doesn't really matter what it is, because the words will not be heard.
At present I have put

'Now you are mine, mine at last beloved for ever.'

but you will think of something better than this kind of slush.
(The music is the same as in Act I where Hugh says

'You are mine and here in Heaven's light I hold you.')

That I believe is all. There are several other places where I have altered or cut and added, but you will be able to improve on my colloquialisms and banalities when you have the whole to revise.

1000 thanks
Yr. R. V. W.

Hotel Suisse,
Ospedaletti-Ligure,
Riviera,
Italy.

On 2nd thoughts—if you have *not* already done anything better for Mary's arioso I think I cd. do it out of 8 lines from your original song, thus

'Oh no! the fighters come—
I hate all hate and cruelty,
Nought suffers, but a sting
Pierces my very heart, while he
Gloats o'er their suffering;
And must I now, I too, I too,
My youth beneath his knife,
And must I fall like you, like you,
His victim—called his wife.'

Do you approve?

R. V. W.

Postmarked 21 Dec. 13.

Hotel Suisse,
Ospedaletti-Ligure,
Riviera,
Italy.

1000 thanks.

They are splendid: now here are two more.

A. Cd. you alter the 1st 3 lines of verse II of Aunt Jane's song so as to make the pause in the *sense* come at the end of the line, as it does in verse I—if *not* I can alter the tune, but wd. rather not. At present they go

O tender blossoming
O little mouths that cling—
a wife—

(pause in music, have it same tune as verse I)

Finds etc.

B. Cd. you make a 2nd verse in the same metre to Mary's 4 lines beginning

In the night time I have seen you
riding, riding—

R. V. W.

Two more episodes remain to be chronicled of the opera's beginnings. In June 1914 Steuart Wilson and Denis Browne (who was killed in Gallipoli in 1915) came to 13 Cheyne Walk, and played and sang through the whole work to Harold Child, Adeline, and Ralph.

A month later Ralph took his score to Oxford to show to Hugh Allen. George Butterworth and Henry Ley were present. Dr. Ley remembered, 'we all spent a day playing and "singing" this delightful opera. At 10.30 V. W. suddenly said "will anyone come for a walk?" I volunteered. I remember well George Butterworth standing on Sir Hugh's doorstep at No. 9 Keble Road, and shouting "Madmen" as we left. We set off on a perfect July evening reaching Cumnor Church as the clock struck 1 a.m. After going down the lane to Bablockhythe Ferry we made our way up to Cumnor Hirst and Boar's Hill, passing Robert Bridges's house en route. We then decided to wait and see the dawn break over Oxford, which was a memorable sight under proper conditions. On the way down to Oxford V. W. saw what he thought was a short cut; with considerable difficulty he got himself over a wall with my help, and found himself on the top of a poultry shed, which caused a great commotion. I begged him, with much persuasion for fear of arrest, to retreat as there was a house just opposite. As I anticipated, the lights of the house soon went on, and with some luck we made a hasty retreat. We eventually reached Allen's house at 6 a.m.' Time has obliterated the conversation of that night walk, except for Ralph's one pronouncement, 'There is no such thing as originality.' Only one more postcard went to Harold Child.

Postmarked
4 August 1914 13 Cheyne Walk, S.W.

Many thanks—I think the alterations are splendid—I'd prefer the milder version of Jane's song. How about 'I have dreamt my arms about you twining'—a woman's arms seem to me more twining than a man's—but this is unimportant. Also how about 'So dawns my last day of freedom'—if not I can do the other tho' it will spoil the flow rather.

I go away for about a week tomorrow if any trains are going.

R. V. W.

Hugh was revised several times, cuts and additions being made.

A final revision was printed in 1958. A note written during the 1950s to Herbert Byard explains itself:

I added the extra scene to *Hugh* because we were told it was too short —that in the provinces they 'wanted their money's worth.' But it was never a success, both dramatically and musically it is poor and in addition entirely spoils the dramatic effect of the sudden hush at the old beginning of Act II coming sharpest after the noisy finish of Act I. So I never want to hear it or see it again.

The distinguished Czech critic Jan Loewenbach, who was a friend of Janaček, met Ralph after a performance of *Hugh the Drover* and told him how much he liked it, adding, 'but I don't know if I dare tell you what it reminds me of more than anything?' Ralph pressed him and he said, '*The Bartered Bride*'. 'But that's splendid, it's exactly what I intended,' said Ralph.[1]

[1] Told to Elizabeth Maconchy by Mrs. Loewenbach in 1963.

APPENDIX II

Vaughan Williams and Bach

After the First World War ended Ralph became conductor of the Bach Choir. He had been a member for about sixteen years and for some of this time he had served on the Committee.

He conducted his first concert with the choir on 14 December 1921, and the programme notes which he wrote for it give his ideas fully.

'The policy of performing the Cantatas of Bach (especially the more intimate ones) with a chorus of three hundred in a hall capable of holding over two thousand, may seem to some to be hazardous. Truly, the ideal way to give such music is by a small choir in a small building. But where are these ideal circumstances to be found?—not apparently in the concert-rooms of London. It seems then to be a question of three hundred voices or no cantatas; for the third course, that of keeping the majority of the chorus silent in all except the noisier numbers, is unthinkable in the case of a society like the Bach Choir, which lives through the enthusiasm of its members; and surely, if the Bach Choir is to be true to its name, it cannot cut out of its scheme those works which contain most of the essence of Bach. It is hoped, therefore, that the beauty of these cantatas will make itself felt under any conditions and in any circumstances, provided that the performers bring their minds and their hearts to the work. This brings us face to face with another problem—in what language are the cantatas to be sung? The Bach Choir have no unreasoning prejudice against the German language, but it is difficult to sing from the heart in any language but one's own: therefore English must be the language of an adequate rendering,[1] provided that the English used has (1) any relation to the German original, (2) any relation to the English language as it exists outside opera libretti. At present only a handful of such translations exist, and the choice is thereby limited. It remains for some enthusiastic

[1] It seems to be a sound principle that no singer should sing in any language with which both he and his audience are not familiar. Perhaps an exception may be found in the case of liturgical music such as the Roman Mass, in which the English equivalent is thoroughly familiar to the audience.

Bach lover to put this right, and arrange for the publication of many of the cantatas in a version in which they can be widely used.

The large chorus requires a (comparatively) large orchestra to support it. This occasionally upsets the orchestral balance and has necessitated a slight modification of the instrumental detail. In one case also where Bach (probably for safety) directed trombones to play with the voices throughout, the conductor has ventured to substitute some unobtrusive horn parts: in another case an obbligato for the obsolete 'violoncello piccolo' has necessitated a slight re-arrangement of the string parts.

Three complete cantatas will be performed tonight—

1. Jesus took unto Him the Twelve (*Jesus nahm zu sich*), which was Bach's 'trial piece' on his installation as Cantor in Leipzig in 1723. This is, so far as is known, the first performance in England.
2. Stay with us (*Bleib' bei uns*), written for the 'Second Easter Festival', probably in 1736.
3. The Sages of Sheba (*Die Weisen aus Saba*), an Epiphany cantata dating from 1724 (?)

There will also be sung the chorus *Now praise my soul* (taken from the cantata *Gottlob, nun geht*). The chorus is founded on the choral *Nun lob mein' Seel'*, and was composed early in the Leipzig period.[1]

At the end of the programme the choral 'Jesu, joy of man's desiring' will be sung by special request. The instrumental part of the programme will consist of the short organ prelude in C (as an introduction to 'Now praise my soul'), the Concerto in D for pianoforte, violin and flute (No. 5 of the Brandenburg concertos) and the French suite in E major for pianoforte solo.

R. V. W.

Ralph gave his first performance of the *St. Matthew Passion* at the Queen's Hall on 7 March 1923. The programme notes he wrote for this performance may be considered in the light of a lecture which he gave to the Leith Hill choirs before their first performance of the Passion in 1931 and which he repeated at Morley College years later—towards the end of the war—to an audience of young service people at the request of his ex-pupil, Inglis Gundry.

[1] This chorus will be sung in the version edited and transcribed by Sedley Taylor, whose name lives in the grateful remembrance of so many generations of Cambridge musicians. [Footnote to original programme.]

After discussing the musical background, he said:

There is one aspect which, though not a musical one, must have strongly influenced Bach in his work, that is, the popular Passion or mystery plays and processions. There is fairly good evidence that Bach must have been familiar with these ceremonies where, after a Church service, a procession to the Cross took place out of doors in which the various characters in the story, including a representative of Christ Himself, with His cross, marched in traditional order, chanting hymns. Surely a procession of this kind must have been in Bach's mind when he planned his great opening chorus in which the opposing choirs cry to each other 'See him—whom?—the bridegroom' and as the procession advances a third choir is heard singing the well-known hymn 'O Lamb of God most holy'.[1]

So it was with visual as well as musical images in mind that Ralph prepared his own performances. The story unfolded with dramatic intensity and he made his soloists and choir understand that singing the notes was not enough. Besides knowing their music they must be the original actors of the story as well as the devout seventeenth century Lutherans for whom the work was written. As with the Cantatas, he was troubled by problems of proportion and language.[2]

It may seem to some a hopeless task to present Bach's St. Matthew Passion in a London concert room, because if we listen to it as a concert piece we shall entirely mistake its purpose. The essence of the 'Passion' form is the recital of the Gospel story as a Church service, interspersed with reflective solos and choruses and the well-known choral melodies of the Lutheran Church (many of which happily belong to the English Church as well, so that here we are on familiar ground), and it is in this spirit that it must be performed and listened to.

However in transferring a work from the Thomaskirche in 1729 to a London concert room in 1923, certain adaptations and compromises are inevitable. To start with, the only possible language in which the gospel history can be recited to an English audience is that of the Authorized Version of 1611: anything else would be an insult to Bach and the Bible. To do this it is necessary to alter a few notes of Bach's recitative, and in a few cases to sacrifice some of Bach's subtlety of phrasing but the compromise cannot be avoided.

[1] Unpublished lecture.

[2] He used the Elgar–Atkins edition with some modification of his own devising.

Bach's original chorus for his cantatas and Passions consisted of not more than 40 voices. What then are we to do when we have a chorus of 300? It seems ridiculous and outside the bounds of dramatic propriety to give the words of the Apostles or the questions of Peter to more than a few voices; these numbers have therefore been assigned to the semi-chorus. One exception, however, has been made: the words 'truly, this was the Son of God' belong not to 'the Centurion and they that were with him', but are the triumphant outcry of the whole world. In a performance such as today's, another question arises. In Bach's time the Passion was divided into two parts with a long interval (and a sermon) between the parts. When such conditions no longer obtain are we justified in making certain omissions? There seems to be no object in performing the whole of the Passion merely to be able to say, like the man who proposed to go down a coal mine, that we have done so. A few cuts are made in today's performance of certain arias which, according to the standard which Bach himself has set, do not reach the high level of the rest (though for any other composer we should consider them as great music), of others which require a virtuoso obbligato on an obsolete instrument, and of parts of the narrative which are not essential to the course of the story.[1] Also certain '*da capos*' have been abbreviated, in connection with which we may quote the wise sentence of Hubert Parry, 'The only respect in which Bach falls under the spell of convention was in following without sufficient consideration the principle of repetition familiar through the direction "*da capo*".' It is as though when he had carried out his artistic scheme with all the technical richness and care in detail he could muster up to a certain point, he felt he had done all that was required of him and wrote '*da capo al fine*'.[2]

The programme of the *St. John Passion*, sung by the Bach Choir on 24 March 1928, was prefaced with a note on translation, much like the one he had written for the *St. Matthew*, then came the innovation:

It is important that an audience should be presented with an uninterrupted view of the text, not obscured by such unnecessary words as 'Recit', 'Aria', etc. To secure this and at the same time make the divisions of the text clear, a different kind of type is used for each of the main sections of the text (the narration, the reflective arias and choruses, and the chorals). In the accompanying text, therefore, the

[1] Robert Sterndale Bennett in an article in *Music & Letters* (Vol. 37, No. 4, 1956) pointed out that R.V.W.'s cuts are very much the same as Mendelssohn made in 1829 and William Sterndale Bennett in 1858.

[2] Bach Choir programme note, 1923.

narration (the Bible words) are printed in ordinary Roman type, the reflective arias and choruses in *italics*, and the chorals in SMALL CAPITALS.

From then on, every programme of either *Passion* given by the Bach Choir has been so printed.

It was a year after the performance of the *St. Matthew* that Ralph wrote to Cedric Glover about another problem that arises in every performance of the *Passion*. Mr. Glover, a member of the Bach Choir Committee, an amateur musician of wide interests, as well as a devoted bass in the Choir, had complained—and was to complain for years—about Ralph's use of the pianoforte. Ralph answered:

I once heard a Bach performance with harpsichord throughout (in Queen's Hall) and it sounded intolerable in a large place. I think a harpsichord and a small organ is ideal for the recitatives (as they do at Amsterdam) but this is out of practical politics—and who is going to play it? Also the harpsichord by itself at once gives an 'antiquarian' flavour to the music which we want to avoid at all costs. I do not propose to use the pfte. in the choruses except to strengthen the bass in one or two places. And we must remember that the modern violin, oboe and horn are about as remote from the instruments of Bach's time as the pfte. is from the harpsichord. As to the figures in the air for the tenor and other places—it does not follow that because Bach did not mark them he did not want them (see Schweitzer).

I think Bach probably wrote no solos for viola because no one cd. play it—his viola parts looked like this—I rather liked the viola in the Agnus.

I am having some of the recitatives done on the organ—but please bring it up at Ctee. I am quite open to argument.

P.S. On Bach's instrumentation generally, read Schweitzer. Do you remember Allen's magnificent trombones at the end of the Mass?

P.P.S. The harpsichord is all right with a small band and a small choir—but 350 in the Q.H.?[1]

This question of pianoforte continuo runs through all the years in which he gave performances of the *St. John* and *St. Matthew* Passions at Dorking—twenty-three performances of the *St. Matthew*, and twelve of the *St. John*. He disliked the sound of the harpsichord and thought it was in any case too thin a sound to consort successfully with modern wind instruments

[1] Queen's Hall, Portland Place, London. Destroyed by enemy action, 1941.

and a large choir. This is discussed in *Bach the Great Bourgeois*[1] and in other places in his writings. He eventually wrote out a continuo pianoforte part for the *St. Matthew* Passion, and this is discussed in letters to Herbert Byard, written after a performance in March 1949 (one of the six performances to which he came).

Thank you so much for your letter. I wish I had seen you on Saturday, and we could have talked things over. I have quoted your kind words in a letter I have written to my choir.

As regards the question of the end of No. 67[2] I know that the B. G.[3] edition has the figured bass, but whenever I have heard the work it has been pure unison—even a performance at Amsterdam, so far as I can remember, which was supposed to be very correct and had all the horrors like harpsichord and other pedantries. I suppose if the harmonies were put in at all they were put in on the organ. I think one is quite justified, however, in leaving them out. In the same way I always leave out the harmonies that[4] have a pure bass in the accompaniment to 'Eli, Eli,' if possible on the organ only.

I should very much like a criticism on my realisation of the figured bass in the Evangelist part.

I remember the very interesting letter you wrote to *The Times* some time ago condemning what you called the 'plops' in the ordinary pianoforte scores. I cannot believe that is what Bach meant and I venture to think he meant something more like what I wrote out for Gritton[5] to play. Some people, however, strongly object to it and say it is not Bach, and other people go so far as to say it is like a pianoforte concerto.

I should very much like to know what you think about this?

The letter from Herbert Byard in answer to this is unfortunately lost. Ralph's answer to the answer followed on 6 April 1949:

Many thanks for your second letter. There is only one point I want to answer—that is the question of the pianoforte going on all through the solos.

[1] *The Listener*, 1950, reprinted in *National Music*. Oxford University Press, 1963.

[2] No. 67. Recit. and Chorus: 'I am the Son of God,' 'And when they were come unto a place called Golgotha——'.

[3] Bach Gesellschaft.

[4] The word 'that' should probably be 'and'.

[5] Eric Gritton, pianist and regular performer in the Dorking *St. Matthew* & *St. John Passions*.

If Bach wanted that why did he have strings occasionally and then drop them at certain moments, unless he meant the keyboard to take it up there? Also I feel that the pianoforte continuo right through would sound very monotonous, and of course the harpsichord would sound unbearable. . . . As you say, the tone of all instruments and the conditions being so different, we cannot give it as Bach meant it, even if we wanted to. The question is whether he will bear transference to modern conditions. A great many of the eighteenth century composers will not bear the transposition and therefore had better be left alone; but Bach obviously can.

Ralph rehearsed his choirs for both *Passions* with great intensity. They had to know their music so well that he could devote his attention to their understanding and interpretation of the story. In the *St. John* he made them sing the first answer to ‘ hom seek ye?’ in a truculent way, the hunting pack in full cry. Then, after that strange description ‘they went backward and fell to the ground’, the second time they answered ‘Jesus of Nazareth’ they had to be a frightened crowd. He made them sing with self-justification, ‘If He were not a malefactor we would not have delivered Him up unto thee’, and this developed into an even more self-righteous mob with ‘We have a law, and by our law He ought to die’—little by little the structure was built up, the lyrical chorals, and the dramatic development of the chorus, but all within the framework of the music. He described how he had differed from Albert Schweitzer over the duet for soprano and alto in the *St. Matthew*: ‘Behold, my saviour now is taken’, which Ralph always believed to be a lament, broken by the crowd’s ‘Thunders and Lightnings’ as if the two Marys were lost in their own grief, oblivious of the darkness, the rending of the temple veil and all such terrifying manifestations. Schweitzer wanted the women’s voices, Ralph said, to be in a strict marching time: ‘He demonstrated, taking my arm and walking me up and down the room while he sang it.’

Whether one agrees with Ralph’s ideas or not, they were the outcome of thought, study and the devotion of a lifetime. Writing of these, Herbert Byard said:

I don’t suppose even in 1958 R. had reached absolute finality over the *Matthew*—for little things did change from year to year . . . certainly the *St. John* changed, I remember being particularly struck in

1953 by the *ff* passionate ending of 'Ah, my soul', and R. explaining why he'd done it that way. Yet in 1956 he did it *pp* and argued quite convincingly for it. . . . What I recognized in the Dorking *Passions*, and what I want other people to recognize, was the impact of one great mind upon another.[1]

[1] Letter to U.V.W., 1960.

Index of Works

Adieu, 67
Along the Field, 156, 343

Bacchae, The, 94, 105
Benedicite, The, 171, 181, 220, 269, 326, 355
Blackmwore by the Stour, 57, 62
Bridal Day, the, 335, 360, 383, see also *Epithalamion*
Bucolie Suite, 61
Bushes and Briars, 66

Ca' the Yowes, 142
Choral Flourish (Psalm xxxiii), 388
Choral Hymns, Three, 181, 196
Coastal Command (film), 245, 250
Concerto for Oboe and Strings, 259, 316, 345
Concerto Grosso, 290, 292, 299, 301
Concerto in C Major for Pianoforte and Orchestra, 194
  version for two pianofortes and orchestra, 269
Concerto in D Minor (*Concerto Accademico*) for violin and string orchestra, 156, 161
Cousin Michael, 67

Death of Tintagiles, The (Maeterlinck), 108
'*Dives and Lazarus*', *Five Variants of*, 230, 296
Dona Nobis Pacem, 210–12, 215, 220, 223, 250, 252, 260, 306, 310
Double Trio for Strings, 225, 234, 250, 257, 277
Dover Beach, 57, 357

Elizabethan Songs, Three, 110
England of Elizabeth, The (film), 65, 368, 379
English Folk Songs, Suite for Military Band, 151, 154
Epithalamion, 218–20, 221, 222, 225, 228, 335, 360, 383, see also *The Bridal Day*

Fantasia on Christmas Carols, 105–6, 193
Fantasia on the Old 104th, 297, 300, 354
Fantasia on Sussex Folk Tunes, for Violoncello and Orchestra, 180
Fantasia on a Theme by Thomas Tallis, *see* Tallis
First Nowell, 202, 397
Five English Folk Songs, 112
Five Mystical Songs, 97, 112, 326
Five Tudor Portraits, 212, 213, 265, 278, 324, 345, 346
Five Variants of 'Dives and Lazarus', 230, 296
Flemish Farm (film), 248
Flemish Farm (Suite), 265
Flos Campi, 156, 160, 161, 170, 276, 278, 326, 347
Flourish for a Coronation, 213
Flourish for Glorious John, 385
Folk Songs of the Four Seasons, 299, 310
49th Parallel (film), 239, 245, 249
Four Hymns, 137–8, 158, 190, 278, 350

Greensleeves, 104, 257

Happy Days at Gunby, 395
Harmonica, Romance for, 324
Heroic Elegy and Triumphal Epilogue, 67, 73
Hodie (*This Day*), 337, 346–7, 359, 374
House of Life, The, 65, 72
Household Music, 245
Hugh the Drover, 96, 104, 113, 134, 150, 154, 155, 181, 214, 226, 306, 335, 339, 399, 400–22
Hundredth Psalm, The, 181, 300, 326
Hymn Tune Prelude on Gibbons's Song 13, 180–1, 260
Hymn Tune Preludes for Orchestra, Two, 211

In the Fen Country, 81, 287
Introduction and Fugue for two pianofortes, 267

In Windsor Forest, 190, 350
It was a Lover and His Lass, 142

Jean Renaud, 67
Job, a Masque for Dancing, 183, 184, 185, 187, 188, 197, 203, 211, 218, 226, 278, 284–5, 286, 338, 362, 383

L'Amour de Moy, 67
Lark Ascending, The, 138, 156, 355, 374
Linden Lea, 57, 62, 158, 219
Lovely Joan, 104
Loves of Joanna Godden, The (film), 267, 271, 280

Magnificat, 191
Mass in G Minor, 138, 160, 171, 232, 284, 298
Mayor of Casterbridge, 300
Menelaus, 354
Merciless Beauty (Three Chaucer Rondels), 158, 159
Motion and Stillness, 158
Mystical Songs, Five, 97, 112, 326

New Commonwealth, The, 249
Nothing is Here for Tears, 210

O How Amiable, 202
O Taste and See, 333–4
O vos omnes, 142
Oboe and Strings, Concerto for, 259, 316, 345
Ocean, The, see *Sea Symphony*
Old 104th, Fantasia on, 297, 300, 354
Old Hundredth, The, 333–4
Old King Cole, 149–50
On Wenlock Edge, 82, 83, 87, 102, 126, 153, 156, 158, 350, 383
Oxford Elegy, An, 297–8, 321, 326, 335

Partita for Double String Orchestra, 277, 282–3
Passacaglia for the Bride on B.G.C., 196
People's Land, The (film), 245
Phantasy Quintet, 110
Pianoforte Suite, 155
Pilgrim Pavement, The, 201
Pilgrim's Progress, The, 87, 138, 163, 216, 260, 286, 299, 304, 306–8, 310–12, 313–51
  Revival, 316
  Cambridge, 342–4
  German Translation, 288–9
  Songs from, 351
Poisoned Kiss, The, 209, 211, 213, 215, 276, 371
  revised version, 381
Prayer to the Father of Heaven, 209, 282, 284
Prelude on Three Welsh Hymn Tunes, 360

Quartet in A minor for Jean on her birthday, 255–6, 259–60
Quartet in G minor, 83, 352
Quintet (clarinet, horn, violin, cello and piano), 64

Rest, 62
Revéillez vous, Piccars, 67
Riders to the Sea, 161, 190, 213, 215, 220, 298, 313, 333, 335, 351
Romance for Harmonica and Orchestra, 324
Running Set, The, 201, 202, 257

Sancta Civitas, 152, 161, 162–3, 164, 210, 220, 278, 284, 312, 340, 355–6, 391
  German Translation, 285, 288
  Latin version, 292
Schmücke Dich. Bach, *arr.* for cello and strings, 378
Scott of the Antarctic (film), 287, 293
Serenade to Music, 221, 222, 223, 321, 340, 351, 366
Shakespeare Songs, Three, 355
Shelley, *Six Choral Songs*, 231, 235
Shepherds of the Delectable Mountains, The, 87, 138, 145, 157, 158, 169, 196, 273
Silent Noon, 64, 65, 134
Sine Nomine, 160
Sir John in Love, 174, 175, 181, 190, 228, 246, 267, 289–90, 308, 312, 369, 397, 398, 399
Six Choral Songs, 231, 235
Sky above the Roof, The, 78, 220
Solent, The, 65

Sonata for Violin and Pianoforte, 343, 346, 347
Song for a Spring Festival, 359
Songs of Travel, 65, 72, 136, 354
Sons of Light, The, 304, 307, 308, 317, 326
Souls of the righteous, The, 284
Sound Sleep, 64
Stricken Peninsula (film), 264
Suite for Viola and Small Orchestra, 203, 211
Symphonic Rhapsody, 67
Symphonies:
A Sea Symphony, 65, 68, 77, 78, 87, 88, 90, 95, 96, 107, 113, 125, 135, 141, 154, 156, 160, 163, 170, 184, 224, 250, 251, 252, 269, 278, 290, 310, 314, 316–17, 340, 357, 359, 380, 388
A London Symphony, 95, 96, 104, 109, 110, 111, 113, 126, 134, 149, 153, 161, 169, 202, 211, 221, 269, 270, 278, 289, 296, 315, 328, 337, 353, 355, 361, 400
A Pastoral Symphony, 121, 134, 140–1, 142, 143, 144, 153, 159, 164, 169, 194, 195, 211, 223, 262, 294, 347, 383
No. 4 in F minor, 190, 205–6, 211, 213, 353, 366
No. 5 in D major, 253, 257, 260, 265, 266, 270, 273, 277, 312, 324, 326
No. 6 in E minor, 267–8, 279, 282–3, 289, 291, 293, 296, 300, 302, 317
No. 7, *Sinfonia Antartica*, 286, 293, 315, 317, 328–9, 330, 382
Symphonies (*contd.*):
No. 8 in D minor, 358, 369, 371–2, 374, 375, 381, 383, 388
No. 9 in E minor, 65, 385, 390–1, 398, 399

Tudor Portraits, Five, 212, 213, 265, 278, 324, 345, 346
Tallis, Fantasia on a Theme by Thomas, 88, 97, 107, 192, 221, 277, 286, 333, 355
Te Deum, 1927, 171
Te Deum, 1937, 213
Thanksgiving, A Song of (Thanksgiving for Victory), 261–3, 265, 292, 326
This Day, see *Hodie*
Thomas the Rhymer, 393, 397
Toward the Unknown Region, 78, 83, 95, 112, 113, 190, 309, 340, 345
Tuba Concerto, 346

Valiant for Truth, 237, 249
Variations for Brass Band, 385
Vision of Aeroplanes, A, 369, 373
Vocalises, Three, 390
Voice out of the Whirlwind, The, 278

Wasps, The, 83, 85, 87, 105, 336
Suite, 355
Where is the Home for Me?, 105
Whither Must I Wander?, 64
Willow Wood, 64, 87, 113
Windsor Forest, In, 190, 350
Winter's Willow, 62

Index

Abinger Chronicle, 230
Abinger Pageant, 202, 289
Ackland, Valentine, 398
Addison, 88
Adler, Larry, 324, 329
Alan, Hervey, 345
Albert, Prince Consort, 46
Alcock, Sir Walter, 222, 396
Aldeburgh Festival, 343
Aldous, Joyce, 371–2
Alexandra, H.M. Queen, 162
Allen, H. P. (later, Sir Hugh), 37, 38, 42, 89, 90, 92, 95, 107, 125, 134, 135, 139, 147, 154, 160, 162, 198, 207, 273, 357, 421
Alvary, Max, 34
Alwyne, Horace, 193
Amos, Maurice Sheldon, 37, 39, 92, 233
Ampthill, Lady, 394
Andrews, Dr. H. K., 136
Anique, Clémence, 117
Ann Arbor, University of Michigan, 350–1
Anson, Hugh, 266
Aristophanes, 83
Armstrong, Robert, 377
Armstrong, Sir Thomas, 108, 284, 321, 389
Arnold, Matthew, 292, 321
Arts Council, The, 286, 328, 343
Arundell, Dennis, 342–4
Ashcroft, Dame Peggy, 340
Askew, Norman, 324
Askew, Violet, 324
Auerbach, Erich, 397
Austin, John, 181
Avril, Elsie, 150
Awdrey, Diana, *see* Oldridge

Bach, J. S., 101, 119, 121, 140, 148, 157, 164, 170, 186, 194, 221, 223, 369, 378, 379, 389, 396, 399, 423–30
Mass in B minor, 154, 162, 164, 385; English translation by R. V. W., 253, 271, 275
Bach J. S. (*contd.*)
St. John Passion, 149, 170, 271, 273, 274, 281, 288–9, 304, 314, 315, 316, 369, 373, 387, 388, 426, 427, 429
St. Matthew Passion, 53, 98, 142, 148, 149, 153, 159, 186, 246, 252, 257, 262, 267, 271, 273, 274, 281, 288, 289, 290, 304, 306, 317, 329, 369, 387, 389, 424, 426, 427, 429
Bach Cantata Club, 178
Bach Choir, The, 56, 106, 107, 125, 139, 141, 148, 149, 153, 154, 157, 159, 162, 164, 168, 170, 171, 179, 246, 423–30
Bagot, Jane (*see* Vaughan Williams, Lady)
Baillie, Isobel, 316, 326
Bainton, Edgar, 126
Baker, Lance, 390
Balakirev, 110
Balcon, Jill *see* Day Lewis, Jill
Balcon, Sir Michael, 326
Balfour, Mr., 109
Bantock, Granville, 126, 273
Barber, Samuel, 357
Barbirolli, Sir John, 180, 203, 277, 291, 302, 315, 317, 324, 328–9, 346, 358, 369, 372, 383, 396–7
Barbirolli, Lady *see* Rothwell, Evelyn
Bardgett, Herbert, 316
Bark, The Rev. Canon L., 159
Barker, Granville, 109, 150
Barnes, William, 62, 219, 282
Barter, Arnold, 95, 96, 314
Bartók, 66, 100, 147, 390
Bate, Stanley, 136
Battell, Robbins, 142
Bax, Arnold, 110, 147, 205, 266, 366
Baylis, Lilian, 184
Bayliss, Mr., 326
Beagley, J., 280–1, 288, 289
Bean, Ernest, 384
Beatty, Earl, 135
Beaux of London City, The, 372–3
Becker, Lydia, 26
Becker, Mr., 26

Beecham, Sir Thomas, 165, 213, 278 287
Beerbohm, Sir Max, 25, 230, 234, 235
Beerbohm, Lady, 235
Beethoven, 190, 226, 228, 230, 231, 267
Choral Symphony, 226, 230, 231, 267
Behrens, Leonard, 329
Bell, W. H., 71
Ben-Haim, Alexander, 399
Benjamin, Arthur, 205, 325, 349, 382, 397
Benson, Sir Frank, 75, 103, 174, 177
Bernhardt, Sarah, 42
Bidder, Helen (Biddy), 182, 190, 199, 251
Bing, Rudolf, 356–7
Birch, John, 373
Bird, Henry, 74, 83
Birmingham, City of, Choir, 149
Symphony Orchestra, 359, 366
Bishop, Morris, 354
Black, Joyce, *see* Finzi, Joy
Blackheath (Surrey) Choral Society, 137
Blake, 183, 187, 188, 284, 386
Blech String Quartet, 245
Bliss, Sir Arthur, 180, 296, 315, 347, 384, 385
Bloomington, University of, 351
Blunden, Edmund, 216
Boatwright, Helen, 355
Boito, 36, 147
Bone, Miss, 290
Booth, John, 153
Borrow, George, 168
Bosanquet, Mr. and Mrs., 28
Bosanquet, Vivian, 12, 19
Boston Symphony Orchestra, 192
Boughton, Rutland, 112, 126, 147, 176, 177, 303, 322, 327, 335, 378–9, 387
Boult, Sir Adrian, 114, 133, 136, 139, 140, 141, 154, 159, 170, 184, 194, 205, 206, 213, 230, 254, 265, 279, 282, 284, 309, 315, 326, 341, 358, 361, 366, 375, 377–8, 383
Bournemouth Daily Echo, *The*, 322
Bournemouth Symphony Orchestra, 67, 322
Boyce, Bruce, 340
Boyle, Ina, 136
Brackenbury, Maud, 60
Brahms, 164, 221
Brandram, Rosina, 410
Brandrum, Mr., 24
Breitkopf and Härtel, 113, 114
Brewer, Sir Herbert, 172
Bridge, Frank, 126
Bridges, Robert, 138, 169, 180, 350, 374, 421
Briggs, The Rev. Canon, 249, 285–6
Briggs, Mrs., 285–6
Bristol, University of, 313–4
British Broadcasting Corporation (formerly Company), 148, 165, 239, 261, 347, 361, 389, 396
B.B.C. Chorus, 213
B.B.C. Symphony Orchestra, 185, 194, 205, 213, 230, 278, 279
British Council, 230, 264, 346, 363
British Music Society, 138, 147, 157, 158
British National Opera Company, 148, 152, 154, 155
British Transport Commission, 379
British Transport Films, 368, 379
Britten, Benjamin, 203, 234, 265, 268, 298, 310, 313, 335, 339
Broadwood, John, 62
Broadwood, Lucy, 62, 63, 70, 74, 89, 140, 141, 179
Brockless, Pauline, 389
Brooke, Rupert, 108
Brown, Bernard, 232, 236, 262, 274, 377
Brown, Honorine (*nee* Williamson), 171, 174, 180, 187, 188, 205, 208, 214, 215, 222, 228, 232, 235, 237
Brown, John, 381
Browne, Denis, 87, 112, 122, 421
Browne, Harold, 374
Brown, Wilfred, 387, 389
Bruch, Max, 36, 52, 57, 147
Bryn Mawr (Pennsylvania): Mary Mary Flexner Lectures, 191, 192, 193, 203
Buck, Sir Percy, 251
Bucks., Beds., and Oxon Festival, 83
Buffalo Philharmonic Orchestra, 353–6
Bulmer, Mr. and Mrs., 195
Bunyan, John, 138
Burke, Charles, 141
Burkhard, Willy, 220
Burnaby, John, 150
Burton, Hal, 306

Busch, Fritz, 114
Bush, Alan, 239, 367
Busoni, 147, 194
Butterworth, George, 89, 92, 95, 98, 105, 109, 111, 113, 115, 122, 136, 147, 421
Butterworth Trust, 377
Buxtehude, 221
Byard, Herbert, 422–8, 429
Byrd, William, 141, 147, 341

Cambridge, Caius College, 361
Cambridge, Madrigal Society, 333
Cambridge Music Festival, 149
Cambridge University Music Society, 150, 342
California, University of (Los Angeles), 351–2
Camargo Society, 184, 187
Calvocoressi, M. D., 79, 80, 260
Cameron, Basil, 383
Cameron, John, 380
Cameron, Mrs. Julia, 48, 90, 305
Canning, Vera, 225
Capell, Richard, 184
Careño, Madame, 60
Carey, Clive, 105, 112, 140, 267, 298, 336
Carnegie Trust Awards, 147
Carnegie United Kingdom Trust, 126, 196, 274
Carol Case, John, 389
Carr, Francis, 294
Carr, Rosamond, 173, 184, 185, 187, 188, 190, 195, 196, 205, 206, 207, 213, 214, 218, 223, 224, 226, 229, 259, 284, 291, 294, 336
Carter, Mary (Mrs. Field Reid), 331
Cartwright, Peggie, 360
Caruso, 147
Casals, 74, 180, 378
Catalinet, Philip, 342–3
Cecil Sharp House, 221, 222, 225, 260, 278, 310, 394
C.E.M.A., 247, 264
Charterhouse, 25–30, 234, 238, 301, 323, 375
  Masque of Charterhouse, 301
  Carmen Carthusianum, 301, 375
Chaucer, 158
Chelmer, Lord, 377
Cheltenham Festival, 358–9, 396
Chicago, University of, 351
Child, Harold, 96, 155, 249, 400–22
Christie, John, 202, 311–12
Church, F. J., 163
Churchill, Sir Winston, 223, 313–14
Clarion Singers, 289, 312
Clarke, Dr. Ian, 288, 300
Clarke, Mary, 1
Clarke, Rebecca (Mrs. James Friskin), 105, 336, 357
Clegg, Edith, 72
Clinton, Gordon, 338, 389
Coates, Albert, 212
Coates, John, 153
Cohen, Harriet, 180, 181, 194, 260, 366
Cobbett, W. W., 110
  Walter Cobbett Medal, 182
Cockerell, Mrs. Sydney, 149
Coghill, Nevill, 304, 306
Cole, Dr. William, 270, 296, 326
Coleridge-Taylor, 139
Collegium Musicum Londinii, 378
Collard, John Clementi, Life Fellowship, 203
Colles, H. C., 148, 184
Collins, Mr., 288
Composers Concourse, 367
Composers Guild, The, 303, 316, 385
Contemporary Music Society, 220
Cook, Ellis, 28
Cook family, 314
Cooper, Gerald, 161
Cooper, Joseph, 225
Cornell University, 342
  à Cappella Chorus, 354–5
  Sage Chapel Choir, 354
  University Orchestra, 355
Corelli, Marie, 104
Cornford, Frances (*née* Darwin), 35, 215, 343, 370–1, 381
Cossart, Ernest, 193
Covent Garden (Royal Opera House), 108, 306–8
Coverdale, Miles, 181
Craig, Gordon, 91, 93, 94
Craig-Sellar, Miss, 74
Cramer, Mr. (music teacher), 19
Cranmer, Arthur, 162, 186, 246, 326
Craufurd, James, G., 340
Craxton, Janet, 316, 387
Creighton, Walter, 72
Crown Film Unit, 250, 316
Croydon Philharmonic Society, 278, 388

Cudworth, Charles, 361, 388, 395
Cullen, Margery, 232, 253, 273, 291, 328, 330, 384, 395
Cumberlege, Sir Geoffrey, 327, 381
Cundell, Edric, 377
Curle, Adam, 145, 301
Curle, Cordelia (*née* Fisher), 48, 49, 85, 139, 144, 145, 159, 169, 173, 197, 205, 290, 210, 214, 236, 245, 248, 255, 258, 259, 262, 265, 266, 268, 269, 270, 271, 273, 274, 285, 287, 288, 294, 297, 299, 300, 301, 302, 304, 307, 309, 310, 326, 331, 373
Curtis Musical Institute, 165, 172
Curwen, Mr., 154
Curzon, the Marquess of, 135
Cuyler, Louise, 350

Daily Mail, *The*, 184, 255, 291
Daily Worker, *The*, 293, 396
Damon, Mr., 202
d'Aranyi, Jelly, 74, 156, 161, 180, 185
Darbishire, Elizabeth, 195, 226, 246, 274
Darke, Dr. Harold, 107, 140, 249, 340, 373
Darwin, Bernard, 12, 21, 295, 373
Darwin, Caroline, *see* Wedgwood, Caroline
Darwin, Charles, 5, 11, 12, 13, 17, 18, 86, 325
Darwin, Emma, 10, 18, 19, 21, 23
Darwin, Erasmus, 11, 372
Darwin, George, 10, 21, 23
Darwin, Nicola, 373
Darwin, Sir Robin, 296, 368
Darwin, Susan, 10
Davies, Meredith, 346, 374
Davies, Mr., 360
Davies, Walford (later Sir), 66, 83, 107, 147, 164, 166, 182, 206, 210, 275
Davison, Archibald, 192
Day, Nora, 203, 251
Day Lewis, Cecil, 326, 328, 329, 384
Day Lewis, Jill, 326, 329, 370, 384
Dearmer, Percy, 70, 71, 157
Dearmer, Mrs. Percy, 78
Debussy, 42, 147, 170, 291
Decca Record Company, 341
De la Mare, Walter, 216
de l'Etang, Antoine, 46
Delius, F., 42, 110, 147, 160, 179, 206
de Maré, Eric, 328
Dent, Edward, 114, 214, 311, 315, 321, 340
Derain, Canon (Malines), 173
Derby, Lord, 189
de Ropp, Robert, 188, 259, 294
de Ropp, Ruth, 259
Desmond, Astra, 186, 191, 198, 212, 278, 345
de Valois, Dame Ninette, 184, 187, 188
Diaghilev, 93, 94, 113, 150, 183
D'Indy, 79, 80
Dodds, Jamieson, 96
Dolin, Anton, 188
Doniach, Shula, 287
Dorking Advertiser, 388–9
Dorking Bach Choir, 271, 273, 294, 388
Dorking and Leith Hill Preservation Society, Pageant, 216
  England's Green and Pleasant Land, 222, 289
Dorking Operatic Society, 289, 315
Dorking Refugee Committee, 224, 229, 237, 246
Dorking: St. Martin's Church, 240, 246, 257, 270
Douglas, Johnstone, 336
Douglas, Roy, 315, 328, 337–8, 358, 385, 390, 392
Dowling, Denis, 228, 316
Downing College, Cambridge, 35, 36
Down Ampney, 6, 7–9, 286, 349
Drake, Bryan, 340
Drummond, William, 338
Duckworth, Stella (m. Jack Hills, d. 1897), 48, 49, 169
Dukas, Paul, 110
Duncan, Isadora, 94, 105, 150
Duncan, Raymond, 94
Dunhill, Thomas, 43, 71, 187, 273
du Val, Lorraine, 266
Dvořák, 141
Dyson, Sir George, 269, 298, 320, 373

Eastman School of Music, Rochester, N.Y., 349
Eaton, Sybil, 170
Ecoives, 120, 121, 134
Edward, H.R.H. Prince of Wales (later H.M. King Edward VII), 46, 92, 207

Edward, H.R.H. Prince of Wales (later H.M. King Edward VIII), 166
Edwards, Sir Eric, *see* Chelmer, Lord
Edwards, Pte., 119
Eglesfield Music Society, 321
Ellaby, Mr., 24
Elgar, Sir Edward, 42, 88, 92, 97, 98, 134, 137, 173, 197, 198, 202, 203, 206, 208, 211, 282, 286
Elgar Blake, Mrs., 198
Eliot, T. S., 396
Ellis, F. B., 110, 111, 115, 122, 315
Elizabeth I, 333
Elizabeth, H.M. Queen [Mother], 302, 324
Elizabeth II, H.M. Queen (Coronation), 333–4
Elwes, Gervase, 87, 126, 147
Elwes, Joan, 343
Engel, Carl, 260
English Folk Dance Society (Cambridge Branch), 149, 150
English Folk Dance and Song Society, 150, 168, 189, 190, 202, 204, 224, 264, 315, 369, 376, 394
  Journal, 293
  New York Branch, 193
English Hymnal, The, 71, 76, 87, 138, 157, 264, 373, 394
  Scottish Supplement, 281
Epstein, 287–8, 296, 386
Erskine, H. C., 26
Evans, Nancy, 338, 361, 389
Evans Williams, Laura, 96
Evening News, The, 270

Fachivi, Adila, 74, 180, 185
Falkner, Christabel, 348–9, 353, 354, 355, 356
Falkner, Julia, 356
Falkner, Keith, 155, 186, 342, 348–9, 354, 355, 356, 361
Farrer, the Hon. Anne, 202
Farrer, The Lord, 74, 207
Farrer, Lady, 32, 73, 74, 178, 207, 232
Farrer, The Hon. Dame Frances, 167, 181, 185, 202, 214, 232, 285, 292
Fauré, 102, 147
Federal Union, 234, 317
Federal Education and Research Trust, 361
Fellowes, 336
Ferguson, Howard, 374
Ferrier, Kathleen, 246, 268, 317
Festival of Britain, 298, 310, 349
Fiedler, Herma, 221, 228
Fiedler, Professor, 217, 221, 226
Field House (St. Aubyns), Rottingdean, 22–4
Finney, Ross Lee, 351
Finzi, Christopher, 341, 359, 374, 389
Finzi, Gerald, 170, 196, 216, 250, 265–6, 267, 269, 277, 286, 291, 294, 300, 302, 312, 315, 321, 331, 333, 338, 341, 346, 359, 369, 374, 375–6, 389
Finzi, Joy, 196, 197, 286, 291, 312, 321, 331, 333, 346, 374, 376, 398
Fisher, Adeline (*see* Vaughan Williams)
Fisher, Charles, 122
Fisher, Cordelia, *see* Curle, Cordelia
Fisher, Edwin, 48, 71, 185
Fisher, Mrs. Edwin, 185
Fisher, Emmeline, *see* Morris, Emmie
Fisher, Florence, *see* Maitland, Florence
Fisher, H. A. L., 151, 162, 170, 181, 230, 237, 294
Fisher, Herbert, 2, 35, 46, 47, 51
Fisher, Hervey, 47, 48, 60, 61, 65, 77, 91, 110, 133, 138
Fisher, Jack, 60, 62
Fisher, Mrs. Herbert (Jackson, Mary), 46, 47, 49, 50, 52, 65, 66, 67, 69, 75, 85, 89, 110, 133, 401
Fisher, Admiral Sir William, 48, 214
Flack, Hoppy, 405
Flagstad, Kirsten, 324
Flecker, James Elroy, 147
Fletcher, Dorothy, *see* Mrs. Robert Longman
Fletcher, Mary, 155, 235, 277
Flower, John, 323
Flügel Horn, 381
Foggin, Myers, 385, 388
Folk Song Society, The, 70, 77, 150
Forster, E. M., 202, 216, 230
Forsyth, Cecil, 64, 143, 359
Foss, Hubert, 101, 157, 207, 218, 244, 281, 316, 325, 336
Foss, Lukas, 351
Foster, Arnold, 204, 205, 254, 317, 390

Fox-Strangways, A. H., 135, 151
Frank, César, 147
Frank, Alan, 315, 343, 385
Friskin, James, 87, 105, 336, 357
Fuller-Maitland, J. A., 62
Furtwängler, 203

Gardiner, Balfour, 66, 107, 206
Gatty, Ivor, 35, 37, 50, 92, 119, 159, 179
Gatty, Margot, *see* Parrington
Gatty, Nicholas, 35, 37, 50, 54, 55, 56, 57, 58, 64, 65, 71, 92, 119, 161, 251, 273
Gatty, René, 50, 52, 53, 54, 55, 56, 57, 58, 59, 68, 92
George V, H.M. King, 92, 206, 210
George VI, H.M. King, 214, 316
Gertler Quartet, 266
Gibbs, Armstrong, 136, 152
Gilbert, Geoffrey, 360
Gilchrist, Anne, 251
Gillespie, Dr., 352
Gipps, Dr. Ruth, 136, 390
Girdleston (Duck), 26, 27
Gladstone, Dr. F. E., 31
Glanville-Hicks, Peggy, 357, 375
Glastonbury Festival, 147
Glover, Cedric, 195, 291, 315, 372, 391, 427
Glyndebourne, 202, 228, 311
Goddard, Scott, 378, 385
Godebski, 103
Godfrey, Sir Dan, 60, 63, 67, 76, 147
Godley, Dr. A. S., 135
Goethe, 387
Golden Age Singers, 333
Goldsbrough, Arnold, 154
Goodchild, Mr. and Mrs., 19
Goossens, Sir Eugene, 139, 147, 395
Goossens, Leon, 259, 262
Gordon, June, 380
Gordon Clark, Barbara (*née* Lawrence), 196
Gordon Clark, His Honour Judge, 196, 359
Goren, Eli, 378
Gough, Miss Beryl, 360
Gow, Dorothy, 136
Gowe, Stewart, 69
Grainger, Ella, 395
Grainger, Percy, 92, 110, 142, 395
Graves, Robert, 180, 375
Gray, Alan, 36, 41, 42, 213
Gray, H. W., 143
Greene, Eric, 186, 312, 338, 388, 389
Grinke, Frederick, 346, 347, 374
Gritton, Eric, 428
Grout, Professor Donald, 348–50, 354, 356
Grout, Margaret, 356
Grove, Sir George, 30
Grove's Dictionary of Music and Musicians, 30, 68, 75, 148
Guilbert, Yvette, 260
Gunby Hall, Lincolnshire, 65, 395
Gundry, Inglis, 267, 290, 424
Gurney, Ivor, 136, 215, 216
Guys Hospital Musical Society, 112

Hadley, Dr. George, 276, 382, 384
Hadley, Mrs. George Hardley, *see* Stewart, Jean
Hadley, Patrick (P.A.S.), 136, 206, 291, 323, 344, 361–2, 388, 391, 395, 398
Hadley, Margaret, 384
Haig, Earl, 135
Haig Brown, Dr., 27, 28, 234
Haig Brown, the Misses, 27
Hall, Marie, 138
Hallé Choir, 316
Hallé Orchestra, 277, 291, 302, 313, 316–17, 328–9, 369–70, 385
Hamburg, University of, 221
Hamilton, H. V., 26, 27
Hancock, Leonard, 299, 306, 307
Handel, 137, 139, 168–9
Handel Society, 139
Hankey, Lord, 320
Hannam-Clark, George, 104, 362
Hardy, Thomas, 42, 84, 85, 300
Harford, Francis, 64, 67
Harling, Edna, 373, 384, 387
Harris, Sir William, 46
Harrison, Anne, 12
Harrison, James, 10
Harrison, Julius, 137
Harrison, Lucy (*née* Wedgwood), 4, 5, 8, 10, 12, 13
Harrison, Tom, 202, 289, 312
Hart, Fritz, 43
Harvey, Evelyn, 294
Haslam, Diana, 295
Hassall, Christopher, 109

Haydn, 178, 249, 328, 347
Heather Festival of Music, Oxford, 162
Heatley, The Misses, 69
Heirs and Rebels, 65, 92, 120, 160, 161, 400
Helpmann, Robert, 203, 284
Henderson, Roy, 212, 224, 278, 290
Henderson (timpanist), 89
Henschel, Sir George, 42, 139
Herbert, A. P., 185, 328
Herbert, George, 2, 97, 138
Herbert, Ivy, 253, 259, 270, 271
Herrick, Robert, 360
Herzogenberg, Heinrich von, 52
Heseltine, Olive, 294
Heseltine, Philip, *see* Warlock, Peter
Hess, Dame Myra, 230, 239, 245–6, 357
Hewitt, Mr. James, 22, 24
Hewitt, Miss, 22
Hewitt, Mr. William, 22, 23
Higley, Mr., 410
Hindemith, 203
Hirsch Quartet, 361
Holbrooke, Josef, 66
Hollingsworth, John, 316
Hollins, Frank, 339, 362–3, 366, 398
Holst, Emil (von), *see* Cossart, Ernest
Holst, Gustav, 43, 44, 50, 56, 60, 61, 62, 63, 64, 65, 68, 71, 72, 74, 75, 78, 80, 83, 84, 85, 91, 92, 93, 107, 111, 112, 120, 122, 124, 126, 127, 128, 130, 131, 133, 136, 137, 138, 141, 142, 145, 146, 152, 153, 154, 156, 160, 161, 166, 169, 170, 171, 172, 174, 176, 180, 181, 184, 188, 189, 190, 191, 193, 197, 199, 200, 201 202, 203, 204, 205, 211, 212, 254, 273, 278, 329, 356, 378, 401
  Assemble all ye maidens, 169, 378
  Choral Fantasia, 189, 378
  Choral Symphony, 160, 161, 170
  Egdon Heath, 85, 170, 378
  Hymn of Jesus, 136, 160, 191, 347
  Planets, The, 133, 137, 185
  Two Songs Without Words, 78
Holst, Imogen, 78, 136, 189, 200, 204, 211, 223, 237, 278
Holst, Isobel, 60, 65, 200
Hornstein, Genia, 237, 269, 271, 285, 310, 358, 372, 382
Hornstein, Yanya, 237, 285
Hôtel de l'Universe et du Portugal, 79, 81, 318
Housman, A. E., 82, 156, 343
Howard-Jones, Evlyn, 43, 54, 64
Howells, Herbert, 126, 194, 216, 325, 338, 347, 373, 374, 378, 385
Howes, Frank, 194, 293, 337, 358, 385
Howland Prize (Yale), 356–7
Hoyte, W. S., 50
Huddersfield Choir, 211
Hudson, W. H., 168
Hull, Sir Percy, 223
Hull, Robert, 354–5
Humperdinck, 147
Huntingdon-Hertford Foundation, 352–3
Hurlstone, William, 67
Hutton, Dr., Dean of Winchester, 159
Huxley, Sir Julian, 357

Ibert, Jacques, 346
Iliff, Noel, 397
Imlach, Molly, 351
Incorporated Society of Musicians, 232, 325
Ingrave, 66, 69
International Folk Dance Festival, 210
International Folk Music Council, 277
International Society for Contemporary Music, 147, 158, 188, 210
Interned Alien Musicians, Home Office Committee for the release of, 236, 247
Intimate opera, 340
Inwards, Haydn, 38, 87, 150
Ireland, John, 43, 54, 147, 327
Irving, Ernest, 271, 279, 280, 293, 315, 326, 329
Isaacs, Colonel, 208, 282
Isaacs, Leonard, 136, 361

Jackson, Mary, *see* Fisher, Mrs. Herbert
Jacobson, Maurice, 277
Jacques Orchestra, 246
Jacques, Dr. Reginald, 321
James Allen's Girls' School, 68
Janaček, 159, 184, 307, 422
Jenkins, Sir Gilmour (Gil), 186, 266, 302, 307, 326–7, 330–1, 336, 339, 340–1, 344, 358, 367, 376, 377, 382, 385, 386, 391, 395, 398

Jochum, Eugen, 221
Joffre, Marshal, 135
Johns, Glynis, 245
Johnson, Dr. Samuel, 372
Jones, Trefor, 155
Jonson, Ben, 175
Jooss, The Ballet, 221, 331
Jooss, Kurt, 246
Juilliard School, 336, 357

Kantrovitch Quartet, 310
Karpeles, Helen, *see* Kennedy
Karpeles, Maud, 95, 151, 168, 178, 192, 193, 201, 204, 224, 225, 235, 267, 277
Karsh, 295–6
Kaye Smith, Sheila, 267
Kells, Iris, 307
Kelly, Sir Gerald, 320, 333, 390, 392, 394, 399
Kempson, Lucy, 386
Kempson, Rachel (Lady Redgrave), 386
Kennedy, Douglas, 95, 218, 219, 228, 394
Kennedy, Eslyn, 316, 328, 344, 381, 399
Kennedy, Helen (*née* Karpeles), 95
Kennedy, Michael, 114, 311, 316, 328, 344, 380, 381, 396–7, 398–9
Kennedy Cooke, Mr. and Mrs., 346
Kennet, Lord, 240
Kensington Festival, 146, 191
Keynes, Anne, 291
Keynes, Sir Geoffrey, 183, 184, 187, 284, 386
Keynes, Margaret (Lady [Geoffrey] Keynes), 183, 184
Keynes, Maynard (Lord Keynes), 187
Kiddle, Frederick, 87
Kingsford, Mrs., 149
King's Lynn Festival, 323–4, 397
Kirby, Alan, 278, 388
Kirkpatrick, John, 354
Kitchener, Lord, 115, 116
Kitson, C. H., 260
Kisch, Eve, 225
Kletschka, Klara, 380
Kneller Hall (Royal Military School of Music), 151
Kodály, Zoltan, 66, 147, 172, 215, 286
Koussevitzky, Serge, 192
Kreisler, 97, 98, 317
Krips, Josef, 292, 339–40, 353, 355, 356, 369, 395

Labey, Marcel, 81
Lambert, Constant, 187, 188, 211
Lanchester Puppets, The, 323
Langstaff, Esther and Meredith, 348
Langstaff, John (Jack), 395
Langton, Stephen, *see* Massingberd
Larpent, Katie and Bee, 336
Lasker, Vally, 182, 184, 186, 187, 190, 199, 202, 203, 251
Laslett, Peter, 396
Lavengro, 393
Lawrence, Barbara, *see* Gordon Clark
Lawrence, Naomi, 196
Lawrence, T. E., 354
Lear, Edward, 25, 90, 233
Leather, Mrs. Ella, 83, 105, 294
Leeds Festival, 45, 79, 87, 89, 96, 160, 215, 339
Leeds Municipal Orchestra, 73
Leeds Philharmonic Society, 340
Leith Hill Musical Festival, 73, 74, 82, 86, 88, 93, 100, 106, 137, 138, 141, 148, 149, 159, 162, 167, 171, 178, 180, 181, 186, 189, 190, 194, 196, 197, 199, 211, 214, 220, 226, 230, 232, 240, 255, 262, 274, 275, 290, 296, 307, 310, 315, 317, 328, 331, 344–5, 354, 359, 395
Le Fanu, William, 41, 285, 389
Le Fleming, Christopher, 136, 277, 290
Le Fleming, Phyllis, 290
Lejeune, C. A., 280
Leoncavallo, 147
Lewin, Colonel, 74
Lewis, Professor Anthony, 289, 333
Lewis, Joseph, 149
Lewis, Richard, 361
Ley, Dr. Henry, 89, 92, 421
Liddell, Henry, 46
Listener, The, 428
Litchfield, Henrietta (Aunt Etty), 10
Litchfield County Choral Union (U.S.A.), 142
Liverpool Philharmonic Society, 52
Liverpool University College (Doctor of Laws), 189
Llewelyn Davis, Crompton, 92, 141
Llewelyn Davies, Theodore, 92
Lloyd, A. L., 394

Lock, Major-General Sir Robert and Lady, 237, 330, 358, 381–2
Lockyer, James, 110
Lodge, Oliver F. W., 230
Loewenbach, Jan, and Mrs. 422
Lofthouse, Charles Thornton, 309
London County Council, 326
London Labour Choral Union, 170
London Philharmonic Orchestra, 203, 253, 257, 340, 341
London Schools Orchestra, 387
London Scottish Rifles, 116
London String Quartet, 110, 126
London Symphony Orchestra, The, 97, 137, 140, 245, 278, 328, 340, 342, 346
London University, 309
London, University College, 315
Londoner, The, 57
Longman, Dorothy (*née* Fletcher), Mrs. Robert Longman, 105, 107, 119, 140, 141, 143, 144, 167, 176, 182, 185, 214, 225, 233, 235, 237
Longman, Lisette, 298, 327, 329, 336, 340
Longman, Margaret, 105, 107, 329
Longman, R. G. (Bobby), 105, 107, 119, 140, 143, 144, 167, 207, 214, 225, 233, 237, 277, 298, 327, 329–30, 336, 340, 398
Lucas, Una, 192, 193
Lushington, Susan, 186, 266
Luther, Martin, 181

M.M. Club, 247, 285, 309
Madrigal Society, The, 340, 369, 390
Maeterlinck, Maurice, 108
Magpie Madrigal Society, 62
Mahler, Gustav, 34, 92
Maitland Ermengard, 51, 96, 338
Maitland, Florence (*née* Fisher, later Darwin), 35, 36, 48, 51, 78, 79, 158
Maitland, Fredegonde, *see* Shove
Maitland, Frederic, Professor of the Laws of England, Cambridge, 35, 48, 51, 77, 78, 158
Major, Joseph, 128
Malleson, Miles, 87
Manchester Guardian, The, 293
Mann, Flora, 140
Margaret, H.R.H. Princess, 310, 324
arianske Lazne, 293
Marsh, Edward (Eddie), 41, 108, 109
Marshall, Mrs. Julian, 74
Marshall, W. A., 129
Martin, Gillian, 323
Mary, H.M. Queen, 145, 155, 156
Mason, Edward, 112
Massingberd, Margaret, 64
Massingberd, Stephen, 17, 31
Mathieson, Muir, 239, 245, 250, 316
Maxse, The Misses, 29
Mazzolini, Ettore, 349
Mendelssohn, 147, 283, 426
Menges, Herbert, 397
Menges, Quartet, 225, 250, 255, 259
Menuhin, Yehudi, 317
Meredith, Hugh, 381
Michelangelo, 30, 345
Middlesex Hospital, 381–2
Milford, Robin, 136, 170, 333, 380
Miles, Bernard, 324
Miles, Napier, 109, 165, 187
Milner, J., 57
Mitchell, Ena, 278, 290
Mitropoulos, 353
Moeran, E. J., 156
Monserrat, 160
Monteverdi, 254, 267
Montgomery, Bruce, 321
Montgomery, Peter, 203, 243
Montgomery - Massingberd, Diana (Lady), 251, 395
Monthly Musical Record, 135, 158
Moody, Dr., 256
Moore, A. J. (Canon), 129, 130
Moore, Enid, 348, 395
Moore, Gerald, 348, 395
Moore, G. E., 37, 39, 41, 65, 92, 336, 343
Moores, Michael, 399
Moreman, Dr. and Mrs., 351
Morley College, 84, 92, 93, 106, 116, 141, 154, 204, 254–5, 267, 329, 424
Morris, Emmeline (*née* Fisher), Mrs. R. O. Morris, 67, 85, 110, 117, 165, 168, 169, 170, 172, 173, 174, 181, 185, 189, 236
Morris, R. O., 115, 117, 165, 168, 171, 172, 174, 181, 185, 189, 196, 205, 236, 247, 248, 259, 262, 263, 266, 275, 276, 283, 286–7
Morrison, Angus, 323
Morse, Rose, 199

Mott, Mr. and Mrs. and Florrie, 90, 91
Moule Evans, David, 202
Mukle, May, 247
Müller-Hartmann, Robert, 237, 252, 277, 283, 285, 288, 297, 302, 310, 399
Mullinar, Michael, 267, 268, 269, 276, 293, 297, 300, 304, 311, 346, 347, 361
Murray, Gilbert, 94
Music and Letters, 134, 135, 137, 163, 216, 426
Music Review, The, 203
Musical Times, The, 151, 159
Musicians Benevolent Fund, 377
Musicians, Worshipful Company of, 182, 273
Musical Autobiography (reprinted in *National Music and Other Essays*), 19, 30, 32, 33, 36, 43, 45, 80, 82, 281
Myers, Rollo, 103
MacCarthy, Desmond, 230, 321
McCarthy, Lillah, 109
McCleary, Fiona, 294, 336
McCleary, Dr. George, 34, 294, 327, 336, 382, 395
McCleary, Gwyneth, 382
McEwen, Sir John, 157
McFall, David, 373–4
Macfarren, 315
Macgibbon Quartet, 360
McGill University, 349
Machray, 119, 301
McInnes, Campbell, 64, 89, 97, 107, 138, 251
Mackail, Clare, 97, 138
Mackenzie, Eila, 352
McKie, Sir William, 382, 396
Mackrill, Charles, 119
Macnaghten Concerts, 369, 384, 388, 389
Maconchy, Elizabeth, 136, 161, 285, 340, 389, 422

Nash, John, 384
Nathan, Paul, 255
National Festival of Schools Music, 300, 309
National Gallery Concerts, 230, 246, 250, 254, 257, 260, 266
National Music and Other Essays, 135, 428, *and see Musical Autobiography*
National Trust, The, 258, 259
Neal, Mary, 150
Neel, Boyd, 349
Neve, William, 371
Nevinson, Evelyn (*see* Sharp, Evelyn)
Nevinson, Henry, 168, 209
Newman, Ernest, 148
Newmarch, Rosa, 184
New Opera Company, The, 371, 382, 396, 397, 398, 399
New Statesman, The, 396
New York Symphony Orchestra, 192
New York World Fair, 230
Nielsen, Carl, 380
Nicholls, Agnes (Lady Harty), 44, 107, 197
Nicolai, 174, 175, 246, 315
Nijinsky, 93, 150
Nikisch, 53
Noble, John, 343–4
Noon, James, 27
Norwich Festival, 156, 169, 184, 212
Noss, Luther, 356
Nottingham Oriana Choir, 339
Nottingham University, 394
Novello, Ivor, 238
Novello Davies, Madame Clara, 238

Observer, The, 280
Oldridge, Diana (formerly Awdrey), 141, 194
Olivier, Sir Laurence, 396
Olympus, Mount, 123, 124
O'Neill, Maire, 109
O'Neill, Norman, 139
Orchestration (of old works), 168–9, 427–9
Ord, Boris, 150, 272, 333, 342–4, 368
O'Sullivan, Seumas, 158
Oxford Bach Choir, The, 135, 284
Oxford Book of Carols, 171
Oxford Festival of Music, 284
Oxford Orchestral Society, 262, 320
Oxford University Musical Club, 64
Oxford University Press, 157, 158, 252, 315, 327, 336, 343

Pakenham, Simona (Mrs. Noel Iliff), 370, 372, 397, 399
Palestrina Society, 105, 336
Palmer, Samuel, 168
Paray, Paul, 277

Parker, Archbishop, 88
Parkinson, Hon. Mrs. Dorothy, 339, 340
Parratt, Sir Walter, 41, 46, 50, 74
Parrington, Hugh, 161
Parrington, Margot, *née* Gatty, 55, 90, 91, 161, 294
Parry, Sir Hubert, 31, 32, 36, 44, 50, 93, 112, 117, 125–6, 134, 137, 147, 164, 170, 178, 214, 282, 284
  As a teacher, 367
  Blest Pair of Sirens, 112, 164, 170, 380
Pattinson, Dorothy, 357
Parsons, William, 346
Pearl, Ruth, 225
Pears, Peter, 339, 340
Percival, Allen, 344
Performing Rights Society, The, 377
Pernell, Orrea, 355
Peter Jones Operatic Society, 308
Petersfield Festival, 73
Philadelphia Orchestra, 192
Pini, Anthony, 378
Piper, John, 284
Plamondon, 102
Plato, 163
Pole Piggott, Wellesley, 3
Pollack, Anna, 267, 268
Poston, Elizabeth, 380
Pottipher, Mr., 66
Potto, Molly, 259, 270
Prescott (*Conquest of Mexico*), 171, 331
Price, Lieutenant Colonel, 238, 239
Pro Canto Singers, 388
Procter, Norma, 346
Promenade Concerts, Introduction to programmes, 1949, 293
Propper, Erica, 396
Puccini, 147
Purcell, Henry, 43, 44, 68, 76, 84, 91, 115, 157, 178
  Fairy Queen, 91, 178
  King Arthur, 84, 178, 291
  Dido and Aeneas, 43, 324
  Soul of the World, 157
Purcell Society (Welcome Songs), 68

Quayle, Anthony, 312
Queen's College, Oxford, 321
Queen's Hall Orchestra, 110, 165, 184
Quilter, Roger, 67
Quirke, Mr., 22

Radford, Robert, 410
Ramsbotham, 26
Raunay, Jean, 102
Ravel, Maurice, 79, 80, 81, 85, 86, 102, 103, 109, 110, 112, 113, 118, 120, 133, 158, 260, 318
Raverat, Gwen, 183, 184, 284, 328, 343
Rawsthorne, Alan, 321
Redgrave, Sir Michael, 312, 340, 386
Redgrave, Lady, *see* Kempson, Rachel
Redgrave, Vanessa, 386
Reed, W. H., 97, 140, 173, 197, 198, 249
Reynardson, H. F. Birch, 62
Rhys, Ernest, 212
Richards, Irene, 225
Richardson, Sir Ralph, 260
Richmond, Sir Bruce, 97, 103, 107, 125, 265, 400
Richmond Elena (Lady Richmond), 125, 265
Richmond, Susan, 336
Riddle, Frederick, 278
Riley, Athelstan, 71
Ritchie, Mabel (Margaret), 170, 268, 280, 291, 329, 390
Ritchie, Mrs., 138, 188
Ritchie, Pegs (Spring Rice) (Meredith), 138, 173, 174, 185, 381
Robertson, J. Tindall, 127, 128
Robinson, Bernard, 168
Robinson, Douglas, 306
Rooper, Jasper, 136
Rose, Bernard, 321
Rosenbaum, Eddie, 399
Rossetti, Christina, 67
Rossetti, D. G., 64, 65
Roth String Quartet, 351
Rothenstein, William, 134, 137
Rothwell, Evelyn (Lady Barbirolli), 345, 358
Roughead, Nicholas, 329
Rowntree, Dr. Ray, 381, 384
Royal Academy of Music, 196, 276, 289, 312, 357, 381, 389
R.A.F. Orchestra, 250
R.A.M.C. (2/4 London Field Ambulance), 116–25
Royal Choral Society, 154, 310
Royal College of Music, 30, 31, 32, 33, 34, 36, 38, 41, 42, 43, 44, 45, 49,

54, 73, 88, 89, 90, 105, 117, 134, 136, 137, 139, 141, 148, 153, 154, 155, 157, 161, 166, 170, 174, 176, 181, 189, 206, 207, 211, 215, 228, 246, 247, 266, 267, 276, 291, 320, 324, 337, 346, 387, 390
Royal College of Music Magazine, 28, 35, 101, 119, 121, 123, 124, 136, 215, 257, 370–1
Royal College of Organists, 256
Royal Festival Hall Organ, 298
Royal Garrison Artillery, 141 Heavy Battery, 125–32
Royal Philharmonic Society, 140, 245, 283, 287, 302, 369, 383, 385, 390–1
Royal Philharmonic Society's Gold Medal, 180, 245–6, 278, 302
Royal Society of Arts, Albert Medal of the, 362, 368
Rubbra, Edmund, 333, 378
Rural Music Schools Association, 290, 301
Russell, Leslie, 387
R.V.W. Trust, 377–8, 380

Sadler's Wells Ballet Company, 188, 284
St. Agnes Mothers Meeting singing class, 146, 191
St. Barnabas, South Lambeth, 45, 50, 53, 54, 58, 64
St. Michael's Singers, 249
St. Pancras Town Hall, 267, 290, 390
St. Paul's Girls' School, 182, 192, 193, 194, 199, 202, 203
Saint-Saëns, 36, 147
Salvation Army Staff Band, 331, 359–60
Sammons, Albert, 110
Samuel, Harold, 140, 153
Sargent, Sir Malcolm, 155, 176, 181, 203, 215, 277, 300, 324, 385, 391
Sassoon, Philip, 108
Schoenberg, A., 147
Schuman, William, 357
Schwarz, Rudolf, 366
Schweitzer, Albert, 170, 427, 429
Schwiller, Isidore, 82, 83, 127, 186, 198, 232, 297, 326
Schwiller Quartet, 83, 87,
Schwiller, Ralph, 337
Scott, Anthony (Tony), 301–2, 338, 391, 398
Scott, Cyril, 66, 102
Scott, Kathleen, 280
Scott, Marion, 216
Scott, Peter, 329, 338
Scott, Captain Robert, 279
Scott, Ruth (Mrs. Anthony Scott), 302, 398
Scott Holland, Canon, 70
Sellick, Phyllis, 267, 269
Shakespeare, 158, 174, 175
Shakespeare Prize (Hamburg), 216, 221
Sharp, Cecil J., 66, 67, 70, 74, 92, 95, 105, 122, 150, 151, 154, 394
Cecil Sharp, A. H. Fox Strangways and Maud Karpeles, 151
Sharp, Evelyn, 209
Sharp, Joan, 390
Shaw, G. B., 42, 134, 189, 336
Shaw, Joan, 367
Shaw, Martin, 90, 91, 92, 157, 171, 180, 367
Sheffield Philharmonic Chorus, 316
Shelley, 231
Shepherd, Victor and Mary, 282, 310
Shirehampton and Avonmouth Choral Society, 110
Shore, Bernard, 300, 301, 307, 360, 377
Shore, Olive, 360
Shove, Fredegonde (*née* Maitland), 51, 90, 158, 166
Shove, Gerald, 158
Shuttleworth, Anna, 399
Sibelius, 92, 139, 142, 278, 296
Silk, Dorothy, 152, 186, 249
Skelton, John, 208, 209, 282
Slade School of Fine Arts, 138
Smith, Cyril, 267, 269
Smyth, Ethel, 152, 260
Society for the Promotion of New Music, 257, 264
Sons, Maurice, 83
Spring Rice, Pegs, *see* Ritchie
Songs of Praise, 157
Sound Broadcasting Society, 396
South London Orchestra, 254
Spenser, Edmund, 218, 316, 325, 335
Spooner, The Rev. Canon W. J., 51
Sprigge, Sylvia, 230
Squire, Barclay, 68
Squire, Sir John, 216

Stafford, Irmgard and Gordon, 373
Stainer and Bramley, 62
Stanford, Sir Charles Villiers, 32, 44, 45, 46, 50, 52, 89, 112, 126, 134, 147, 148, 149, 153, 154, 157, 164, 325, 367, 387
Stanton, Dr., 314
Starey, Rev. L., 262
Steggles, Harry, 118, 119, 120, 121, 123, 124, 127, 229, 290, 324, 336
Steggles, Myrtle, 229
Stephen Sir Leslie, 48, 49, 67, 169
Sterndale Bennett, Robert, 426
Sterndale Bennett, William, 149, 426
Sternhold and Hopkins, 297
Stevenson, R. L., *see Songs of Travel*
Stewart, Jean (Mrs. George Hadley), 225, 247, 255, 256, 259–60, 262, 266, 269, 276, 360, 382, 387
Stewart, Marjorie, 187
Stewart (Mr.), 26
Stinchcombe Festival, 141, 149, 194
Stoeckel, Carl, 142, 143, 144
Stoeckel, Mrs., 144
Stokowski, Leopold, 381
Strachey, Oliver, 336
Stratford on Avon (Revels), 74
Stratton, George, 245
Straube, Dr., 164
Strauss, Richard, 108, 112
Stravinsky, 92, 113
Sturgess, A. B., 377–8
Sucher, Rosa, 34
Suddaby, Elsie, 191
Suggia, Madame, 270
Sullivan, Lieut.-Col. G. A., 132
Sumsion, Alice, 189, 197, 277, 286, 362
Sumsion, Herbert, 165, 172, 189, 197, 277, 286, 362
Sunday Express, The, 330
Sunday Times, The, 328
Surrey County Council Education Committee, 264
Surrey County Music Association, 331
Susskind, Walter, 277
Suttlery, Mr., 24
Swaffham Primary School, 397
Synge, J. M., 161, 352
Sytowski, Mr., 352

Tallis, Thomas, 88, 385
Tatham, Mrs., 167
Tatler, The, 396
Taylor, Jeremy, 138
Taylor, Noel, 389
Taylor, Sedley, 424
Tchaikovsky, 36
Tennyson, 90, 162
Terry, Ellen, 42, 91
Terry, Richard R., 147, 149
Tertis, Lionel, 161, 199, 203, 395, 397
te Wiata, Inia, 308, 313
Teyte, Maggie, 410
Thatcher, Sir Reginald, 340
Three Choirs Festival, *Gloucester*, 88, 107, 172, 173, 189, 191, 202, 215, 277, 300, 338, 374
Hereford, 83, 105, 106, 156, 169, 195, 211, 223, 228, 269, 294, 325
Worcester, 97, 138, 164, 191–2, 210, 285, 312, 346–7, 383
Thirkell, Angela (*née* Mackail), 97
Thistleton, Frank, 377
Thomson, Katherine, 289
Thorndyke, Dame Sybil, 260
Thurston, Frederick, 294
Times, The, 89, 96, 97, 184, 190, 213, 220, 264, 293, 316, 335, 376, 396, 400, 428
Times Literary Supplement, The, 75, 97
Tippett, Michael, 254–5, 266, 359, 377, 388, 396
Toscanini, 225
Tovey, Donald F., 67, 74, 114, 176, 178, 195, 224, 237
Townsend Warner, Sylvia, 398
Toye, Geoffrey, 110, 111, 115
Trevelyan, Elizabeth (Bessie), 74, 180
Trevelyan, George (G.M.T.), 37, 39, 41, 74, 92, 165, 233, 236, 252, 327, 343, 375
Trevelyan, Humphry, 344
Trevelyan, Robert (R.C.), 74, 92, 98, 176, 180, 230, 277
Trew, Arthur, 290
Trinity College, Cambridge, 34, 35, 150, 236, 252
Trinity College, Dublin, 226
Tudor Singers, 226, 284, 297
Turner, W. J., 126

University of California, at Los Angeles, 351, 352

Vaughan Williams, Adeline (*née* Fisher), 35, 46, 47, 48, 49, 50, 51
marriage to R.V.W., *passim*
Death, 309
Vaughan Williams, Rev. Arthur, 2, 6, 8, 9
Vaughan Williams, Constance (Mrs. Hervey Vaughan Williams), 140, 195, 196, 212, 213
Vaughan Williams, Sir Edward, Judge of Common Pleas, 1, 5
Vaughan Williams, The Rev. Edward (Edwardie), 2, 17, 65
Vaughan Williams, Henrietta Maria, 2
Vaughan Williams, Hervey, 6, 8, 10, 15, 20, 22, 25, 29, 97, 140, 180, 195, 213, 247, 252, 258, 318
Vaughan Williams, Hervey (1829), 2
Vaughan Williams, Lady (Jane Bagot), 1, 6, 8, 49
Vaughan Williams, Laura, 6
Vaughan Williams, Lewis, 2, 6
Vaughan Williams, Margaret (*née* Wedgwood), 4, 5, 6, 8, 9, 10, 12, 13, 17, 18, 19, 20, 21, 29, 66, 90, 98, 115, 152, 165, 166, 195, 208, 212, 213, 215, 318
Vaughan Williams, Margaret (Meggie), 7, 8, 15, 19, 20, 21, 23, 27, 29, 66, 73, 74, 90, 93, 98, 105, 107, 165, 166, 167, 186, 318
Vaughan Williams, Sir Roland (Lord Justice of Appeal), 2, 15
Vaughan Williams, Roland and the Hon. Grace, 285
Vaughan Williams, Ursula, 218, *passim*
Vaughan Williams, Walter (Wattie), 2
Verdi, 101, 174, 246
Verlaine, 42, 78
Verrall, Mrs., 68
Vigeland, Hans, 355
Vincent, John, 352–3
Vincent, Ruth, 352–3
Viñes-Roda, Ricardo, 110
Vocalist, The, 61, 68, 400
Vogue, 168, 305
Vulliamy, Mrs. Edward, 149
Vyvyan, Jennifer, 380

Waddington, S. P., 92, 155, 181, 251
Wager, Henry, 14
Wager, Sarah, 11, 13, 15, 16, 21, 24, 251
Wagner, *Tristan and Isolde*, 34, 328, 329, 362, 394
Wakefield, Mary, 73
Wakefield, Dr. Russell, Bishop of Birmingham, 159
Wales, University of, 182
Waley, Arthur, 368
Walker, Ernest, 67
Wallace, William, 56
Waller, Edmund, 268
Wallis, Dorothy, 282, 312
Walpole, The Rev. Mr., 6
Walter, Bruno, 277
Walthew, Richard, 32, 33
Walton, Sir William, 147, 203, 205, 278, 289, 315, 392
Walton, Lady, 392–3
Warrack, Guy, 136, 316, 321, 385
War Transport, Ministry of, 250, 265–66
Warlock, Peter (Heseltine, Philip), 153
Watson, Dr. Sydney, 321
Watson, Miss, 144
Wedgwood, Caroline, 3, 4, 10, 13, 18, 23, 33, 98
Wedgwood, Iris, 135, 249, 276, 290, 314, 326, 374–5
Wedgwood, Josiah (III), 3, 6, 16, 18
Wedgwood, Lucy, *see* Harrison
Wedgwood, Margaret, *see* Vaughan Williams
Wedgwood, Sir Ralph, 35, 37, 38, 39, 51, 59, 60, 65, 135, 251, 259, 290, 314, 326–7, 336, 362, 374–5
Wedgwood, Sophy, 4, 5, 8, 10, 13, 14, 17, 18, 19, 20, 29, 33, 98, 166, 258, 318
Wedgwood, Veronica (Dr. C. V.), 135, 338
Weelkes, Thomas, 200, 341
Welch, Dr., 261
Wellesz, Egon, 313
Wemys, Lord, 135
West, A. C., 22
Westrup, Professor, Sir Jack, 284
Whalley, George, 295
Whistler, Rex, 238
Whitman, Walt, 65, 78, 94, 101, 129, 144, 158, 210, 212
Whitsuntide Singers, 138, 171, 188, 200, 214

Whyte, Ian, 136
Wigram, Sir Clive, 207
Wilkinson, Norman, 109
Willcocks, David, 337, 374
Williams, Grace, 136, 331
Williams, Harold, 198
Williams, John, 1
Williams, Joseph, 100
Williamson, Honorine (*see* Brown, Honorine)
Willoughby, Ernest, 193
Wilson, General, 135
Wilson, Marie, 343
Wilson, Mary (Lady Wilson), 244, 306, 307
Wilson, Oriana, 280
Wilson, Sir Steuart J., 87, 105, 107, 112, 137, 140, 158, 159, 186, 191, 197, 198, 244, 252, 268, 277, 297, 306, 308, 311, 321, 326, 329, 421
Winger, Walter, 351
Winship, E. R., 131
Wiseman, Herbert, 277
Wolverhampton Musical Society, 149
Women's Institutes, 232, 292, 299, 310
Wontner, Arthur, 109
Wood, Charles, 36, 154
Wood, Sir Henry J., 42, 63, 68, 76, 160, 161, 169, 221, 223, 257, 260
Wood, Lieut.-Col. Michael Forrester, 218, 247
Wood, Thomas, 283
Wood, Ursula (*née* Lock), *see* Vaughan Williams, Ursula
Woodhouse, Gordon, 26
Woodhouse, Violet Gordon, 26
Woolf, Virginia, 169, 235
Workers' Educational Association, 93
Worsdell, Guy, 305
Wright, J., of Derby, 372
Wuillaume Quartet, 102
Wurm, Stanislas, 127

Yale University, 356
Young, Dr. Percy, 298
Young, Wayland, 240